Epic Sound

STEPHEN C. MEYER

Epic Sound

Music in Postwar Hollywood Biblical Films

INDIANA UNIVERSITY PRESS

Bloomington and Indianapolis

This book is a publication of

Indiana University Press
Office of Scholarly Publishing
Herman B Wells Library 350
1320 East 10th Street
Bloomington, Indiana 47405 USA

iupress.indiana.edu

Telephone   800-842-6796
Fax   812-855-7931

Manufactured in the United States of America

Library of Congress Cataloging-in-Publication Data

Meyer, Stephen C., [date] author.
   Epic sound : music in postwar Hollywood
biblical films / Stephen C. Meyer.
   pages cm
   Includes bibliographical references and index.
   ISBN 978-0-253-01443-6 (hardcover : alkaline paper)
— ISBN 978-0-253-01451-1 (paperback : alkaline paper) —
ISBN 978-0-253-01459-7 (ebook) 1. Motion picture music—
History and criticism. 2. Bible films—United States. 3. Film
composers. I. Title.
   ML2075.M48 2015
   781.5'420973—dc23

                                                  2014017905

1 2 3 4 5   20 19 18 17 16 15

*For my sons, Gavin and Dylan,
lovers of music and the moving image*

Contents

Acknowledgments

I have developed the ideas for this book in dialogue with many friends and colleagues, and I am indebted to all of them. My starting point for this entire project was the Miklós Rózsa Papers in the Special Collections Research Center of Syracuse University, and I am grateful to the entire staff of this department for their cheerful professionalism and generous assistance. I also wish to acknowledge staff at other libraries and institutions: in particular, Warren Sherk of the Margaret Herrick Library at the Academy of Motion Picture Arts and Sciences; Edward Comstock of the Cinematic Arts Library at the University of Southern California; and Anne Woodrum of the Robert D. Farber University Archives and Special Collections Department at Brandeis University. Without their help, I would not have been able to complete my work.

Some of the ideas in this book were first presented as conference papers: at the New York University "Music and the Moving Image" conferences from 2010, 2011, and 2013; the 2012 conference "From Nineteenth-Century Stage Drama to Twenty-First-Century Film Scoring: Musicodramatic Practice and Knowledge Organization," sponsored by the Society for American Music and California State University, Long Beach; and at chapter meetings of the New York State–St. Lawrence Chapter of the American Musicological Society from 2012 and 2013. I benefitted greatly from the opportunity to share my work with these supportive communities of energetic scholars. In addition, I wish to thank many specific individuals for their help. Maurizio Corbella was extraordinarily generous with his work on electro-acoustical music in postwar Italy, and I also wish to thank Maurice Mengel for his help with the chapter on *Barabbas*. Bill Rosar gave many useful comments on early plans for this book, and I thank him for sharing some of his seemingly universal knowledge of film music with me. In addition to helping me discover the probable source for the main theme of *Barabbas*, Matthew Balensuela provided a sympathetic ear for the duration of this project. Closer to home, I wish to thank Johanna Keller for her thoughts on Barber's *Adagio for Strings*. I owe much to my colleagues in the Department of Art and Music Histories, who have helped to improve this book in countless ways and who have provided a wonderfully supportive work environment. In particular, I wish to thank Carol Babiracki, Theo Cateforis, Laurinda Dixon, and Amanda Winkler. Many ideas are the result of conversations with personal friends, on long bicycle rides and kayak trips, and over copious amounts of excellent food and wine: in particular I wish to thank David Brackett, Lisa Barg, Suzanne Mettler, Wayne Grove, Gail Hamner, and Dan Bingham. I also wish to thank Raina Polivka of Indiana University Press for her consistent enthusiasm and support. Lastly, I want to thank Jim Buhler, who read a draft of the entire manuscript with great care and attention. I owe much to his perceptive insights.

It is customary in acknowledgements such as these to thank one's family for their love and support, and I certainly do that here. But I have been doubly blessed in this regard. My brother, Donald Meyer, has read many of the individual chapters and offered extremely helpful comments gleaned from his work as a musicologist and a composer. Many of the ideas in this book came out of long conversations with him, on topics ranging from childhood family dynamics to Bernstein's use of the Mixolydian mode. My wife, Eileen Strempel, has given me tremendous support throughout the entire writing process. But she has been more than simply a loving partner to me and a wonderful mother to our children. She also read much of the manuscript and offered help and advice on matters great and small. I thank her not only for her love, but for her intellectual engagement with this project.

I will end by thanking my mother, Norma Meyer, who decades ago tried to help me through one of my many adolescent crises of faith by presenting me with her copy of Lloyd Douglas's *The Robe*. "Everything I know about Christianity," she told me, "I learned from this book." The crises of faith are still with me, but so is her copy of Douglas's novel, which I used in the preparation of this book. I honor this gift, along with all of her other gifts to me.

* * *

Some aspects of research that appears in chapter 6 is based on a paper that I delivered at the 2012 conference "From Nineteenth-Century Stage Drama to Twenty-First-Century Film Scoring: Musicodramatic Practice and Knowledge Organization" and was subsequently published as "'Leitmotif': On the Application of a Word to Film Music," *Journal of Film Music* 5/1–2 (2012), 101–108.

Note to Readers

When timings appear in the text, they refer to the following commercially released DVDs of the films:

Samson and Delilah: ASIN B004A30XO6
David and Bathsheba: ASIN B000CNE0M4
Quo Vadis: ASIN B00005JN8Z
The Robe: ASIN B001NSLE5I
The Ten Commandments (50th Anniversary Collection): ASIN
    B000CNESNA
Ben-Hur: ASIN B000056BP4
King of Kings: ASIN B002AT8KBU
Barabbas: ASIN B00DMZCEI6
The Greatest Story Ever Told: ASIN B0002BO05S

Unless otherwise indicated, I am responsible for all transcriptions (both from the scores and from the film scripts) as well as for translations.

Epic Sound

Introduction

"It could be that M-G-M's *Quo Vadis* will be the last of a cinematic species, the super super-colossal film," begins Bosley Crowther in his review of Mervyn Le-Roy's 1951 blockbuster.

> If so, it should stand as the monument to its unique and perishable type, to an item of commerce rendered chancy by narrowing markets and rising costs. For here, in this mammoth exhibition, upon which they say that M-G-M has spent close to $7,000,000 and which runs for just shy of three hours, is combined a perfection of spectacle and of hippodrome display with a luxuriance of made-to-order romance in a measure not previously seen. Here is a staggering combination of cinema brilliance and sheer banality, of visual excitement and verbal boredom, of historical pretentiousness and sex.[1]

Crowther continues in a similar manner, analyzing specific scenes and focusing on the performances of the leading actors. Although he has some positive words for Leo Genn's portrayal of Petronius and for the authentic presence of Finlay Currie as St. Peter, the bulk of the review is sharply critical. "We have a suspicion," he concludes, "that this picture was not made for the overly sensitive or discriminate. It was made, we suspect, for those who like grandeur and noise—and no punctuation. It will probably be a vast success."

Known for his urbane sophistication, Crowther was one of the foremost film critics in postwar America. While his review certainly shows his trademark caustic wit, it also illuminates a theme that is central to the reception and interpretation of films such as *Quo Vadis* and other postwar biblical epics. By any measure, films of this type were enormously successful. *Quo Vadis* would be the second-highest-grossing film of 1952, and (according to *Variety* magazine) biblical epics would be the most popular type of movie in six of the ten years of the 1950s. Yet this popular success was not, for the most part, accompanied by critical praise. The faintly supercilious tone with which Crowther predicts the future popularity of LeRoy's film was typical of other critics as well. Indeed, this kind of response to the biblical epic was so prevalent that Bruce Babington and Peter Evans, in *Biblical Epics: Sacred Narrative in the Hollywood Cinema*, begin their book-length study of the biblical epic genre with a subsection entitled "Problems of Discourse: Beyond the Valley of the Wisecrack." The authors rightly point to the ways in which these attitudes "block the way forward" for serious research into the biblical epic.[2] Indeed, after the decline of the genre during the 1960s, historians and cultural critics chose simply to ignore the biblical epic rather than mock it. In the chapter "Film and Television" from his book *American Culture in the 1950s*, for example, Martin Halliwell mentions the genre only in passing, focusing instead on films such as *Rear Window* and *Blackboard Jungle*. In their survey *American Film and Society since 1945*, Leonard Quart and Albert Auster do not mention the biblical epic at all.[3] Indeed, considering the popularity of the genre during the postwar period, the bibliography for the biblical epic is remarkably thin.[4]

Critical responses such as these—whether of neglect or mockery—indicate a certain embarrassment with respect to the postwar biblical epic, an embarrassment that I regard (*pace* Babington and Evans) not merely as an obstacle to analysis but also as a symptom. The postwar biblical epic was dismissed or ignored not because it was tangential to American cinematic history, but rather because it exposed all too clearly so many of its ideological and aesthetic tensions. Many of these—such as those between commerce and art; between inward religious devotion and external (superficial?) display—are implicit in Crowther's *Quo Vadis* review. But there are other tensions in these films as well, concerning historical authenticity, technological innovation, and the nature of religious experience (among other topics). These films articulate America's identity as a Christian nation, as well as its problematic relationship to the idea of empire during the postwar period. They present notions about ethnic or racial identity, about sexuality and gender relationships that are frequently troubled and occasionally contradictory. Above all, they embody a sense of unreflective excess that lies at the heart of American cinema—and perhaps at the heart of postwar American culture more generally.[5] Responding without embarrassment to this quality of unreflective excess has proven to be a difficult task.

The purpose of this book is to contribute to such a response by focusing on one aspect of the biblical epic, namely, its musical sound track. Although music—for reasons that I discuss below—played a disproportionately large role in these films, there is by no means a unitary biblical epic musical style. Mario Nascimbene's score for *Barabbas* (1962) included innovative textural effects that would in many ways presage the more elaborate sound design of subsequent films. Other scores, such as Elmer Bernstein's for *The Ten Commandments* (1956), seem more indebted to the techniques of the thirties and forties. And if the scores to the postwar biblical epics contained a wide variety of different styles, so too did the function of music differ greatly from film to film. In some of the epics—most notably *Quo Vadis*—music helped to create an aura of historical authenticity (or at least a sense of the archaic), whereas this idea played little or no role in other films under consideration here. Music was also needed to accomplish various kinds of suturing, and to help articulate the oftentimes rambling and complex narratives in these films. More generally and (most obviously), music contributed to the grandeur and "epicness" that was so central to the genre. The soundscapes of these films, in short, served many different purposes, purposes that did not always harmonize with one another. In this sense, they reflect the ideological and aesthetic tensions within the genre and, more generally, within postwar American society.

Defining a Genre

Before introducing some of the technological and social contexts that impinge upon the films that I discuss, it is useful to examine the ways in which these films constitute (or do not constitute) a genre, and what is at stake in applying that term to them. The title of this book references three potential generic qualifiers—"epic," "Hollywood," and "biblical"—each of which articulates a category with porous and sometimes indistinct boundaries. The distinction between a film that is epic and one that is not—to begin with the most obvious example— is by no means clear. "Epic," as Steve Neale points out,

> is essentially a 1950s and 1960s term. It was used to identify, and to sell, two overlapping contemporary trends: films with historical, especially ancient-world settings; and large-scale films of all kinds which used new technologies, high production values and special modes of distribution and exhibition to differentiate themselves both from routine productions and from alternative forms of contemporary entertainment, especially television.[6]

Quo Vadis certainly belongs in this category, as do films such as *The Robe* (1953), *The Ten Commandments* (1956), and *Ben-Hur* (1959). These films are closely related to other epics concerned with the history of ancient Rome: films such as *Spartacus* (1960), *Cleopatra* (1963), and *The Fall of the Roman Empire* (1964). *The Fall of the Roman Empire,* for example, contains a chariot race that—although it is quite different in cinematographic terms than the analogous scene in *Ben-Hur*— serves a very similar plot function. Like *Ben-Hur, Quo Vadis,* and other biblical epics, both *The Fall of the Roman Empire* and *Cleopatra* contain magnificent scenes in which the hero or heroine enters into Rome. In addition to these kinds of common traits, shots, and scenes—what Rick Altman has called "semantic" markers of genre—there are also important plot similarities (or, to use the parallel term, "syntactic" markers) that link the postwar biblical films not only to other epics, but also to more generically distant works.[7] What I call the "two-woman" plot archetype, for example, was common to many kinds of films; so too was the plot dynamic in which political differences cause an intimate friendship between two men (e.g., Judah Ben-Hur and Messala in *Ben-Hur,* or Livius and Commodus in *The Fall of the Roman Empire*) to turn to enmity. In some ways, then, the films that I consider form a sub-genre of the broader category of historical epics, a category that includes not only *Spartacus* and *Cleopatra,* but also films such as *El Cid* (1961) or *Lawrence of Arabia* (1962) that are set in different epochs and places.

In other ways, however, postwar biblical films have a more ambiguous relationship to the category of the "epic." A film such as *The Silver Chalice,* for example, contains only a few of the grandiose or spectacular qualities that characterize the typical blockbuster of the period, and although *David and Bathsheba* was advertised as an epic film, it also seems in many ways to be cut from a different cloth.[8] With its cinematographic austerity and doubt-wracked central character (to cite another example), *Barabbas* approaches the aesthetic of the European art film. An even stronger claim for cross-generic influence may be made with regard to *The Greatest Story Ever Told.* Unlike directors such as DeMille (who filmed much of *The Ten Commandments* in Egypt) or King Vidor (who used Spain as a stand-in for the Middle East in *Solomon and Sheba*), George Stevens shot this film in the high desert landscapes of the intermountain West. Much of the cinematography in this film directly references the style of the western made famous by John Ford and other directors (including George Stevens himself, whose *Giant* is a kind of epic unfolding in the West Texas oilfields).

What distinguishes the films under consideration here from the broader category of the historical epic, or indeed from other films such as *Giant* or *How the West Was Won,* is their biblical subject matter. Here too, however, generic boundaries are unclear. Films such as *The Ten Commandments* or *King of Kings* are tied closely to biblical narrative. The plots of films such as *The Robe, Quo Vadis,* and *The Silver Chalice,* on the other hand, have only a tangential connection to scripture. The category of "biblical film" could conceivably exclude these latter films, which center on characters that are not directly mentioned in the sacred texts. Alternately, the category could be expanded in order to include what we might call "para-biblical" films such as *Demetrius and the Gladiators* (the sequel to *The Robe*) or *The Egyptian* (in which the followers of Akhnaton function essentially as proto-Christians). Indeed, Hollywood has appropriated the Bible in such diverse ways that it might be more useful to divide the category of the biblical epic into subgenres according to source material. The two most important books on the biblical epic—Babington and Evans's aforementioned *Biblical Epics* and Gerald E. Forshey's *American Religious and Biblical Spectaculars*—take this approach. Babington and Evans, for example, distinguish three subcategories of the biblical epic: the Old Testament epic, including *David and Bathsheba, The Ten Commandments,* and *Samson and Delilah;* Roman-Christian epics such as *Quo Vadis, The Robe,* and *Ben-Hur;* and finally Christ films, including *King of Kings* and *The Greatest Story Ever Told.* The generic borders suggested by the term "Hollywood" might initially seem to be more secure than those that surround the categories of "biblical" or "epic" film. Indeed, most of the films under consideration here (particularly those that were produced during the late 1940s and early to mid-1950s) were the products of big Hollywood studios such as Paramount and MGM. But as the studio system that had dominated production and distribution of films during the 1930s and 1940s broke down, moreover, a distinctive Hollywood style became increasingly difficult to define. Films such as *David and Bathsheba* are clearly products of the Hollywood system, but the creation of *Barabbas* and *Solomon and Sheba* (and, to a lesser extent, *Quo Vadis* and *Ben-Hur*) was an international affair. Like other generic qualifiers, then, the terms "Hollywood," biblical," and "epic" are subject to potentially endless rearticulation, qualification, and contestation.

My choice of films has been determined not in order to make an argument about generic coherence, still less to challenge conventional generic classifications. Although I consider all of the most popular biblical films from the postwar period, this book is not meant to be a comprehensive guide to the music of a genre whose borders are in any case somewhat permeable. Instead, I have chosen specific films in order to investigate certain key topics that inform the music used in what we might call the postwar cinematic interpretation of the Bible. These topics lie at the intersection of music-historical themes (such as the ideals of historical authenticity, the development of electro-acoustic music, and, more generally, the course of musical modernism during the postwar period) and the evolution of more broadly articulated attitudes toward politics, religion, and society. Therefore, within each chapter, I avoid a scene-by-scene description of the music in favor of more focused discussion of certain key sequences chosen in order to illuminate the topic at hand. Music in the postwar biblical epic, I argue, functioned as a kind of cultural allegory: an essential part of the fantasy image through which postwar audiences could mediate the newfound experience of American empire and the idea of America as a Judeo-Christian nation. The decline of the genre (and its attendant musical transformations) seemed to portend the end of American empire, at least as a grand spectacle.

Meeting the Challenge of Television

Scholars have frequently attributed the revival of biblical epic film to technological and economic factors. Central among these was the rapid rise of television, which (according to the historian Alan Nadel) reached two-thirds of American homes by 1953. Attendance figures for the movies, which had hit an all-time high during the 1940s, plummeted precipitously during the following decade. In his book *America at the Movies; or "Santa Maria, It Had Slipped my Mind,"* Michael Wood quotes some statistics that make this decline quite apparent. "Between 1951 and 1958," he writes, "the weekly moviegoing public in America fell from 90 million to 42 million; between 1946 and 1959 the number of cinemas in America—excluding drive-ins—fell from 20,000 to 11,000."[9] The ensuing financial crisis for the film industry was compounded by the 1948 Paramount decision, in which the U.S. Supreme Court divested the major movie studios of their distribution networks. The epic films of the 1950s were in many ways simply a response to these extraordinary pressures. In order to draw people away from their television sets and into the movie houses, films needed to present something that was impossible to duplicate on the small screen. With their lush colors, spectacular special effects, and extraordinary attention to visual detail, the epic films of this period did just that. They gave audiences a taste of what Vivian Sobchack (quoting advertising slogans for the films themselves) calls the "surge and splendor" of an epic story.[10] By offering audiences a new kind of cinematic experience, studio executives hoped to regain the dominant and extraordinarily popular position they had held in the American entertainment industry during the so-called "golden age" of Hollywood cinema.

One of the key characteristics of the historical epic, Sobchack points out, is the homology between the complex and spectacular worlds depicted in the film and the complex and spectacular means by which these worlds are brought to the screen. The genre, she writes, "*formally repeats* the surge, splendor, and extravagance, the human labor and capital cost entailed by its narrative's *historical content* in both its *production process* and its *modes of representation*."[11] We may see this process of formal repetition most simply, perhaps, in the extraordinary length of the postwar biblical epics. By the standards of postwar epic film, *King of Kings* and *Quo Vadis* are relatively short, clocking in at 168 and 171 minutes, respectively. Both *The Ten Commandments* (220 minutes) and *Ben-Hur* (212 minutes) approach the four-hour mark, while *Cleopatra* (244 minutes) surpasses it. The original running time for *The Greatest Story Ever Told* (later substantially reduced) was an astounding 4 hours and 20 minutes.

But the "surge and splendor" of the genre is manifest in other ways as well. Although the earliest of the postwar biblical epic films (*Samson and Delilah* and *Quo Vadis*) used conventional aspect ratio, the genre became closely associated with the widescreen formats that were developed and used during the 1950s (such as VistaVision, Todd AO, and Cinemascope).[12] The expanded field of vision that these formats provided clearly contributed to the sense of grandeur that was so central to the genre, and helped to create what we might call a distinctive visual signature for the biblical epic film. Both literally and figuratively, the expanded screen made room for the enormous sets, extravagant costumes, and "casts of thousands" that were so typical of the postwar epic. Conspicuously, the promotional materials for these films are full of hyperbolic references to their production (including references to their enormous budgets). They advertise the film, but they also (not so subtly) advertise the achievements of the studio and of the film industry more generally. As part of its effort to generate enthusiasm for *Ben-Hur,* for example, Metro-Goldwyn-Mayer produced an elaborate promotional book with full-color glossy stills from the film, as well as line drawings and descriptions of each of the major characters. With its inflated language and painstaking accounts of sizes, numbers, and expenses, the book is typical of promotional materials for the postwar epic film. Both in production and on the screen, the epic was suffused with the sense of the hyperbolic.

This sense of the hyperbolic also informed another characteristic feature of postwar epic films, namely, the extraordinary length and complexity of their musical scores. The elaborate orchestras that recorded the scores for these epic films, along with the salaries and prestige of composers such as Alfred Newman and Miklós Rózsa, were in this sense simply part and parcel of this generic sensibility. In comparison to other cinematic genres, the biblical epic did indeed seem to call forth an extraordinarily large amount of music. While there is a certain amount of diegetic music for bacchanalian dances, religious ceremonies, trumpet fanfares, and the like, postwar epic films are most notable for the large amount of underscoring that they contain.[13] This is especially true for films produced in the latter part of the period under consideration here: films such as *Ben-Hur* and *King of Kings*. Sobchack understands this extensive—or excessive—nondiegetic music very much as part of the spectacle of these films. "The Hollywood epic," she writes, "also defines History as occurring to music—pervasive symphonic music underscoring every moment by overscoring it."[14]

The spectacular nature of these scores is undeniable, but they serve other purposes as well. As in other cinematic genres, music works to assist (or even compel) immersion in the film's narrative. Long and complex underscoring, it can be argued, is most important precisely in those cinematic genres (fantasy, science fiction, historical epic) in which the gap between everyday life and the film's diegetic world is the greatest. In this sense, the scores to the biblical epics helped to bridge the gap between postwar America and the reimagined fantasy of ancient Rome, Israel, or Egypt. But the biblical epic was also beset by other, more generically specific contradictions: between materiality and transcendence; or between the glorification of freedom and the (implicit) celebration of power and control. Music needed to help overcome these contradictions—or at least to help make sense of them. Borrowing a term from film theory, we might view the extraordinary length and complexity of the underscoring for postwar epic film not merely as a manifestation of the hyperbolic, but also as an index of the number and extent of the sutures that it is called upon to perform.[15]

However composers and filmmakers construed the function of music in the postwar biblical epic, its effect on audiences was greatly enhanced by the new sound technologies that were being developed during this period. To be sure, these developments were less readily apparent than the new widescreen aspect ratios: the technological history of film sound during this period does not include revolutionary events such as the introduction of sound-on-film during the mid- to late 1920s or the development of Dolby sound during the late 1970s. Nevertheless, what the film scholar Paul Reinsch calls the "post-war/pre-Dolby" period witnessed some important technological changes.[16] Foremost among these was the introduction of magnetic tape technology into the motion picture (introduced, significantly, for DeMille's *Samson and Delilah*).[17] This technology captured a wider range of frequencies than the older optical technology and led to a much improved sound-to-noise ratio. Magnetic tape technology also facilitated the introduction of stereo sound into motion pictures. During the 1950s, theater managers also began to add additional speakers, in order to immerse their audiences in a more complex soundscape. We should note that these kinds of technological changes were not adopted universally. Despite the seemingly inevitable tendency to regard films (particularly those produced before the era of "director's cuts" and "expanded editions") as fixed texts, postwar biblical epic films were and are screened in a wide variety of different venues, venues that created (and continue to create) quite different aural experiences for different audience members. Not surprisingly, technological innovations were more important in the large movie houses with elaborate speaker systems, and less relevant for smaller and/or more provincial venues. Indeed, the spotty and incomplete adoption of these new technologies has led John Belton to speak of a "frozen revolution" with regard to the development of film sound during this period.[18] But although observations about the audience experience of postwar epic film must be conditioned by an understanding of the particular circumstances in which they were screened, it is clear that the producers of these films were clearly interested in taking advantage of these technological possibilities. In the crucifixion sequence from Koster's *The Robe,* for instance, the sounds of thunder are reproduced stereophonically, producing (in properly equipped theaters) a novel and presumably thrilling sense of acoustic immersion that anticipated the more elaborate sound designs of films such as *Star Wars.* These kinds of stereophonic and surround-sound sonic environments were a key part of the epic film experience during this period, and further distinguished the cinematic experience from the more domestic pleasure of the small screen.

Epic Religion

The challenges to the old studio system posed by the Paramount decision and the rise of television may help to explain why so many of what Crowther called "super super-colossal" films were produced during the 1950s and early 1960s, but it cannot account for the particular *content* of these films, and especially for the fact that so many of them were based on biblical material. In many ways, of course, the Bible was simply a convenient and familiar source for distant historical backdrops: the Egypt of the Pharaohs or Nero's Rome were in this sense no different from the "barbarian North" depicted in *The Vikings* (1958) or the medieval Spanish landscapes of *El Cid* (1961). But the popularity of the biblical epic also reflected one of the most important cultural developments of the postwar period, namely, religious revival and the expansion of Christian (and Jewish) institutions. Church membership during this period grew more quickly than the U.S. population, and (at least according to Gallup polls) church attendance on an average Sunday reached its historical peak, at 47 percent in both

1955 and 1958.[19] The popularity of the biblical epics during the postwar period is clearly bound up with this broader movement in American life.

In order to understand the ways in which the biblical epic reflected this broader movement, it is not enough simply to note the close correspondence between church attendance figures and box office statistics. We must also examine the theological and emotional qualities of what William McLoughlin has called the "fourth great awakening." McLoughlin notes similarities between the rise of popular postwar Christianity and previous religious movements (e.g., the first Great Awakening of the early to mid-eighteenth century and the Second Great Awakening during the period from 1795 to 1835). "In each of these periods," he writes, "a theological and ecclesiastical reorientation coincided with an intellectual and social reorientation in such a way as to awaken a new interest in the Christian ethos which underlies American civilization."[20] Perhaps the clearest manifestations of this "awakening" were the famous crusades led by Billy Graham. In these mass meetings, as well as in his numerous books and broadcasts, Graham articulated a narrative of spiritual crisis and personal transformation that was deeply resonant for Americans during this period. This narrative also informs many of the plots of the postwar biblical epics. The heroes of these films—Marcus Vinicius in *Quo Vadis,* Marcellus Gallio in *The Robe,* Moses in *The Ten Commandments,* Judah Ben-Hur in *Ben-Hur*—are typically figures of some authority within the existing imperial power structure. In the course of the narrative, the hero is stripped of his power or compelled to renounce this authority. He moves from being an insider to being an outsider, and through an internal process of conversion reconstructs his identity in opposition to the regime in which he once played an important role. Not all the postwar biblical epics, of course, follow this same plot trajectory. In *David and Bathsheba* (1951), David begins and ends the narrative as king of Israel, and Jesus in *King of Kings* (1961) is never part of any earthly hierarchy of wealth or power. Yet even in these films, we find elements of the topos of conversion and personal renewal. As the hero of the 1951 film, King David is chastised for his adulterous relationship with Bathsheba and must rededicate himself to God in order to save himself and his nation. *King of Kings* handles the conversion topos in a different way, by displacing it onto the figure of the centurion Lucius and (to a lesser extent) the role of Claudia (wife of Pontius Pilate). The pattern of conversion and reconstruction is perhaps not so ubiquitous as to be called the master narrative of the biblical epic, but it nevertheless played a central role in the genre.

In creating music to accompany and express this narrative pattern, the composers of the postwar epics engaged an extraordinarily rich tradition. This engagement took many forms. Some of these—such as the insertion of the "Hallelujah Chorus" from Handel's *Messiah* into Alfred Newman's score for *The Greatest Story Every Told*—were blatant or even coarse. The plainchant hymns that Miklós Rózsa adapted for the Christians in *Quo Vadis* to sing are less jarring, but they are also an appropriation of sacred music (albeit less direct ones). The engagement with these traditions, however, might also take a more oblique form. The choral music that so frequently appears at the end of the postwar biblical epics is clearly a marker of transcendence; so too might certain purely instrumental gestures in films such as *Ben-Hur* and *Samson and Delilah* be heard as musical expressions of the sacred. Indeed, as I describe in the chapters that follow, music was one of the key ways in which these films conveyed their religious and theological messages.

Authenticity

The conversion topos that informs so many of these films clearly has a specifically religious meaning. But it may also be linked to a persistent strain in the criticism with which the biblical epics were so frequently greeted, a strain that centered around the idea of authenticity. In the conversion narratives of the postwar biblical epics, the hero has been led away from his true self by the false allure of power, status, and/or decadent sexuality. Conversion is typically a process of turning back, a stripping away of everything that is superficial so that the authentic self may emerge (or reemerge). If we place cinema itself in the space occupied by the epic hero, then we might sense a curious, quasi-inversional resonance between the plots of these films and the ways in which they were critically disparaged. Deploying phrases from Crowther's review of *Quo Vadis* as quoted at the beginning of this introduction, we could say that the "mammoth exhibition" of "hippodrome display" and "historical pretentiousness" are the analogues of the decadent luxury and morally compromised power structures that the epic hero must reject. The technological marvels and audiovisual grandeur of the epics are superficially attractive, but they do not convey any genuine or authentic truth.

What we might call the "authenticity anxiety" surrounding the epics—the sense that despite (or because of) their technological sophistication they remained fake—may help to account for one of their more curious features, namely, the extent to which producers, directors, and studio executives attempted to establish their historical credentials. As I discuss in more detail below, the studios often went to great lengths in order to assure that sets and costumes were historically accurate. Voiceovers and introductory titles often provided sources for the stories that were about to unfold, much in the manner of academic footnotes. The major studios employed academic technical consultants such as Hugh Gray (MGM) and Henry Noerdlinger (Paramount) in order to provide expert advice on such matters. These efforts to establish the authenticity of the epic reached their apogee, perhaps, with DeMille's 1956 remake of *The Ten Commandments*. Sponsored by Paramount and DeMille, Noerdlinger published selections from his research as a 200-page book entitled *Moses and Egypt,* with the complete scholarly apparatus of footnotes, bibliography, index, a list of biblical references, and another list of references to the Qur'an. "To acknowledge the vast research work for the film," Noerdlinger writes in the introductory acknowledgments for his book, "950 books, 984 periodicals, 1.286 clippings and 2.964 photographs were studied."[21]

In *Moses and Egypt,* it should be noted, Noerdlinger has little to say about music, and in the composition of his score for *The Ten Commandments,* Elmer Bernstein does not seem to be very much concerned with historical authenticity. Quite the reverse is true for Miklós Rózsa, at least in the context of his work for *Quo Vadis.* As I discuss in chapter 3, Rózsa made historical authenticity a guiding principle of his work for this film. To a lesser extent, ideas about historical authenticity also seem to have informed Mario Nascimbene's work on *Barabbas* and Newman's score for *The Robe.* What is of interest here is not so much the success or failure of these efforts (however they might be judged), but rather the ways in which the music for the biblical epic intersected with and articulated the more general authenticity anxiety that haunted the genre.[22]

Freedom and Empire

The plots of the biblical epics—as I have suggested above—may have resonated with a broader cultural anxiety about authenticity, but they had a more overt relationship to postwar domestic politics and international relations. The ancient Hebrews and early Christians in the biblical epics are typically persecuted by vast and decadent empires: empires whose power ultimately depends upon the toil of slaves. And if the conversion topos might be understood in terms of the "fourth great awakening," so too can this plot motif be seen as a reflection of what Robert Ellwood has called the "dominant theme" of the 1950s, namely the relationship between the individual and "mass society."[23] This theme is manifest most prominently in American Cold War ideology, through which the rivalry between the United States and Soviet Union was cast in terms of an epic struggle between freedom and totalitarianism, democracy and dictatorship. In many ways, the biblical epics simply transposed these ideological dichotomies into a distant historical past. Indeed, the films themselves often insist upon the contemporary relevance of the events and characters that they depict. Nowhere is this theme made more explicit than in the prologue to *The Ten Commandments,* in which Cecil B. DeMille emerges from a projected curtain in order to address the audience directly about the "highly unusual subject" of the film. This subject, DeMille continues, is quite simply the birth of freedom. The central question of the film—again according to DeMille—is whether or not men shall live according to the rule of law or according to the whim of a brutal dictator. DeMille then affirms the topicality of the subject by telling the audience that the struggle for freedom is still going on today, virtually commanding us to read Yul Brynner's Rameses as a counterpart of the mid-century totalitarian dictator: a beefcake version of Stalin, perhaps, only one beset by marital difficulties. While the appearance of a director presenting his own prologue to a film is (to quote DeMille) "highly unusual," the fundamental trajectory of his comments is not. The voiceover narrations that feature so prominently in the postwar epics adopt much the same tone. As Babington and Evans point out, these narrations typically "lay out in binary antagonism oppositions from whose encounter the ultimate dynamic of history will be born: Conquering Rome/Conquered Judaea; Empire/Slavery; Power/Helplessness; the Whip and the Sword/Suffering."[24] Like DeMille's prologue, they situate the movie's plot in a specific historical time and place, such as Rome and Palestine during the reign of Tiberius (*The Robe*) or of Nero (*Quo Vadis*) or ancient Israel during the period of Judges (*Samson and Delilah*), even while they position the plot as part of a larger, more epic story. As members of the "most powerful nation in the free world," audiences for the biblical epic could understand themselves as a part of this story, the successors to the heroic Christians or early Israelites depicted on the screen.

The Cold War forms an inescapable backdrop to the postwar epic films, and decades of scholarship have explored their latent (or explicit) anti-Soviet messages. The images of ancient Rome or Pharaonic Egypt presented in these films, however, are more than simple analogues for the Soviet Union. Indeed, scholars have articulated other, more nuanced accounts of the ways in which these movies reflected national and international politics of the 1950s and early 1960s. In her book *Projecting the Past: Ancient Rome, Cinema and History,* for example, Maria Wyck explores ways in which the cinematography of *Quo Vadis* evokes the visual culture of Nazi Germany and Mussolini's Italy, situating twentieth-century fascism and not the Soviet Union as the contemporary analogue of decadent Neronian Rome.[25] Melani McAlister frames the postwar epic in somewhat different terms. Drawing on the work of earlier scholars such as Michael Wood, she notes that representatives of the Roman Empire are typically cast with actors sporting British or quasi-British accents (Peter Ustinov as Nero in *Quo Vadis,* for example, or Frank Thring as Pontius Pilate in *Ben-Hur*). The heroes of these films, by contrast, are typically played by all-American actors such as Robert Taylor or Charlton Heston. The postwar period, she points out, was precisely the time in which the United States was replacing Britain as the predominant hegemonic power, and it is possible to read the plots of the biblical epics in terms of the anti-colonialism that (intermittently and inconclusively) informed aspects of American foreign policy during this period.[26]

Still another line of interpretation would understand at least some of the biblical epics as a reflection of more localized struggles surrounding the establishment and early years of the State of Israel. In his discussion of *Ben-Hur,* for example, Gilbert Forshey writes that "one of the factors that persuaded [director William] Wyler to make the film was the story's political implications. He thought of the film in terms of the Egypt–Israeli 1956 war, which President Eisenhower refused to support. He was attracted partly because *Ben-Hur* told the story of Jews fight-ing for their freedom."[27] In America of the 1950s and early 1960s, in short, the biblical epic could engage a variety of different geopolitical topics in a variety of different ways.

If the biblical epic reflects some of the complexities of postwar international topics, we might also understand its rhetoric against the backdrop of domestic politics. The fact that many of the actors and directors so prominent in the biblical epic, such as Heston and DeMille, lent their support to conservative agendas both inside and outside government might tempt us to read the genre as a product of Hollywood's right wing. Indeed, DeMille was a key figure in the anti-communist attack on the film industry that was so damaging during the late 1940s and early 1950s. In 1944, DeMille co-founded the Motion Picture Alliance for American Ideals, and a year later he started his own Foundation for Political Freedom. Both these organizations worked in support of government organizations devoted to rooting out Communism and other "un-American" ideas from the film indus-try.[28] But the political associations of the postwar epic were not always so clear. The character of Petronius in *Quo Vadis*—who eventually commits suicide when it is no longer possible for him to participate in Nero's corrupt regime—is an in-teresting figure in this regard. According to Maria Wyck, some critics of the early 1950s understood the Petronius plot line as a thinly veiled critique of McCar-thyism. Babington and Evans make a similar argument with respect to the plot of *The Robe*: interpreting the anti-Christian Roman tribunals in this film as al-legorical representations of the House Un-American Activities Committee.[29] If we enlarge our view of the postwar epic to include films such as *Spartacus,* the political and ideological associations of the genre become still more complex. Spartacus, after all, was the leader of a slave revolt, and his mythologized his-tory had already been appropriated by communist groups such as the Spartacus League in Germany following World War I. In the extreme anti-communist en-vironment of 1950s and early 1960s, scriptwriters for the film needed to trans-form a crusader against capitalism into a progenitor of the American virtues of freedom and liberty. But although the script for the film infuses the Spartacus story with hefty amounts of respectable domesticity, the plot nevertheless stakes out left-wing positions on pressing issues of social justice and racial equality. Just as with regard to foreign policy, then, the postwar epic references domestic poli-tics in a wide variety of different ways.

Rather than subscribing to any one particular reading of these films, then, it is more fruitful to understand their plots more generally in terms of what Ger-aldine Murphy calls "cold-war imperial anxiety."[30] The enormous sets, the thou-sands of extras, the countless technicians, and, not least, the sound technicians and musicians that the epics demanded were marshaled with what can be called imperial power. Directors such as Wyler and DeMille were frequently likened to generals, and it is easy to understand the production of epic films as a metaphor for the global projection of American military and economic might during the postwar period. As the hyperbolic advertising rhetoric for the epics reminds us, audiences for these films were encouraged to enjoy their magnificence and their expense: their identity as exemplary products of American industry. The plots of the movies, on the other hand, encouraged audiences to identify with the heroic men and women standing against the imperial forces: with the underdogs fighting for freedom. The epics thus allowed audiences simultaneously to celebrate imperial power and to disavow it. They could take pleasure both in the power of Imperial Rome or the Egypt of the Pharaohs *and* in the knowledge that that power would ultimately be destroyed.

Just as the composers for biblical epic films engaged a long musical tradition for the representation of the sacred or transcendent, so too could they draw upon a wealth of preexisting musical topoi for the expression of military or political power. Marches and trumpet fanfares—traditional markers for military might— are abundant in these scores. We might also hear the massed parallel chords that feature so prominently in the scores to *Ben-Hur, The Robe,* and *Quo Vadis* (as well as other films) as aural symbols of totalitarianism, in which individuals—like the musical notes of the score—are forced to move in lockstep with one another. In a more general sense, the full orchestral timbres that typify so much of the biblical epic scores might connote a sense of monumentality that resonated with certain recurring visual motifs in these films. With their distant shots of parade grounds and massed blocks of soldiers, for example, the triumph scenes in *Quo Vadis* and *Ben-Hur* recall the cinematography of Leni Riefenstahl. The colossal architecture of *The Ten Commandments* or *Samson and Delilah,* while different in style from that of Soviet Russia, nevertheless carries a similar sense of overwhelming monumentality. And if pleasure in this visual monumentality—as I have suggested above—must in some sense be disavowed, so too did the composers for these epics bracket the aural topoi of military or political power that circulate through their scores with what can only be called musical irony. This irony takes many forms: from the interaction between trumpet fanfares and monophonic hymns in the arena scenes of *Quo Vadis* to the distorted and dissonant marches that are woven through *The Robe* and *Barabbas.* In this sense, the music of the postwar biblical epic resonates and expresses the idea of "imperial anxiety" that Murphy identifies as such a central part of postwar American culture.

Gender and Sexuality

The ironic combination of celebration and disavowal that informs the idea of the monumental in the biblical epic is even more sharply expressed in another facet of the genre, namely, its presentation of sexuality. As many scholars and critics have pointed out, the religious content of the biblical epic also provided producers and directors a culturally sanctioned way to explore the erotic and to offer their audiences voyeuristic pleasure. Viewing the sins of the flesh and the temptation of illicit sex in the context of a biblical story allowed audiences the opportunity simultaneously to indulge in this voyeuristic pleasure and to disavow it. This simultaneous disavowal and indulgence of the erotic was a key part of the genre from its very beginning, and it is nowhere more marked than in the work of Cecil B. DeMille. It is aptly expressed, for example, by a passage from a novelization of DeMille's 1923 version of *The Ten Commandments* written by Henry MacMahon and illustrated (as the frontispiece tells us) by scenes from the photoplay. In this passage, MacMahon describes the orgy scene, in which the Israelites—temporarily abandoned by Moses—worship the Golden Calf. In the 1923 version of the scene—in contrast to the 1956 remake—Moses' sister Miriam is one of the leaders of the apostates. "Fire was in her eye," MacMahon writes,

> the lust of the flesh inspired her. Turning to the outstretched hands and bodies of the Israelites, she cried in dulcet, coaxing tones:
> "Come, worship ye the Golden God of Pleasure, for the God of Israel heareth not, neither doth He see!"
> She footed it in a wild measure before her Deity, lost to sense of self, expressive only of the abandon that would submit—and clutch eagerly after—the embraces of the He-Master.
> It was the signal for a sex-dance the obscenity of which has not been exceeded in history. Men and women joined in figures interpretative of the orgy of lust that was to follow.
> No sex-imagination of that primitive people was beyond what they tried and did, and ever in the lead was Miriam, fawning upon her Beast, rubbing its legs and flanks, contorting about it in her ecstasy.[31]

The pagan orgy scene was to be a staple of the biblical epic in both the prewar and postwar period, appearing not only in the 1956 remake of *The Ten Commandments,* but also (albeit in different forms) in films such as *Samson and Delilah, Quo Vadis,* and *The Story of Ruth.* It reaches its apogee, perhaps, in the famous "pagan revel" from *Solomon and Sheba.* On one level, these displays of eroticism are merely gratuitous. But they are also framed by broader questions about the role of the erotic and the nature of gender relations that are central to the genre. As I argue in chapter 1, the most prominent way in which the postwar biblical epics explored these questions was through the two-woman plot archetype, in which the hero must choose between a domestic and a foreign woman. The choice of the hero is always linked to the fate of the people that he leads; his erotic and his historical destiny are inextricably intertwined.

It is not difficult to understand the gender dynamics of the postwar biblical epic in terms of what Alan Nadel has called "containment culture." In his article "God's Law and the Wide Screen: *The Ten Commandments* as Cold War 'Epic,'" Nadel depicts DeMille's film (and, by extension, the entire genre of which it is a part) as the cinematic expression of "containment culture."[32] By this term, Nadel is referencing not only the principle of containment that guided American foreign policy with regard to the spread of Communism during this period, but also a more general conservatism whose goal was to contain the sexual, racial, and intergenerational tensions that were to transform American society in subsequent decades. In *The Ten Commandments* as in the other biblical epics, the lust of the flesh that is so provocatively enacted in the pagan orgy scenes is indeed ultimately contained within the bounds of a domestic marriage (or marriage-like relationship). And yet to understand this aspect of the biblical epic as nothing more than a kind of cautionary tale about uncontrolled sexuality does not do justice to the complexities of the gender dynamics in these films. The end of the period under consideration in this book, after all, saw the beginnings of cultural movements that would present radical challenges to supposedly normative ideas about gender and sexuality. These challenges are articulated in books such as Betty Friedan's *The Feminine Mystique* (1963), but also in more diffuse changes in cultural attitudes toward sexuality. Some of this complexity, I argue, is adumbrated even in those films that seem most informed by conservative notions of gender and the erotic.

It is hardly surprising that music should play such an important part in the articulation of gender dynamics in the postwar biblical epics. The pagan orgy scenes feature prominent solo and/or group dances, with ample opportunity for diegetic music. A typical strategy for these dances, as we shall see, was to employ orientalist musical topoi. Orientalist gestures also typify much of the music that composers wrote for the "foreign" women of the two-woman plot archetype. As I discuss in more detail in subsequent chapters, composers freely employed musical conventions for the femme fatale that stretch back through early film music to the nineteenth-century operatic and symphonic repertoire. But in this field as well, composers found interesting ways to nuance and transform these musical conventions.

A Conservative Aesthetic?

With their affirmation of traditional social and religious values and their emphasis on escapist spectacle, the postwar biblical epic is typically understood as a conservative cinematic genre. The apparently inherent cultural conservatism of the genre would by necessity also seem to distance the scores for the biblical epics from the most important musical developments of the postwar period. The 1950s and 1960s were arguably two of the most transformative decades in the history of American music: witnessing (among other developments) the emergence of rock 'n' roll, the development of new styles and forms of jazz, and the development of electronic music and electronic instruments. Many of these new styles and timbres were reflected in film scores as well. Rock 'n' roll famously made its cinematic debut with *Blackboard Jungle* in 1955, and in the following year Louis and Bebe Barron created the first all-electronic film score for *Forbidden Planet*. Film music composers of this period were increasingly interested in jazz and modernist techniques such as serialism, as well as new instrumental combinations and timbres. It is hardly accidental that these new kinds of musical procedures were associated with cinematic genres that directly addressed contemporary social and/or technological problems. In this context, the lush orchestral textures and quasi-leitmotivic structure of the scores that Rózsa, Bernstein, Newman, and others wrote for the biblical epic film during this period would seem to be anachronistic.

The music of the postwar biblical epic, however, cannot so easily be consigned to the dustbin of history. As I mentioned, biblical epics such as *Samson and Delilah* and *The Robe* were among the first films to take advantage of new technologies such as magnetic tape and multi-speaker stereo sound. Although the biblical epic scores—particularly from the early part of the period under consideration here—typically employed a more or less traditional symphonic orchestra, some of these scores (most notably, Mario Nascimbene's music for *Barabbas*) incorporate new sound textures and new techniques for sound production. More germane to my topic are the ways in which the music of the postwar biblical films seems in certain crucial ways to anticipate the revival of the epic in works such as *Gladiator* and Peter Jackson's *Lord of the Rings* films, as well the soundscape of more generically distant films such as the *Star Wars* prequel trilogy. Particularly important in this regard is music's contribution to what we might call the density of the time-space image that they render. The widescreen formats and extended length of the historical epic film is a manifestation of this density: the suggestion that the characters, settings, and events depicted in the film are too big and full and complex to be contained by a "normal" film. On the most basic level, the full orchestral timbres that are featured so prominently in many of the postwar epics are a clear analogue of the widescreen image, connoting size and grandeur by association and simply by virtue of their volume. Yet the more sophisticated scores for the postwar epic—such as Rózsa's music for *Ben-Hur*—reflect the density of the time-space image in another way: by associating the various geographical settings of the film with distinct soundscapes. In this sense, the music for the postwar biblical epics seems to be less a throwback to the classic Hollywood styles of the 1930s and 1940s and more of an adumbration of contemporary practices.

The revival of the epic in the period since *Gladiator*, of course, represents a transformation rather than a simple recapitulation of the genre. Apart from the technological changes that have revolutionized the production of epic films, their plots no longer reflect the hegemonic social position of Christianity (Mel Gibson's *The Passion of the Christ* is the exception that proves the rule in this regard). Nevertheless, I would like to suggest that the connections between the music for movies such as *Ben-Hur* or *The Ten Commandments* and that written for more contemporary films points toward a certain broader continuity in the epic style. Perhaps the epic emerges precisely in those periods in which Americans are more profoundly questioning their sense of destiny and their country's role in world history. The postwar period was just such a time, as are, perhaps, the times in which we now live. If the anxieties of this imperial age are not exactly the same as those of the postwar period, neither are they completely different.

1 A Biblical Story for the Post–World War II Generation?

Victor Young's Music for DeMille's *Samson and Delilah*

When Cecil B. DeMille was preparing to pitch his idea for a film on Samson and Delilah to Paramount, he was—at least according to the account in his autobiography—far from confident. "A new generation of executives had grown up since *The King of Kings*," he wrote, referring to his 1927 Christ film,

> and most of them greeted my suggestion of *Samson and Delilah* with the expected executive misgivings. A Biblical story, for the post–World War II generation? Put millions of dollars into a Sunday school tale? Anticipating this familiar chorus, before the meeting held in my office to decide on my next production, I asked Dan Groesbeck to draw a simple sketch of two people—a big brawny athlete and, looking at him with an at once seductive and coolly measuring eye, a slim and ravishingly attractive young girl.
>
> When the executives trooped in, ready to save me and Paramount from the ruinous folly they were sure I had in mind, I greeted them, saw them to their seats, and brought out the Groesbeck sketch.
>
> "How is that," I asked them, "for the subject of a picture?"
>
> They were enthusiastic. That was movies. That was boy-meets-girl—and what a boy, and girl!
>
> "That, gentlemen, is *Samson and Delilah*."[1]

Like so many of the other anecdotes in his autobiography, this brief story provides a simple answer to a complex question—in this case, about the viability of a biblical film in the postwar period. Despite (or perhaps because of) its jovial, commonsense tone, however, the anecdote reveals some important truths about the social and aesthetic contexts for the biblical epic in the postwar period. It is clear that the executives at Paramount—and most likely others as well—saw the entire genre as old-fashioned. In this context, it is worth remembering that DeMille was himself the most important director of epic film during the 1920s and 1930s. By the time that DeMille was making his pitch, he was already in his mid-sixties. It is entirely possible that the new generation at Paramount was inclined to look upon the *Samson and Delilah* project as an attempt by DeMille to relive the glory days of his young adulthood. In hindsight, of course, their skepticism seems entirely misplaced. *Samson and Delilah* would not only turn out to be enormously successful, it would also inaugurate a decade in which the biblical epic would arguably be Hollywood's most profitable genre.[2] In the immediate postwar period, however, it was clearly seen as a risk.

DeMille was able to overcome the skepticism of the Paramount executives by the simple and time-honored strategy of foregrounding the eroticism of his material. In this sense, DeMille's promotional pitch simply recapitulated a central feature of his prewar epics. In *The Sign of the Cross* (1932) and *Cleopatra* (1934), he had already combined lavish historical spectacle with the ravishing sexuality of Claudette Colbert; Dan Groesbeck's beefcake sketch may simply have evoked the promotional materials for these earlier, highly successful films. And although the idea of linking grandiose spectacle with the erotic may have reached its apogee in DeMille's oeuvre, it was hardly unique to his movies. Foregrounding the erotic was central to the epic genre, and it seems to have been particularly important for those films whose subject matter was based on Old Testament narratives. Even a cursory glance at this subtype of the postwar biblical epic will reveal the extent to which producers and directors were drawn to plot lines in which sexual desire and/or romantic love played a central role: not only the tale of Samson and Delilah, but also the stories of Esther, Ruth, and Jezebel, of David and Bathsheba and of Solomon and the Queen of Sheba. Indeed, the titles of these films— *Samson and Delilah, David and Bathsheba, Solomon and Sheba, Esther and the King*—often indicate this insistent focus on gender dynamics, a focus that is present even in films in which it is not so blatantly advertised. *The Ten Commandments*—or at least its first half—could in this sense easily have been titled *Moses and Nefretiri*. In this sense, the anecdote about the Paramount executives speaks to the "eroticization of the Old Testament" that was such an important part of the postwar biblical epic.

Of course, there was more to the genre of the biblical epic than simply "boy meets girl, and what a boy, and girl!" As in genres such as grand opera and the historical novel, the plots of these epics frame the erotic by a grand historical narrative. When Samson loses his hair as a direct result of his sexual dalliance with Delilah, for instance, his "folly" (to use the words of the film's introductory voiceover) is not merely a personal misfortune. The forces of tyranny and superstition—embodied by the Philistines and their "devil god" Dagon—achieve a temporary victory as a result of Samson's inability to control his desires, and the "dream of liberty for his people" is momentarily eclipsed. The fundamental idea—that sexual incontinence leads inevitably to historical/political catastrophe—is driven home in other Old Testament epics as well. In *David and Bathsheba*, for instance, the king's relationship with the wife of Uriah the Hittite leads to drought and political dissolution. In *Solomon and Sheba*, the king's unbridled lust for the Queen of Sheba makes him vulnerable to a coup attempt by his brother Adonijah, and exposes his kingdom to attack by external enemies. Even in *The Ten Commandments,* it is perhaps the soft arms and ruby-red lips of Nefretiri, and not the chariots of Rameses, which most seriously threaten the destiny of the Hebrew nation. In the postwar epic (to put it another way), sexual desire has world-historical consequences.

It seems unlikely that the Paramount executives to whom DeMille made his *Samson and Delilah* pitch were particularly interested in these historical ramifications. Their biggest concern was with what we may call the third defining characteristic of the genre—the religious nature of the material. For mainstream Christianity and Judaism, the 1950s were halcyon days, and from the perspective of the early twenty-first century, it is easy to see the biblical epic as part of the "fourth great awakening" of American religious life. To the movie executives of the 1940s, however, the religious subject matter of *Samson and Delilah* was clearly a potential liability. In prewar epic films such as *The Ten Commandments* (1923), *King of Kings* (1927), and *The Sign of the Cross* (1932), DeMille had found effective ways of representing the transcendental or supernatural aspects of the story. But the Paramount executives were clearly worried that the audiences of the postwar period had grown too sophisticated for these techniques. The idea of a *Samson and Delilah* film seemed too outdated and moralistic to succeed with a new generation of filmgoers.

The fears voiced by the Paramount executives in DeMille's story, of course, never materialized. Helped no doubt by the star power of Victor Mature and Hedy Lamarr in the title roles, *Samson and Delilah* was the highest-grossing film of 1950. The film garnered two Academy Awards (for Best Color Art Direction and Best Color Costume Design) and was nominated for several others. As the first of the postwar biblical epics—and by virtue of the fact that it was directed by Cecil B. DeMille—*Samson and Delilah* was (perhaps inevitably) firmly rooted in the generic conventions of the prewar era. It shares neither the psychological subtlety of later epics such as *David and Bathsheba* and *Barabbas,* nor the widescreen grandeur of *Ben-Hur* and the 1956 version of *The Ten Commandments.*[3] The music for the film may be seen in similar terms. Paramount executives used their in-house composer Victor Young for the musical score, which was eventually nominated for an Academy Award (although it did not win). Young was a well-respected craftsman, known especially for skill in scoring exotic themes and locales.[4] Like the scores to so many other films during this period, Young's music for *Samson and Delilah* is essentially leitmotivic in structure. The writing is very much in the tradition of classic Hollywood film scores by composers such as Max Steiner and Erich Wolfgang Korngold. Like DeMille himself, Young was in many ways simply relying on tried and true techniques in order to craft entertainment for the new post–World War II generation.

If I have concentrated on sexual desire, history, and the religious in this preliminary discussion, it is not because these form a complete list of generic characteristics, but rather because it was in these three areas that the underscoring—at least potentially—could make the greatest contribution to DeMille's film. The most memorable theme in the movie is surely the melody that Young wrote for the Delilah character—it dominates the score in much the same way that Hedy Lamarr's performance of the role dominates the visual narrative. Young seems less assured with regard to the historical/geographical frame of the film. Despite his reputation as a master of musical orientalism, Young seems to have had little interest in the kind of historical authenticity that was to be of such importance to other biblical epic film composers (most notably, Miklós Rózsa). And while it is possible to hear certain sections of the score as references to a specific Jewish identity, a particular ethnic sound plays a much smaller role in Young's music than it does in other film scores (such as Mario Nascimbene's work for *Solomon and Sheba*). In a similar manner, Young's music for the transcendental moments of *Samson and Delilah* seems to look backward to the tropes and conventions of the prewar era (if not to symphonic and operatic tropes of the nineteenth century). Like the Paramount executives listening to DeMille's pitch, Young was perhaps most comfortable with the parts of the film that had to do with "boy meets girl, and what a boy, and girl!"

Gendering the Opening Credits

The essential character of Young's score is readily apparent from the music that he wrote for the opening credit sequence. As with most typical mid-century Hollywood films, the opening credits for *Samson and Delilah* function both to provide data about the external reality of the film (principally, the names of the stars and those involved in its production), and to suggest key elements of the imaginary world that is about to unfold. Visual elements such as typeface and/ or scenic backdrop are often an important part of this process, but it is primarily through the underscoring that the opening credit sequence typically introduces the fundamental character and emotional mood of the film. The opening credit sequence for *High Noon* (1952)—to take a particularly well-known example of this technique—is accompanied by the ballad "Do Not Forget Me O My Darlin'." "Do Not Forget Me O My Darlin'" returns as nondiegetic music at various points in the film (most notably at the end), but Dmitri Tiomkin uses it as source material for other parts of his score as well. Examples such as these illustrate the links between the music industry and film that were becoming increasingly important during this period, but they grow out of a practice that stretches back into the world of nineteenth-century opera and operetta overtures. Like these overtures, the opening credit music primes the perceptual pump. When themes and melodies from the opening credit music return in the remainder of the film, they are (if only subconsciously) recognized and emotionally marked. In this way, the opening credit music introduces the semiotic logic of the film, drawing the au-

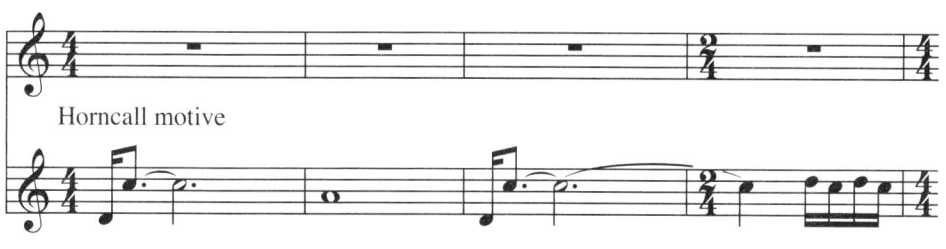

Example 1.1. Samson motive.

dience into its essential soundscape—as well as its attendant mood or emotional ambience—even before the diegesis begins.

Needless to say, the emotional ambience of *Samson and Delilah*—as well as the bulk of its plot—will be largely determined by the erotic/romantic relationship between the two principal characters. The music for the opening credits to the movie—like those to many other mid-century Hollywood films—prepares the ground for this diegesis. It follows what James Buhler, David Neumeyer, and Rob Deemer have called the "conventional musical design" for this music, articulating two distinct theme groups, whose gender associations are impossible to deny.[5] The credit music begins with a three-note call-like motive featuring an upward leap of a minor seventh, a motive that will soon become associated with Samson himself. In both its texture and in its intervallic profile, the motive clearly evokes the horn call and fanfare, musical topoi traditionally associated with masculine vigor and energy (see Example 1.1). With some imagination, we may perhaps also hear in this motive a reference to the blast of the shofar, a suggestion of the specifically Jewish identity of its hero. This music accompanies an image of two hands unrolling an ancient scroll, upon which the title of the film appears. The font used for this title, as well as for the credits that follow, is built up from short angular lines, in imitation of ancient cuneiform writing. As these appear on the screen, we hear a short extension of the fanfare theme (appearing in the upper staff in my transcription), whose distinctive melodic profile will return

Example 1.2. Delilah motive.

at various points in the film in which the plot references the Jewish people or the Jewish land. This extension, with its distinctive augmented second melodic interval, is closely related to the Miriam motive that I discuss below.

Here in the opening credits, this motive leads directly into a brief statement of the Philistine march music that will later be associated with the forces of tyranny. Young uses this march idea to bring the music to a full cadence. An abrupt change in texture and tempo marks the beginning of the second part of the opening credit music: a full, A-A-B-A statement of the melody that will soon be associated with Delilah (see Example 1.2). In its rhythmic and melodic profile, as well as its basic texture, this theme provides a stark contrast with the masculine musical gestures from the very beginning of the opening credit music. Instead of the leaping angularity of the Samson motive, Delilah's music is characterized by scalar motion. It suggests a triplet subdivision of the beat, while Samson's motive (as well as the march idea with which it is occasionally linked) is firmly in duple meter. The quasi-military instrumentation of the Samson motive is set against the lush sound of the strings, playing the Delilah theme in their middle range, accompanied by occasional harp chords. The opening credit music, then, creates what we might almost call an aural analogue of Groesbeck's sketch, focusing our attention firmly on the big brawny athlete and the ravishing sexuality of the leading lady.

Young's music is able to function in this manner, of course, precisely because it conforms so closely to firmly established musical topoi. If Samson's motive is essentially a modified fanfare, so too does the music for Delilah echo that used to depict similarly dangerous women, not only in other postwar biblical epics, but in other cinematic genres as well. The Delilah theme most directly recalls, perhaps, the music that Rudolph Kopp wrote for Cleopatra in DeMille's 1934 epic of the same name. The (anti-) heroines in film noir (to take another example) are also frequently given themes featuring rhythmic ambiguity and slippery or turning melodic figures. Like many other aspects of mid-century Hollywood film scoring technique, this convention is firmly rooted in the long operatic tradition of the femme fatale.[6] Carmen's "Habañera" is probably the proximate source for the film music associated with these dangerous women. Like the music for Bizet's famous character, these themes operate according to an old and very widely distributed semantic logic, in which tonal and rhythmic stability are associated with social and emotional stability.[7] Like the bodies of the women with which they are associated—and in contrast to the masculine angularity of the hero motives— these melodies curve and flow. As in *Carmen,* the sinuous lyricism of these cinematic themes is bound up with sexual seduction and moral turpitude. Young's opening credit music, in short, operates within a very widely distributed and firmly established semantic system.

Women, Domestic and Forbidden

The musical contrasts in the opening credit music, of course, become legible precisely because of the ways in which the film's plot is informed by a familiar narrative archetype, in which the hero must choose between two women who offer contrasting types of erotic/romantic relationships. One of these women is safe and domestic, while the other is a femme fatale, charged with dangerous sexual energy. Bizet's *Carmen* clearly conforms to this plot archetype (with Micäela serving as the domestic woman and Carmen as the femme fatale). In mid-century Hollywood, however, the clearest expression of this plot structure probably comes in film noir. In her article "Women in Film Noir," Janey Place uses the two primary female characters in *Out of the Past* (Ann and Kathie) as example of what she calls the "two poles of female archetypes."[8] In Alfred Hitchcock's *Vertigo,* to cite a well-known example, the nurturing Midge is the domestic woman, while the mysterious Madeleine/Judy (played by Kim Novak) is the femme fatale. The archetype of the "choice between two women" was an especially important part of the plots to the postwar biblical epics, in which (aside from epics about the Christ story such as *King of Kings* and *The Greatest Story Ever Told*) it appears with remarkable frequency. The plot archetype, of course, may find different resolutions in these films. In *Quo Vadis* and *The Ten Commandments,* the hero is able to resist the seductive sexuality of the femme fatale (Poppaea and Nefretiri, respectively) and turns instead to the redemptive power of the domestic woman (Lygia in *Quo Vadis* and Sephora in *The Ten Commandments*). Delilah's seduction of Samson in *Samson and Delilah* is to some extent repeated in *Solomon and Sheba,* in which the hero rejects the virtuous domestic woman Abishag in favor of the sexual allure of the foreign queen. What is significant at this point is not the divergent resolutions of the two-woman plot archetype, but rather the ways in which this archetype becomes the vehicle to explore the connection between the personal and the political, and, more specifically, between world history and sexual desire.

In this regard, an important distinction can be made between what Babington and Evans call the "Roman/Christian epics" (e.g., *Quo Vadis, Demetrius and the Gladiators,* and *Ben-Hur*) and those that are based on material from the Old Testament. In the Roman/Christian epic, the forbidden woman of the plot archetype represents the decadence of the empire (indeed, she is typically herself an empress), while the domestic woman represents the emerging values of Christianity. The romantic/erotic tension in these films thus parallels an essentially religious tension between Christianity and paganism. Unlike his counterparts in the Roman/Christian epics, however, the Old Testament epic hero is typically a king or religious leader. His romantic/erotic crisis is thus inevitably bound up with crises of leadership and national identity.

When the two-woman plot archetype appears in the Old Testament epic, the domestic woman therefore represents the values of the tribe or nation with which the hero—for good or for evil—must in some way make his peace. Largely de-eroticized, she is closely bound up with the family and with family life. In *Samson and Delilah,* for example, Miriam almost always appears accompanied by the child Saul. Conveniently collapsing several generations of the Old Testament historical narrative, the screenwriters for *Samson and Delilah* eventually identify this figure as the very same person who will become the first king of Israel. Miriam functions essentially as a surrogate mother to the future king, but the domestic woman in these epic films more typically inherits her familial/dynastic status from the authority of her father. In *David and Bathsheba,* for instance, the domestic woman Michal is the daughter of Saul (not his surrogate mother), and David's legitimacy is at least to some extent bound up with his loveless marriage to her. In a similar manner, Ahab (the leader of the tribal elders in *Solomon and Sheba*) has confirmed his submission to royal authority by sending his daughter Abishag—the domestic woman of this 1959 film—to be raised at the court in Jerusalem. In *The Ten Commandments* it is Jethro, the sheik of the Midianites, who offers Moses his choice of one of his seven daughters. At the climax of a scene that I describe in more detail in a subsequent chapter, Moses chooses the eldest daughter, Sephora, to be his wife. By marrying her, Moses secures his position in bedouin society. And although Sephora is technically a Midianite, not (yet) a full member of the Hebrew community, her romance with Moses unfolds both literally and figuratively in the shadow of Sinai, the mountain of God. Courting her, Moses finally sheds his residual Egyptian identity and embraces his destiny as a tribal and national leader.

If the domestic woman of this plot archetype is typically associated with home and nation, then the forbidden woman is literally and figuratively foreign. So subsumed is Gina Lollobrigida's character (in *Solomon and Sheba*) in this foreign identity that she is never given a proper name: she remains "the Queen of Sheba" (or "the foreign harlot") throughout the film. Delilah is a daughter of the Philistines, who will deliver the hero into the hands of his foreign enemies. Nefretiri is queen of the Egyptians, tempting the hero to forswear his destiny and embodying the moral corruption against which he must struggle. Unlike an alliance with the domestic woman, a marriage or a sexual relationship with the femme fatale threatens to undermine or destroy the hero's strength and authority. In this context, the motor of the plot is thus the hero's relationship with the forbidden woman, because it is that relationship that threatens his identity as a national and or religious leader. The two-person title format of so many of the Old Testament epics (e.g., *Samson and Delilah, Solomon and Sheba*) in this sense reflects not simply the eroticization of the biblical narratives but also the fact that—in these films—the hero's relationship with the forbidden woman will occupy center stage.

Miriam's Virtue, Delilah's Desire

The plot archetype of the two women intersected only obliquely—or incompletely—with the Old Testament narratives that the screenwriters for the postwar epics used as source material. The greatest challenge, perhaps, was to expand and augment the rather sparse treatment of these gender dynamics in the biblical stories. In the Samson and Delilah story from Judges chapters 13–16, for example, Delilah is only one of a number of women with whom Samson has some kind of sexual relationship. There is no character corresponding to the film's Miriam, only the discontent of Samson's parents that their son could not choose a wife from the tribe of their own people. Instead, much of the biblical narrative is devoted to the relationship between Samson and an unnamed "daughter of the Philistines" who dwells in Timnah. Delilah disappears from the narrative as soon as she is able to extract the secret of Samson's superhuman strength. Neither the scenes in which Delilah visits Samson in his Philistine prison nor the final Samson/Delilah interchange in the Temple of Dagon are present in the Bible. The biblical story of Moses is considerably longer than the story of Samson, but screenwriters for the 1956 film still needed to augment the narrative. The love story of Moses and Nefretiri, upon which the plot of *The Ten Commandments* lavishes so much attention, is not present in the book of Exodus. The Old Testament is even more laconic with regard to the Solomon and Sheba story. Although the two-woman archetype is, so to speak, latent in many biblical narratives, screenwriters needed to expand and modify these stories in order to make the archetype the main motor of their respective plots.

In this process of expansion and modification, screenwriters often made use of various nineteenth- or twentieth-century novelizations of the biblical stories in order to provide interesting plot detail. For his *Samson and Delilah* script, for example, Jesse L. Lasky used certain important plot ideas from Vladimir Jabotinsky's novel *Judge and Fool*.[9] Foremost among these was the idea of linking the Philistine "woman of Timnah" (with whom Samson makes a marriage contract) with the figure of Delilah. Following Jabotinsky's novel, the film script gives this woman a name (Semadar, played by a young Angela Lansbury), and makes her Delilah's older sister.

The character of Miriam—the domestic woman of the two-woman archetype in this film—also finds its antecedent in Jabotinsky's novel.[10] Many of the early scenes in *Samson and Delilah*—including a significant one in which she is not on-screen herself—are devoted to establishing her essential character. In the second scene of the film, for example, Samson's mother Hazel is berating him for his inappropriate marriage choice. She asks him why he can't choose a woman from his own village, and Samson tells her merely that "forbidden figs are sweeter." His mother's reply is telling: "But the sweetest figs grow right in your own garden! Why, from morning to night, Miriam's hands are never idle. And no cross words ever cross her lips." When Miriam herself arrives moments later, Hazel cajoles Samson into revealing his plans to marry a "daughter of the Philistines." Miriam confesses her desire for Samson, but resigns herself to the fact that he does not want to marry her. "I'll always be here," she promises at the end of the scene. The marriage choice of the hero's parents, Miriam is a paragon of industry, virtue, and constancy. Marrying her instead of a Philistine woman would reinforce Samson's role as the leader of the Danite tribe. Rejecting her means, at least to some degree, rejecting home, tribe, and nation.

According to Lasky, the film's screenwriter, DeMille had a great deal of trouble casting this role. The account that Lasky gives in his autobiography is interesting for the light that it sheds on Miriam's character:

> The one part that hadn't been and apparently couldn't be cast was the hometown-girl-next-door, the honest Hebrew maiden that Samson should have married. She had to look like what any Jewish mother would choose for her son, practical, religious, unglamorous, and marvelous about the house. Miriam, the good girl, marriage with whom would have deprived the Bible of its most spectacular love story.[11]

Lasky was friends with the Jewish actress Olive Deering and presented her to DeMille as a "walking synagogue" who would be ideal for the role. DeMille agreed to consider her for it. "I hardly needed [the] warning," Lasky continued, "that DeMille would have my scalp if Olive turned out to be insufficiently Semitic."[12] We do not need to believe all the details of Lasky's account to recognize

Example 1.3. Miriam motive.

Miriam as a kind of stereotypical figure. Her status as an embodiment of Jewish identity is clearly reflected in the underscoring (see Example 1.3). During the scene with Samson—and throughout the film—the shots of Miriam are consistently accompanied by a clearly articulated motive, a motive built from typical orientalist topoi such as the double harmonic minor scale (a harmonic scale with a raised fourth-scale degree) and sob-like appoggiatura figures.[13] In the context of this film, these gestures clearly mark Miriam's Jewish ethnicity.

As I mentioned above, the Miriam motive is very closely related to the extension of Samson's theme, a motive that appears at many points in the film in which the plot foregrounds Jewish history or identity. This minor-mode theme accompanies certain shots in the first scene of the film, for instance, in which an old man is narrating the story of Exodus to a group of children. When Samson's wedding feast with Semadar turns into a violent confrontation between Samson and the Philistine wedding guests, we hear a militarized version of this theme accompanying Samson's heroic victory. The close association between the Jewishness theme and the Miriam motive, in short, reinforces the idea that Miriam character is wholly subsumed into her religious/ethnic identity.

Semadar dies during the fight between Samson and the Philistines, and her position as Samson's principal love interest is taken by her younger sister Delilah. Although Delilah is clearly identified as a Philistine, she is not—as Miriam is—essentially a representative of her nation. The associations of the Miriam motive slip between the personal (Miriam herself) and the communal (the Jewish people), but the Delilah motive is bound up with a unique individual. Following the typical procedures of classic Hollywood film scoring, the texture and orchestration of the Delilah theme are modified to reflect the dramatic situations in which the character finds herself. As we might expect, we hear the theme prominently in the underscoring for the first scene in which Delilah appears, as she flicks plum pits at Samson from her perch atop the wall surrounding her father's house. Here Delilah acts as a young coquette, attempting to attract Samson's attention. Her theme accordingly appears with harp and flute instead of the full strings that articulated her music in the opening credits. Later in the film, as she leads a caravan through the Valley of Sorek, her theme is accompanied by a rocking counterpoint that imitates the gait of the camels. As Delilah comes to dominate the diegesis, so too does her motive—in all of its various manifestations—come to dominate the underscoring.

Her centrality in this respect is most readily apparent during the middle section of the film, which dramatizes the complexities of her relationship with Samson. At this point in the plot, Samson has become the leader of what amounts to a guerrilla war against the Philistines. Motivated in part by Samson's earlier rejection of her, Delilah devises a plan to capture the hero and deliver him into the hands of his enemies. The rich caravan that she leads into the Valley of Sorek is essentially the bait she will use in order to lure Samson into a trap. When Samson comes to raid her caravan, Delilah seduces him. Instead of returning to his role as a guerrilla captain, Samson lingers with her by a pool and in the indulgent luxury of her tent. Eventually he reveals to her the secret of his strength. Despite her earlier promises to the Philistine princes, Delilah is reluctant to take advantage of her knowledge. It is clear that she genuinely loves the Hebrew hero and suggests escaping with him to Egypt. But their love idyll is interrupted by the arrival of Miriam, who tells Samson of the depredations that have been visited upon his family and the rest of the Danites by the Philistines. Miriam's words call Samson back to his duty. He leaves Delilah's tent in order to prepare for the journey back to his homeland, leaving Miriam and the Philistine seductress alone together. Their conversation—as we might expect—reads as a kind of distillation of the two-woman plot archetype:

DELILAH: "You love him. Women cannot deceive each other. It is in your face when you look at him. You want him for yourself!"

MIRIAM: "Yes I love him. In his face I see all that is strong and good. His name is like a cry of hope for us. I dreamed that one day Samson would take me for his wife. But he has never looked upon me as a woman."

DELILAH: "His face, his name! Shadows on a wall! You think that is love? You worship him with prayers and downcast eyes. I love him as a man of flesh and blood."

MIRIAM: "He is not leaving you for me. There is a higher voice that speaks through him, and he will always answer its call. Even your treacherous beauty cannot turn him from it."

DELILAH: "I cannot fight against his god. But no woman will take him from me."

In this scene, as in many other parts of the film, the underscoring functions essentially to articulate the shot/counter-shot structure of the cinematography. In this regard, the use of music in *Samson and Delilah* conforms to the conventional techniques of classic Hollywood film scoring. As the camera shifts back and forth between Miriam and Delilah, we hear distinctive motives on the sound track. The ferocious gleam in Hedy Lamarr's face as she voices this last line helps us to understand it as a turning point in the plot: the moment at which Delilah decides to abandon the idea of escaping with Samson to Egypt. Accompanied by a surging rearticulation of her motive (of course), Delilah instead decides to drug Samson so that she may cut off his hair and deliver him up to the Philistine soldiers. Far from having its desired affect, then, Miriam's intervention thus ends up sealing Samson's fate. By arousing Delilah's jealousy, Miriam condemns Samson to destruction.

Like so many other films that employ the two-woman plot archetype, the script for *Samson and Delilah* typically situates both Miriam and Delilah as objects of the male desire. The Philistine soldiers that march into the first scene of the film refer to Miriam as a "jug of Danite wine that we have not yet tasted," while in the subsequent scene Samson speaks of his potential marriage partners as figs that he will consume. This particular confrontation between Miriam and Delilah, however, opens up a different way to interpret the characters, not merely as objects of male desire but also as (potentially) desiring subjects. Indeed, this scene suggests feminine desire as the primary motor of the plot. In the biblical account on which the film script is based, Delilah betrays Samson for money. In the libretto to Saint-Säens's opera *Samson et Dalila* (although not perhaps in the music), Delilah is motivated by the love of her own people. There is a shadow of this, perhaps, in DeMille's film as well.[14] But the primary motivation for the character in *Samson and Delilah* is jealousy: jealousy that is the consequence of Delilah's physical or sexual desire for the hero.

Turning around the two-woman plot archetype so that it articulates feminine desire rather than the desire of the hero suggests another reading of the *Samson and Delilah* plot, one that places the film in the context of postwar anxieties and hopes concerning gender identities. Changing gender identities and questions about women's independence, of course, had been central to American culture at least since the end of the nineteenth century, crystallizing around figures such as the "New Woman" of the pre–World War I era and the long struggle for women's suffrage. Questions of gender roles and identities were foregrounded again during the middle years of the century. During the war, many women stepped into traditional male occupations and found a new sense of satisfaction in their work. But when the veterans returned to civilian life, many of these female workers were displaced. "Rosie the Riveter" was forced to return to the domestic sphere. Difficulties with this social transition were—at least on the part of conservative commentators—frequently attributed to the rise of the independent woman. Nowhere are anxieties about this independent woman more clearly articulated than in the bestselling 1947 work *Modern Woman: The Lost Sex,* by Marynia Farnham and Ferdinand Lundberg. The first demand of the independent woman, according to Farnham and Lundberg,

> is for sexual gratification. . . . This is the core of the goal—sexual, orgastic [*sic*] equality with men. These women have intellectualized and rationalized their sexual lives, determining that they will have for themselves the experiences and, therefore, the satisfactions that men have. So far as the experiences are concerned, they can carry out their intentions, but where the gratifications are concerned, they meet with dismal, tragic failure. Sexual gratification is not an experience to be obtained through the simple performance of the sexual act. To a very great extent the unconscious exertions of these women to obtain absolute parity with men have resulted in crippling them precisely for this much-desired objective. Dr. Helene Deutsch, among many other psychiatrists, affirms this when she states, "In the light of psychoanalysis, the sexual act assumes an immense, dramatic and profoundly cathartic significance for the woman—but this only under the condition that it is experienced in a feminine, dynamic way and is not transformed into an act of erotic play or sexual 'equality.'"[15]

Delilah may not have "intellectualized and rationalized" her sexual life, but she does conform in many ways to the stereotype of the modern woman, concerned with her own sexual desire, willing and fully able to operate in public realms that were heretofore exclusively male. Miriam, on the other hand, continually deflects her desire for Samson. Even if, as Delilah says, Miriam wants the hero for herself, she functions essentially as the superego of the plot, calling Samson back to his divinely ordained destiny as the champion of the Hebrew people.

The quasi-Freudian scientific tone of *Modern Woman: The Lost Sex* is quite different from the aesthetic of DeMille's film, and it would be a mistake to understand the Delilah character as nothing more than a dramatization of Farnham and Lundberg's hypothetical virago. Nevertheless, their widely quoted book may enrich our understanding of those links between sexual desire and world-historical processes that I have already identified as a key element of the epic style. At the end of the first chapter of their work, the authors foreground these links. "The crisis of contemporary civilization," they write,

> is fundamentally psychic in original cause and in present effect. It is economic, too, and social and political. That we recognize. But it is, fundamentally, psychic. And it revolves around women although originally set into motion by men.
>
> Throughout, it will be seen, women are the principal transmitting media of the disordered emotions that today are so widely spread throughout the world and are reflected in the statistics of social disorder.[16]

When Farnham and Lundberg were trying to discover the root causes of "the disordered emotions" of postwar society, the story of Samson and Delilah, it seems safe to say, was quite distant from their thoughts. Nevertheless, their words return us to the fundamental ground of the postwar biblical epic: namely, to the idea that gender relationships have world-historical consequences. Both DeMille's epic and Farnham and Lundberg's book—albeit in very different ways—reflect the profound anxieties about these consequences that emerged during the postwar period.

Underscoring History

There is little in the original biblical narrative of Samson and Delilah that speaks to these anxieties: little, indeed, that might elevate the story to the world-historical plane. Other biblical narratives make clear links between the hero's actions and their consequences for the Jewish people. In the first and second books of Kings, for example (which narrate the events of the divided monarchy that followed the death of Solomon), the national leaders are continually "doing what was hateful in the sight of the Lord": worshipping false idols or cavorting with foreign women. God's wrath is kindled, not only against kings such as Ahab, but also against the entire nation. Samson, on the other hand (as Michael Stanislawski points out), is the most "un-Jewish" of all biblical heroes.[17] Above I mentioned the ways in which Lasky (and other screenwriters of the Old Testament epics) augmented biblical narratives in order to accentuate the erotic and romantic tensions of their scripts. In the case of the Samson and Delilah narrative, however, screenwriters also needed to "epicize" the original story.

One way in which the screenwriters provided the necessary historical dimension to the Samson and Delilah story, as I suggested above, was to overlay the "two-woman" plot archetype upon it. But Lasky and DeMille also employed the more direct method of prefacing the main diegesis of the film with a voiceover prologue. These kinds of prologues—for reasons that I examine in more detail in a subsequent chapter—were particularly important in the postwar biblical epic. But they also figure prominently in other mid-century cinematic genres.[18] Sometimes—especially in films such as *Laura* (1944) and *Sunset Blvd.* (1950) in which the introductory narration is given by a character in the film's plot—the voiceover accompanies the opening sequence of the cinematic diegesis. In other films, the voiceover constitutes a discrete and quasi-independent cinematic narrative.[19] The voiceover narration in *Casablanca*—to take one particularly well-known example—describes the circuitous route sometimes taken by refugees from Nazi-controlled Europe: leading from Paris south to Marseilles, then across the Mediterranean, and eventually to the eponymous Moroccan city. This perilous journey is represented visually by a line slowly unfolding on a map, an image that is intercut with scenes of planes and ships. Here, as in many other mid-century films, the voiceover presents an essential backstory to the plot: providing information about a specific place and time so that the diegesis may properly begin *in medias res*. The voiceover to *Samson and Delilah,* however, does more than this. It anchors the narrative within a vast mythical/religious history. Like Geoffrey of Monmouth's *History of the Kings of Britain* or Gregory of Tours's *History of the Franks,* the voiceover narrative for DeMille's 1949 film starts quite literally with the creation of the world:

> Before the dawn of history, ever since the first man discovered his soul, he has fought against the forces that desired to enslave him. He saw the awful power of nature arrayed against him—the evil eye of the lightning; the terrifying voice of the thunder; the shrieking, wind-filled darkness—enslaving his mind in shackles of fear. Fear bred superstition, blinding his reason. He was ridden with a host of devil gods. Human dignity perished on the altar of idolatry. And tyranny rose, grinding the human spirit beneath the conqueror's heel. But deep in man's heart, still burned the unquenchable will for freedom.

By definition, the voiceover is distinguished from synchronized dialogue by the fact that it does not belong to any particular body. As Kaja Silverman pointed out in her influential book *The Acoustic Mirror,* this fact gave the speaking voice a special "theological" status. The special status of the voiceover, she wrote,

> is the effect of maintaining its source in a place apart from the camera, inaccessible to the gaze of either the cinematic apparatus or the viewing subject—of violating the rule of synchronization so absolutely that the voice is left without an identifiable locus. In other words, the voiceover is privileged to the degree that *it transcends the body.* Conversely, it loses power and authority with every corporeal encroachment, from a regional accent or idiosyncratic "grain" to definitive localization in the image. Synchronization marks the final movement in any such localization, the point of full and complete "embodiment."[20]

The examples of voiceovers that Silverman cites are almost exclusively from film noir and mid-century woman's films, perhaps because it is in these genres that the embodiment (or transcendence) of the voiceover is so often problematic or ambiguous. There is no such ambiguity in the voiceovers to the postwar biblical epics. In these films, the voiceover is set apart from the diegesis not only because it lacks "an identifiable locus," but also by its syntax and vocabulary. Although the *Samson and Delilah* prologue does not—as the analogous voiceover in *The Ten Commandments* does—literally quote the book of Genesis, it employs a similarly exalted diction. In DeMille's later epic—as in *Solomon and Sheba*—the theological status of the introductory voiceover is further enhanced by its similarity to that other transcendental voice: the voice of God.

In this context, the analogy between the first chapter of the *History of the Kings of Britain* or the *History of the Franks* and the prologue to *Samson and Delilah* is perhaps less gratuitous than it first seems. Like the beginnings of these medieval texts, the prologue to DeMille's film presents a radically abbreviated world history. Each stage of this history is accompanied by appropriate images and sound effects. The first image of the film—a spinning globe, partially shrouded by clouds—recalls similar mid-century cinematic gestures. The spinning globe (without clouds, to be sure) also accompanies part of the voiceover to *Casablanca;* and it appeared as well during the 1930s and 1940s as part of the introductory logo for the widely viewed Universal newsreels. In *Samson and Delilah,* as in these other instances, it serves to contextualize the subsequent diegesis, investing it with world-historical importance. For the remainder of the voiceover prologue, DeMille's cinematography becomes more specific. As we might expect, the director illustrates the "awful power of nature" by violent storm scenes, replete with roiling clouds and flashes of lightning. Out of the "wind-filled darkness," images of idols (looking somewhat like stylized versions of Easter Island megaliths) successively loom. The rise of tyranny is symbolized by images of soldiers' feet marching inexorably across the screen. But when the voiceover turns to the unquenchable will for freedom that burns in the heart of man, these military images are replaced with benign clouds, glowing yellow and orange against a deep blue sky. The camera literally turns its eyes toward heaven, invoking—as in the image of the spinning globe with which the voiceover begins—the creative power of God.

If the spinning globe suggests the world-historical character of the introductory voiceover, so too does the voiceover as a whole frame the specific story of Samson and Delilah as but one chapter in a much more elemental and universal conflict. That conflict is presented in starkly oppositional terms, as a conflict between slavery, idolatry, and fear against freedom, faith, and human dignity. The musical contrasts of Victor Young's underscoring reinforce this opposition in direct and conventional ways. The cosmic chronology symbolized in visual terms by the spinning globe, for instance, finds its musical counterpart in swirling harp arpeggios that accompany a descending chromatic melody. The marching feet of the soldiers—symbolizing the rise of tyranny—are synchronized with an angu-

Example 1.4. Philistine march.

lar A-minor theme in $\frac{4}{4}$ time (see Example 1.4). And as the camera turns its eye toward the heavens at the end of the sequence, we hear shimmering strings in the upper register playing rising diatonic melodies: traditional topoi of transcendence that may be found in any number of nineteenth-century choral, orchestral, and operatic works.[21] Young's underscoring, in short, conforms entirely to traditional patterns. Together with the conventional cinematographic images, and the unambiguous certainty of the voiceover script, it provides a clear moral frame for the filmic diegesis. The dichotomous nature of the imaginary world is expressed by binary oppositions: light versus dark, glimmering clouds or clattering armor; shimmering string melodies versus ominous minor-mode marches. Framed by these totalizing binary oppositions, the filmic diegesis becomes something akin to a moral fable. It is—to invoke the hyperbolic style of the voiceover—simply another chapter in the eternal struggle between freedom and slavery.

The musical contrasts in this opening voiceover anchor the semantic logic of the underscoring for the remainder of the film. In the very first sequence of the main diegesis, for example, we see an ancient street in which an old man is recounting the story of Moses. Youngsters crowd around him, hanging on his words and interrupting his narrative with energetic interpolations at appropriate moments. This idyllic scene is interrupted by a troop of soldiers, dressed very much like the mythical forces of tyranny referenced in the introductory voiceover. It is hardly surprising that they are accompanied by exactly the same A-minor march theme as well. The sound-image clarifies (if any clarification should be needed) that these particular servants of the Philistine king are merely local instantiations of the rise of tyranny, which is "grinding the human spirit beneath the conqueror's heel." The march theme, indeed, will function through the rest of the film as a leitmotif for the Philistine soldiers, a musical symbol for characters who are themselves little more than symbols.

In this respect, Young's practice may fruitfully be compared to scoring for epic films during the silent era. Although—for obvious reasons—these films do not begin with voiceover narrations, they often feature mythic/historical prologues that frame the main diegesis.[22] In his epochal film *The Birth of a Nation,* for instance, D. W. Griffith frames the Civil War narrative of the Stoneman and Cameron families with several sequences that depict "the coming of the African to America." In his score for the film, Joseph Carl Breil emphasizes the importance of these events by associating them with a distinctive, menacing musical theme: the so-called "Motif of Barbarism."[23] According to the ideology of the film, enslavement and forced immigration is morally wrong not so much because it dehumanized Africans, but because it made miscegenation possible. The film holds the mixing of the races responsible for the evils of the Civil War and its aftermath. The literal and figurative embodiment of miscegenation is the mulatto villain Silas Lynch, and when this character appears later in the film he is consequently associated with the same motive that is first used to accompany images of African slaves. In a similar manner, the Philistine march in *Samson and Delilah* helps us identify the specific Philistine soldiers in the main diegesis as the embodiment of a fundamental force: in this case, tyranny rather than miscegenation. In both films, musical repetition encourages us to understand the filmic diegesis in terms of a broader historical sweep.

Underscoring Conversion

In the voiceover prologue to *Samson and Delilah,* this historical sweep is articulated in both political and religious terms. The opening narration presents a straightforward sequence—fear, superstition, idolatry, tyranny—that strongly implies causality. Distorted spirituality leads inevitably to political oppression. And if tyranny is bound up with worship of "devil gods," so too is "the unquenchable will for freedom" bound up with worship of what the film obviously holds as the one true God. The political story of the film—the story of the Israelites' struggle for freedom from their Philistine overlords—will therefore be paralleled by a religious story: the conflict between idolatrous worship of the Philistine god Dagon and the true worship of the God of Israel.

This conflation of the religious and the political was central to DeMille's concept of the biblical epic, and it will return with even greater force in *The Ten Commandments.* For DeMille—as well as for many other conservatives during the immediate postwar period—the intersection of politics and religion had unique topicality and relevance. Like many other Americans, DeMille understood the Cold War as a struggle that was both spiritual and geopolitical. In this—as in so many other ways—the approach of the enormously influential evangelist Billy Graham was representative. As Steven Miller points out,

> Graham offered an emphatically spiritual interpretation of the Cold War. Communism was "Satan's religion," a "great anti-Christian movement" whose gains had been "masterminded" by that same force. The evangelist viewed communism as a

rival faith, complete with its own trinity (to quote the book *Communism and Christ,* which Graham mailed to every member of Congress, along with President Harry Truman and his cabinet): "Marx the Lawgiver, Lenin the Incarnate Truth, Stalin the Guide and Comforter."[24]

If DeMille's postwar biblical epics shared with Billy Graham an "emphatically spiritual interpretation of the struggle between freedom and slavery (whose current instantiation was the Cold War), so too do the films reflect Graham's soteriology, a soteriology that centered around the act of conversion. As scholars such as Robert S. Ellwood and James Gilbert have pointed out, personal conversion was at the heart of Graham's message.[25] Beginning in 1947, and for many decades thereafter, Graham led "crusades" in major cities—at first in the United States and then around the world—in which thousands of people dedicated or rededicated themselves to Christ. In many ways, of course, these crusades were simply the postwar expression of an American revivalist tradition, stretching back through figures such as Dwight Moody and Charles Grandison Finney to the Camp Hill revival, and even further to the Great Awakening of the eighteenth century. But if the message was in some ways similar to that preached by these earlier figures, the medium of that message was distinctly modern. During the postwar period, Graham developed a vast media and publishing empire that he used to broadcast his message to unprecedented numbers of people. Like the producers of so many of the postwar biblical epics, Graham thus used new technologies and organizational principles to convey an essentially conservative message.

Graham turned to the topic of conversion at many points in his voluminous writings, and his description of the process reflects the fact that his explicit goal was to bring the Gospel to as many people as possible. In his best-selling 1953 book *Peace with God,* for instance, Graham acknowledges that "conversion may take many different forms. The way it is accomplished depends largely upon the individual—his temperament, his emotional balance, his environment, and his previous conditioning and way of life."[26] Nevertheless, the archetypal conversion experience for Graham—as for so many others—begins with the "dark night of the soul": with the subject's experience of profound loss. Here again, Graham's description of conversion in *Peace with God* may serve as a representative example:

> In these tragic moments, as the individual stands stripped of all his worldly power
> . . . he recognizes how terribly and completely alone he really is. In that moment, the
> Holy Spirit may cause the worldly bandages to fall from his eyes and he sees clearly
> for the first time. He recognizes that God is the only source of real power, and the
> only enduring fountainhead of love and companionship.[27]

The image of bandages falling from the eyes—of worldly blindness giving way to spiritual illumination—obviously derives from the archetypal account of Paul's conversion from the Acts of the Apostles (this image will feature prominently—albeit in a much different form—in the later biblical epic *Barabbas*). Like so many other biblical references in Graham's writings, however, it appears here more as an idiomatic expression than as a fully developed metaphor. In *Samson and Delilah,* on the other hand, the link between blindness and conversion becomes explicit.

This conversion process happens in two distinct stages. The first of these comes—to use Graham's words—at the moment when Samson has been "stripped of all his worldly power," namely, after he loses his divine gift of supernatural strength. Immediately after the scene between Miriam and Delilah that I discussed above, Miriam sets off on her return journey. Delilah returns to her tent and pours two glasses of wine. Into one of these she drops powder from a vial that she had kept hidden in the base of her feather fan. Samson tells Miriam that he will follow her shortly, and he strides back into Delilah's tent in order to gather his belongings. Once there, Delilah cajoles him to drink the cup of drugged wine, and while he is asleep she cuts off his hair. Since this hair is the source of his superhuman strength, Samson is now defenseless before his enemies. The Philistine soldiers promptly arrive and bind the Israelite hero in chains. Their leader Ahtur promises Delilah not to shed a drop of Samson's blood, but this promise does not preclude other types of punishment. Heating his sword in the coals of a brazier, the Philistine captain prepares to blind the hero. Before he does so, however, Samson prays to God (1:33:40): "O Lord, my eyes did turn away from you to look upon the fleshpots of my enemies. Now you take away my sight, that I may see again more clearly. Blessed be the name of the Lord." In the musical semantics of mid-century Hollywood cinema, conversion—like other inward emotional experiences—seems to call out for musical underscoring. It is hardly surprising, then, that Victor Young provided a distinctive leitmotif to accompany Samson's prayer (see Example 1.5). The characteristic timbre of this passage—shimmering strings playing high in their upper register—stands in stark contrast both to the modal fanfare motives with which Samson is typically associated and to Delilah's sinuous triplet-dominated melodies. With its slow tempo, *sostenuto* articulation, diatonic (B-major) tonality, and homophonic texture (together with typical $\hat{4}$-$\hat{3}$ suspensions), this music strongly evokes the sacred chorale. Victor Young also used this music for a scene in the first part of the movie, in which Samson prays for strength against his enemies. More distantly, it resembles the music associated with "the unquenchable will to freedom" from the introductory voiceover, although it does not quote it directly. Like the music for Delilah and many of the other themes in the score, the prayer leitmotif evokes traditional musical markers for transcendence that stretch back into the nineteenth-century symphonic and operatic repertoire. At the beginning of the prelude to *Lohengrin* (to confine ourselves to an example with which Young was almost certainly familiar), Wagner uses a similar homophonic shimmering-string texture as a musical symbol for the transcendent spirituality of the Holy Grail. This kind of musical association was already a well-established staple of film scoring in the prewar period,

Example 1.5. Samson's prayer.

and similar kinds of music will be linked to transcendence in the later biblical epics as well. As the camera moves back to a shot of the glowing sword and the face
of the Philistine captain, this shimmering string chorale is replaced by underscoring typical of the first part of this scene: the second phrase of the Delilah
melody and then the three-note fanfare idea that is strongly associated with Samson himself. In musical terms, the string chorale thus functions very much as an
interpolation, setting Samson's prayer apart from the normal diegesis of the film
and marking it as sacred speech.

After his blinding, Samson is imprisoned by the Philistines and forced to serve
them as a slave. He spends his days as if he were nothing more than a beast, pushing a millstone to grind the Philistine's grain. Successive camera shots of a wheat
field undergoing the seasonal changes of sowing, ripening, and harvesting establish the passage of time. Delilah has triumphed, and yet she still cannot forget
Samson. A shot of the grinding millstone with the minor-seventh fanfare idea is
enough to introduce the idea of the Israelite hero. A dissolve takes us to Delilah
awakening in her luxurious bed, accompanied—as we might expect—by a statement of her theme. She hears the voices of the Saran ("You cannot undo what has
been done") and that of Samson ("My eyes can never find more beauty than they
see in you"). Delilah rises from her bed and comes to the window, where she begins to pray to the God of Samson: "Give back the light to his eyes," she says; "take
my sight for it."

Delilah's offer to exchange her own sight for that of her beloved, of course,
evokes the central image of blindness that informs Samson's prayer, and it may
at first seem that she has undergone a transformation similar to spiritual awakening of the hero. The plot motif whereby the forbidden woman is converted
to the true faith will return in the 1959 epic *Solomon and Sheba* (although not
in DeMille's next and final foray in the genre, *The Ten Commandments*). Unlike the analogous scene in *Solomon and Sheba*, however, the sequence depicting Delilah's inward transformation in *Samson and Delilah* is not underscored.
This lack of underscoring has many potential meanings. It may simply indicate
that in *Samson and Delilah*—as in *The Ten Commandments*—DeMille's primary

focus is on the spiritual transformation of the hero. The scene also seems to cry out for a feminist interpretation; namely, that the director—by presenting Delilah's prayer without music—is denying her subjectivity, confirming (to paraphrase Laura Mulvey) the woman's "to-be-looked-at-ness." Since music typically functions in *Samson and Delilah* as a marker for emotional affect, its absence in this scene may also have the curious effect of undermining our faith in the genuineness of Delilah's conversion. However we might understand the spiritual dimension of the scene, it is clearly the moment in which Delilah fully realizes the depth of her love for the hero.

Prompted by this love, she now resolves to visit Samson and to offer herself wholly to him. As she enters the dungeon, she finds Samson chained to a millstone, offering another prayer to God. "Be not far from me," Samson prays, "for there is no other help. My strength is melted like wax. My heart is dry of hope. I am blinded and among enemies. O Lord, o my strength! Send me your sign!" At this moment, Delilah places her hand on Samson's naked shoulder. Startled, he turns toward her and asks, "Are you flesh and blood, or an angel of the Lord? . . . Who are you?" Delilah is genuinely remorseful for her actions, but Samson—at least initially—is unappeased. For many months, he tells Delilah, he has asked God for vengeance, and her visitation now provides him the opportunity to take revenge. He lifts Delilah above his head, with the intention—we are led to believe—of smashing her body against the millstone.

At that moment, however, Delilah cries out: "Samson, Samson! Your chains are broken!" In the year since Samson's degradation, his hair has grown back and, unbeknownst to the hero, his supernatural strength has also returned. The camera pans to Samson's uplifted face, and as it does we hear a recapitulation of the shimmering string chorale. The music encourages us to interpret the return of Samson's strength as the direct answer to his prayer. Indeed, this is how Samson himself understands the return of his strength. He sets Delilah down and begins to imagine how he might once again go out against the Philistines. Stumbling amid the amphorae, however, he realizes that this hope is in vain. Delilah offers an alternate plan: to escape with her to Egypt. He must hurry, she says, for in a few hours the Philistine guards will be coming to take him to the Temple of Dagon, where he will be chained between two pillars and forced to humble himself. Upon hearing these words, Samson realizes what he must do. Purged of anger and lust, he has at last been converted into a vessel for God's will; he has at last accepted his heroic destiny.

For those viewers familiar with traditions of European opera and drama, this scene would certainly have resonated (or perhaps continues to resonate) with the famous dungeon scene from the second act of Beethoven's *Fidelio* and the analogous moment in Goethe's *Egmont,* in which the imprisoned hero has a vision of his beloved. Indeed, the screenwriters for this scene may have been influenced (if only subconsciously) by these classical models.[28] As in *Egmont,* the hero's fortunes are bound up with those of his people, and like Florestan, Samson confuses his beloved with an angel. All these scenes dramatize a moment of psychological or spiritual transformation. In this sense, the shimmering string chorale in *Samson and Delilah* occupies the same structural position as the famous ascending oboe line that inaugurates the final section of Florestan's aria in Beethoven's opera. But the prison scene in *Samson and Delilah* ultimately unfolds as a kind of inversion of its famous predecessors. Delilah, after all, is no angelic vision, but a "flesh and blood" woman who—despite the chaste mantle in which she has literally and figuratively robed herself—still represents temptation for the hero rather than transfiguration. More significantly, the scene ends not, as it does in *Fidelio*, with the spiritual intoxication and exhaustion of the hero, but with Samson's voluntary reenslavement. Abandoning the possibility of freedom with Delilah, Samson wraps the chains around his body so that he may be led before the pagan priests in the Temple of Dagon.

The Temple of Dagon sequence begins with a marketplace scene that establishes a mood in which festive celebration and orientalist menace are mingled in equal measure. The underscore begins with the Philistine march, but it is soon followed by exotic triple-meter music, music accompanying an acrobatic dance that presumably forms part of the pagan ritual about to unfold. The appearance of Miriam and Saul is clearly marked with another statement of Miriam's motive; then Delilah enters the temple wearing a magnificent cloak that appears to be made almost entirely of peacock feathers. Last to arrive is Samson himself, who is led out into an arena-like space at the feet of the gigantic idol of the pagan god. Miriam then throws herself at the feet of the Saran to plead for Samson's life. The Philistine king—played by George Sanders with an air of urbane detachment—asks Delilah to determine the hero's fate. Miriam then turns to the Philistine seductress in what amounts to a recapitulation of the previous confrontation between the two women in the Valley of Sorek scene that I described above. Indeed, Miriam directly references this confrontation. "Once in the Valley of Sorek," she says, "you said you loved him. Then set him free. If there is love in you, let me take him back to his people." Just as in the previous scene, however, Miriam's presence enflames Delilah's jealousy and causes her heart to harden. "You want him for yourself," Delilah replies. "You want to feel the strength of his arms about you; to hold him close and comfort him. You want to bear him children. I'd rather see him dead than in your arms."

Delilah's reference to Miriam's potential motherhood, of course, clarifies and extends the dynamic of the two-woman archetype that informs the plot of the film, a dynamic that is reinforced by Victor Young's score. As in the Valley of Sorek scene, Victor Young's underscoring here follows the shot/countershot pattern of the cinematography: shifting between iterations of Delilah's motive and Miriam's motive as the camera changes its perspective. We may see the exact correlation between dialogue and underscoring in a representative page from the conductor's score of this cue, reproduced here as Figure 1.1. Both literally and figuratively, the music thus underscores the tragic consequences of

Figure 1.1. The conductor's score for Miriam and Delilah in the Temple of Dagon from *Samson and Delilah*. Robert D. Farber University Archives and Special Collections Department, Brandeis University.

what Farnham and Lundberg would call Delilah's destructive desire for sexual gratification.

The Saran dismisses Miriam and Saul, and Samson is brought before the mocking crowd. A band of pygmies torments the hero until Delilah intervenes. Pretending to further humiliate Samson, she leads the hero in between the two main pillars of the temples and begs him to save himself by kneeling before the idol. But Samson has other plans. He tells Delilah to leave, and once he is convinced that she has gone, he prays to God for strength. As he does so, the shimmering strings return once more, briefly alluding to the fuller chorale that has underscored earlier moments of sacred speech in the scenes described above (2:03:01). The underscoring continues with Samson motives, together with a brief allusion to Delilah's music as the camera lingers for a few moments on her suffering face. But this music is obscured by crowd noise, which now rises to a climax of mocking laughter. Then the soundscape suddenly collapses into silence as a new camera shot shows the base of the column beginning to crumble and move. Cries of agony mingle with the crashing thunder of falling stones as the temple—together with the giant statue of the idol Dagon—collapses into rubble. Samson perishes among the ruins, along with his Philistine enemies.

Forward and Backward with the Biblical Epic

By the standards of later epic films such as *Ben-Hur* and *The Ten Commandments,* the special effects of the Temple of Dagon scene are simple and crude. The powerful effect that the sequence made on postwar audiences was nevertheless one of the reasons that *Samson and Delilah* had such enormous success at the box office. As was so often the case with postwar biblical epic film, however, the popular success of *Samson and Delilah* was not always accompanied with critical praise. An anonymous reviewer from *Variety,* for instance, notes the "corniness of [the film's] storytelling" and "its old-fashioned technique," even while acknowledging the film's lavishness and size.[29] A review appearing in the *New Yorker* on the last day of 1949 is still more critical:

> It may be said of Cecil B. DeMille that since 1913, when he teamed up with Jesse Lasky to create *The Squaw Man,* he has never taken a step backward. He has never taken a step forward, either. . . . Perhaps DeMille's survival is due to the fact that he has decided in his movie nonage to ally himself with God as his co-maker and to get his major scripts from the Bible, which he has always handled with the proprietary air of a gentleman fondling old love letters. In *Samson and Delilah,* DeMille is back on his usual beat, but this time I'm not at all sure that he has produced a work that enhances the glory of him or his Associate.[30]

The comments of these critics echo the fears voiced by the Paramount executives quoted at the beginning of this chapter. They suggest that—at least for a significant section of the postwar audience—DeMille's film was seen as a generic holdover from an earlier epoch. Indeed, none of the major themes of *Samson and Delilah*—the idea of male conversion, the two-woman plot archetype, the connection between personal drama and grand historical novel—were particularly novel. In historical terms, then, *Samson and Delilah* represented a paradox: a backward-looking film that nevertheless inaugurated the most popular cinematic genre of the postwar period.

The major themes of *Samson and Delilah* would to a greater or lesser degree inform all the postwar biblical epics that were to follow. In the 1950s and early 1960s, however, these themes were inevitably shaped and transformed by new cultural contexts: the political anxieties of the Cold War; the religious awakening of the postwar period (and its subsequent transformation); and the new attitudes toward gender dynamics and sexuality that were beginning to appear on the horizon. Precisely because of its ideological links to the epic of the prewar period, then, the genre of the biblical film became increasingly contested and problematic.

If the ideology of the subsequent biblical epics came to articulate the tension between old and new that was so central to the culture of the postwar period, so too—to adopt the language of the *New Yorker* review—does the music for these films look both backward and forward. Although the review from *Variety* did not single out the ways in which music contributes to the "corniness of the storytelling," Young's score for DeMille's first postwar epic is very much a part of its "old-fashioned technique." His leitmotivic approach to the epic score would remain important for the entire period that I consider in this book. Indeed, the music for the two most popular postwar epic films (*The Ten Commandments* and *Ben-Hur*) can in many ways be understood as a development ("intensification" may be a better word) of Young's basic technique. And yet the film scores that followed in the wake of *Samson and Delilah*—those of Bernstein and Rózsa included—also began to reflect the profound changes in postwar music: the idea of authenticity (manifested both in the impulse toward historically informed performances and also in the emerging folk music revival); the development of new techniques for the manipulation of sound; and, above all, the deepening divide between art music and popular music. In this sense, the conventionality of the *Samson and Delilah* score was less a model than a point of departure for subsequent composers of biblical epic scores.

2 Turning Away from "Concocted Spectacle"

Alfred Newman's Score for
David and Bathsheba

By 1951—the year in which both *David and Bathsheba* and *Quo Vadis* premiered—the practice of supplementing box office receipts by commodifying cinematic music was already well established. This commodification took a variety of forms. Later in the decade (after the long-playing record became established as a commercially viable medium for recorded sound), "original sound track" albums became important. But in the late 1940s and early 1950s, the principal media for the dissemination of film music (outside of the films themselves) were concert music (such as the *Spellbound* Concerto that Miklós Rózsa created from his score for Hitchcock's *Spellbound,* or the Sinfonia Antarctica that Vaughn Williams developed from his score for Charles Frend's *Scott of the Antarctic*) and popular songs, either taken directly from the film or else cobbled together by adding words to prominent themes from the film score. These songs (and, to a lesser degree, the concert music as well) could then be recorded and/or sold as sheet music. Along with various picture books, novelizations, and other kinds of material, these ancillary products orbited around mid-century films like so many moons around a central planet.

The density of this orbital field—needless to say—varied greatly from film to film. None of the movies from the 1950s—not even blockbusters like *The Ten Commandments* and *Ben-Hur*—were accompanied by anything approaching the panoply of books, posters, lunchboxes, and action figures that surrounded (and continue to surround) the *Star Wars* film franchise. For other films under consideration here—such as *The Robe* and *The Silver Chalice*—the primary cross-marketing relationship was with the book upon which they were based. In these cases (to extend my metaphor), book and film were like twin planets orbiting around each other. During the 1950s, the income generated by these supplementary materials was no doubt dwarfed by the box office income for the film. For studios and publishers, they were on the whole little more than ephemera. But for the historian, they provide a valuable index of the ways in which various films intersected with (and helped to shape) more general cultural and aesthetic categories. Just as an examination of the material and kinetic properties of a moon may provide information about the main planet that it orbits around, so too does a study of this ancillary material provide interesting insight into the film with which it was associated.

We might use this ancillary material to approach the aesthetic differences between *Samson and Delilah* and what we might consider its successor in the genre of the postwar biblical epic: Henry King's *David and Bathsheba.* In musical terms, the most significant moon to orbit Cecil B. DeMille's film was almost certainly the popular "Song of Delilah," with words by Jay Livingston and Ray Evans.[1] The sheet music cover features Hedy Lamarr and Victor Mature in a reclining embrace and announces that the song is "inspired by the Paramount Picture, Cecil B. DeMille's Masterpiece *Samson and Delilah.*" Livingston and Evans's verses have no direct connection to the plot of the film (Samson is never mentioned) but they are set—as we might expect—to a foursquare iteration of Victor Young's Delilah theme. It appears here very much as it does in the opening credit sequence of the film, only shorn of the thematic interpolations (Samson's minor-seventh horn calls; the fragments of the Philistine march) that accompany its cinematic version. With its brief mood-setting introduction and thirty-two-bar A-A-B-A structure, "The Song of Delilah" conforms easily to the expectations for popular songs during the period. The sheet music is written for voice and piano, but (like other songs of the period) includes ukulele chords in tablature as well. Nat King Cole recorded "The Song of Delilah" on the Decca label in 1950, adding a bolero-like beat and orientalist orchestration (bongo drums, solo flute, etc.), presumably in order to capitalize on the exotic allure of the Hedy Lamarr character. In "The Song of Delilah," in short, Young's film music takes its place alongside countless other products of postwar popular culture that simultaneously celebrate and warn against the dangerous allure of the forbidden woman.

The dangerous allure of the forbidden woman was also central to the plot of *David and Bathsheba,* and a quick search of popular sheet-music titles from 1951 will uncover a "David and Bathsheba" published by Twentieth Century–Fox (the studio that released the film). The cover of this sheet music shows a seminude Bathsheba being bathed by two black female servants, reproducing (albeit indirectly) the most famous scene from the film. The song "David and Bathsheba" would thus seem to have the same relationship to the Henry King film as "The Song of Delilah" bears to the *Samson and Delilah* movie. There is, however, one crucial difference. "The Song of Delilah" is almost a direct transcription of Young's film music. Neither the words nor the music to "David and Bathsheba," however, have anything to do with Alfred Newman's score.[2]

The most logical source material for a counterpart to "The Song of Delilah" would have been the evocative theme that Newman wrote for Bathsheba (the for-

Example 2.1. Bathsheba theme (as it appears in the opening credit music).

bidden woman in the 1951 film). Like many of the themes for other forbidden woman characters, this music features a distinctive chromatic slip, a gesture that is typically bound up with the threat of moral slippage (see Example 2.1). Another typical forbidden woman thematic gesture is the turning quarter-note triplet figure that Newman uses as a kind of contrapuntal answer to the first phrase of the Bathsheba theme, a gesture that recalls similar turns in the Delilah music.

Although the screenplay for *David and Bathsheba* does not identify Bathsheba as a foreign woman, the orchestration of her theme includes certain exotic touches (such as the finger cymbals that punctuate the ends of each sub-phrase) that recall similar kinds of textures used for certain appearances of the Delilah theme in *Samson and Delilah*.[3] Apart from its unusually disjunct melodic contour, then, Newman's Bathsheba theme is saturated with gestures that (as I discussed in the previous chapter) were well established musical markers for seduction and dangerous feminine sexuality.

Despite the features that link the Bathsheba motive to music for other mid-century cinematic femmes fatales, however, its irregular phrase structure and awkward chromatic leaps seem to have made it unsuitable for translation into popular song. There was, in other words, no "Song of Bathsheba" for Nat King Cole (or some other postwar singer) to record. For cross-marketing sheet music sales, the film and music industries turned instead to other music: the choral rendition of the Twenty-third Psalm that appears near the end of the film. In place of a sultry embrace between two lovers, the cover features a generic religious image of a stained-glass window. Newman's unusual harmonic progressions are presumably too complex to be rendered by the typical ukulele player—the music seems intended instead for performance in church. Even though *David and Bathsheba* and *Samson and Delilah* share similar settings, plot structures, and dramatic themes, the orbital field of ancillary materials that surrounds each film is thus quite different.

Example 2.2. David's war march.

These differences do not necessarily indicate that *David and Bathsheba* is an inherently more religious film than *Samson and Delilah,* or that Susan Hayward (who plays Bathsheba in King's film) is any less erotically provocative than Hedy Lamarr. But they do suggest some of the stylistic differences between Newman's music and the more conventional score that Young wrote for DeMille's film. Less constrained by musical topoi (e.g., Samson's horn-call motive or the minor-mode march used for the Philistines), Newman's fundamental musical language for *David and Bathsheba* is much more harmonically and rhythmically complex than the score to *Samson and Delilah.* The stylistic differences between the two scores are cast into higher relief by the fact that the films share so many other qualities. Both, of course, use the Old Testament as their source, and the sets and costumes that DeMille and King use to represent the world of ancient Israel have much in common. More significantly, the narratives of both films are informed by the two-woman plot archetype that I described in the previous chapter. King's film, to be sure, also includes many incidents from the Old Testament narrative in which erotic relationships play no role: the battle with the Philistines before the gates of Rabbah, and (as flashbacks) the fight between David and Goliath and the battle on Mt. Gilboa. But just as *Samson and Delilah* concentrates on the attraction between its two main characters, the focus of Philip Dunne's script is the relationship between David (played by Gregory Peck in his only biblical epic role) and Bathsheba. This relationship begins in adultery, when Bathsheba is still the wife of Uriah the Hittite. Even after Uriah's death (for which David is largely responsible) and David's subsequent marriage to Bathsheba, the relationship remains tainted by sin. In this sense, Bathsheba is the forbidden woman of the two-woman plot archetype, holding a position similar to that of Delilah in DeMille's 1949 film.

The similarity between the plot structures of *Samson and Delilah* and *David and Bathsheba* is reflected in the musical structure of the films' opening credits. As in Young's score, and in accordance with the conventions that dictated such music in mid-century Hollywood, the feminine theme in the opening credit music to *David and Bathsheba* is juxtaposed with masculine motives. If Young frames his Delilah music with Samson's motives and the Philistine march, the analogous function in Newman's score is filled by another march-like motive: one that is associated throughout the film with David's warlike energy in both its positive and negative aspects (see Example 2.2). Despite the stylistic differences that distinguish Newman's score from Young's, the opening credit music for *David and Bathsheba* fills much the same function as in *Samson and Delilah*. In each case, this opening music adumbrates the central relationship of the hero and the forbidden woman: the relationship that will dominate the plot of both films.

But if the large-scale semantic strategy—the juxtaposition of "seductive woman" music with warlike masculine themes—is broadly similar, the nature of the individual musical gestures is not. Both the Bathsheba theme and David's war march are far more dissonant and (in the case of the Bathsheba theme) harmonically unstable than their counterparts in *Samson and Delilah*. The same qualities that render the Bathsheba theme less suitable for repurposing as a popular song also color this opening credit music, inflecting the semantics of the gendered juxtaposition of masculine and feminine music in new sorts of ways. The complexities made Newman's music more difficult to assimilate into the popular musical culture of the early 1950s, and helped to place King's film in a different generic context than *Samson and Delilah*. Indeed, certain aspects of the film have led some scholars to associate *David and Bathsheba* with the woman's film rather than the epic, and there are also strong generic connections to the psychological films that were so popular during the 1940s.[4] In their extensive discussion of *David and Bathsheba,* Babington and Evans also foreground its links to other genres: "Traces of three genres are visible: Film Noir, 1940s Melodrama (particularly the romantic 'Woman's Picture'), and the Western pastoral."[5]

It was perhaps these different generic contexts that Bosley Crowther had in mind when he noted in his 1951 review of the film that *David and Bathsheba* "avoids to a great extent the pageantry and overwhelmingly concocted spectacles of some Biblical productions which have emanated from Hollywood." Instead of spectacle, interpersonal relationships and processes of psychological transformation are the main focus of King's film. Although Crowther does not mention Newman's score, music plays a central role in articulating the moral ambiguities and emotional complexity that are at the heart of the story. In terms of cinematic history, then, Newman's *David and Bathsheba* score offers a very different model of what music in biblical film might be.

Music, Dialogue, and Surveillance:
The Two Women of *David and Bathsheba*

The generic differences between *Samson and Delilah* and *David and Bathsheba* first emerge in connection with the domestic woman of the two-woman plot archetype. The character who fills this role in *David and Bathsheba* is Michal: the daughter of Saul and (as we learn in the first scene between her and David) the first of David's wives. In contrast to Miriam (and other similar characters such as Sephora from *The Ten Commandments* and Abishag from *Solomon and Sheba*), Michal is not the representative of a general Hebrew ethnic/religious identity, but rather the embodiment and carrier of dynastic legitimacy. In the first and second books of Samuel—which include the most detailed biblical accounts of this period in Israel's history—the relationship between David and Michal is somewhat ambivalent. After David proves his excellence in battle, Saul gives him his daughter as a wife. Later—when Saul turns against David and attempts to slay him—Michal protects her husband and allows him to escape into exile. Michal, however, does not follow her husband, but instead returns to the control of her father. Saul then gives her away a second time to another man (presumably to obtain a new ally in his struggle against David). When David secures the kingship after the death of Saul, he takes Michal as his wife once more. Michal is mentioned again in the context of David's entry into Jerusalem. Looking out a window at the new king dancing before the Lord, Michal "despises him in her heart" and speaks scornfully to him about his impropriety. It is this latter account of Michal—which shows her as a mocking shrew rather than as a loving helpmate—that provides the touchstone for her character in *David and Bathsheba*. In the film, it is Michal's coldness and hostility that is to a large degree held responsible for David's adulterous affair with Bathsheba. Michal's shrewishness—to put this another way—partially exonerates David's sin.[6] Indeed, by giving Michal a sharp tongue and a willingness to indulge in political machinations, Philip Dunne (the scriptwriter for the film) seems to justify and valorize David's relationship with Bathsheba. Alone among the domestic woman characters in the Old Testament epics under consideration in this book, then, Michal is a deeply unsympathetic character.

Her first appearance comes early in the film, immediately after David has rather unsatisfactorily brokered a dispute between his two sons Amnon and Absalom (an unsuccessful attempt, we might say, to deal with question of dynastic legitimacy manifesting itself in the next generation). Both have laid claim to a vineyard, and David is compelled to award the land to Amnon (his elder son and heir to the throne). By way of compensation, he gives Absalom a gilded dagger and then strides upstairs toward his private chambers. A brooding ostinato figure in the underscoring—representing, perhaps, David's troubled thoughts—accompanies the transition into the next scene. When David enters his chambers, he sees Michal waiting for him. The underscoring abruptly stops, creating a perceptual edge that draws attention to the significance of this moment of recognition. We may think of this musical gesture as an inverted stinger, marking an event not by a sudden burst of sound but by a sudden silence. For obvious reasons, it is especially effective in films like *David and Bathsheba* in which underscoring plays such a large role. In this context, the lack of underscoring for the ensuing scene articulates the prosaic and essentially loveless nature of Michal's marriage with David. Their conversation, tense and charged with hostility, eventually turns to the topic of their own relationship. Michal accuses David of loving only himself. "My love was wasted," she tells her husband; "you had no need of it." In his defense, David brings up painful events from the past:

DAVID: "Is your memory so short? I had great need of it once. I begged you on my knees, but you deserted me. You refused to follow me into exile. You even dishonored your vows, and let your father marry you to another."

MICHAL: "Against my will!"

DAVID: "You can say so. But I cannot help thinking that real love would have fathered a stronger will."

MICHAL: "Then why did you take me back?"

DAVID: "You might have guessed. Without Saul's daughter at my side, the northern tribes would never have acknowledged me as king. By taking you back, I made Israel one."

This hard truth evidently strikes Michal to the heart, for she turns aside her face and begins to sob. This emotional change is marked by the reintroduction of the underscore: a low, mournful melody in the Phrygian mode, played by a solo bassoon. David says a few more words about the need "to go on living," but Michal remains silent. Recovering her composure, she walks proudly out of the chamber without a word of farewell. David strides out of the chamber as well, but in the opposite direction: onto a balcony that overlooks the house of Uriah the Hittite.

A brief moment of silence articulates a sea change in the orchestral texture of the underscoring: from the dark counterpoint of low woodwinds to high, suspended notes in the violins. What this shift in the underscoring articulates is a basic cinematic topos that appears in countless films in nearly every film genre, namely, the moment when the (male) hero first sees the object of his desire. It has more direct analogues, of course, not only in countless visual representations of the David/Bathsheba story, but also in many other biblical epics.[7] For his 1934 epic *The Sign of the Cross,* for example, DeMille essentially imported the bathing femme fatale motif for the famous scene in which Claudette Colbert (playing Messalina) bathes in asses' milk. There is a similar—and largely gratuitous—bathing scene for Gina Lollobrigida in *Solomon and Sheba.* Like these analogous scenes from other films, the sequence from *David and Bathsheba* is accompanied by prominent underscoring. The gaze is first articulated by sustained chords played in the upper register of the strings, a shimmering sound that recalls similar transcendent music from *Samson and Delilah* (as well as music in similar dramatic contexts). These textures serve—in musical terms—as a prologue to a full exposition of the Bathsheba theme, played by the strings in their middle register (see Example 2.3). The link between the Bathsheba motive and the character on the screen is unambiguous here; in this sense Newman's music functions very much like the Delilah theme in Young's score. But this correspon-

Example 2.3. David sees Bathsheba.

dence masks a deeper difference between the two films: a difference that has to do with the relationship between the two principal female characters.

In *Samson and Delilah,* the scenes between Miriam and Delilah are central to the plot: it is arguably Delilah's jealousy of Miriam that provokes her decision to cut off Samson's hair. The confrontation between the domestic and forbidden women (between Miriam and Delilah) is articulated through the contrasting leitmotifs with which the two characters are associated. In *David and Bathsheba,* however, the domestic woman and the forbidden woman do not confront one another directly—indeed, they never appear together in the same cinematic frame. In aural terms, the opposition between these two characters does not take the form of a juxtaposition between two contrasting leitmotifs (as it does in DeMille's film), but rather as an opposition between speech and music, or better, the opposition between two different kinds of silence. In the Michal/David scene, it is music—the traditional analogue of the emotional life—that is silent. In a film that is so saturated with underscoring, Michal's confrontation with David stands out simply because it lacks music. Unlike Miriam, Michal has no leitmotif: or, perhaps better to say, her leitmotif is the silencing of music. Michal and David negotiate but they no longer love. When David sees Bathsheba, it is instead speech that is stricken dumb. He cannot bargain, he cannot justify; he can only feel.

Henry King and Alfred Newman, of course, were not the first to use music as a generalized marker for the erotic desires that that might undermine the rationality of the word.[8] The foregrounding of the underscore during the gaze sequence, then, is hardly surprising. More interesting are the ways in which the juxtaposition between music-less text and text-less music functions in two other scenes: scenes that articulate the complex emotional relationships between the hero and the two principal female characters. The first of these occurs only a few minutes after the scene in which David watches Bathsheba bathing. Aroused by sexual desire, he sends his servant to command Bathsheba to dine with him that very night. As the king issues his orders, Bathsheba's motive sounds continually. But when the woman herself arrives in his chambers (17:49), the underscore ends. It is replaced by awkward dialogue in which David speaks obliquely about his "hot blood," and tries to get information from Bathsheba about her sexual intimacy with her husband Uriah. The lack of music during this exchange, we might say, mirrors the dryness of the previous exchange between David and Michal. In both cases, the absence of music references the absence of genuine emotional connection. When David kisses her, Bathsheba is unresponsive, and no music underscores the clinch. Unwilling to force sexual intimacy, David dismisses Bathsheba, proud in the belief that he has never taken anything that has not been freely offered. "At least," he says to Bathsheba, "I can console myself with the thought that your modesty matches your beauty." Instead of leaving, however, Bathsheba takes control of the conversation. "Perhaps you would prefer truth to modesty, sire," she replies. She admits to watching David walking on the terrace, and to knowing that he would be watching her that very evening. Before he gazed on Bathsheba bathing, then, he was himself the object of Bathsheba's gaze.

Bathsheba's confession marks a turning point in the filmic diegesis, but it also carries more significant theoretical freight. If the description in 2 Samuel chapter 11 of David watching Bathsheba bathing herself is not the *locus classicus* of the voyeuristic male gaze, then it is certainly one of its archetypal manifestations. The cinematic narration of this scene in *David and Bathsheba,* then, calls out for interpretation in terms of classic feminist film theory, theory that postulates audience identification with the voyeuristic gaze of the male hero. This central notion of identification is neatly summarized by Julie Kelso, who describes the process whereby "the spectator identifies first with the gaze of the camera and then with the gazes of the characters. As such," she continues, "the spectator comes to be sutured into the world of the film as its 'subject,' with meaning arising at this very juncture."[9] Cheryl Exum's analysis of the bathing scene is directly informed by this idea. The male viewer of the film, she writes, "like the male reader of the biblical story, is invited to take David's symbolic position as the focalizer of the gaze: he can look through David's eyes; he can fantasize himself in David's place. The woman is naked for his pleasure."[10] By reversing David's gaze, then, Bathsheba is not simply observing a lonely man (although she is certainly doing that). She is also inverting a foundational spectatorial archetype.

The Bathsheba of Henry King's film, of course, is hardly the first female cinematic character to assume the (male) position as the "focalizer of the gaze." In her book *The Desire to Desire,* Mary Ann Doane writes extensively about such characters as they appear in a different cinematic genre, namely, the women's films of the 1940s. In these films, she writes, "one can readily trace . . . recurrent suggestions of deficiency, inadequacy, and failure in the woman's appropriation of the gaze. It is the very concept of subjectivity and its place in feminist theory which is in question. The predicament is specified most succinctly in the question posed by Ann Kaplan, 'Is the gaze male?'"[11] If the gaze is by definition male, then the image of a female spectator—such as Bathsheba confesses herself to be—is inherently problematic. As an example of this kind of character, Doane focuses on the figure of Helen in the 1946 film *Humoresque.*[12] At the climax of *Humoresque,* Helen commits suicide by walking into the ocean (to the strains of the "Liebestod" from *Tristan und Isolde*). Her death seems to confirm the impossibility—

Example 2.4. David and Bathsheba love theme (beginning).

or at least the instability—of the female spectator in the context of mid-century Hollywood cinema. Bathsheba's fate, on the other hand, suggests a more complicated or ambivalent interpretation of this cinematic topos. *David and Bathsheba* will not end with Bathsheba's suicide, but rather with the reconfirmation and reinvigoration of her marriage with David. How, then, are we to interpret the meaning of the reversed gaze?

In their analyses of *David and Bathsheba,* both David Gunn and Julie Kelso (albeit in very different ways) take up this very question. The fact that the object of the gaze (Bathsheba, in this case) might be looking back, according to both Kelso and Gunn, undermines the stability of male subjectivity within the film. Neither of these scholars has anything to say about the music in this scene, and although their arguments are certainly convincing, they may be enriched and modified by a consideration of the film's underscoring. For just as in the previous scene (in which we see David looking at Bathsheba), the desiring gaze is marked by the introduction of music.

As Bathsheba reveals her own secret surveillance of the king, the underscoring begins again, first with a new theme in the woodwinds and then—as we might expect—with Bathsheba's own melody. As in the previous sequence, then, the introduction of underscoring is bound up with desire. And yet this (feminine) desire is—at least at this point in the film—markedly different from David's lust. Bathsheba is not interested only in sexual intimacy. "Think not of this one night," she says to David, "but of all the days and all the nights to come. Think if I can give you all that you need, for as long as you live, as your wife." It is of course easy to understand Bathsheba's words cynically, as a disempowered woman's attempt to bargain sexual intimacy for the status of marriage. The underscoring, however, suggests a different interpretation. The word "wife" is marked by the introduction of a new theme, played first by the flute and then by the strings, that I have transcribed as Example 2.4. This theme forms the foundation of the underscoring for the remainder of the scene, in which David discloses his true desires. What he wants is not merely—or even primarily—the enjoyment of Bathsheba's body, but rather a companionate marriage based on true understanding, freed from the power relationships attendant upon his royal status. This is the kind of understanding—the kind of love—that Bathsheba longs to offer him. The underscoring helps to make it clear that Bathsheba's desiring gaze is not simply a mirror of David's voyeuristic lust. The love theme, after all, is quite distinct from the Bathsheba motive. In this context, the quasi-sequential upward melodic gestures may be understood as successive waves of passion: the prominent two-voice contrapuntal texture as a musical representation of two personalities twining around each other. Bathsheba does not so much return David's gaze as transform it. Her desire is domestic, and it domesticates his desire in return.

That is not to say that Bathsheba's gaze successfully challenges the gender dichotomies articulated by the film, still less that it inverts the gendered power dynamics typically encoded in mid-century cinema. David still occupies the subject position in the film, and his mastery over Bathsheba is never questioned. In this sequence, however, the interplay of music, speech, and silence, of gazing and the reversal of the gaze, does not serve primarily to reinscribe these power relationships. Its main role is rather to articulate the essential conflict of the film, the conflict between sovereignty and desire. The plot will turn on the possibility—or impossibility—of reconciling David's love for Bathsheba with his duties as king.

Encountering the Past

In this broadest sense David's dilemma is essentially the same one that Samson faces in the Valley of Sorek scene from *Samson and Delilah,* in which Samson must decide between Delilah's seductive sexuality and his duties as judge and protector of the Danites. The characters in *David and Bathsheba* are drawn with much more psychological (and musical) complexity, to be sure, but the fundamental tension is the same. A more important distinction between *Samson and Delilah* and *David and Bathsheba* concerns the way in which the two films treat another topos of the biblical epic plot; namely, the hero's conversion experience. In DeMille's film, as we have seen, the steps of Samson's conversion are articulated by prayer. In *David and Bathsheba,* on the other hand, the hero can only find his path to God by coming to grips with his past; it is not simply a turning, but also a turning back.

As with Samson, David's turn to God unfolds in distinct stages. The first of these takes place in the sequence that follows immediately upon the David/Bathsheba scene that I described above. We may think of this scene as the conclusion of the first act of the film.[13] It operates—to use Rick Altman's terminology once again—through both syntactic generic markers (the two-woman plot archetype) and semantic ones (the bathing scene) in order to introduce and articulate the film's primary relationships. The second act begins with another of these generic markers, namely, the pastoral/romantic idyll in which the hero and the forbidden woman develop their love in the context of some relaxed, idealized, natural setting. As with so many of the other generic markers of the postwar bib-

Example 2.5. Shepherd's tune.

lical epic, we may find analogues of the pastoral/romantic idyll in other filmic genres, in spoken plays and in operas.[14] In the specific context of the biblical film, these scenes ultimately reference the *fons et origo* of the topos: Adam and Eve in the Garden of Eden.[15] These kinds of scenes occur in many of the postwar biblical films. Samson and Delilah, for instance, share idyllic moments bathing by a pool in the Valley of Sorek, while in King Vidor's 1959 film Solomon and Sheba float on a small boat among the reeds, twined together in an indolent embrace. The scene near the beginning of the second half of *The Ten Commandments,* in which Nefretiri invites Moses onto her barge in order to seduce and/or humiliate him, may be understood as an unrealized romantic idyll that alludes to the generic topos without developing it.

The analogous sequence in *David and Bathsheba* begins with bucolic images of sheep and a rustic peasant boy. A solo oboe sounds in the underscoring, playing a simple tune in the Lydian mode, unaccompanied. Here, of course, Newman is drawing on conventions that stretch back into the nineteenth-century symphonic and operatic literature and beyond, conventions that link the solo oboe with the shepherd's pipe and with the pastoral more generally. In the context of *David and Bathsheba,* however, the solo oboe carries a more specific association with David's childhood. David was a shepherd before he became a king; the solo oboe thus comes to symbolize the simplicity of his early life in contrast to the convoluted politics and emotional tensions of the court. In the conversion scene that I describe below, this contrast becomes the locus of David's emotional/psychological crisis. And although there is little in the visual composition of this scene that might suggest emotional tension, the Lydian mode in which the shepherd's tune is cast might perhaps adumbrate the deflating sense of loss with which this complex of scenes will end (see Example 2.5).

This crisis is adumbrated by the drama of idyll. After the opening shot of the shepherd with his flock, the camera pans to David and Bathsheba lying together on a blanket, on a hillside dotted with flowering trees. Bathsheba asks David to tell her about his past, to tell her "of the boy you once were."[16] The love theme from the previous scene plays in the underscoring, suggesting that the ensuing narration is a prelude to lovemaking. The lovers' kiss is interrupted by the shepherd boy with his bleating sheep, and David turns once more to stories of his own childhood tending his father's herds. "Once when I was a boy," he tells Bathsheba, "we had a year when even the wells ran dry. . . . That was the year that I fought the wolves." Eight wolves attacked his flock, David explains, but he was able to kill six

Example 2.6. Mt. Gilboa fanfare motive (beginning).

of them with his sling. Inspired by his own story, David decides to show his skill to Bathsheba, to replay, in other words, the heroic events of his childhood. He borrows a sling from the shepherd boy and chooses a tree as a target. But David has lost his skill. The young boy takes his sling back and hits the tree on his first attempt. Bathsheba's flirtatious laughter deflects David's embarrassment, but we nevertheless understand David's failure as a symbol of a deeper crisis. If David can no longer defend the sheep from the wolves, how can he defend his human flock—the people of Israel—from their enemies?

If the first part of the idyll—the scene with the shepherd boy—represents David's encounter with his childhood, the second part of the idyll concerns the more recent past. The two lovers hear the bleating of a young lamb whose mother has been caught in the brambles. David helps an old shepherd free the ewe, and in so doing discovers that the man has only one arm. "I'm an old soldier, sir," he says to David as he helps the man out of the brambles. "Fought for the king." In the underscore, Newman places a dissonant fanfare-like motive, in which muted trumpets play the principal melodic line (see Example 2.6). Preferring honesty to flattery, David does not reveal his true identity: "For David?" he asks. "No, not him," replies the old soldier, "For the king . . . King Saul." Responding to David's questions, the old soldier describes the battle on Mt. Gilboa. The rocky summit itself looms nearby, and the old soldier is able to tell David of how Saul and his son Jonathan perished heroically at the hands of the Philistines. Jonathan was David's best friend, and David's feelings of inadequacy, as we will soon discover, are enormously heightened by the sense that he has betrayed this friendship. "'Twas a black day for Israel: the king gone, Jonathan gone, and none worthy to take their place," says the soldier in conclusion. "Yet Israel found a king," David replies, "in David." "Saul was king," says the old soldier, momentarily straightening his crooked spine; "Jonathan should be king today." As in the earlier scene in his chambers with Michal, David has no answer to the charge that he is unfit to inherit Saul's sovereignty.

Example 2.7. Mt. Gilboa theme (beginning).

David's sense of his essential inadequacy is enormously intensified in the following scene. Night has fallen, and Bathsheba and David have found shelter in a rustic hut at the base of the mountain. But David is unable to sleep. He stands under the eaves, staring up at the mountain's shadowy slopes. In the underscore, new material introduced by the bassoon launches the longest cue in the film—indeed, one of the longest cues in any of the biblical epics. For nearly four minutes, there is no dialogue at all: the drama is carried forward solely by the cinematography and by the continuous underscoring (see Example 2.7). Its tempo—as well as certain aspects of the rhythm—resemble that of a slow march (albeit one in triple meter), and, indeed, the theme accompanies David as he leaves the shelter of the hut and begins to climb toward the summit of Mt. Gilboa. Bathsheba, too, is restless, and the camera temporarily cuts away to show her rising from her bed inside of the hut and watching her beloved. Newman continues the Mt. Gilboa theme in the underscore but adds a passionate violin counterpoint to it in a kind of textural echo of the contrapuntal treatment of the love theme in the earlier scene. We are reminded, perhaps, that David and Bathsheba's love is bound up, not only with David's voyeuristic gaze, but also with Bathsheba's more surreptitious observation.

The camera then returns to David's restless ascent of the mountain. Momentarily adopting the hero's point of view, it focuses briefly on the shattered wreck of a battle chariot. As it does so, the underscoring recalls the dissonant fanfare first heard in conjunction with the old soldier's narrative in the previous scene. The abrupt chords—here played *forte* in the trumpets—function like a stinger. We may hear them as a kind of psychic eruption—as the moment when David's guilt-ridden thoughts about the battle rise up to take control of his consciousness. As David arrives at the summit of the mountain, the camera adopts his point of view in a striking tracking shot (one of only three such shots in the film). A vibraphone in the underscoring creates an uncanny soundscape that corresponds to the unusual cinematographic effects. This uncanny soundscape may have reminded some mid-century audience members of another film in which Gregory Peck plays another psychologically disturbed hero: the 1945 mystery *Spellbound*.[17] This film features hallucinatory sequences (for which Salvador Dali created the sets) in which Peck's character attempts to remember his dreams. By understanding these dreams, it is hoped, Peck's character will discover the trauma that has induced his amnesia and thereby remember his true identity. For the underscore to these sequences, Miklós Rózsa used a combination of the novachord, the vibraphone, and the theremin in order to create an aural world similar to the one that Newman evokes in the Mt. Gilboa scene in *David and Bathsheba*. And yet in the later film, unlike *Spellbound,* we do not actually see the hallucination or dream on the screen. Instead, David's psychic disturbance is expressed primarily by means of sound.

The Mt. Gilboa theme returns briefly as David wanders among the isolated boulders that are strewn around the summit, but it is again interrupted by the stinger-like chords of the dissonant fanfare, now associated with the image of a broken sword. The gesture functions as a semantic recapitulation of the first interpolation of this fanfare. In each case, the detritus of battle (chariot and sword) acts as a visual analogue of the distorted musical topos of war (the dissonant fanfare). Insofar as we understand the Mt. Gilboa theme as a kind of traumatized march, we can extend this analogy to other parts of the scene as well. Saul and Jonathan marched into battle at the head of their people; David marches to the summit of the mountain accompanied only by his guilt.

In the next part of the scene, this guilt precipitates what we might call an episode of hallucinatory audiation. David picks up the hilt of the broken sword, and the camera moves to a medium shot of the king. The underscoring is replaced by sound effects: first muted trumpets and a ram's horn, then with cries, rolling chariot wheels, and the neighing of horses. David seems to be imaginatively recreating the battle as if he himself had taken part in it. The camera moves to a close-up of David's face, as he cries out the name of his former friend. Just as the hallucinatory audiation reaches its climax, David shouts out "Jonathan" for a second time. This brings the auditory episode to a close. For a brief moment, we hear only the empty sound of the wind. As David sits down on a rock, a solo oboe sounds in the underscore. Its melody begins as a restatement of the Mt. Gilboa theme, but its plaintive character recalls the shepherd tune that accompanies the romantic idyll (transcribed above as Example 2.5). Indeed, the second

Example 2.8. Solo oboe recapitulation/variation of the Mt. Gilboa theme.

phrase of the theme (beginning with the third measure of my transcription), the melody is deflected toward a recapitulation of the shepherd melody (see Example 2.8). The camera momentarily cuts away from David to show Bathsheba standing behind a boulder, watching David while remaining unobserved (recalling again the surveillance motif that is such a prominent feature of this film). As she appears, David recites the famous passage taken from the end of the first chapter of the second book of Samuel: "How are the mighty fallen, in the midst of the battle? O Jonathan! Thou wast slain in thine high places. I am distressed for thee, my brother Jonathan. Very pleasant hast thou been unto me. Thy love for me was wonderful, surpassing the love of women. How are the mighty fallen, and the weapons of war perished!"[18]

Newman adds increasingly dissonant contrapuntal lines to the oboe melody, obscuring its connection to the Mt. Gilboa theme. In the final gesture of this complex of scenes—the second act of the film—David lets the broken sword fall from his hand. The weapons of war have perished; so too (it seems) have David's hopes of recovering the heroic sovereignty of Saul.

The Empty Gaze

The next section of the film—what we might call its third act—recounts David's failures. It opens with a ceremonial procession. In order to honor Yahweh—and also to buttress his own quasi-sacred authority—David has arranged to bring the Ark of the Covenant into his royal city of Jerusalem. David arrives with Bathsheba in order to witness what should be a glorious moment. But as the caravan approaches, a young woman runs screaming out of the city gates. She is an adulteress, condemned under the law to be stoned to death. So too—under the law—is Bathsheba, and David might be expected to intervene. But he merely sends Bathsheba into the city so that she will not have to witness the punishment. David's moral cowardice seems to bring divine retribution. As the caravan climbs the stony path up to the city gate, the Ark starts to slip off its wagon. A soldier keeps the ark from falling, but as he lays his hands on the sacred object he is stricken down. The prophet Nathan—who is leading the procession—declares that the Ark may not enter the city until God's wrath is appeased. He commands that a tabernacle be erected to house the Ark, while David retires back into the city. As Nathan issues his command, we hear a new melody in the lower strings, a

Example 2.9. Prophet theme (beginning).

motive that will assume special importance in the remainder of the film (see Example 2.9). This motive is directly linked with Nathan, not only in this scene but throughout the third act of the film; I have for that reason elected to label it the prophet theme. But it would be equally apt to call this the motive of David's sacred kingship. Nathan's role, after all, is essentially to call David back to his duty as the anointed one of Israel.

The first section of the motive is best understood as being cast in G♯ Aeolian; its steadfast character might suggest something of Nathan's personality or, perhaps, of the rigorous law for which he is the principal voice. But the second part of the theme (beginning in measure 7 of my transcription) modulates first to the parallel major mode (B major) and then (in measure 11 of my transcription) toward what sounds like C Mixolydian. As David Lewin and others have pointed out, these kinds of chromatic third relationships (such as that which obtains between G♯ and C) are an essential part of the harmonic syntax of the mid-late nineteenth-century symphonic and operatic music repertoire.[19] This repertoire (and, in particular, the operas of Wagner) formed the basis of Newman's stylistic approach to *David and Bathsheba* (and many of his other film scores as well). Although it is dangerous (and potentially misleading) to make generalizations about the semantics of these kinds of harmonic relationships, they are often linked with a sense of propulsion and/or transformation. The abrupt modulation to the mediant in the prophet theme, I would like to suggest, carries a similar adumbration of transformation, a sense, perhaps, that the rigors of the law are mitigated or enriched by grace.

At this point in the film, however, such transformations are still impossibly distant. Instead, David's failures in the public sphere become more and more evident. They are echoed and intensified by problems in his private life. Bathsheba announces that she is pregnant, and David must find a way to preserve her reputation and his own. Instead of acknowledging his relationship with Bathsheba, he calls Uriah to his court. At a banquet ostensibly held to honor him, David arranges for an erotic dancer to perform. His hope is that Uriah will become so enflamed with desire that he will visit the conjugal bed. David could then—presumably—pass off Bathsheba's child as Uriah's rather than as his own.

It is a shabby solution, and David knows it. Indeed, his shame and frustration have led him to the brink of a psychological and emotional crisis. It is hardly accidental that this crisis should unfold in David's private chambers, and on the very terrace from which he first spied the bathing Bathsheba. As in the scenes that I described above, it is Michal who initiates the drama. She enters David's chambers unannounced (59:44), accompanied by minor-mode underscoring which continues from the previous scene. Her eye is captured by something outside of the room, and in the next shot the camera adopts her point of view. The object of her gaze is David, who is pacing anxiously back and forth on his terrace. Here—perhaps—is another desiring gaze: an echo of David's voyeurism or, more appropriately, of Bathsheba's clandestine surveillance of the king. Indeed, the underscoring recapitulates the love theme that was first associated with Bathsheba's promise of companionate marriage. Is there a suggestion here that—despite the biting satire with which she speaks to her husband—Michal, too, yearns for a loving relationship with him? Or does the music reflect a kind of premature nostalgia on the part of David, a nostalgia for an ideal love relationship with Bathsheba that seems as if it has gone before ever truly coming to be? As is so often the case, the question of to whom—if anyone—the underscoring belongs is left ambiguous. The camera follows David in a medium shot and then shifts briefly back to Michal in order to confirm our knowledge that he is the object of her gaze. But David, too, is watching. As he looks out over the edge of his terrace, the camera adopts his point of view instead of Michal's. His gaze, naturally, is directed toward Bathsheba's house: to the very terrace that once held her naked body (discreetly screened, of course). Indeed, the camera reproduces the exact angle and distance of the original voyeuristic gaze. What we have, then, is a structure of nesting surveillance: we watch Michal watching David, who gazes toward Bathsheba's terrace. Only this time, Bathsheba is absent. In the center of the network of surveillance is an empty frame.

The idea that David's gaze is a failed recapitulation of his original voyeurism is accentuated, perhaps, by the fact that it is underscored by a continuation of the love theme and not by the seductive Bathsheba music that accompanied the earlier scene. This Bathsheba theme enters only later, after the camera releases us from the empty gaze. After a close-up shot of the king, it accompanies David as he strides back into his apartment, where Michal is waiting for him. When she begins to speak, the underscoring fades away, reinforcing her status as the silencer of the emotional life with which music is so closely associated. As in the previous scene, her tone is biting and satirical. "I thought I might be of comfort to my husband," she says. "It's a terrible thing—to know that your beloved is in the arms of another." Michal is fully aware both of Bathsheba's pregnancy and of David's elaborate plan to avoid responsibility for it. She also knows that the plan has failed. Uriah, she tells David, is sleeping not with Bathsheba but rather in the palace, with the officers of David's guard. David shoves her roughly onto a divan and strides angrily out of the room. His outburst is accompanied by a renewal of the underscoring: a violent variation of the Bathsheba theme that carries us into the next scene. Taken as a whole, then, this second confrontation between David and Michal thus reads as a kind of musico-cinematic inversion of the previous sequence. In the first sequence, music-less dialogue leads through the Bathsheba seduction music to the love theme. In the second sequence, this process is reversed. Now the love theme accompanies David's empty gaze; it leads back through the seduction music to another frustrating, emasculating argument with Michal. The first sequence climaxes in the (presumably sexual) union of the king with his beloved, while the second sequence ends in anger and humiliation.

Michal is only able to humiliate David because she speaks the truth to him. In each of the chamber scenes that I have described, her focus is on David's inadequacy: on the ways that he fails to fulfill the role of the king. In the first of these chamber scenes, Michal compares David unfavorably with the model of kingship embodied by her father Saul. "Do you think," she asks David, "that hanging his spear on your wall will make you royal?" "I do not deny that Saul was every inch a king," David replies, anachronistically referencing *King Lear*. "And his successor, every inch a fraud," Michal replies. In the second chamber scene, Michal returns to the theme of David's dynastic illegitimacy, describing his plan to pass off his own child by Bathsheba as Uriah's offspring as "a cunning trick, worthy of the son of goatherds."

In the language of the twenty-first century, we might say that David's problems stem from his inability to take responsibility for his own actions. In this sense, David's "cunning trick" (whereby he might deny his paternity of Bathsheba's child) is but one manifestation of a deeper character flaw. In the Mt. Gilboa scene that I described above, David cannot acknowledge his true identity, because by doing so he would have to acknowledge that he failed to stand by Saul and his son Jonathan when they met their deaths in battle. After Uriah is killed while leading the Israelite troops against their enemies, David similarly fails to acknowledge his own role in the Hittite's death. In both of these cases, to be sure, the scriptwriters are at pains to minimize David's guilt. Uriah, for instance, volunteers to lead the Hebrew troops into battle, and David merely accedes to his request. David remains a sympathetic character, but he is nevertheless deeply flawed.

After Uriah's death, David is at last free to marry Bathsheba. But the ceremony is a stilted and joyless affair, marred by an argument between the lovers. Their partial reconciliation is interrupted by an extended montage sequence, depicting the drought that has afflicted Israel. The director shows us images of fierce windstorms and dying sheep. Onscreen we see the same shepherd boy and old soldier that appeared in the Mt. Gilboa sequence from the second act of the film, only now they are suffering from famine. For the underscoring, Newman brings back themes and musical textures from the earlier sequence, reinforcing the links between David's personal failures (e.g., his absence from the battle, his adulterous affair) and their political, religious, and even ecological consequences. Since David is an anointed king, the punishment for his sins falls on the entire people of Israel, not simply on his own head. As in *Samson and Delilah*— and indeed, the entire genre of the biblical epic—the personal and the political are inextricably interlinked.

Brokenness and Reconstruction

The third act of the film reaches its climax in another ceremonial scene, in which Nathan comes before the king. The prophet enters the throne room to a full-throated restatement of the prophet theme, now shorn of its transformative modulation. Nathan's role—as always—is to call David back to his duty. As in the biblical narrative, he does this by means of a parable. The script for this scene follows very closely the account in 2 Samuel chapter 12, in which Nathan asks for the king's judgment on the man who took and slew the only ewe lamb of a poor neighbor, even though he was rich in flocks and herds. David condemns the hypothetical rich man, and in so doing condemns himself. David accepts the verdict that he has himself pronounced and is willing to die as punishment for his sins. But Nathan refuses to accept this solution. Instead, he demands that Bathsheba be punished. The sequences that follow may be regarded as the fourth act of the film: David's spiritual atonement and reconciliation with God.

Seemingly defeated, David retires to his private chambers in order to bring Bathsheba before the people. Once there, however, he hurriedly begins to plan their escape. But escape is impossible. Angry crowds have surrounded the palace, demanding Bathsheba's death as atonement for the sins of the royal couple. David vows to die in defense of his beloved, but as he reaches for a spear that is hanging on the wall, Bathsheba stops him. Acknowledging her own guilt, she seems resigned to death. Instead of a spear, she takes a lyre from off the wall and hands it to David. "In all of our years together," she says, "you have never played for me. Play for me now, David, something from your childhood, when you were a shepherd." Sitting down on the couch, David nestles the lyre into his lap and begins to strum (see Figure 2.1).

Cast in B minor, unharmonized except for a repeating tonic pedal in the bass, David's lyre music is simple enough to have been invented by a shepherd boy (see Example 2.10).[20] Indeed, many aspects of the lyre melody—its monophonic texture, the emphasis on the G♮-C♯ interval, its reduced melodic compass, and certain aspects of its rhythmic profile—evoke the tune associated with the shepherd boy at the beginning of the second act of the film. Its slow tempo together with the downward trajectory of its melodic lines evoke a sense of deep melancholy. After the melody comes to a resting point, the king begins to recite the familiar words of the Twenty-third Psalm, words, we should remember, that the Bible explicitly credits to David. Although the lyre is silent, David keeps the instrument

Figure 2.1. Gregory Peck and Susan Hayward in the recitation/musical performance scene from *David and Bathsheba*. From the core collection production files of the Margaret Herrick Library, Academy of Motion Picture Arts and Sciences.

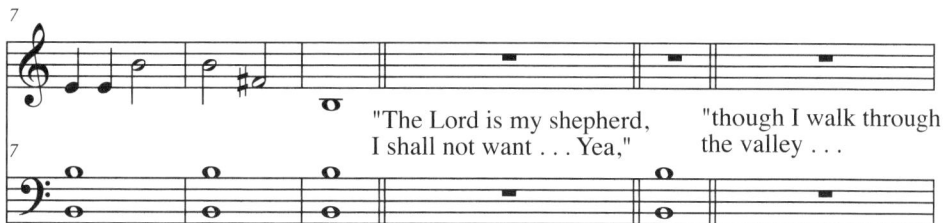

"The Lord is my shepherd,
I shall not want . . . Yea,"

"though I walk through
the valley . . .

. . . thy rod and thy staff,
they comfort me"

Thou preparest a table . . .
house of the Lord forever.

Example 2.10. David's recitation/musical performance of the Twenty-third Psalm.

on his lap, suggesting, perhaps, that the words of the psalm were originally sung to the melody that he has just played. Indeed, at certain points in the psalm, David interrupts his recitation to strum a few notes on the lyre. After "Yea" (and before "though I walk through the valley of the shadow of death"), he simply plucks the tonic. But after "Thy rod and thy staff, they comfort me," he plays most of the second phrase of his original melody. After his recitation ends, he repeats the first phrase of the melody in what amounts to a kind of abbreviated *da capo* repeat of the lyre music. The performance thus takes on some of the characteristics of an operatic melodrama, or—more aptly, perhaps—of a half-forgotten song in which text and melody have somehow become dismembered.

Words from the penultimate line of the psalm function as a textual transition for the next part of the scene, in which David reflects on what we may call his personal spiritual history. "Goodness and mercy," he begins:

> When I wrote these words, I was only an ignorant shepherd boy. There was no one to teach me about God, so I taught myself. I saw him in the hills, in the trees, in the miracle of the birth of lambs. I felt his mercy when the wolves had fled and my flock was safe. When spring broke the grip of snow and ice, when the cool wind blew, after the heat of the day. I saw his splendor in the flowers blazing on the hillsides, and the stars burning in the sky, and knew his hand in everything. Then I wandered from him, and when I tried to find him again, I had lost him. Somewhere in Saul's court, or when I roamed the desert in exile, or in the camps of the Philistines. His image paled in the lights of the city, and his voice was drowned in the quarrelling and scheming of the ambitious and the mighty.

With its parallel constructions and elevated poetic diction, this personal spiritual history in many ways extends and develops the style of the psalm. Newman's underscoring for this sequence—which begins with a restatement of the lyre melody after the words "I was only an ignorant shepherd boy"—may be heard in a similar manner: as an extension and development of the dismembered song. Newman gives the melody here to the solo oboe, invoking—as he does throughout the film—the traditional association between the solo oboe and the shepherd's pipe. But the appearance of this melody in the underscoring also acts retrospectively on David's diegetic performance of the psalm. This performance, we remember, comes in response to Bathsheba's request that David play something from his boyhood. In this context, the solo oboe evokes the beginning of the Mt. Gilboa scene, in which the young shepherd boy functions as a kind of substitute for the young David himself. The lyre melody that we hear in this later scene, to be sure, is not a direct recapitulation of the shepherd's tune from earlier in the film. And yet the two themes do share some similar melodic gestures and are cast in more or less the same tempo. Psalm text and melody are thus clearly associated (in a way that they are not in the Bible itself) with David's childhood and (more importantly) with the innocent, unmediated experience of God. But David has lost this direct experience of the divine. The brokenness of David's performance—the fact that the words of the psalm are spoken and not sung—emerges as a potent metaphor for this loss.

As David continues his personal spiritual history, Newman's underscoring grows more complex. Contrapuntal lines are added to the original melody that modulates through several keys before arriving on F with the words "and knew His hand in everything." For the next section of David's monologue, in which he recounts his loss of faith, the underscoring loses its connection to the original lyre melody. Instead, we hear sustained dissonant chords, from which new melodies eventually emerge. David speaks further of his spiritual alienation, recalling the moment in which God struck down one of his soldiers who touched the Ark of the Covenant in an attempt to keep it from falling to the ground. The dissonant underscoring reaches its point of greatest intensity when David reimagines this moment by reaching out his own hands. At this point, however, David seems to undergo a spiritual transformation. The underscoring falls silent as he lowers his hands and tells Bathsheba that she shall not die. It has, we might say, already done its work: illustrating the king's spiritual passage by leading the audience from the monophonic shepherd's tune, through increasing levels of contrapuntal and harmonic complexity to the dissonant chords that precede (indeed, almost seem to provoke) the crisis. In the silence that follows this crisis, we sense, a new idea is born, an idea that will lead David (and by extension, the people over which he rules) out of his seemingly intractable problems.

With newfound resolve, David strides out of the palace and into the Tabernacle in which the Ark of the Covenant is housed. As he does so, we hear the prophet theme again in the underscore, now with its distinctive chromatic mediant modulation restored. We might regard this cue as an example of semiotic migration: a motive once associated with Nathan is now linked to the king. A more fruitful interpretation would understand the underscoring in terms of David's spiritual growth. Similar shots earlier in the film, in which we see David purposefully striding toward some goal, are accompanied by variations of the war-march motif first heard at the beginning of the filmic diegesis. The presence of the prophet theme in this scene suggests that he is now moving forward into a different kind of space: the space of sacred kingship.

The underscoring stops abruptly as David enters the Tabernacle. He falls on his knees before the Ark and begins to pray. Eventually he lays his hands on the sacred vessel itself, reenacting the gesture that marks the climax of the spiritual crisis scene in the palace. As he does so, the same dissonant chords that accompanied this crisis return. But they do not—as David himself might be imagining—bring instant death. Instead, a thunderbolt initiates a flashback scene. The camera shows us a sunny hillside upon which sheep gently graze. In the underscoring—naturally enough—we hear the same melody that David first played on his harp, the melody that underscored the first part of the spiritual autobiography quoted above. As at the beginning of this spiritual biography, the melody is again played on the solo oboe—alluding again to the tradition of the shepherd's pipe. Both image and music thus return to the state of primal innocence that David has lost—and, incidentally, to the sound-image that initiated the Mt. Gilboa sequence from earlier in the film. They reverse, albeit in an abruptly truncated manner, the process of alienation that the king has narrated in the preceding scene.

A shepherd boy appears, running in haste toward a companion. "David, David!" he calls, "come quickly!" Prompted by a vision from God, the prophet Samuel has come to the tents of the shepherd Jesse in order to anoint a new king over Israel. The following scene of the film shows this pivotal event in the young David's life. It is significant here that David's anointing is accompanied by the same extended version of the prophet motive that Newman used to underscore the adult David's passage from the palace to the Tabernacle of the Ark. In terms of orchestration, however, the underscoring seems more closely connected to the simple shepherd music that we have already heard at various points in the film. It thus alludes both to pastoral innocence and to David's sacred kingship, signaling, perhaps, that this kingship can only be recovered by an act of return.

A second thunderclap initiates a brief return to an image of the adult David before the Ark of the Covenant, but this brief scene is in effect only a bridge to a second flashback. This sequence narrates the second key event in David's youth: his encounter with Goliath. Like the first flashback, this Goliath sequence has continual underscoring, heightening the tension that climaxes when the young David strikes Goliath dead with a stone from his sling. Still another thunderclap returns us to the scene in the Tabernacle, where David still has his hands on the Ark. Touching the Ark, of course, is forbidden, and earlier in the film we have already seen this sacrilege lead to instant death. But the thunderclaps of God have in this instance brought revelation instead.

Taken in isolation, it is difficult to understand why or how this spiritual revelation should be mediated by these twin flashbacks. Indeed, it's possible to attribute their presence here simply to a desire to insert famous incidents from the David story into a plot in which they would otherwise have no place. A more sympathetic interpretation, on the other hand, would see these flashbacks in light of what is arguably the central problem of the plot: David's inability to take responsibility for the past. In this context, the flashbacks in the Tabernacle might be understood as being in dialogue with David's auditory hallucination at the summit of Mt. Gilboa. From this interpretative standpoint, the auditory hallucination functions as a dismembered sound-image, in which the visual reimagination of the battle (which we would normally expect) is strangely absent. It thus forms an analogue of the dismembered or broken recitation of the Twenty-third Psalm that David recites for Bathsheba. The Tabernacle flashbacks, from this perspective, represent a holistic reexperiencing of the past.

It is altogether appropriate, then, that the end of the flashbacks should be articulated by a moment of silence, a moment in which (we presume) David experiences a spiritual reorientation. The silence is broken by the sound of rain, the sign that God has heard the king's supplication. With a prayerful gaze toward the

Example 2.11. Final cue (beginning).

heavens, David steps out of the Tabernacle and into the downpour. As he does so, we hear a male chorus in the underscoring, singing (a cappella) a new setting of the Twenty-third Psalm (see Example 2.11). As David walks out of the Tabernacle and back into his palace, the melody spins out into full polyphony. Women's voices and eventually orchestral accompaniment are added, so that the underscoring takes on the lineaments of the choral anthem. Returning to his chambers, David lifts up Bathsheba and with her turns toward an open door, the door that leads out into the rain-filled beauty of the night. Uplifting choral music suffuses the soundscape, signaling the unambiguous resolution of the spiritual, domestic, and political conflicts that have driven the plot of the film.

These kinds of choral endings were a well-established topos of the biblical epic. They may be found in prewar epics such as *The Sign of the Cross,* and the tradition stretches back into the late nineteenth-century melodramas from which early film music drew so much of its musico-dramatic semantics.[21] *Ben-Hur, Quo Vadis,* and *The Robe* end in very much the same manner as *David and Bathsheba.* Although the specific settings of these three movies are quite different, each of their final scenes show the hero united with his wife or bride (in a newly sanctified relationship) and at one with his God. But if the plots of these films end, so to speak, in the same place, they nevertheless arrive there via different routes. In the course of *Quo Vadis,* Marcus Vinicius leaves behind his self-centered militarism in order to embrace Christianity; the Marcellus character in *The Robe* similarly converts to the new faith by leaving behind his tepid quasi-pagan agnosticism. David—by contrast—must experience a reconversion, a turning back to God, or (to use the Hebrew term) *tshuvah.*

Newman's score offers a kind of musical analogue for this theological concept, at least as it unfolds in the plot of the film. The music that begins the final musical cue—the setting of the Twenty-third Psalm that accompanies the moment in which David steps out of the Tabernacle and into the pouring rain—is clearly a variant of the prophet motive that I transcribed above. It begins with the same $\hat{5}$-$\hat{1}$-$\hat{3}$-$\hat{2}$-$\flat\hat{7}$-$\hat{1}$ melodic contour and includes a prominent transcendental modulation, first to a major key (in this case the relative rather than the parallel major) and then to the chromatic mediant (with the text "Yea though I walk"). But if the melodic/harmonic materials of the cue largely recycle those of the prophet motive, its text ("The Lord is my shepherd") and, to a lesser degree, the simple vocal texture with which it begins recall the dismembered song that David played for Bathsheba (see Example 2.10). The choral music at the end of *David and Bathsheba,* then, represents a reintegration that is more than a reintegration, a return that is more than a return. It unites the text that—in the film, at least—is associated with David's boyhood (e.g., "The Lord is my shepherd"), with an expanded version of the prophet motive: music associated with the politico-religious responsibilities of kingship. David's return to God, after all, cannot mean a return to his life as a shepherd. *Tshuvah* is more than a recapitulation; it is a movement into a new space.

Genre and the "Religious Boom"

At the beginning of this chapter, I used the ancillary sheet music associated with *Samson and Delilah* and *David and Bathsheba* to illustrate the contrasting musical styles of the two scores and to suggest ways in which these different styles helped to articulate different generic spaces for the two films. The fact that this final cue from *David and Bathsheba* was arranged and sold as a choral anthem (presumably suitable for liturgical use), however, also bears witness to the curious location of the film—and by extension, the biblical epic genre as a whole—at the intersection of what Steven Cohan calls the postwar "religious boom" and the entertainment industry.[22] Alongside their other motivations, studio executives in the early 1950s were attempting to capitalize on this boom by combining biblical stories and moral content with different sorts of generic topoi. In this light, we might see the first two postwar biblical epics (*Samson and Delilah* and *David and Bathsheba*) as experimental efforts to articulate a commercially successful style. In many ways, *Samson and Delilah* can be viewed as an extension of the prewar epic. But *David and Bathsheba,* as we have seen, is linked not only to films such as *The Sign of the Cross,* but also to more modern genres such as the woman's film and the psychological drama. The "turn away from concocted spectacle" was also a turn into a new—and hopefully even more profitable—generic model.

The generic hybridity of *David and Bathsheba* is one of the principal reasons that the film has generated a fairly large amount of scholarly discourse—despite the fact that it was by no means the most popular of the postwar biblical epics. *David and Bathsheba* was a successful film (although not as successful as either *Samson and Delilah* or *Quo Vadis*), but in many ways it had no successor. *The Robe*—Twentieth Century–Fox's next biblical epic—would be a very different film from *David and Bathsheba*. Filmed in CinemaScope and loaded with spectacular scenes, *The Robe* was in many ways a response to the grandeur and magnificence of MGM's first postwar foray into the biblical epic genre: *Quo Vadis*. It is to this film that we now turn.

3   Spectacle and Authenticity in Miklós Rózsa's *Quo Vadis* Score

In "The Romans in Films"—one of the lesser-known *feuilletons* from the *Mythologies* collection—Roland Barthes turned his caustic wit on a seemingly inconsequential detail from Joseph L. Mankiewicz's *Julius Caesar* (1953): namely, the hair styles of the leading actors. In this film, he writes,

> all the characters are wearing fringes. Some have them curly, some straggly, some tufted, some oily, all have them well combed, and the bald are not admitted, although there are plenty to be found in Roman history. . . . What then is associated with these insistent fringes? Quite simply the label of Roman-ness. We therefore see here the mainspring of the Spectacle—the *sign*—operating in the open. The frontal lock overwhelms one with evidence, no one can doubt that he is in Ancient Rome.[1]

Barthes places the omnipresent forelock in what he calls an "ethic of signs." "Signs," he continues,

> ought to present themselves only in two extreme forms: either openly intellectual and so remote that they are reduced to an algebra, as in the Chinese theatre, where a flag on its own signifies a regiment; or deeply rooted, invented, so to speak, on each occasion, revealing an internal, a hidden facet . . . (as in the art of Stanislavsky, for instance). But the intermediate sign [such as the fringe] reveals a degraded spectacle, which is equally afraid of simple reality and of total artifice.[2]

Although the score to Mankiewicz's *Julius Caesar* was written by Miklós Rózsa, the movie bears only a tangential relationship to the biblical epics that are the subject of this book. For despite its Roman setting, *Julius Caesar* is ultimately a film version of a play rather than an epic film. Rózsa himself made a distinction between his music for *Julius Caesar*—which he described as "apt for a Shakespearean drama"—and the score that he had recently finished for *Quo Vadis*.[3] Indeed, Barthes does not include music in his critique of cinematic Roman-ness: he either accepted Rózsa's score as adequately "apt" or (as is more likely) paid no attention to it. A discussion of the *Quo Vadis* score, then, must take place at some distance from Barthes's "The Romans in Films." Nevertheless, I argue in this chapter that Barthes's "ethic of signs"—his notions of the intermediate sign and the degraded spectacle—has unique applicability to Rózsa's music for this film. In none of his other film scores from what he called his "historico-biblical" period is Rózsa so preoccupied with questions of musical authenticity, and Rózsa took great pains to write music that was—to use Barthes's terms—"deeply rooted" in the world of first-century Rome. Rózsa outlined his efforts to create historically authentic music for the film in a fascinating article that he wrote for *Film Music Notes,* to which I turn below. With *Quo Vadis,* however, Rózsa needed to balance these efforts with another kind of musical authenticity that was woven into the plot of the film: a plot that turns on the conflict between the authentic faith of early Christianity and the inauthentic, spiritually empty empire in which that faith first developed. Music plays a central role in articulating this conflict. This chapter, then, examines the creative tension between these two kinds of authenticity: between historical verisimilitude and the narrative demands of the film.

The colorful characters and dramatic historical events portrayed in Henryk Sienkiewicz's novel *Quo Vadis?* (1895) made it a logical choice for cinematic adaptation, and Mervyn LeRoy's 1951 film is only one of many versions of the story that have been made for the large and small screen. Earlier *Quo Vadis* films include an influential Italian version directed by Enrico Guazzoni (1913), and the 1925 version starring Emil Jannings.[4] Cecil B. DeMille's early sound epic *The Sign of the Cross*—released by Paramount in 1932 with a score by Rudolph Kopp—follows essentially the same plot as *Quo Vadis* and shows many other similarities to the films that are more explicitly based on Sienkiewicz's novel. MGM had plans for their own *Quo Vadis* as early as the late 1930s, but the project began in earnest only in 1949. The studio originally enlisted producer Arthur Hornblow Jr. and director John Huston to make the film, which was to have starred Gregory Peck and a young Elizabeth Taylor. Technical problems and a serious conflict between Huston and studio head Louis B. Mayer regarding the nature of the film eventually led both Huston and Hornblow to withdraw from the project, and *Quo Vadis* ended up in the hands of LeRoy and the producer Sam Zimbalist.

Although the story of the postwar biblical epic properly begins with *Samson and Delilah, Quo Vadis* brought a new sense of spectacular grandeur to the genre. With 110 speaking roles, 30,000 extras, colossal sets, and an enormous number of costumes, *Quo Vadis* eventually cost $7 million to produce. The size of its budget was later eclipsed by other epic films, but in 1951 it nevertheless represented an enormous gamble for the studio. The ability of *Quo Vadis* to recoup these expenses and to generate profits for MGM helped to establish the financial viability of the biblical epic and paved the way for the even grander, more expensive films that were to follow. Of course, *Quo Vadis* incorporates many specific themes and general cinematic strategies from earlier films: not only *Samson and Delilah,* but also prewar epics such as *The King of Kings,* DeMille's first version of *The Ten Commandments,* and *The Sign of the Cross.* But *Quo Vadis* nevertheless also helped to establish new forms and conventions, especially through its use of large-scale spectacle and (as I argue in this chapter) through its new approach to music. From this perspective, then, *Quo Vadis* stands at the beginning of a new, specifically postwar approach to the biblical epic film.

Cinematic Music and Historical Authenticity

Like other aspects of the film, the music for *Quo Vadis* has a complicated history. According to Frank K. DeWald, managing director L. K. Sidney originally asked Miklós Rózsa (on staff at MGM) for his advice on a suitable composer. Rózsa suggested William Walton, who had already had success scoring epic films such as *Henry V.* But Sidney eventually persuaded Rózsa to take on the project himself.[5] In many ways, it was an unusual assignment. Rózsa's nearest approach to the genre of historical or epic film had been his score to *The Thief of Bagdad* (1940). He was probably best known as a composer for noirish psychological dramas such as *Spellbound* (1945) and *A Double Life* (1947), films for which he earned his first two Academy Awards. Rózsa was later to enjoy tremendous success as a composer for epic films: not merely those based on biblical themes (like *Ben-Hur* and *King of Kings*), but also those on other subjects (most notably *El Cid*). In the late 1940s and early 1950s, however, he was still a newcomer to the genre.

From his autobiography and especially from his *Film Music Notes* article, it is clear that Rózsa approached the music for *Quo Vadis* with a sense of doing something novel and innovative. Indeed, Rózsa begins his article by explicitly differentiating himself from previous practices. "The motion picture with historical background," he writes, "always presents interesting problems to the composer. There have been innumerable other historical pictures produced before 'Quo Vadis,' and they were all alike in their negligent attitude toward the stylistic accuracy of their music."[6] Rózsa's assessment of earlier historical films is not entirely accurate, and more than a little unfair. The inclusion of tunes such as "Dixie" and "Maryland, My Maryland" in both *The Birth of a Nation* and *Gone with the Wind* (to cite only the most obvious examples) might be understood in terms of historical, if not perhaps stylistic, accuracy. Closer to *Quo Vadis,* the score that Rudolph Kopp created for *The Sign of the Cross* includes some selections that might—with a generous imagination—be understood as efforts to reproduce the sound of early Christian hymnody. But Rózsa is less interested in evaluating previous film scores than in articulating a striking gap between these scores and the idea of historical authenticity that—in his opinion—informs other aspects of film production. "When a period picture is made," he writes,

> the historical background of the script is naturally based on historical facts and the dialogue tries to avoid any anachronistic term or reference. The art director, interior decorater [sic], costume designer, hair stylist and makeup man start their work only after thorough research, and the greatest care is taken that every building, every

piece of furniture, every costume and every hairdo is absolutely authentic according to the period of the picture. During the actual photographing a historical adviser, usually a scholar of reputation, supervises this procedure so that nothing can slip in and spoil the absolute authenticity. Why is it then that when we come to music an exceptionally lofty attitude is felt and no one seems to care much about the genuineness of this most important factor of picture making?[7]

The fact that Rózsa references hairstyle as an example of authenticity in historical film helps to put his remarks into dialogue with the Barthes essay that I cited above. For Barthes, the quasi-Roman hairstyles (or, to use his word, "fringes") in *Julius Caesar* are the prime example of the "degraded spectacle" and, more specifically, of cinema's failure adequately to signify ancient Rome. "The Romans in Films," we might say, is haunted by the suspicion that cinema itself—at least in the hegemonic production systems developed by the Hollywood studios—may be incapable of creating a historical film that would not be simply another degraded spectacle. Rózsa, obviously, does not share this sense of cinema's failure. Like film scripts, sets, and costumes, hairstyles can be historically authentic, just as long as proper care is taken. In *Quo Vadis,* he implies, music will be brought up to the level of historical authenticity enjoyed by other aspects of the cinematic art.

As the above quotation makes clear, Rózsa's remarks reveal a certain degree of defensiveness with regard to musical aspects of film production. Especially at this point in his life, Rózsa had a highly ambivalent attitude toward film music composition. On one hand, he felt it to be a distraction from what he regarded as his more important and serious work: the composition of concert music in the classical central European tradition. On the other hand, he was clearly interested in elevating the cultural status of film music scoring: not only vis-à-vis activities such as set production or costume design, but also in the general field of music composition.

Rózsa's ambivalence toward the practice of film music composition and his own relationship to serious music figure prominently in my discussion of his *King of Kings* score in chapter 7. More germane to my concerns in this chapter is the central role that scholarship played in Rózsa's attempt to elevate the cultural status of film music composition (and, perhaps unconsciously, to validate his own work as a film music composer). "When *Quo Vadis* was assigned to me," he writes,

I decided to be stylistically, absolutely correct. First, thorough research had to be made. Though my old studies of the music of antiquity came in handy now, I am most indebted to the librarian of Metro-Goldwyn-Mayer studios, Mr. George Schneider, who with unfailing enthusiasm and unceasing effort produced every reference to the period that could be found in the libraries throughout the four corners of the world.[8]

The "old studies of the music of antiquity" that Rózsa mentions probably refer to his study in Leipzig during the late 1920s. In his autobiography, Rózsa specifically mentions the teaching of Theodor Kroyer, who (according to the composer) "seemed to live in the twelfth or thirteenth century." "The University [of Leipzig]," he continues, "gave me a grounding in musicology that was to stand me in good stead later."[9] One is reminded that Rózsa was writing and composing during the early stages of the twentieth century's early music revival, before the extensive performance practice debates of the 1980s and 1990s deconstructed and problematized the whole notion of historically authentic music performance backed up by rigorous scholarship. For Rózsa, the path from ancient manuscript, inscription, or iconographical source to contemporary (cinematic) realization is untroubled and direct.

Rózsa devotes the bulk of his *Film Music Notes* article to a discussion of the specific sources that he used for the individual musical cues in *Quo Vadis*. But although the musical relationships between source materials and film cues are his chief concern, Rózsa begins his article not by speaking about sound, but rather by describing how models of antique instruments such as lyras, kitharas, cornua, and tubae were constructed.[10] The blueprints for these instruments, Rózsa explains, were created from careful study of sculptures and bas-reliefs in the Naples and Vatican museums. It is important to understand that these newly created models of ancient instruments (which appear prominently in the film) are essentially props. Although we see the ancient cornua—to take just one example—we do not hear them. Modern trumpets (and other brass instruments) sound when we see them played, just as the small Scottish harp sounds when we see an ancient lyre. Authenticity—at least in this case—does not fully extend into the field of instrumentation.[11]

In this context, the comparison that Rózsa makes between the visual aspects of film production (set and costume design, makeup and hair styling) and the creation of the film score is particularly interesting. Although film audiences of the postwar period could not be expected to understand—for example—fine distinctions between the uniforms of a first-century tribune and those of a legate or centurion, they did have a certain familiarity with the visual culture of ancient Rome—or at least with the ways in which that culture was reproduced for modern audiences. The ancient world was an important theme in nineteenth- and twentieth-century art, both in Europe and in America. As Maria Wyke and other scholars have pointed out, the cinematography of the biblical epics (and other epics set in the ancient world) was profoundly influenced by this nineteenth- and twentieth-century heritage. Indeed, specific scenes in these epics were sometimes directly modeled on well-known prints or paintings. In his 1913 version of, for example, Guazzoni used Jean-Leon Gêrome's *Ave Caesar, Morituri Te Salutant* (1859), and *Pollice Verso* (1872) to construct his mise-en-scène, supposedly eliciting applause from cinematic audiences who recognized the familiar paintings.[12] From the standpoint of studio executives, then, spending time and money to ensure the historical authenticity (or at least a certain degree of fidelity to preexisting concepts) of sets and costumes made sense. The musical frame of reference for the ancient world, by contrast, was far less fully developed. The answer to the rhetorical question with which Rózsa ends the opening paragraph of his essay—"Why is it then that when we come to music . . . no one seems to care much about [its] genuineness . . . ?"—is thus fairly straightforward. Without a more fully developed frame of reference for ancient music, it simply did not make sense to worry about the "genuineness" of the *Quo Vadis* score.

That is not to say that music had no role to play in the ways in which cinematic audiences imagined the world of ancient Rome. By the time that Rózsa began his work on *Quo Vadis,* there was already a set of expectations about the ways that the ancient world should sound, and not merely about the ways it should look. In the book of photoplay music compiled by Sol P. Levy, for instance, we find a whole category of selections for "Roman or Biblical" scenes.[13] The first of these is a march suitable "for Processional, return of Victorious Armies, Gladiators, etc."; there are also selections for scenes of worship and even for an arena scene that features the roaring of lions. What makes Rózsa's score for *Quo Vadis* unique, then, is not the musical depiction of ancient Rome per se, but rather its relationship to the idea of historical authenticity. For the costume or set designer, history could be called forth by copying the surviving sculptures and paintings of ancient Greece and Rome (or, more probably, the nineteenth- and early twentieth-century imaginative reconstructions of those sculptures and paintings). Audiences of the 1950s (and later periods as well) had comparatively little knowledge about early music. The epic films of the fifties and sixties—as I show in this book—helped to establish a new repertoire of musical topoi for the representation of the ancient world. But in 1951, these topoi had yet to crystallize. In the context of ideas about historical authenticity that were circulating in the postwar period—we might say—the soundscape of ancient Rome could not merely be reproduced, but also had to be reimagined.

Roman-ness

The first musical cues in the *Quo Vadis* score exemplify two of the principal styles that Rózsa used to create this soundscape. As is the case with so many of the postwar biblical epics, the filmic diegesis begins with a voiceover. For *Samson and Delilah,* as we have seen, Victor Young wrote full symphonic underscoring for this narrative. But in *Quo Vadis,* it is accompanied only by a steady drumbeat. This drumbeat emerges directly from the music for the opening credits and then passes over into the filmic diegesis as the cadence of a cohort of kettle-drum players. This cohort—as the voiceover tells us—is a part of the fourteenth legion, which is returning victorious to Rome along the Appian Way. Commanding the legion is the hero of the story, Marcus Vinicius (played by the veteran American actor Robert Taylor). In the first scene after the voiceover,

Example 3.1. Marcus's Chariot (Vinicius motive).

Marcus receives an order requiring him to make camp outside of the city. Both he and his men yearn for the comforts and delights of Rome, and Marcus is incensed by the idea that he should forgo them. Driving his chariot into the city with reckless abandon, he demands an immediate audience before Emperor Nero.

The cue that Rózsa wrote for this scene—labeled in the conductor's score as "Marcus's Chariot"—is based around a clear theme that will be closely associated with the hero during the first part of the film (see Example 3.1). Like other hero motives from the postwar biblical epics (and in postwar Hollywood more generally), it is replete with masculine musical topoi. Its angular melodic profile, for instance, recalls that of Samson's horn call in *Samson and Delilah,* and the leaping fourths that characterize the end of the Marcus Vinicius theme can be heard as a kind of modified fanfare. Like David's war music from *David and Bathsheba,* the Vinicius motive also references the topos of the march, principally by virtue of the firm and regular $\frac{4}{4}$ meter and the repeated quarter notes that begin its second phrase. Although the Vinicius theme appears in many different guises, it is most typically orchestrated so that brass and percussion ("military" instruments) are highlighted. Indeed, the Vinicius theme has many commonalities with the diegetic or quasi-diegetic marches that Rózsa wrote for *Quo Vadis:* the Hail Nero cue that accompanies Marcus's grand entry into Rome and the Hail Galba cue that accompanies similar scenes of marching legionnaires in the penultimate scene of the film. The first theme of the Hail Nero cue is repro-

Example 3.2. Hail Nero (beginning).

duced as Example 3.2. Indeed, Rózsa employed the Vinicius motive as the second theme of the Hail Nero cue, reinforcing the connections among these various musical ideas.

In structural terms as well, this Vinicius motive plays a role in *Quo Vadis* similar to that of its analogues in *Samson and Delilah* and in *David and Bathsheba*. The introductory music in both films is built around motives associated with the hero and his principal love interest. In a similar manner, the overture to *Quo Vadis* begins with the Vinicius motive and continues with the music that will be associated with the virtuous maiden Lygia (whom Marcus will eventually marry). And yet the music also has a special character that distinguishes it from anything found in the scores to these earlier biblical epics. In intervallic terms, its melody is generated primarily by fourths and (to a lesser degree) by major seconds; semitones and thirds appear much more rarely. Rózsa uses parallel chords (often lacking a third) to harmonize the melody, suggesting a Dorian or Mixolydian tonality for the motive. These harmonic and melodic features form a central component of what I call Rózsa's "imperial style," one of the principal means by which he constructs an imaginary soundscape for the ancient world.

Rózsa addresses precisely these tonal features in the latter pages of his essay, when he turns—with some reluctance, one senses—toward the question of harmonization. "As the music for *Quo Vadis* was intended for dramatic use and as entertainment for the lay public," he writes,

> one had to avoid the pitfall of producing only musicalogical [*sic*] oddities instead of music with a universal, emotional appeal. For the modern ear, instrumental music in unison has very little emotional or aesthetic appeal; therefore, I had to find a way for an archaic sounding harmonization which gives warmth, color, and emotional values to these melodies. A parallelism with open fifths and fourths came in most handy and also a modal harmonization suggested by the different (Lydian, Phrygian, Dorian, Mixolydian, etc.) modes of the melodies in question.[14]

"A stylistically, strictly correct music corresponding to our period," he continues a few pages later,

> could not have supplied these aims to the modern spectator and listener. Although I have constructed my themes on classical principles and was able to use a few fragments from historical relics, these had to be harmonized to make them emotionally appealing. A romantic, chromatic harmonization would have been out of place and a simple modal harmonization seemed to me the closest to the character of this music.[15]

The "historical relics" of ancient Greco-Roman music that Rózsa discusses in the first part of his article (The Epitaph of Seikolos, the spurious Ode of Pindar, etc.) may have provided models for some of the melodic features of this imperial style, and they are by no means the most important source of inspiration. In his biography of Rózsa, Christopher Palmer argues that this style had its roots in Magyar folksong. "The roots of Hungarian peasant song," he writes, "are in the church modes and the pentatonic scale, its predominant intervals are the fourth and the fifth and therefore suggest a harmonic treatment derived from those intervals, i.e. superimposed chords of parallel fourths and fifths. Now these are precisely the means whereby an atmosphere of antiquity may be conjured up for western ears."[16] We might refine Palmer's argument by drawing attention to another source, namely, the dramatic music of Rózsa's countryman Béla Bartok. The modal harmonies and massed parallel chords that Rózsa used so effectively recall certain passages in Bartok's music, such as the moment in his opera *Bluebeard's Castle* in which the heroine Judith opens the fifth door of the castle in order to reveal the riches of Bluebeard's kingdom. Although Bartok and Rózsa may ultimately be drawing on the same Magyar folk sources, it is important to recognize the latter composer's roots in a specific kind of twentieth-century Hungarian nationalist art music: a style which (like so many other national styles from the period) had ironically cosmopolitan roots. To describe this music solely in terms of its Magyar connections is, in any case, to oversimplify a far more complex stylistic genealogy. In addition to Hungarian sources (in both folk and concert music), Rózsa may also—consciously or unconsciously—have been drawing on pieces such as Carl Orff's *Carmina Burana* and Stravinsky's *Firebird Suite*: works

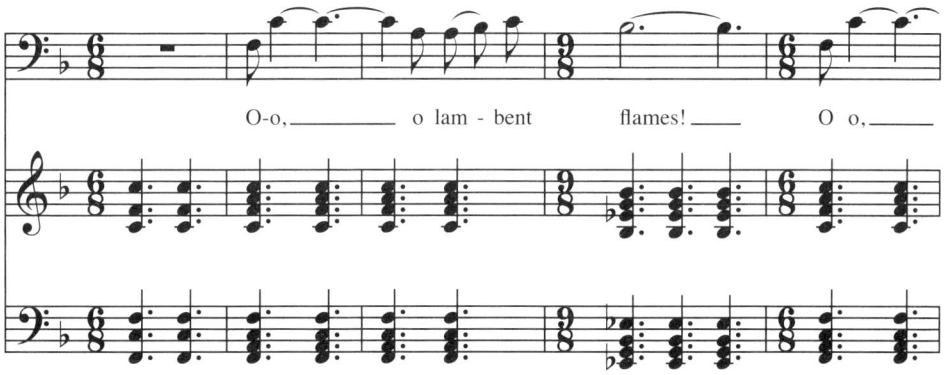

Example 3.3. "O lambent flames" (Nero's song).

in which modal scales and parallel harmonies play an important role. In any case, the prehistory of this style is less significant here than its cinematic function in the film. For this imperial style is only one of the means through which Rózsa constructs his imaginary ancient soundscape. It operates, we might say, in dialogue with one component of the historicist music that Rózsa discussed in his article, namely, the diegetic music that he wrote for Emperor Nero.

After Marcus's furious chariot ride, the camera follows him inside the palace. Nero is here, reclining on a divan, surrounded by slaves and courtiers. The emperor is played with obvious relish by Peter Ustinov, sporting luxurious bangs that would have provided grist for Barthes's mill. Nero is at work on his latest song, the melody of which (as Rózsa tells us in his *Film Music Notes* article) is based on the Epitaph of Seikolos. Nero is struggling to choose between the words "omnipotent" and "omnivorous." Vain, pompous, comically self-centered, he comes to embody many of the stereotypical features of Roman decadence (see Example 3.3).

Nero's music is clearly differentiated from the imperial style of the triumphal march and of the Vinicius theme. In addition to the clear distinction between diegetic and nondiegetic music, there is a strong contrast between the fanfare-like melodies and march rhythms of the underscoring for Marcus and the strumming lyre and pressed vocalism of Nero's music. Marcus and Nero clearly represent two aspects of Roman-ness, aspects of an empire that, as the voiceover prologue informs us, is ultimately doomed to fail. One aspect of Roman-ness is the inordinate love of power, symbolized most directly in the military march. Another is the inordinate love of luxury manifested by Nero and his court. In this sense, both Marcus and Nero—at least at this point in the film—are little more than stereotypical representations of generalized historical forces.

Luxuria and Sexual Desire

The representation of Roman-ness in *Quo Vadis* draws upon conventions that were centuries if not millennia old. As Martin Winkler writes:

> Military power and excessive luxury have been regarded as the two major contributing factors of Rome's fall since Montesquieu published his *Considerations of the Causes of the Greatness of the Romans and Their Decline* in 1734. His perspective echoes that of the ancient Romans themselves, primarily that of Sallust. The moralizing historian, who was to influence Tacitus's negative perspective on the imperial system, attributes Rome's decline to *luxuria* and *lubido dominandi*.[17]

While Nero's "O lambent flames" certainly functions as an expression of *luxuria*, it is certainly not the only music in *Quo Vadis* that fills this role. Roman decadence is also expressed through the music and drama of another topos of the biblical epic plot, namely the banquet scene. In addition to the ostentatious consumption of food and drink, the banquet scene in the postwar epic also features a dance—often erotic in nature—performed for the delectation of the guests (and, needless to say, of the cinematic audience as well). We find banquet scenes not only in *Quo Vadis*, but also in *Ben-Hur, Esther and the King, Demetrius and the Gladiators*, and many other films. In *Salome* and in *King of Kings*, Salome's dance before Herod functions as part of a banquet scene; while in *David and Bathsheba*, as we have already seen, the king stages the erotic dance in order to enflame Uriah's sexual desires. The scene in *The Ten Commandments* in which the daughters of Jethro dance before Moses and the other sheikhs of Sinai may be regarded as a variant of this cinematic topos. In *Quo Vadis*, the banquet scene occurs fairly early in the film. Marcus has been seized by desire for Lygia and has asked to have her guardianship transferred from the virtuous General Plautius to himself. Nero agrees, and at his command Lygia is abducted from the general's home and brought to the imperial palace. She is commanded to attend the em-

Example 3.4. Assyrian Dance.

peror's banquet, where she is presented to Marcus as if she were a slave. As she enters the banquet hall, the first of two erotic dances is already in progress. Indeed, the banquet scene in *Quo Vadis* is quite extended: it contains not only dances but also a great deal of dialogue as well as Nero's complete performance of "O lambent flames." The most distinctive music in the banquet scene, however, is probably the cue that Rózsa wrote for the second of the dances, labeled in the conductor's score as the "Assyrian Dance" (see Example 3.4).

Like "O lambent flames," the Assyrian Dance is based on ancient sources, and the solo bassoon that plays the melody in this cue might be understood as a stand-in for the ancient aulos. In this sense, it is similar to Nero's "O lambent flames." But the bacchanalian music also references many features prominent in nineteenth- and early twentieth-century musical orientalism. These include ostinato patterns (in both melody and accompaniment), accents that create a sense of mixed meter or cross-metrical patterning and turning, arabesque-like melodic patterns. Prominent E♭s in the Assyrian dance push the sense of tonality toward the Phrygian mode, another typical feature of orientalist themes.[18] The Assyrian Dance, we might say, inhabits the space in which the categories of orientalist and historically authentic overlap.

In the Hollywood biblical epics, as in the older operatic and symphonic tradition, the orientalism of the bacchanalian dance is typically a marker of dangerous sexuality. As such, it is often associated with an attempt at seduction. In *David and Bathsheba,* as we have seen, it is Uriah who is the object of this attempt, while in *The Ten Commandments* it is Moses' desires that are meant to be aroused. In *Quo Vadis* this seduction motif operates on two levels, more or less simultaneously. Marcus is attempting to impress Lygia with the luxury and splendor of the imperial court in order to weaken her resistance to his sexual advances. But while he is conversing with Lygia, he is himself being watched by the empress Poppaea. Indeed, the motif of the female gaze is at least as strongly articulated in *Quo Vadis* as it is in *David and Bathsheba*. Poppaea first appears in the film as part of the emperor's suite as they watch Marcus's triumphal entry into Rome. During the second section of the march (the section that is based on the Vinicius theme) she queries the leader of the Praetorian Guard, Marcus's rival Tigellinus. "Marcus Vinicius," she asks, "isn't he the one who came to see Nero yesterday?" "An arrogant man," answers Tigellinus, "one who bears watching." "From what I hear," Poppaea responds with a provocative leer, "he might bear watching at much closer range." During the Assyrian Dance, Poppaea essentially recapitulates her predatory gaze. She uses a ruby-colored lens to focus her attention (and ours) on Marcus and Lygia. She suggests to Nero that he "might have overlooked something for [him]self"—in other words, that Nero should claim Lygia in order to leave Marcus free to be the object (or victim) of her desires.

The fact that both *David and Bathsheba* and *Quo Vadis* include the motif of the female gaze foregrounds more basic structural similarities between the plots of the two films. For like *David and Bathsheba, Samson and Delilah,* and indeed nearly every other postwar biblical epic, the plot of *Quo Vadis* can be understood in terms of the two-woman plot archetype. Lygia embodies the purity and domesticity represented by Miriam in *Samson and Delilah,* and (in a negative sense) by Michal in *David and Bathsheba.* Poppaea's desire, like Delilah's, threatens to deflect the hero from his historical destiny. As I mentioned in chapter 1, however, the two-woman plot archetype typically operates differently in the Roman/Christian epics (such as *Quo Vadis* and *The Robe*) than it does in those films that are based on material from the Old Testament. The ancestral/tribal elements of the two-woman plot archetype that are so important in *David and Bathsheba* and *Samson and Delilah* are consequently lacking in *Quo Vadis.*[19] In this plot, sexual desire thus functions in different sorts of ways. It is not only the hero who is tempted by illicit sexuality, but the heroine as well.

Christian Music

In this context, it is useful to look at the banquet scene in *The Sign of the Cross.* As I mentioned above, the plot of this movie is so similar to that of *Quo Vadis* that the latter could almost be regarded as a remake of the earlier film. The hero of *The Sign of the Cross* is Marcus Superbus (instead of Vinicius), but he, too, is the object of Poppaea's desires. The heroine's name is Mercia instead of Lygia, but her relationship to the hero is much the same as her counterpart's relationship to Marcus Vinicius.[20] Like *Quo Vadis, The Sign of the Cross* contains a banquet scene in which Marcus attempts to seduce the heroine away from her virtuous Christian faith and into the world of *luxuria* and illicit sexuality. The banquet scene in *The Sign of the Cross* is filled with diegetic, orientalist dance-like music that is likewise quite similar to Rózsa's "Assyrian Dance." In the earlier film, however, the hero calls upon a courtesan (Ancaria) to aid him in his seduction attempt. At his command, the courtesan recites an erotic poem ("The Naked Moon") to the accompaniment of the orientalist dance as she slinks seductively around the unresponsive heroine. Her performance is interrupted, however, by the sounds of Christians singing a hymn as they are led to prison (see Example 3.5).

In many ways, the music that Rózsa wrote for the Christians in *Quo Vadis* is quite similar to Kopp's hymn. Apart from a very brief excursus into two-voice harmony, Kopp's Christian music—like Rózsa's—is essentially monophonic. The restricted range and moderate *tactus* of the music in *Quo Vadis* also recalls the Christian music in *The Sign of the Cross.* Nevertheless, the approach to the Christian music in *Quo Vadis* differs from Kopp's practice in many significant ways. The first of these concerns the question of historical authenticity. As Rózsa makes clear in his article, he based all three of the monophonic Christian hymns in *Quo Vadis* on historical sources. The first example of Christian music in *Quo*

Glo - ry   o - ver the   earth and seas,   glo - ry and peace - a - bove

Example 3.5. Christian hymn from *The Sign of the Cross* (beginning).

Vadis appears roughly halfway through the movie. At this point in the film, Lygia has escaped from the imperial palace, and Marcus (along with two men that he has hired) has tracked her to a secret meeting of the Christians. Paul is baptizing new converts, while other Christians are singing a cue that Rózsa titled the "First Quarry Hymn," based (as he notes in his article) on a Babylonian Jewish liturgical melody. The music thus functions in a quasi- (or proto-) liturgical manner. The Christian meeting ends in a similar way, with another monophonic hymn that operates essentially as a recessional. This, too, is based on historical material: the "Hymn to Nemesis," discovered by Vincenzo Galilei (see Example 3.6). What distinguishes Kopp's "Glory over the earth and seas" hymn from the "Second Christian Hymn" (as well as the other music that Rózsa wrote for the Christians) is the abrupt chromatic shift that takes place between its first two phrases. This shift is probably best understood as a marker of (potential) spiritual transformation, akin to the kinds of chromatic mediant juxtapositions that I discussed in the context of Newman's *David and Bathsheba* score. While it is possible to interpret the monophonic texture of Kopp's hymn as a reference to the simplicity of early Christian faith, then, its musical semantics seem to have more to do with the chromatic transformational harmony of late nineteenth- and twentieth-century concert music.

If the musical style of Rózsa's Christian music stands in an oblique relationship to its antecedents in *The Sign of the Cross,* so too is the function of this diegetic hymnody within the two respective films similar in some ways and different in others. In both films, the decision to include Christian hymnody at certain key moments in the plot was surely inspired by certain passages in the original novel in which Sienkiewicz depicts this music in evocative terms. Here, for example, is his description of Marcus's emotions as he witnesses the secret service of the Christians:

> After a while the crowd began to sing a certain strange hymn, at first in a low voice, and then louder. Vinicius had never heard such a hymn before. The same yearning which had struck him in the hymns murmured by separate persons on the way to the cemetery, was heard now in that, but with far more distinctness and power; and at last it became as penetrating and immense as if together with the people, the whole cemetery, the hills, the pits, and the region about, had begun to yearn. It might seem, also, that there was in it a certain calling in the night, a certain humble prayer for rescue in wandering and darkness.[21]

Example 3.6. "Second Christian Hymn" from *Quo Vadis* (based on the "Hymn to Nemesis").

The strange and powerful singing of the Christians, in other words, was a central part of the *Quo Vadis* story that could not be overlooked. Sienkiewicz describes their singing not only in the context of this secret service, but also in his narration of the arena scenes toward the end of the novel, in which the Christians are being fed to the lions.[22] Both of these scenes figure prominently in *The Sign of the Cross* and in the 1951 film. Yet the striking juxtaposition of Christian singing and the erotic dance in *The Sign of the Cross* has no counterpart either in the novel or in the 1951 film. Like many other aspects of the 1932 film (such as the augmented role for the highly sexualized Poppaea), the insertion of this banquet scene into the *Quo Vadis* story reorients the plot of Sienkiewicz's novel, so that its central tension is between lasciviousness and virtue.[23] The Christian music in *The Sign of the Cross* functions largely in the service of this tension. Indeed, it is hard to imagine a clearer musical expression of the conflict between Christian faith and decadent sexuality than this heterophonic juxtaposition of the hymn and the orientalist dance.

As I discuss below in my interpretation of the climactic arena sequence, Christian music plays an even more central role in the 1951 *Quo Vadis* film. But it functions, so to speak, along a different semantic axis. The central tension in the plot of Mervyn LeRoy's film is not between lascivious and virtue, but rather between faith and power. That is not to say, of course, that eroticism plays no part in the 1951 film. The banquet scene in *Quo Vadis* contains plenty of writhing half-naked bodies (both male and female), and Poppaea is garbed in a succession of clinging gowns, each more revealing than the last. And yet in comparison to *The*

Sign of the Cross, her role is somewhat attenuated. In the 1951 film, there are no bathing scenes, and Poppaea has no musical motive of her own. The emphasis (to use Sallust's terms again) is on *lubido dominandi* rather than on *luxuria,* and the plot of the movie turns on the hero's conversion from this love of power to the self-sacrificing ethos of the new Christian faith.

In musical terms, we can trace the process of conversion in Rózsa's transformations of the Vinicius motive: the music that represents what the composer in his *Quo Vadis* article calls "pagan heroism and self confidence." Marcus's identification with the martial valor and pride of the empire is at its peak during his triumphal entrance into Rome, when his own motive forms the second theme for the triumphal march. But this identification is progressively undermined, first by Marcus's blossoming love for Lygia, and then by the power of the Christian faith with which she is aligned. Marcus attempts to abduct Lygia as she and her companions are returning from a secret Christian service, but the virtuous maiden is protected by her gigantic bodyguard, Ursus. Ursus injures Marcus, but then brings him into the home of a fellow Christian so that he may recover from his wounds. Here he is tended by Lygia, and as he comes more and more under her influence, his musical theme is transformed. Reorchestrated and played at a slower tempo, it loses its march-like characteristics so that it may be more seamlessly blended with Lygia's music. As he becomes more and more convinced of the truth of the Christian message (and as his love for Lygia deepens), Marcus becomes even less closely associated with the Vinicius motive. Eventually, this theme disappears from the score altogether.

Marcus's conversion unfolds against a broader historical (or quasi-historical) backdrop, namely, the ideological conflict between the secular power of Rome and the spiritual power of the nascent church. This conflict is dramatized in a spectacular sequence of scenes that unfold in the Coliseum. Nero has blamed the Christians for the fire for which he himself was responsible, and has commanded that they should all be fed to the lions. Facing certain martyrdom, the Christians turn their souls to God and lift their voices in song. The conflict between faith and arbitrary secular power plays out not least in terms of music.

In the climactic arena scenes of *Quo Vadis,* imperial power is manifested—at least musically—primarily through the trumpet fanfares: fanfares that to some extent take over the semiotic position of the Marcus Vinicius theme with which they have so many affinities. Heard in the final part of the film essentially as source music, the fanfares represent *lubido dominandi,* reduced to its barest essentials. Together with the hymn, the sound effects and the underscoring, the fanfares function as part of an acoustic complex that dramatizes the central ideological conflict of the film in a particularly potent way.

The Coliseum scenes begin in a festival atmosphere, enhanced by Rózsa's dance-like underscoring. With its siciliano rhythmic gestures and energetic tempo, this music recalls the Dance of the Vestals that precedes Marcus Vinicius's triumphal entry into Rome. A brief fanfare announces the entrance of Nero and Poppaea, together with other members of the court. As in the triumphal procession sequence from the first part of the film, the chief vestal virgin intones a prayer, which sacralizes the event and marks it as a public demonstration of the Roman state. In the sound mix for the film, her voice is strangely amplified, so that it sounds almost as if it is being projected through a loudspeaker—one wonders if there is perhaps an acoustic reference here to the use of the loudspeaker during the war years. Nero gives the signal to drive the Christians into the arena, and his gesture is accompanied by a second trumpet fanfare, reinforcing the connection between this musical gesture and imperial power. Sounds of the cheering crowd combine with the roars of the lions, illustrating (not too subtly) the destructive and animalistic energy of an inflamed mob. These cacophonous sounds end abruptly, however, when Peter appears in the upper part of the Coliseum. In an acoustic gesture that both echoes and answers the earlier prayer of the vestal, Peter prays for the Christians and assures them that they will be received into Paradise. Newly inspired by their leader, the Christians begin to sing the "Second Christian Hymn" that earlier functioned as the recessional to their secret service, the hymn that stands as the musical marker of their spiritual power.

The fact that the Christians sing this hymn in unison, of course, demonstrates their spiritual unity. With its Mixolydian modality and its rising second and third phrases, the "Second Christian Hymn" eloquently expresses the Christians' confidence in eternal life, even in the face of death. Nero is both dumbfounded and agitated by their singing, and cuts it off with another physical/acoustic gesture. When he lowers his hand, a third fanfare sounds, and the lions are again released into the arena. But neither the trumpets nor the lions can permanently quell the hymn, which rises again even as Peter is seized and thrown into prison. Individual Christians may die, but their song and their faith endures.

The sound mix for this moment in the film is in many ways analogous to that of the banquet scene in *The Sign of the Cross* that I described above. But in the 1951 film, the heterophonic juxtaposition is between Christian hymnody and imperial power (manifested by the fanfares) rather than decadent lascivious dance. The juxtaposition thus presents *in nuce* the conflict between spirit and empire that is at the core of the plot. The ultimate victory of the spirit is aptly foreshadowed in a kind of epilogue to the Coliseum sequence, in which Nero walks the arena with members of his Praetorian guard, looking with consternation at the smiles on the faces of the corpses. Rózsa's underscoring for this epilogue—based on the "Second Christian Hymn"—carries the song of the Christians past death into the realm of the spirit.

Authentic Song?

At many points during the arena sequence, Nero himself draws attention to this spiritualizing function of music, expressing disbelief that the Christians can be singing even as they are about to die. The song of the Christians is galling not merely because it spoils the demonstration of imperial power (which depends upon the terror of its victims), but also because of Nero's own aspirations as a creative artist. These aspirations, of course, have been central to the characterization of Nero at least since Suetonius. But they are particularly marked in the 1951 *Quo Vadis* film. Indeed, the plot of this film explains the burning of Rome as a mad attempt on the part of Nero to create a kind of colossal *Gesamtkunstwerk*. In this light, we might understand the Christian music as a kind of authentic answer to the tragicomic presentation of "O lambent flames" (and the other music that Nero sings). Nero longs to create music of transcendent power, but he is unable to do so. He recognizes it—to his torment and chagrin—in the simple monophonic hymnody of the Christians.

The juxtaposition of the Christian music with "O lambent flames" returns us to the questions of authenticity with which I began this chapter. Of all the musical cues that Rózsa discusses in his article, it is probably in the three Christian hymns that the ideal of historical authenticity is most directly aligned with the narrative demands of the plot. As Rózsa points out, the last of these three cues ("Evensong") was based on the Ambrosian anthem "Aeterna rerum conditor," and it seems likely that many audience members of the postwar period would have identified it as an example of Gregorian chant. In a similar way, the "First Christian Hymn" would probably have been understood as ancient religious music even though its specific source almost certainly went unrecognized. The fact that Rózsa asked that the music be sung by a "genuine Jewish cantor" no doubt accentuated the aura of authenticity generated by the monophonic texture and the relatively free rhythmic structure of the song. The music could thus serve both as a marker of historical authenticity—as genuine music from the time of Nero—and in a narrative/symbolic sense as a marker of spiritual authenticity vis-à-vis the secular power of the empire. Similar claims, however, are more difficult to make with regard to "O lambent flames." The Epitaph of Seikolos was widely available in transcription—it appears in both Curt Sachs's *Musik des Altertums* (1924) and in the first editions of the *Harvard Anthology of Music* (1949)—and it is possible that it might have had some currency as a musical marker for the ancient world. And even if few members of the audience would have recognized the source, the lyre accompaniment and the modal nature of the melody would probably have suggested a certain degree of historical authenticity. But it is also possible that these very musical qualities would also have suggested other kinds of authenticity as well. In this regard, it is relevant to compare "O lambent flames" to musical cues with similar musical styles and textures, both in other postwar biblical epics and also within *Quo Vadis* itself. Objectively speaking, the closest analogue to Nero's "O lambent flames" in other postwar biblical epics is probably the recitation/performance that David gives of the Twenty-third Psalm in *David and Bathsheba*. David, to be sure, is speaking rather than singing. But like Nero, he is a ruler performing his own composition to the accompaniment of an ancient lyre. Another point of comparison for "O lambent flames" can be found in a scene from *The Robe* (1953, directed by Henry Koster with a score by Alfred Newman), in which the lame Christian woman Miriam sings before an attentive audience of fellow villagers, just as Nero sings for his courtiers (I examine this scene in more detail in the following chapter). It is highly unlikely (although not impossible) that Newman based his cues on historically authentic music such as the Epitaph of Seikolos. With their relatively free rhythm, modal melodies, and strumming lyre accompaniment, both Miriam's song and David's recitation nevertheless locate the characters in a chronologically and geographically distant culture, and in this sense are quite similar to the music that Rózsa composed for Nero.

The similarities between "O lambent flames" and David's recitation or Miriam's song from *The Robe,* however, only foreground their important semantic differences. In both *The Robe* and *David and Bathsheba*, solo song connotes simplicity, earnestness, directness, and truth. It is aligned, we might say, with the force of the Spirit, which (at least in the ideological framework of the ancient epic film) is opposed to the decadent machinations of secular power. Indeed, this musical style—apart from the songs of Nero—also plays a similar role in *Quo Vadis*. It appears, for example, in another of the historicist examples that Rózsa describes in his article, namely, the song that the slave woman Eunice sings approximately halfway through the film (disc 1, 1:26:57).[24] Eunice is in love with her master Petronius, one of Nero's most trusted courtiers who also happens to be the uncle of Marcus Vinicius. With its poetic description of romantic devotion, Eunice's song is the musical embodiment of her passion for Petronius, an emotion that Petronius eventually comes to return. In part because of Eunice's love, Petronius will leave behind his pose of cynical detachment. Eventually—in the scene in which he commits suicide—he speaks truth to power, defies Nero, and frees Eunice from slavery. Although Eunice's song is not associated with religious faith, it functions as a musical embodiment of the kind of selfless love that (at least in the plot of the film) stands in opposition to Nero's narcissism. It is possible, of course, to understand the musical style of "O lambent flames" ironically: as a reference to the kind of spiritual authenticity that Nero will never have. But (with apologies to Rózsa) it can also be seen as a moment in which the demands for spiritual authenticity and the demands for historical authenticity were too distant to be reconciled. In the musical semantics of the postwar biblical epic, in any case, Nero's songs remained an anomaly.

Both the Christian music and (to a lesser extent) the diegetic songs of Nero and Eunice probably carried an aura of historical authenticity for mid-century audiences. In other cases, however, Rózsa's efforts to base his music—as much as possible—on authentic historical sources had little bearing on how the film was understood. The fact that the underscoring for the scene in which Lygia is abducted from the house of General Plautius uses a chromatic motive from the second Delphic hymn, for example, almost certainly had little or no relevance for the cinematic audience. In a similar way, the diegetic music for the bacchanal at Nero's palace was most likely heard simply as a species of musical orientalism familiar from countless sources, stretching back from *Casablanca* well into the nineteenth century. Without the aid of explanatory notes (such as the ones that Rózsa himself provided in his article), then, it seems that his extensive efforts to create a historically authentic score would have gone largely unnoticed by the postwar cinematic audience.

In his attempt to create historically authentic music for *Quo Vadis*, Rózsa was hampered not only by issues of semantic legibility, but also by the relative paucity of notated music that survived from this period. In this context, it is hard to imagine how Rózsa could have treated the relationship between the musical cue and its corresponding source material without a certain degree of freedom. We can thus speak about a process of compromise or mediation through which Rózsa adapted the ideal of historical authenticity to the exigencies of the postwar biblical epic. This process takes place along a number of axes, the first of which has to do with musical function. The Epitaph of Seikolos, for example, was discovered on a tombstone in Asia Minor during the 1880s. The context in which it appears in the film is hardly funereal in nature. Similarly, the source material for Nero's second song—the Gregorian anthem "Omnes sitientos venite ad aquas"—has little to do with the dramatic context in which the song occurs. Nero is singing to a small group of his courtiers as they look out over the fires that are consuming Rome. While the source material might be considered an ironic reflection on the inferno ("Omnes sitientos venite ad aquas" may be translated as "Let all who thirst come to the waters"), it is far more likely that Rózsa simply found a compelling melody in the Gregorian anthem, and used it without regard to the meaning of the text.

Music, of course, is continually being repurposed, and it is difficult to imagine a melody that has not served a variety of different functions. A more interesting axis of compromise, therefore, has to do with historical and geographic specificity. Again, if Rózsa were to restrict himself only to music that could be dated to first-century Rome, he would have had very little to work with. He was therefore compelled, so to speak, to cast a wider historical and geographical net. The third hymn of the Christians, to take one example, is based on the Ambrosian "Aeterna rerum conditor," part of a repertory that dates from many centuries after the events depicted in the film are supposed to have taken place. While it is certainly possible that the Babylonian Jewish melody that Rózsa used for the first Christian hymn might have been sung in first-century Rome, we cannot be sure that it was. As Rózsa freely admits, his work is informed by a kind of imaginative reconstruction based on informed deduction rather than an abundance of source materials.

I make these observations regarding the *Quo Vadis* score not in order to critique the composer, but rather to point out some of the difficulties that attended the task of writing historically authentic music for an epic set in the ancient world. Rózsa was keenly aware of all these problems, and his thoughts on film music and historical authenticity evolved quite dramatically during his "historico-biblical" period (roughly from *Quo Vadis* through *The Last Days of Sodom and Gomorrah* in 1962). Indeed, when he returned to the biblical epic genre with *Ben-Hur*, Rózsa made far less use of historically authentic sources. In his *Quo Vadis* article, Rózsa implicitly treats the movie as a new model for epic film music, a model in which this ideal of historical authenticity would play a central role. But although this ideal would continue to influence the music of the postwar epic, its musical manifestations—as we shall see in the context of *King of Kings* and *The Greatest Story Ever Told*—would take a very different form.

We might therefore frame the oblique relationship between the music of *Quo Vadis* and the ideals of historical authenticity in the terms that Barthes uses to describe the omnipresent forelock in *Julius Caesar*. With some charity and imagination, "O lambent flames" might be understood as a "deeply rooted" sign that reveals an "internal, hidden facet" of ancient Rome, and if "Aeterna rerum conditor" cannot be traced all the way back to the first century, it does at least suggest the early years of the Christian church. But Miriam's song from *The Robe*—or, for that matter, the Marcus Vinicius music or the Marcia Romana from *Quo Vadis*—occupies different ground. Their links to the genuine music of ancient Palestine or imperial Rome (insofar as we may judge these) are tenuous, but neither can they be regarded as "a kind of algebra," as completely abstract musical symbols. They seem to be—to use Barthes once again—yet another example of a "degraded spectacle of the intermediate sign," the aural equivalents of the ahistoric hairstyles that the author so despises.

But with apologies to Barthes, I would like to argue that the construction of these "intermediate signs"—the offending hairstyles or (in my reading) the pseudo-authentic music of *Quo Vadis*—is to be praised rather than despised. Balancing between familiarity and strangeness, this music evoked just the right amount of historical and geographical distance. For it was precisely the pseudo-authenticity and semiotic "in-between-ness" of these films that made them so powerful for postwar audiences. Ironically, it was not the historically authentic music that Rózsa describes with such care in his article that proved ultimately to be the most important legacy of the *Quo Vadis* score, but rather the "dramatic accompanying music" that he discusses (in an almost offhand way) toward the end of his essay. This pseudo-authentic music—the triumphal marches, the music for Lygia, the Assyrian Dance—became in many ways the archetypal sound of the ancient world for postwar American cinematic audiences. If we are to believe the chronological evidence from the source materials (and Rózsa's own description of his compositional process in the *Film Music Notes* article), this style emerged in a provisional, almost accidental manner. It was the result of compromise and adaptation: the by-product rather than the result of the quest for a historically authentic style of cinematic music. It was these sounds—and not the more historically authentic style typified by the Evensong cue and "O lambent flames"—that Rózsa himself would extend and develop in his score for *Ben-Hur*, the score that in many ways represents the apogee of the postwar biblical epic.

4   Novel and Film, Music and Miracle
Alfred Newman's Score to *The Robe*

The postwar religious revival that I referenced in the introduction to this book was manifest not merely in film, but also in many other aspects of American culture, and one index of its strength was the prevalence of religious works atop the best-seller lists during the period. Although the completion of the Revised Standard Version in 1952 propelled the Bible itself briefly to the top of the nonfiction list in the following year, works such as Fulton Oursler's *The Greatest Story Ever Told* (a retelling of the basic Gospel narrative) and Catherine Marshall's *A Man Called Peter* (an inspirational biography of her husband, the preacher Peter Marshall) were more typical.[1] Perhaps the most popular and influential of these postwar religious nonfiction works was Norman Vincent Peale's *The Power of Positive Thinking,* which stayed on the New York Times best-seller list for 186 weeks, 48 in the No. 1 nonfiction spot.[2] Other popular titles included Billy Graham's *Peace with God* and Dale Evans Rogers's *My Spiritual Diary.*[3] The hunger for religious books was also reflected in the popularity of historical novels based on biblical events and characters. The beginnings of this trend may be traced back into the war years, which saw the publication of Lloyd Douglas's blockbuster novel *The Robe* (1942). Douglas followed up this success with his novel *The Big Fisherman* (1949), in which Peter is the central character.[4] But Douglas was by no means the only novelist to take advantage of this hunger. Sholem Asch's *Moses* (1951) and Frank Slaughter's *The Galileans: A Story of Mary Magdalene* (1953) found their way onto the best-seller lists of the time, although their popularity was eclipsed by that of Thomas B. Costain's *The Silver Chalice.*[5] For the book trade in the postwar period, in short, religion sold, and sold well.

In light of this popularity, it is hardly surprising that some of these best sellers should be adapted for the silver screen as epic films. In addition to *The Robe,* which Twentieth Century–Fox turned into a blockbuster in 1953, other cinematic adaptations of mid-century religious novels include Victor Saville's 1954 *The Silver Chalice* (based on Costain's work), Frank Borzage's adaptation of *The Big Fisherman* (1959), and the 1961/62 adaptation of Pär Lagerqvist's novel *Barabbas* (to which we turn in chapter 8). The practice of basing film scripts on best sellers, of course, was already well established during the prewar period, and *The Hunger Games* and *Harry Potter* films bear witness to its vitality in our time. What is interesting for my purposes in this chapter is not this adaptation process per se, but rather the ways in which it intersected with the idea of the miracle.

Demythologization

In many ways the works upon which these postwar biblical films are based are the successors to Sienkiewicz's *Quo Vadis?* and Lew Wallace's *Ben-Hur: A Tale of the Christ*. In both *The Robe* and *The Silver Chalice* (to focus for a moment on the two most significant of these mid-century works) the hero is a fictional character living at or immediately after the time of Christ. Like Marcus Vinicius in *Quo Vadis?* and Judah Ben-Hur in Wallace's novel, the heroes of these later works come into contact with biblical characters such as Peter, Paul, or (in the case of *The Silver Chalice*) Simon Magus. Historical characters from Roman history also figure prominently. Emperor Nero, for example, appears in Costain's novel, just as he does in *Quo Vadis?*, while both Tiberius and Caligula are important characters in *The Robe*. More significant are the ways in which the plots of these twentieth-century novels recapitulate the conversion motif that is so important in their nineteenth-century predecessors. As in *Quo Vadis?* and *Ben-Hur: A Tale of the Christ,* the male heroes of both *The Robe* and *The Silver Chalice* make the passage from an indifferent paganism to Christianity with the aid and love of a virtuous woman, a love interest who is either already a Christian or who becomes one in the course of the novel. In these books, as in the films that are based upon them, romantic love is thus tightly bound up with the spiritual transformation of the hero.

Given the similar plot trajectories of these novels, it is hardly surprising that they should touch on similar themes and problems. As in most of the postwar biblical epics (and the earlier novels and plays from which they drew), the relationship between secular and sacred power is of central importance. The novels also critique the institution of slavery and position Christianity as a liberating force (we return to this theme below). But in one important aspect, the mid-century novels stake out different ideological ground than that occupied by their nineteenth-century predecessors. Unlike Sienkiewicz and Wallace, both Douglas and Costain are particularly concerned with the cognitive dissonance between the practical, rationalist worldview of their heroes and the truth-value of the miracles ascribed to Jesus (and, to a lesser extent, his disciples) in the Gospel narratives. The heroes of the mid-century novels are essentially skeptics, and they are attracted to Christianity on ethical rather than soteriological grounds. For these characters, stories about Jesus' supernatural powers—at least initially— are impediments rather than aids to conversion. In this sense, the miracles are epiphenomena surrounding the essential truths of the Christian message.

The problem of the miracle encountered by the heroes of these novels, of course, was also one faced by their mid-century readers, and—more importantly for our purposes here—by the audiences of the films that were based upon them. In this sense, these novels—and their film adaptations—reflected a broader topic in mid-century and postwar religious life, namely, the problem of demythologizing. A central text for this problem was Rudolf Bultmann's 1941 essay "New Testament and Mythology." "[For] men and women today," Bultmann writes in this essay,

> the mythical world picture [embodied in the Gospel narratives] is a thing of the past. Therefore, contemporary Christian proclamation is faced with the question whether, when it demands faith from men and women, it expects them to acknowledge this mythical world picture of the past. If this is impossible, it then has to face the question whether the New Testament proclamation has a truth that is independent of the mythical world picture, in which case it would be the task of theology to demythologize the Christian proclamation.[6]

Although Bultmann was one of the most influential theologians of the postwar period, his impact on American culture was not nearly as great as that of more popular figures such as Billy Graham and Norman Vincent Peale.[7] None of the mid-century religious novels can be regarded as novelizations of his theology. And yet all these works evidence a certain ambivalence toward the supernatural and miraculous elements in the traditional Gospel narratives, an ambivalence that was especially marked during the postwar period. In this sense, mid-twentieth-century religious novels can be understood in terms of a broader demythologization of the Christian message, and their enormous popularity testifies to the ways in which this impulse resonated broadly in mid-century American culture.

Cinematic Demythologization?

In this context, we might expect the cinematic adaptations of these religious novels to partake of the same general attitude toward the miraculous. Indeed, something of this attitude is articulated in the autobiography of Philip Dunne, who was the screenwriter for *David and Bathsheba, The Robe, Demetrius and the Gladiators,* as well as many other films with religious themes. "I don't deny anyone's right to believe in miracles," Dunne writes,

> but as a non-believer myself . . . I think I should be both presumptuous and hypocritical to imply belief by writing this into my scripts. . . . But I do believe in some miracles. . . . Jesus was a miracle, not because he did conjuror's tricks with water and wine, but because he brought a message of hope to the hopeless and love to those who were hated and despised.[8]

Dunne's attitude toward cinematic miracles is echoed by Gerald Forshey's comment that for postwar audiences, the miracles recounted in the Gospel narratives "must not appear to be optical illusions or cinematic tricks."[9] With regard to the genre as a whole, Forshey may be overstating his case. But with regard to certain films at least, his observation is quite apt. Conflating his words with those of Dunne, we could say—at least with regard to these films—that those responsible for the cinematic presentation of ethical truth could not be conjurors dealing in illusion. And yet there was another impulse in the mid-century American cinema, which was pressuring producers and directors to be precisely that. Widescreen technologies and attendant innovations in cinematic sound were transforming the viewing experience, while creating new expressive opportunities (and presenting new challenges).

The impulse to demythologize the Gospel narratives intersected in a particularly potent manner with these new technologies of the spectacular in the 1953 film version of *The Robe* (directed by Henry Koster, with a score by Alfred Newman)—the first to use the widescreen CinemaScope format. CinemaScope was just one of the various processes that used anamorphic lenses in order to increase the aspect ratio of films. The novelty of this new technology was central to the strategy that Twentieth Century–Fox used to market the film. Publicity posters described CinemaScope as "the modern miracle you see without glasses," positioning the new technology in opposition to the brief craze for three-dimensional films (which required—and still require—special glasses to view properly) that was competing for audience attention during the early 1950s.[10] As I described in the introduction, the cinematic innovations of the 1950s—the various widescreen techniques; 3-D films; new technologies for sound recording and reproduction—were part of Hollywood's broader strategy to meet the challenges posed by the rise of television and the implications of the landmark Paramount decision of 1948. The studios, to put the matter simply, were quite literally banking on audience desire for the miraculous.

Widescreen technology and stereophonic sound would quickly become central to the biblical epic. The technology was particularly effective in presenting the mass crowd scenes, triumphant processions, and panoramic vistas that were to be so essential to the genre. But this technology—at least hypothetically—had a much more troubled relationship to the miracle. The miracles of *The Robe* are true only insofar as they occur in the heart of the believer. In a novel, this completely internal and spiritual arena could be described with power and eloquence. But how could it be filmed? How could the camera capture the sudden surge of exultation in the hero's heart, or the moment when he first accepts the saving love of Jesus?

While is it perhaps unfair to describe CinemaScope and new kinds of sound reproduction as cinematic tricks, the popularity and effectiveness of postwar epics nevertheless rested to a large degree on the technological marvels of the spectacular. In these films, then, there was a potential conflict between the two discourses of the miraculous that I discussed above. The genre of the epic film seemed to demand ever more spectacular—ever more miraculous—special effects, even while cinematic plots of biblical film demanded a demythologized presentation of sublime truth. In the novel-based biblical epics of the 1950s, then, there are two discourses of the miraculous: one inside of the diegesis (in the subject matter of the film) and the other outside of it (in its production and presentation). The subject of this chapter is their intersection.

Musicalizing the Robe

Precisely because of its ambiguous semantic function, music could play a special role at the intersection of these discourses of the miraculous. Together with cutting-edge sound effects, piped through new stereophonic speaker systems with which the first-run theaters of the postwar period were being equipped, music could be a vital part of the modern miracle of the new widescreen cinematic experience. And yet precisely because nondiegetic music made no claims of verisimilitude, it ran no danger of being dismissed as a mere "optical illusion" or "cinematic trick" (to use Forshey's language). The powerful effects that music helped to create—to put this another way—could be interpreted both as supernatural external events and also as internal psychological manifestations of spiritual truth. As such, music could help to overcome the potential contradiction between demythologization and the spectacular.

In Douglas's novel as well as in its cinematic adaptation, the question of the miracle centers around a specific physical object: the plain homespun Robe that Jesus wore. The hero of the story is the tribune Marcellus Gallio, who oversees the crucifixion of Christ and comes into contact with this apparently magical garment. Marcellus's spiritual progress from narcissistic paganism to Christianity unfolds in relationship to the Robe. It is therefore hardly surprising that the opening credits for the film should be accompanied by music that will be associated with the Robe itself, or, rather, with the psychological effects with which it is connected. For this music, Newman employs the transformational chromatic harmony that we have already identified as one of his basic approaches to the scoring of epic film. The opening credit music falls into three sections (see Example 4.1). At least in the first two sections, its most distinctive feature is its harmonic progression. In terms of traditional Roman-numeral harmonic analysis, Newman's progression is difficult to understand. It is more useful to see the succession of chords as being generated by semitonal or tonal voice leading. Following this logic, the E♭ minor sonority of the second measure is derived from the original C minor triad by shifting the root down a whole step and the fifth down a half step. The remaining chords of the progression can be derived using similar operations.

The transformational chromatic harmonies of this main title music recall similar kinds of progressions in the score to *David and Bathsheba* (particularly the final cue of the film). But with regard to *The Robe*, I would like to suggest another context, namely what (for lack of a better term) I call "ominous priests'

Example 4.1. *The Robe* main title music.

music" in nineteenth-century opera. We find examples of this in Saint-Säens's *Samson et Dalila,* or in the priests' music from the first-act temple scene of *Aïda.* For the priests' music in this scene, Verdi uses a homophonic texture with a distinctive rhythm (half notes followed by four eighth notes) that might have been in Newman's ear as he wrote the music for *The Robe.* Verdi used a similar rhythmic pattern for the chanting monks in *Don Carlos,* whose theme contains interesting harmonic shifts that follow the same kind of chromatic transformational logic that Newman employs. Meyerbeer used similar kinds of harmonic transformations in the fourth act of *Les Huguenots.* Like Newman's opening credit music, third-related chords that begin the monks' theme in the "Sanctification of the Swords" scene (from Act 4 of the opera) are played by the brass. In each of these operatic examples, the idea of sacredness is combined with a certain amount of

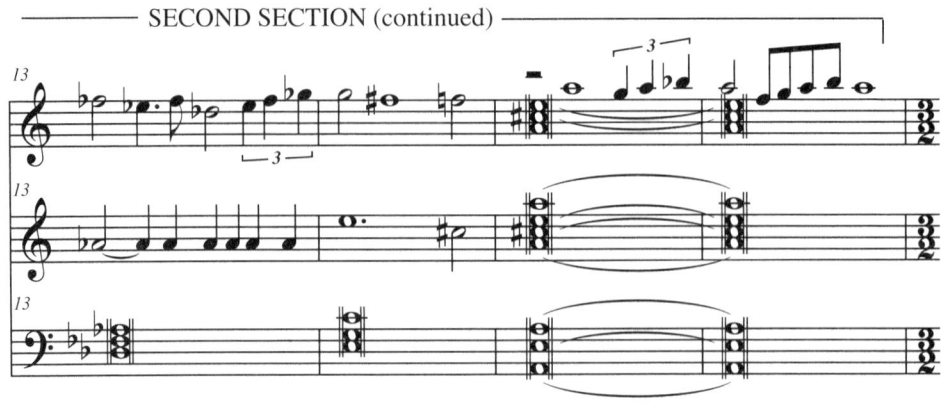

danger; it is easy to understand how these qualities might be relevant to the music for *The Robe* as well.

Although Newman's music for *The Robe* might resonate with these examples, its dramatic implications are in at least one crucial respect quite different from these nineteenth-century operatic precursors. The sacredness of the operatic priests and monks whose music I have cited is dogmatic rather than transcendent, and, with the possible exception of the monks from *Don Carlos,* these religious figures stand in opposition to the hero. In Henry Koster's film, on the other hand, the Robe will be the vehicle for the hero's salvation. Unlike the "ominous priests' music" from these nineteenth-century operas, then, Newman's opening credit music for *The Robe* needed to be not only menacing, but also transcendent. This idea of the transcendent is suggested not so much by the tonal and semitonal shifts between individual chords, but rather by the relationship among the three phrases that constitute the first section of the theme. The first two phrases of this section (measures 1–2 and 3–4, respectively) collapse back into the original sonority. It is possible to hear these first two phrases as failed attempts to break through into a new harmonic plane. The breakthrough comes with the third phrase, which moves from the original C minor chord through B major to a radiant A♭ major sonority. In structural terms, then, the three phrases of this section suggest something akin to the "rule of three" that Vladimir Propp and others identified as a key narrative element in folktales, whereby two thwarted impulses are followed by a third that achieves fulfillment.[11] In this connection, I would like to invoke yet another nineteenth-century example: the sequence of chords that Dvořák uses to introduce the second movement of his Symphony no. 9 (*From the New World*). The specific harmonic relationships among the chords in the Dvořák example, to be sure, are not equivalent to those in the opening credit music to *The Robe;* and the sense of a progression collapsing back into itself is perhaps attenuated by the fact that Dvořák places an A major chord instead of another E minor chord at the beginning of the third measure (the third phrase, so to speak, of the opening gesture). Both these examples nevertheless trace a three-step process that—taken as a whole—articulates the same kind of chromatic mediant relationship (from C minor to A♭ major in the case of *The Robe,* or from E minor to D♭ major in the Dvořák example) that is a persistent marker for transformation in so much of the operatic and symphonic repertoire of the nineteenth and twentieth centuries.

In his article "The Music in *Quo Vadis*," as we have seen, Rózsa left a detailed account of his compositional process and of the ways in which he modeled his score on preexisting source material. Newman left no analogous document and, indeed, there is no evidence that he composed the title music for *The Robe* with the score to *Don Carlos* or the *New World* Symphony in mind. There is no sense here of quotation or borrowing, but rather of an imaginative recycling of deeply rooted musico-dramatic topoi. Newman was a master of what I would like to call the intermediate level of musical reference: of music that seems to hover at the edge of recognition in order to create—at least for some audience members—a rich network of associative relationships. I return to this topic in more detail in the final chapter of this book. At this point, however, it is enough to cite a classic example of his skill in this regard, namely, his title music for King Vidor's *Street Scene* (1931), the first Hollywood film for which he wrote a complete score.[12] While avoiding direct quotation, Newman's *Street Scene* music nevertheless clearly references Gershwin's *Rhapsody in Blue*. The relationship between the title theme for *The Robe* and its analogous nineteenth-century prototypes is admittedly not as close as that which obtains between *Street Scene* and the Gershwin piece, and it seems likely that Newman's appropriation of earlier music in *The Robe* took place on a more subconscious level. In any case, what is significant here is not Newman's compositional process, but rather the dramatic effects of his underscoring. These are apparent not merely on the micro level of chordal relationships or those among the three phrases that constitute the first section of the theme, but also at the macro level. As I have indicated in my transcription, the title theme for *The Robe* unfolds in three sections. For the second of these three sections, Newman takes the A♭ in the upper voices (the arrival point of the first section) and reharmonizes it as part of a D♭ minor chord. This initiates what is essentially a varied repetition of the first section: beginning now on D♭ minor rather than C minor. It is perhaps this idea of a varied repetition over a repeated harmonic pattern that led Harold Brown (in an analysis of the score published in the journal *Film Music* shortly after the film's premiere) to refer to the main title music as the "chaconne theme."[13] In the second section, to be sure, Newman casts the theme in $\frac{4}{2}$ rather than $\frac{3}{2}$. He also adds a sinuous chromatic counterpoint to the basic chordal structure. The orchestration of this section is also quite different: the brass-heavy soundscape of the opening gestures is abandoned in favor of the strings. In the third section of the opening credit music, Newman returns to triple meter and presents a new theme. In marked contrast to the chromaticism of the preceding music, this theme has a clear tonal center and articulates harmonies that are related by fourth and fifth. Its stalwart character seems to evoke the heroic music from other biblical epics, such as the Moses theme from *The Ten Commandments* or the Vinicius music from *Quo Vadis*. It would be possible, then, to understand the opening credit music as a kind of Bar form: the heroic music functioning, in this interpretation, as the Abgesang to the two chromatically transformative Stollen. In the context of the biblical epic, however, such terms have little meaning. A far more fruitful approach would be to understand the tripartite structure of the opening credit music as another reference to the rule of three, which therefore operates on two different temporal levels. On both the intermediate and the macro level (to put this another way), Newman presents the idea of struggle and breakthrough.

By invoking the rule of three, I am implying a connection between the musical structure of the opening credit music and the filmic narrative. In classic mid-century Hollywood film scoring, of course, this kind of connection is more or less taken for granted. As we have seen, a typical strategy for the opening credit music in the postwar biblical epic—as well as in other films—is to present themes that articulate the central love interest of the plot. The principal theme of the opening credit music for *The Robe* (its first and second sections) is somewhat different. It would be misleading to think of this music as a leitmotif for the Robe itself: as the analogue of the Delilah theme in *Samson and Delilah* or the Bathsheba motive in *David and Bathsheba*. Although it does occasionally appear in this manner, it is also used to accompany scenes in which the Robe is not seen. The music is best understood not as a leitmotif, but rather as the music of spiritual crisis. Labeling this music as the Robe motive—as I do in this chapter—is only a convenient shorthand, not a full reflection of its semantic function. This semantic function is essentially to prepare the way for the transcendent resolution of doubt, in short, to prepare the way for conversion. If the transformational harmonies of the first two sections function as the music of spiritual crisis, the tonic/dominant progressions of the third section—following this logic—are the

Example 4.2. The Robe theme as a funeral march.

music of Christian heroism. In this sense, the opening credit music acts as an adumbration of the basic plot trajectory of the film as a whole: a plot trajectory that recapitulates a central dramatic topos of the biblical epic.

Musicalizing the Crucifixion

In the broadest sense, then, Newman's task in *The Robe*—namely, to find music to accompany and represent the hero's conversion—is similar to that which he faced with the score to *David and Bathsheba*. In this earlier film—as I discussed in chapter 2—the key to this conversion is the hero's relationship to the past or, more specifically, to his own childhood faith. In *The Robe,* by contrast, the key to the hero's conversion is his relationship to the miraculous. The musical procedures that Newman uses to articulate conversion in the two films are consequently quite different. In order to understand these differences, I would like first to turn to what was probably the most famous sequence in *The Robe*: the group of scenes that depict the crucifixion of Christ. With the help of his orchestrator Edward B. Powell, Newman manipulates the main Robe theme (the harmonic/melodic progression that he introduced with the first two sections of the opening credit music) so that it may function in myriad dramatic contexts. As underscoring for the procession to Calvary, for example (35:50), the theme appears in the guise of an ominous funeral march (see Example 4.2). The procession is being led by Marcellus, as the tribune's Greek slave Demetrius looks on from his place in the crowd. When Jesus stumbles, a centurion begins mercilessly to beat him. Demetrius tries to stop the violence, and the centurion strikes him down. By the time Demetrius regains consciousness, the procession has passed by. The camera focuses on the face of the slave as he is tended by an unnamed woman. The sky is preternaturally dark, and a sense of wonder is created not least by Newman's evocative underscoring. This consists of short phrases song by a wordless choir. With their turning melodic contours and modal inflections, this music is clearly related to the contrapuntal lines that Newman added to the Robe chords in the second section of the opening credit music. In this scene, however, they first appear in extremely free rhythm and as independent musical gestures.

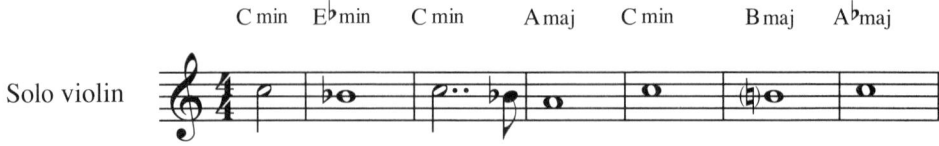

Example 4.3. Violin melody from the crucifixion scene.

They accompany a tracking medium shot that follows Demetrius as he stumbles and then walks toward the object of his gaze: the hill of Calvary with its three crosses silhouetted on the horizon.

In the next scene, Demetrius approaches the cross upon which Jesus has been hung. The wordless choral phrases continue, but now Newman adds two more elements: another set of voices sustaining the basic chords of his progression and a solo violin whose melody articulates one of the voice-leading possibilities inherent in the succession of chords (see Example 4.3). Demetrius's attention is drawn by activity at the foot of the cross, where Marcellus and some other Roman soldiers are casting dice.[14] One of them commands Demetrius to fetch the Robe from where it has fallen to the ground. The centurion claims it by right of possession and then uses it as his wager. As he casts it into the center of the game, the main Robe theme sounds again in the full strings. Thunder rattles the sky, and a fierce wind begins to blow. The sound effects here, reproduced with the new stereophonic technologies that accompanied the introduction of the widescreen format, made a great impression on postwar audiences.[15] Sound effects and underscoring are briefly attenuated so that we can hear Jesus' words from the cross: "Father, forgive them, for they know not what they do." A succession of powerful chords (not derived from the main theme) brings the scene to a close as Demetrius buries his face in the Robe.

In the next scene, the thunderstorm continues to rage as Marcellus and Demetrius walk back toward the city. Demetrius carries the Robe, and at one point Marcellus commands him to throw it over his shoulders. Demetrius stares dumbly at his master until Marcellus strikes him and grabs the Robe himself. But when he tries to shelter under it, it seems to sear his flesh. He falls to the ground in pain, yelling for Demetrius to take it away. In the underscore, as we might expect, is the Robe main theme in its most ominous orchestration: played fortissimo in the lower brass, accompanied by a wordless chorus and bell chimes. Demetrius takes the robe from Marcellus's shoulders, but only after declaring that he will never serve him again.

In the underscoring for this extensive sequence—although not for the film as a whole—Newman approaches something like monothematicism. The tempo, voice leading, and orchestration of this underscoring is so continually varied that the casual listener/viewer of the film is probably only subliminally aware of the musical connections among the individual sections. The unifying element is the harmonic progression. In all its various guises, this progression helps create both the sense of dread and the suggestion of transcendence, or perhaps the idea that dread and transcendence are inextricably linked.

Miriam's Song

Back in Rome, Marcellus's beloved Diana intercedes on his behalf with Emperor Tiberius, and the young tribune is recalled to the imperial court. But Marcellus has been plunged into a debilitating mental illness, and it seems unlikely that he will ever be cured. He is haunted by memories of the crucifixion, and it seems possible that the Robe has somehow cursed or corrupted his spirit. Tiberius then sends the tribune back to Palestine, to recover the Robe and to discover all he can about the "strange sect" of Christianity.

Marcellus travels to Cana, where he meets the Christian elder Justus and the lame singer Miriam. This section of the film contains the only extensive cue of diegetic music in the score, in which Miriam accompanies her solo singing with a lyre. As I mentioned in the previous chapter, monophonic singing with lyre accompaniment is also very important in both *Quo Vadis* and *David and Bathsheba*. And yet the melodic-harmonic qualities of Miriam's song—as well as its narrative or symbolic function—are quite different from those of either "O lambent flames" (from *Quo Vadis*) or the Twenty-third Psalm from *David and Bathsheba*. The most immediately striking quality of Miriam's song is its rhythmic freedom (see Example 4.4). Miriam delivers her song as a kind of recitative, without a clear sense of a repeating rhythmic pulse. In terms of its melodic material, Miriam's song centers around the pitch B: so much so, indeed, that the note seems almost to function like a reciting tone in early medieval chant. Newman places this pitch, however, in a variety of modal contexts. The first phrase of the song ("Now upon the first day of the week") seems cast in the Dorian mode—a typical harmonic marker for antiquity in the films of the postwar period. The prominent D♯ in the second phrase of the song ("very early in the morning"), however, deflects the melody into a modally mixed (major/minor) environment. In the third phrase ("we came unto the sepulchre and found the stone rolled away"), the C♮ introduces a Phrygian element into this environment. Combined with the D♯ in the fourth phrase of the song ("the great stone was rolled away"), the C♮ creates the augmented second that was such a strong indicator of Jewishness in the postwar biblical epics, making the music sung by the lame Christian Miriam of *The Robe* sound a bit like the leitmotif that Victor Young used for her namesake in *Samson and Delilah*.[16]

At least in a general way, the modal fluidity of Miriam's song seems to correspond to the kinds of chromatic third-related harmonies that are so promi-

Example 4.4. Miriam's song (beginning).

nent in other parts of the score (most notably, of course, in the main title). In this sense, the monophonic song serves almost as a distillation of Newman's melodic-harmonic approach to the soundscape of the film. But if Miriam's song is a kind of musical microcosm of Newman's score, its dramatic presentation also implicates music in the film's central theological message, namely, the relationship between miracle and true faith. When in a later scene Marcellus questions Miriam about her disability, and how it is that Jesus—who supposedly healed lepers and restored sight to the blind—left her lame, she gives a telling response. "I used to wonder at that myself," she tells Marcellus,

> until faith taught me the answer. He could have healed my body, and then it would have been natural for me to laugh and sing. And then I came to understand that he had done something even better for me. He had chosen me for his work. He had left me as I am, so that all others like me might know that their misfortune needn't deprive them of happiness, within his kingdom.

Miriam frames her extraordinary musical gifts as a compensation or substitute for the absent miracle, and as the drama of the film makes clear, it is principally through her singing that she is able to inspire others and lead them toward salvation. Miriam's song, we might say, is the vehicle through which the external or superficial miracle—the unrealized healing of the body—is transmuted into the internal miracle: the conversion of the soul.

Music and the Demythologized Miracle

Although Marcellus is powerfully affected by his encounter with Miriam, it is essentially a diversion from the ostensible purpose of his journey. For personal reasons, as well as to fulfill his duty to the emperor, Marcellus must find the Robe again. When he hears that Demetrius has arrived in Cana (presumably with the Robe in his possession), Marcellus rushes to the inn where his former slave is staying. Demetrius does indeed have the Robe, and in its presence, Marcellus becomes extremely agitated. By this point in the film, the former slave has become an ardent Christian, but a Christian of a decidedly Bultmannian orientation. "You think it's the Robe that made you ill," he tells Marcellus in Dunne's script, "but it isn't. It's your own conscience, your own decent shame. Even when you crucified Him you felt it. The spell isn't in you: it's in your heart and in your mind. Face it, Marcellus. Don't be afraid of it! He'd understand you. He had compassion for all men." But Marcellus refuses to accept Demetrius's new condition. He continues to treat him as a slave and commands him to destroy the Robe. "If you want the Robe destroyed," Demetrius says, "you'll have to do it yourself." Marcellus attempts to pick up the Robe with his sword and lift it into the fire. But as he does so, the garment slips back and onto his shoulders. In the novel, Douglas describes this climactic moment with the following passage:

> Marcellus stood transfixed, his fingers buried in the long-feared and hated garment. Then he sat down on the edge of the couch and slowly drew the Robe toward him. He stared at it uncomprehendingly; held it up to the light; rubbed it softly against his bare arm. He couldn't analyze his peculiar sensations, but something very strange had happened to him. His agitation was stilled. Rising, as if from a dream, he laid the Robe over his arm and went out into the peristyle. He sat down and draped it across the broad arms of his chair. He smoothed it gently with his hand. He felt a curious elation; an indefinable sense of relief—relief from everything! A great load had been lifted! He wasn't afraid anymore! Hot tears gathered in his eyes and overflowed.[17]

In the film, it is mainly the underscoring (rather than a chain of exclamatory sentences) that carries the burden of expressing this momentous transformation. When the Robe falls on Marcellus's shoulders—as we might expect—we hear the now-familiar sequence of chromatically related chords. For the transformative moment itself, however, Newman uses the third theme from the opening credit music, a theme that I referred to above as the motive of Christian heroism. Apart

Example 4.5. Peter's motive.

from its appearance in the opening credit music, this is the first time that the motive has appeared in the film. It is held in reserve, so that it has the effect in this scene both of something new and of something long remembered.

This music leads directly into the next musical cue, which accompanies a new camera shot of Demetrius and Marcellus walking purposefully across the village square (see Example 4.5). The Apostle Peter is approaching, and this cue introduces a new melody that will be associated with him. The melody begins with the same rising fourth gesture that is so prominent in the motive of Christian heroism, and the two themes have very much the same character. In these scenes, then, the musical process of the opening credit music acquires a distinctive dramatic meaning. Like so many other aspects of his style, Newman's strategy in this instance is deeply rooted in the traditions of European opera and concert music. The clear tonic center of the motive of Christian heroism and the straightforward diatonicism of Peter's motive discharge the tension created by the chromatic harmonies of the Robe theme. As in countless examples from the canon of European art music, this discharge of harmonic tension is used to express the resolution of dramatic tension. It is too glib to say that Marcellus becomes a Christian when he finally accepts D♭ major as his tonic key, but the musical symbolism is hardly less straightforward.

Newman uses this same basic musical strategy for the denouement of the plot, which comes at the end of an extended trial scene. Marcellus has been accused of treason and is now brought before the new emperor, Caligula, to answer for his crimes. Against her will, Caligula has commanded Marcellus's beloved Diana to sit at his side, in the place of a consort or fellow judge. Marcellus reaffirms his oath to the empire but refuses to abjure his new Christian faith. He acknowledges Christ as King, and for Caligula this is enough. The emperor calls on the assembled senators and other courtiers to condemn Marcellus, and they comply. Diana rushes to Marcellus's side and insults Caligula so that she, too, is sentenced to death. As the centurions march the hero and heroine out of the court, the Robe motive plays in the underscore, sounding very much like the funeral march that accompanied the procession to the cross in the scene that I described above. As in the opening credit music, the Robe motive is then repeated at a higher pitch level, with the addition of a chromatic contrapuntal line. At the climax of this second section, the underscoring is abruptly attenuated, while Diana gives the Robe it-

Example 4.6. Transition from the Robe theme to the final Alleluia at the end of the trial scene.

self into the hands of a Christian slave—"For the Big Fisherman," she tells him, referencing Peter and, incidentally, paving the way for a cinematic sequel. The contrapuntal line begins again, but now with the text "Alleluia." Another "Alleluia" quickly enters, however, as a replacement and transfiguration of this vocal line (see Example 4.6). In functional terms, this diatonic music in $\frac{6}{8}$ occupies the same position vis-à-vis the Robe motive as the motive of Christian heroism holds to this music in the opening title sequence. But its character is far more jubilant. The camera focuses on Marcellus and Diana as they walk forward, and in the background images of the imperial court give way to a vision of the sky. The two lovers are walking into the heavenly kingdom, and the vocal counterpoint to the Robe theme has become a chorus of angels. As Fred Steiner has pointed out, Newman adapted this $\frac{6}{8}$ Hallelujah music from his earlier score for *The Hunchback of Notre Dame*.[18] In stylistic terms, the Hallelujah has little in common with the rest of the score to *The Robe*. The transition into the final Hallelujah is admittedly abrupt, and the decision to use a section of the score to *The Hunchback of Notre Dame* for the finale to *The Robe* may simply have been a response to the time pressures of the studio system. But even if the effects of this transition may have been unintentional or inadvertent, they nevertheless reinforce the idea—so prominent in *The Robe*—of music as the vehicle through with the demythologized miracle is expressed. The fadeout whereby the imperial court is replaced by images of the sky does not show a supernatural transformation of material reality; rather, it adumbrates the spiritual transformation that Marcellus and Diana will undergo as they come into the kingdom of God. That kingdom is not of this world: it is noumenal rather than phenomenal. In the context of *The Robe,* one might almost say, its sovereignty dwells in music and not in the image.

Screening the Miracle

The idea of demythologization that, as I have argued above, was so important in *The Robe* by no means informed all the postwar biblical epics. Indeed, the producers, directors, and composers of these films took a wide variety of different approaches toward the miracles described in the Bible. In some of the biblical epics—such as the 1961/62 *Barabbas* produced by Dino De Laurentiis—there are no miracles per se, only seemingly random acts of nature and extreme psychological states. Although the leprosy that afflicts the hero's mother and sister in the 1959 epic *Ben-Hur* is not necessarily psychosomatic (unlike Marcellus's derangement), their miraculous healing is in many ways analogous to the conversion scene in *The Robe* that I described above. In both *The Robe* and *Ben-Hur,* the miracle is associated with the lifting of a tremendous psychological burden. *King of Kings,* on the other hand, takes a very different approach to the miracle: contrasting the illusory enticements of the Devil with the true miracles of Jesus. The most famous examples of miracles in the postwar biblical epic, however, surely come from *The Ten Commandments.* Miracles—such as the visitation of the Angel of Death, the parting of the Red Sea, and the inscription of the Tablets of the Law—are absolutely central to the story of this film. It is safe to say that DeMille shared none of Philip Dunne's ambivalence about the miraculous, and that the theology of Rudolf Bultmann had little influence on his thinking.

At best, Hollywood offers only a distorted lens through which to view broader trends in American culture, and it is misleading to draw conclusions about American religious life from the commercial products of the major studios. Nevertheless, in the diversity of approaches to the idea of the miracle in the postwar epic, we might perhaps see reflected some of the fault lines along which the consensus Christianity of the 1950s would fracture. The question of the miracle exposed one of the most significant of these fault lines, which concerned the inerrancy of the Bible. Postwar American Christians held increasingly divergent views about whether biblical miracles really happened (as they seem to happen in *The Ten Commandments*) or if instead they should be considered fable-like encrustations that needed to be stripped away from the biblical narrative so that its true meaning might better be discerned. In the shifting political and cultural climate of the 1960s, as these fault lines became deeper and more pronounced, it would become increasingly difficult (and ultimately impossible) for the genre of the biblical epic to solve the problem of the miracle in a satisfactory manner.

The postwar biblical epics did not present a unified theology, still less one that could be identified with a particular Christian denomination. Nevertheless, it is important to recognize that the collapse (or transformation) of the Hollywood biblical epic occurred precisely during the period in which mainline American Protestant churches entered a period of accelerating decline. To make direct causal links between these phenomena would be reductive and misleading. We may instead speak of parallel histories—of a cinematic genre and of a particular kind of American religious institution—that interact in various ways. A full account of these parallel histories is beyond the scope of this book and the competence of its author. But certainly, the problem of the miracle is a point at which these histories intersect most significantly. In this sense, the aesthetic and ideological issues that I have placed at the center of this chapter articulate deeper changes in American Christianity—changes that are still resonating today.

5   Spirit and Empire
Elmer Bernstein's Score to
The Ten Commandments

Like many other critics writing during the 1970s, Michael Wood had an essentially negative attitude toward the biblical epics of the previous decades. In a striking phrase from his book *America in the Movies,* Wood describes the epics as "articulations of a genuine American myth: the myth of excess, the myth that suggests, in many places and in many forms, that only those things that are too big are big enough for American appetites, and that only too much is really sufficient."[1] "The basic elements of the epic," he continues a few paragraphs later,

> seem to run from the relatively minor ones like the music (preferably by Miklos Rozsa or Elmer Bernstein, and always a martial, pompous affair, with lots of organs and trumpets, a mixture of Elgar, Episcopalian hymns, and Handel, alternating with exotic-sounding slow movements for the love scenes, variations on the tunes we usually associate with snake charming) to relatively major ones like certain sturdy, straight-faced acting styles to absolutely essential elements like the big scenes (the orgy, the ceremonial entry into the city, the great battle, the individual combat, and where possible, a miracle or two) and big, earthshaking themes.[2]

In this passage, Wood follows the basic strategy of generic parody, the first step of which is to identify the key semantic markers through which films—or any other kind of cultural product, for that matter—are grouped together. We understand such lists as a seemingly inevitable part of film criticism, even while we recognize their inadequacy and their provisional nature. Almost by definition, these lists obscure the stylistic differences among films, and the ways in which they intersect with other generic traditions. The "ceremonial entry into the city" which is so important in *Quo Vadis,* for instance, is absent from *Samson and Delilah,* and the music for the love scenes between Diana and Marcellus in *The Robe* is very distant from the exotic-sounding "snake charming" themes that Wood seems to have in his ear. Setting aside for the moment Wood's disparaging comments about the music of Bernstein and Rózsa, there is little in either of the Newman scores that we have explored (with the possible exception of the final "Hallelujah" in the finale to *The Robe*) that could be described as "a mixture of Elgar, Episcopalian hymns, and Handel."

Like all generic classifications, then, Wood's list inevitably includes both too much and too little. It is the result of a negotiation between generalization and specificity, and enumerating its inadequacies is ultimately less informative than investigating the nature of this process. Drilling down more deeply into the Wood quotation, we realize that although he is speaking in general terms of the entire biblical epic genre, what he really has in his mind is an amalgam of *The Ten Commandments* and *Ben-Hur*.[3] It is easy to understand why Wood should develop his generalizations from these two films. Judging by box office receipts, these two epics were perhaps the most popular movies of the postwar period. Unlike most of the other postwar biblical epics, moreover, both *Ben-Hur* and *The Ten Commandments* enjoyed a prolonged afterlife during the 1970s, 1980s, and 1990s, when they were periodically rebroadcast on television.[4] By 1975, *The Silver Chalice* had largely been forgotten, and even popular films such as *The Robe* and *Samson and Delilah* were receding into the past. But *The Ten Commandments* and *Ben-Hur* remained a part of the informal canon of films with which Wood might have expected his readership to be familiar. They were the biblical epics that endured. But while both films exemplify the "myth of excess," it is (for reasons that I explore more fully below) *The Ten Commandments* that Wood's critique more provocatively describes. *The Ten Commandments,* after all, was the final film of Cecil B. DeMille, who—arguably more than any director—embodied and inhabited this myth. Indeed, for generations of film audiences, DeMille and *The Ten Commandments* have come to define everything about the biblical epic that is exaggerated, overblown, and pretentious. Film and director have taken on an iconic status, functioning—we might say—as a synecdoche for the entire genre.

Wood's use of the word "myth" can be understood as equivalent to "false consciousness." In this sense, the epic articulates the mistaken belief that bigger is always better, that "only too much is really sufficient." As Wood points out, the epics used the extravagant consumption of resources and exorbitant expenses required for their production as a central part of their marketing. And yet, he continues, "the expense of an epic is not only an item in an advertising campaign, it is an aspect of the movie as you see it. Only epics, I think, insist on our thinking so much about money while we are in the cinema. Every gesture, every set piece bespeaks fantastic excess." The myth, in this sense, is simply the false idea that "anything that had cost that much had to be good."[5]

Later in Wood's chapter, however, the meaning of the myth of excess begins to modulate. Wood begins to speculate about the cultural—or perhaps even the religious—meanings of this cinematic exorbitance. In his view, the epic is (at least in part) a "ritual expression of lack of need":

America is often seen as a parsimonious place, and much is made of its thrifty, practical traditions. Yet waste strikes me as a far more impressive feature of American life. I don't mean casual, careless waste. I mean planned prodigality, spectacular waste, waste as a way of life: glass skyscrapers and cars that give you seven miles to the gallon of gasoline.

I don't think this is a reaction against a past of puritan prescriptions. It is rather the oblique expression of a faith. Here is God's plenty, or what was later known as technological abundance, and to save money or gasoline or energy is to doubt the profusion of God's gifts or the reliability of his covenant with America.[6]

In this passage, the myth of excess is more than simply false consciousness. Epic film is one of the means by which Americans might confirm the abundance that marks their special covenant with God.

Although Wood's focus in this chapter remains resolutely on the production values of the postwar biblical film, his language nevertheless invites us to think about another level upon which the myth of excess might operate. "Covenant" is a word with rich biblical associations, appearing (among other places) in the story of Abraham, in the story of Noah and the flood, and in many sections of the book of Exodus. In that book (the principal source, of course, for the plot of *The Ten Commandments*), "covenant" refers primarily to the special promises that God makes with the Hebrew people. In chapter 6, for instance, God reminds Moses that he has "established my covenant with them [the Hebrew people], to give them the land of Canaan, the land of their pilgrimage, wherein they were strangers."[7] Later, God promises the Hebrews that if they "will obey my voice indeed, and keep my covenant, then ye shall be a peculiar treasure unto me above all people: for all the earth is mine."[8] By using the idea of a special covenant, Wood is invoking this biblical tradition, implicitly placing postwar Americans in the position of the ancient Hebrew people.

The notion that Americans—or certain groups of Americans—had in some sense taken over the special status of the ancient Hebrews, of course, did not originate in the 1970s. It runs like a red thread through American history, stretching back through nineteenth-century figures such as Joseph Smith all the way to the Puritans.[9] What is interesting here is the ways in which this metaphor manifests itself in the postwar biblical epics, and more specifically in *The Ten Commandments*. To some degree, the idea that the ancient Hebrews are veiled representations or spiritual ancestors of postwar Americans informs all the postwar epic films that draw their subject material from the Old Testament. In *Solomon and Sheba*, for instance, the dying King David consecrates his son Solomon by holding a sacred tablet before his eyes, in which each of the twelve tribes of Israel has its own mark. "I leave but one monument to my name," King David says, "the unity of Israel. Symbol of the Twelve Tribes, once separate, each striving for dominance, but now you, the elders of the tribes stand before me, banded together in an indestructible oneness." The tablet functions very much like the American flag on which the thirteen original colonies are symbolically represented by the thirteen stripes, and the total number of states by the white stars on a field of blue. Similar if more subtle examples of this metaphorical link between

America and ancient Israel may be found in other Old Testament films as well. And yet it is in *The Ten Commandments* that this metaphor is perhaps most potent and meaningful.

The special relationship of *The Ten Commandments* to this metaphor is clearly articulated in one of the most peculiar sections of the film, namely, the prologue in which DeMille himself appears on screen in order to address the audience directly. In structural terms, this prologue is essentially a parenthetical insertion into the conventional sequence of audio-visual materials that introduce the film. It functions, we might say, as an additional overture (albeit a non-musical one), augmenting by its very presence the epic grandeur of the film. But it also articulates a particular ideology that is central to DeMille's concept of the biblical epic: an understanding of history as a quasi-Manichean struggle between light and darkness, between freedom and slavery, between true faith and idolatry.

DeMille begins the prologue by acknowledging its strangeness. "This may seem an unusual procedure," he says in a voice of grandfatherly authority,

> speaking to you before the film begins. But we have an unusual subject: the story of the birth of freedom. . . . The theme of this picture is whether men ought to be ruled by God's law, or whether they are to be ruled by the whims of a dictator like Rameses. Are men the property of the state, or are they free souls under God? This same battle continues throughout the world today.

The prologue thus underscores the metaphorical connections between the story of Exodus and Cold War geopolitics. It suggests—or even commands—an allegorical reading of the film, in which Yul Brynner's Rameses is a stand-in for Stalin or Mao, and Charlton Heston's Moses is an embodiment of the spirit of America.[10] The subject of *The Ten Commandments*, in other words, is not merely the events of three thousand years ago, but also those of the present day.

It is hardly surprising, then, that many film scholars have understood the film through a similar lens. In his book *Containment Culture*, for example, Alan Nadel explores ways in which *The Ten Commandments* articulates hegemonic cultural constructions in postwar America: normative ideas about race, gender, and sexuality.[11] Melani McAlister—to whose arguments I turn in more detail below—writes about the ways in which the film articulates Americans' sense of their place in the world during the postwar period.[12] Babington and Evans develop similar ideas about the ways in which *The Ten Commandments* constructs notions of ethnic identity.[13] The idea that a film might function as a mirror in which the audience sees itself reflected, of course, is not limited to *The Ten Commandments*. The postwar biblical epic, in particular, is a genre that insists upon its own topicality. But in DeMille's film, this sense of topicality takes on special power and significance.

Returning to Wood's argument, we might then say that the myth of excess manifests itself not merely in the elaborate sets and costumes, the enormous numbers of extras, and the pompous music, but also in the narrative of the film.

Postwar Americans might understand their special covenant with God not simply in the film's profligate grandeur, but also in its plot: the story of a chosen people blessed by God and charged with a unique historical destiny. And yet on this narrative level, the implications of the myth of excess become more conflicted and complex. In the context of the plot, after all, magnificence, splendor, and (excessive?) grandeur are associated not only with the power of God, but also with the power of the evil Egyptian empire. In this sense, *The Ten Commandments* resembles later epic (or quasi-epic) movies such as *Avatar* and *The Matrix*, in which the plot of the film may be understood as a critique of its own conditions of production. The excessiveness of *The Ten Commandments,* to put this differently, engenders its own disavowal, not simply in the critiques of writers such as Wood and Nadel, but even within the film itself.

On the metaphorical level, we might understand this disavowal in terms of America's unique position during the postwar period. The "epicness" of *The Ten Commandments* certainly reflects American wealth and power and Americans' status (so to speak) as the "chosen people" of God. And yet, as McAlister points out, *The Ten Commandments* (as well as other biblical epics) must also be read as an "anticolonial [narrative], situated at the moment when the United States took over from the European colonial nations the role of a preeminent world power."[14] *The Ten Commandments* celebrates that power even while distinguishing it from the imperial orders that it was replacing. In what follows, then, I consider not only the ways in which Elmer Bernstein's score for *The Ten Commandments* contributes to the film's "ritual expression of lack of need," but also how it reflects some of the ambivalence that attended America's position of global preeminence during the postwar period.

Bernstein and "Musical Storytelling"

In the quotation with which I began this chapter, Wood invoked Elmer Bernstein and Miklós Rózsa as characteristic composers of the biblical epic, doubtless because they wrote the scores for the two most successful films in the genre. Neither Bernstein nor Rózsa, however, was the first choice of the man whom Wood acknowledged as the master of the epic style—Cecil B. DeMille. For his remake of *The Ten Commandments,* it seems, DeMille planned to use the veteran composer Victor Young. DeMille had worked with Young before, not only on *Samson and Delilah* but also more recently with *The Greatest Show on Earth* (1952). Young was on staff with Paramount during the 1940s, and he also provided the music for other DeMille films during this period such as *North West Mounted Police* (1940), *Reap the Wild Wind* (1942), *The Story of Dr. Wassell* (1944), and *Unconquered* (1947). Yet by 1955, Young was in poor health, and it became increasingly clear that he would not be up to the task of scoring *The Ten Commandments.* A new composer needed to be found.

A memo from Roy Fjastad to DeMille on July 27, 1955, sheds light on the process whereby Bernstein was eventually chosen.[15] Fjastad was the music director for Paramount Pictures, and he wrote to DeMille in response to a brief conversation that he had with the director earlier in the day. DeMille had evidently asked Fjastad about a suitable composer for the film. In the memo, Fjastad recommended Bernstein by emphasizing his Wagnerian credentials. "During our short discussion on the set today," he begins, "you asked whether Bernstein could compose music like Wagner, and I answered you that he could. By that I mean only that he could write in the style that Wagner composed and orchestrated, but I did not mean to infer that he possessed the genius of Wagner." Despite his support for the relatively young composer, Fjastad was also careful to give DeMille other choices. In addition to Young (who "did not feel that he could take this assignment"), Fjastad suggested Dimitri Tiomkin, Max Steiner, and Franz Waxman. "I have avoided mentioning any of the better known so called 'modern composers' i.e. Aaron Copland, Bernard Herrmann, etc.," Fjastad writes, "as I am sure we both feel the score should be 'melodic' in the traditional sense of the word." It is interesting that neither Rózsa nor Alfred Newman—arguably the most significant composers for biblical films during the first half of the 1950s—are mentioned as possibilities. It could be that Fjastad and/or DeMille grouped them together with the modern composers such as Copland and Herrmann, whose style (they felt) would be inappropriate for the film. It is clear that DeMille and, by extension, Fjastad were looking for a traditional score, probably along the lines of what Young had provided for *Samson and Delilah*.

As Bernstein recounted in an interview with Katherine Orrison, he was originally contracted to provide pre-production music for certain scenes—including the arrival of the Ethiopians at the Egyptian court and the engagement dance in Jethro's tent—that would be played during the actual filming.[16] When it came time to decide on a composer to create the full score for the finished picture, then, Bernstein already had one foot inside the door. In deciding to use Bernstein—instead of a more established composer such as Waxman or Steiner—DeMille may simply have been following the path of least resistance. The transcripts of meetings at which DeMille and Bernstein spoke about the music nevertheless suggest that the two men enjoyed an amicable relationship. Bernstein quickly adapted himself to DeMille's style by giving the director precisely what he wanted. In the interview with Orrison, Bernstein spoke about DeMille's musical desiderata:

> [DeMille] saw music as a storytelling device. That was what he wanted. He didn't necessarily want the music to add another dimension to the film, but to really just support the storytelling. So he wanted a theme for each character, and when those particular characters were on the screen, you played their theme. If there were more than one, you sort of interwove them somehow. The music was basically retelling the story that you saw on the screen.[17]

Example 5.1. Moses theme (as it appears in the main title music).

Bernstein is speaking about *The Ten Commandments* here, but his description of music as a storytelling device would be equally applicable to *Samson and Delilah.* The similarity between Bernstein's score and Young's music for DeMille's earlier biblical epic is apparent even before the filmic diegesis begins. As in *Samson and Delilah,* the main title sequence of *The Ten Commandments* introduces themes that will be associated with the hero and the forbidden woman. The Moses theme with which the main title begins is more extensive than the three-note fanfare with which Samson is associated, but it is built around the same kinds of upward leaping intervals and other typically masculine musical topoi (see Example 5.1).

As in *Samson and Delilah,* the musical antipode and complement to the hero's theme is that which is linked to the forbidden woman. In *The Ten Commandments,* this character is Nefretiri, the seductive daughter of the Pharaoh (see Example 5.2). Like the music for so many other femmes fatales of the mid-century Hollywood cinema, Nefretiri's theme exemplifies the slippery chromaticism and metrical ambiguity that are conventional markers for dangerous sexuality. Indeed, of all the forbidden woman themes from the postwar biblical epics, it is perhaps the most closely related to the Carmenesque prototypes from the nineteenth century. It's likely that Michael Wood's disparaging comments about "variations on the tunes we usually associate with snake charming" refer precisely to this music.

As in the main title music for *Samson and Delilah,* Bernstein's underscoring for the opening credits to *The Ten Commandments* introduces several other themes that will be important in the main filmic diegesis. Foremost among these is the music that Bernstein himself—in a brief one-page document that outlines the principal themes for the film—refers to as the "theme of God." Bernstein also incorporates other key musical motives that will be associated with the idea of slavery and the power of Moses' enemy Rameses. Although Bernstein's music is both longer and more highly sectionalized than the main title sequences for

Example 5.2. Nefretiri theme.

other films that I have examined, it follows the same basic formal strategy. The opening credit music for *The Ten Commandments* in this sense represents what we might call an "epicization" of the typical mid-century Hollywood pattern, in which a composer uses the main title sequence to introduce one or more of the major themes that will be used in the underscoring for the remainder of the film. The main title sequence, to use Fjastad's words, is "melodic in the traditional sense of the word," and it sets the tone for the remainder of the score.

"Benevolent Supremacy"

In this, as in his treatment of the underscoring for the filmic narrative itself, Bernstein shows the essential conservatism of his approach. We might understand this conservatism in terms of the power dynamics behind the production of the film. When he was hired to create the score for *The Ten Commandments,* we should remember, Bernstein was a relatively young and unknown composer, while DeMille was arguably the most famous personage in Hollywood, a director who exercised control over nearly every aspect of the film (including the music). As Bernstein himself says, DeMille "didn't necessarily want the music to add another dimension to the film." In his essentially traditional approach to *The Ten Commandments,* Bernstein was simply giving the director what he wanted.

When complexities and ironies emerge in what we might call the musical dramaturgy of the film, therefore, they do so as a result of DeMille's basic vision, and not because of any conflict of interest between director and composer. These complexities are the consequence of the film's excessive topicality to which I referred above. We may sense some of these complexities in the sequence that follows directly from the image of the adult Moses receiving the acclamations of the crowd. As Wood says, the "ceremonial entry into the city" was one of the essential qualities of the epic. What Wood fails to mention, however, is the extent to which this ceremonial entry is problematized by narrative elements that cut across the grain of its celebratory impulse. In *David and Bathsheba,* for example, the ceremonial progression of the Ark of the Covenant into Jerusalem is disastrously interrupted when the sacred vessel begins to slip from its litter. The soldier who saves it from falling to the ground is struck dead by lightning, and Nathan proclaims that the Ark must rest outside the city gates. In *Ben-Hur* the ceremonial entry takes the form of a triumph for the Roman consul Quintus Arrius. The hero of the film—Judah Ben-Hur—has recently saved the consul's life and is consequently awarded a place of honor beside Arrius in the triumphal chariot. But Judah's attitude toward the ceremony is at best ambivalent. Earlier in the film, after all, he is condemned to the galleys for his supposed role in assaulting a tribune. In the postwar epic, in short, the ceremonial entry into the city is more often than not ironic.

The closest analogue to Moses' triumphal procession in *The Ten Commandments* might be found in the triumph scene from *Quo Vadis.* At this point in the respective films, both Marcus Vinicius and Moses are victorious military leaders associated with the forces of empire rather than those of the spirit. During his triumph, Marcus Vinicius is being watched from afar by the lascivious empress Poppaea, just as Moses is observed by Nefretiri. In *Quo Vadis,* the crosscurrents to the general mood of celebration are voiced by an elderly man who rides with Marcus Vinicius in the chariot, holding a laurel wreath above his head even while periodically intoning, "Remember, thou art only a man!" In *The Ten Commandments,* these crosscurrents take a different and perhaps more interesting form. The last stage of Moses' ceremonial progress takes place in the throne room of the Pharaoh Sethi, who is flanked by Nefretiri and Rameses. Trumpet fanfares announce Moses' arrival, and he enters the throne room accompanied by the ceremonial acclamation of the high priest. A brief exchange before Pharaoh's throne establishes Rameses' jealousy of Moses. Moses then presents the king of Ethiopia and his sister, presumably so that they may do obeisance to Egyptian power. Rameses instructs Moses to command them to kneel before Pharaoh. "Command what you have conquered, my brother," Moses replies. "I bring the Ethiopian king and his sister in friendship, as an ally to guard our southern gates." The scene thus presents what we might call hard and soft models of imperialism, juxtaposing the hierarchical relationship obviously favored by Rameses with Moses' ideal of a friendly alliance. Melani McAlister characterizes this latter relationship as one of "benevolent supremacy." In the chapter on postwar biblical epics in her book *Epic Encounters,* she convincingly argues that this ideal of benevolent supremacy provided an idealized representation of the relationship between the United States and the Middle East during the postwar period. Following McAlister, we can read Rameses as a representation of the authoritarian and/or colonialist imperialism against which postwar America wished to differentiate itself. In this interpretation, Moses stands in for a theoretically new kind of peculiarly American hegemony, based on friendship and mutual esteem rather than on coercion.

In the subsequent scene, a troupe of Ethiopian dancers enters and lays tribute from their land at Pharaoh's feet. At the end of the dance, Moses tells Sethi that twenty barges, filled with similar bounty, are on their way up the Nile to fill the new treasure city of Pharaoh. It would be easy to read this promise in light of America's postwar geopolitical strategy. The tribute, in this sense, represents the material benefits to be reaped by benevolent neocolonialism, and the barges stand in for tankers transporting petroleum to the new suburbs springing up around postwar American cities. Other aspects of the scene, however, suggest additional or alternative metaphorical meanings. The presentation of the Ethiopian tribute, we should note, is essentially a dance, accompanied by stereotypical African drums and featuring exotically clad acrobatic African bodies. Bernstein introduces a characteristic rhythmic complex for these dancers that we hear again in association with other images of Africans (such as the Nubians who later in the film bear Bithia's litter). Tambourines, bongos, finger cymbals, tenor drums, and timpani play different ostinato patterns in order to generate a quasi-polyrhythmic texture: a kind of musical analogue to the visual play of elaborate costumes and gifts that the Ethiopians lay before Pharaoh's throne. The scene resembles nothing so much as a Cotton Club revue, a performance that reproduces stereotypical sounds and images of "darkest Africa" for the benefit of a white audience. These resonances encourage another metaphorical reading of the scene, in which Moses' attitude of benevolent supremacy references domestic race relations rather than international geopolitics. In this reading, Moses articulates the stance of certain elements of the white establishment toward the nascent civil rights movement. He reaches across the racial divide to offer the hand of friendship, but he retains his dominant position and collects cultural rather than purely material tribute.

However we might understand the metaphorical implications of Moses' relationship to the Ethiopians, this scene clearly establishes key elements of his character. He is a natural leader, gracious in victory, loyal to his pharaoh, and beloved of the people. But the scene also articulates some of the key interpersonal dynamics that will drive the plot forward. The disagreement between Moses and Rameses concerning the proper treatment of the Ethiopians, of course, is but one facet of a broader conflict, here cast in terms of rivalry between two men who are supposedly cousins. More interesting—at least for an account of the ways in which music inflects and shapes the emotional meaning of the film—is the brief exchange among Nefretiri, the Pharaoh Sethi, and the sister of the Ethiopian king. After Sethi endorses the friendly alliance that Moses has made with the Ethiopians, the princess boldly approaches his throne. "Great king," she says, "I will ask but one favor of your friendship. This green stone from our mountains, that I may give it to your Prince of Egypt, for he is kind, as well as wise." Esther Brown, the actress portraying the role of the Ethiopian princess, delivers her lines to Moses with an unmistakable look of desire. "It is pleasing to the gods to see a man honored by his enemies," Sethi replies. "Especially one so beautiful," Nefretiri adds.

Her own passionate desire for Moses has been established in the previous scene, and at this particular moment she clearly regards the Ethiopian princess as a potential rival.

The idea of some kind of romantic or erotic relationship between Moses and the Ethiopian princess finds its origins in ancient sources. In his book *Moses and Egypt,* which summarizes the research that he did in his role as historical advisor for DeMille's film, Henry Noerdlinger notes that in Numbers 12:1 Moses is said to have married an Ethiopian woman. In Josephus, he continues, "her name is Tharbis, the daughter of the Ethiopian king. When, during his campaign as commander of Egypt's army, Moses is unable to conquer the Ethiopian stronghold, Tharbis offers him the city under condition of marriage."[18] The image of a black woman expressing her desire for a white man is extraordinarily rare in postwar Hollywood film, and DeMille's decision to include such a scene in *The Ten Commandments*—despite its provocative implications—might be understood as an index of his self-proclaimed desire to be true to his ancient source material. But it can also be read in the context of the two-woman plot archetype that informs so many of the postwar biblical epics. In the latter part of the film, of course, Nefretiri functions as the forbidden woman whose powerful allure threatens to seduce Moses away from his historical destiny. At this point in the story, however, Moses is still a prince of Egypt. Tharbis is the dangerous foreign beauty, and it is Nefretiri who is the daughter of the "tribe." Like Abishag in *Solomon and Sheba* or Michal in *David and Bathsheba,* Nefretiri is the daughter of a patriarchal authority figure: by marrying her, Moses would establish himself as Sethi's successor. In this context, the scene before Pharaoh's throne resembles the moment in *David and Bathsheba* in which the forbidden woman—Bathsheba, in this case—reveals that she has been surreptitiously watching the king as he paced on his terrace at night. The gaze is reversed, and the exoticized Other is suddenly looking back. As Mulvey, Kaplan, and Doane remind us, the gaze expresses power. Tharbis's turn to Moses, then, poses questions about the limits of Moses' policy of benevolent supremacy. Are the Ethiopians tribute-bearing vassals, or are they comital allies? Could the relationship between Ethiopia and Egypt ever be reversed, so that Pharaoh might send his subordinates to dance and play before the Ethiopian king?

In subsequent sequences from the film, this same question about the viability of soft power is transposed from the field of foreign relations to that of domestic power relationships. At the end of the throne room sequence that I described above, the Pharaoh Sethi commands Moses to the land of Goshen, in order to complete a vast new treasure city. Moses will accomplish this task with the labor of the Hebrew slaves. The first of the two Land of Goshen sequences (27:24ff.) begins with images of the Hebrew slaves dragging and pushing gigantic stones, toiling under the whips of the Egyptian overseers. In visual terms, these images clearly recapitulate a specific shot from the voiceover prologue that comes immediately after the main title music. Like the prologue to *Samson and Delilah,* the voiceover to *The Ten Commandments* frames the main filmic diegesis as but a single chapter in the "eternal struggle between freedom and slavery." Just as the prologue to *Samson and Delilah* begins "before the dawn of history," so too does the voiceover for *The Ten Commandments* begin with a reference to the opening of the book of Genesis:

> And God said, "Let there be light," and there was light. And from this light, God created life upon earth, and man was given dominion over all things upon this earth, and the power to choose between good and evil. But each sought to do his own will, because he knew not the light of God's law. Man took dominion over man; the conquered were made to serve the conqueror; the weak were made to serve the strong; and freedom was gone from the world. So did the Egyptians cause the Children of Israel to serve with rigor, and their lives were made bitter with hard bondage.

During the last sentences of the prologue, we see seemingly endless columns of slaves placed against the background of a lurid orange-black sky. They labor beneath immense ropes to drag a gigantic statue—whose features strongly suggest the images of Pharaoh that will appear later in the film—across the desert sands. The visual repetition underscores (as if any underscoring were needed) the fact that the filmic diegesis—the particular story of these particular slaves in this particular place—is part of an epic story that stretches back to the creation of the world.

This cinematic technique has clear analogues with *Samson and Delilah.* In the prologue to his 1949 film, DeMille used a shot of marching soldiers to accompany the line about tyranny grinding the human spirit beneath the conqueror's heel. When we see a similar image a few minutes later in the film, we understand the Philistine soldiers as a specific instantiation of a more fundamental historical principle.[19] The slavery images from *The Ten Commandments* operate in a similar manner. In both films, moreover, the visual recapitulation is accentuated by the underscoring. In *Samson and Delilah,* as I observed in chapter 1, Victor Young used the Philistine March to accompany the images of the soldiers in the prologue as well as in the main diegesis. In *The Ten Commandments,* Bernstein underscores the image of toiling slaves with a short melody that I call the slavery motive. Beginning with a leaping fifth and built around a pentatonic scale, the motive is most frequently harmonized in the Dorian mode. The slavery motive may be seen in the bass line in the last measures of Example 5.3 below.

This motive first appears in the underscoring for the voiceover prologue, but it also figures prominently in both of the Land of Goshen sequences (as well as in numerous other points throughout the film). In both *Samson and Delilah* as well as *The Ten Commandments,* then, the underscoring helps anchor individual narrative events in a mythic/religious history: in both films, we might say, music helps to integrate the main diegesis with its mythic/historical frame. In this sense, the topicality trumpeted by the framing material in DeMille's epics extends not only to the content of the films (the struggle between tyranny and "the unquenchable will for freedom"), but to issues of cinematic style as well.

In this sense, we might understand Bernstein's use of the slavery motive as yet another example of his old-fashioned approach to the film, yet another example of musical storytelling. Bernstein seems to be following directly in the footsteps of Victor Young, and his slavery motive bears more than a little resemblance to the horn calls with which the older composer depicted the hero Samson. Despite—or perhaps precisely because of—the stylistic and technical similarities between the scores for *Samson and Delilah* and *The Ten Commandments*, however, Bernstein's musical dramaturgy ultimately takes a different shape. This different shape is a direct reflection of the plot of the 1956 film and, in particular, of the different positions occupied by the two heroes in their respective narratives. In *Samson and Delilah*, Samson is always the enemy of the Philistines. He first appears at the beginning of second sequence of the film, joking with his mother and admiring her cooking. If his homespun mantle and leather vest contrasts with the glimmering armor of the Philistine soldiers, so too does Young's underscoring serve to distinguish Samson from his enemies. In *The Ten Commandments*, however, the hero occupies a position of power and authority in the evil empire against which the forces of freedom must struggle. Although he is the personal enemy of Rameses, he is nevertheless a prince of Egypt, not (yet) an enemy of the state. Of course, the film must establish Moses' inherent goodness even while he operates within the power structure of the empire. Throughout the entire first Goshen sequence (narrating the construction of the monumental city), Moses continually ameliorates the harsh rigor of the Hebrews' bondage. When an old woman (a woman who later turns out to be Moses' true mother, Yochabel) is nearly ground to death under a gigantic moving stone, Moses intercedes to save not only her life, but that of the impetuous Joshua as well. "Blood makes poor mortar," he tells the master builder Baka. Moses opens the temple granaries for the slaves and grants them one day in each week as a day of rest. Nevertheless, Moses is still a servant of Pharaoh. His position vis-à-vis the Egyptian state is ambiguous at this point in the film, although not precisely in the ways in which Rameses or Sethi (or, for that matter, Moses himself) imagine. He cannot fully subscribe to the moral code of the state (as exemplified by Rameses and Nefretiri), and yet he is nevertheless Egypt's greatest warrior and greatest builder.

In the logic of musical storytelling, these kinds of ambiguities could present potential problems. One possible way to express the ambiguity of Moses' position might have been to modify his theme—perhaps through changes in orchestration or in its intervallic content—so that it would more closely resemble other musical cues in the score. Bernstein chooses a different path. We may understand his approach by looking more closely at the second Goshen sequence (begin-

Example 5.3. The erection of the giant obelisk.

ning at 43:40), which climaxes with the erection of the giant obelisk. The operation is enormously complex, with mallet men, snubbers, various signalers, and (as Moses himself says) "over 2,000 slaves on the ropes."[20] Sethi arrives just before the climactic moment. Accompanied by Rameses, he is unsure whether Moses is truly a loyal servant, or if perhaps he is pandering to the Hebrews in order to raise them up as an independent force so that he may seize the throne. Bernstein begins his underscoring for this scene with a reference to the slavery theme: a reference that quickly dissolves into a statement of Moses' motive (see Example 5.3). Fragments of this motive are then treated in a rising sequence and accompanied by drum-like block chords. At various points, fragments of the slavery theme are woven into the musical texture. The underscoring for the second Goshen sequence, then, is a kind of conjunctive play between the two motives: an approach, of course, which is facilitated by their resemblance. In addition to their modal similarity, both begin with a prominent upward leap and use similar kinds of rhythmic gestures. When the stone itself finally settles into place, this conjunctive play reaches its climax. We hear heroic music compounded of both the Moses motive and the slavery theme, so that they sound like two halves of a single musical gesture. In the narrative context of the film, the conjunction of the Moses motive and the slavery theme thus becomes legible on a variety of different levels. We may understand this conjunction as a musical analogue of Moses' relationship to the Hebrew slaves (whether that relationship be one of affinity or domination). It could also signify Moses' complicity in the oppressive rule of the Egyptian system or, by contrast, his true identity as one of the oppressed. It is perhaps best understood as suggesting all these relationships at once, helping to articulate or enhance the ambiguity of the hero's role.

Sephora and "Epic Judaica"

From the standpoint of the twenty-first century, it is difficult to avoid a metaphorical reading of this ambiguity. If Moses embodies the spirit of postwar America, then his ambivalent relationship with the Ethiopians and their princess articulates the potential contradictions in the policy of "benevolent supremacy" that McAlister delineates. In a similar manner, Moses' position as chief technocrat in the Land of Goshen sequences might be understood against the background of postwar economics: in particular, the rise of what Dwight Eisenhower so famously called the "military-industrial complex." For audiences in the postwar period, however, these kinds of quasi-ironic critical readings of the hero's ambivalent position—insofar as they existed at all—were almost certainly overshadowed by more widely distributed generic conventions: in particular, the topos of conversion that was such a central part of the postwar biblical epic. In this context, Moses' position in the first section of *The Ten Commandments* resembles that of Marcus Vinicius in *Quo Vadis* or Marcellus in *The Robe*, before their identification with the Roman Empire is softened and undermined by exposure to Christianity. Like David in *David and Bathsheba* or Samson in *Samson and Delilah*, Moses must undergo a physical and/or spiritual ordeal so that his heart and soul may be transformed.

In *The Ten Commandments*, as in these other epics, the conversion of the hero takes place in stages. Moses first learns of his true identity as a Hebrew in the hut of his family. He joins the slaves in the mud pits, but he does not yet understand his true destiny. When the stonecutter Joshua is caught trying to free his beloved Lilia from sexual slavery in the house of the Egyptian master builder, Moses intervenes. He kills the master builder and is eventually brought to justice before Pharaoh. His punishment is to be sent out into the desert with only a single day's ration of bread and water. It is here, in the desert, that his residual identity with Egypt is at last cast off.

DeMille shows us this transformation in a sequence of shots (beginning at 1:44:02) in which Moses struggles blindly against the elements while a voiceover provides the necessary narrative. "Into the blistering wilderness of Shur," the portentous voice begins, "the man who walked with kings now walks alone." As Moses grows more and more exhausted, the voiceover describes his physical and spiritual crisis. The continuous underscoring that accompanies this sequence is based—as we might expect—primarily on the Moses theme, albeit in a de-heroicized guise: transferred from its home texture of the brass into the softer sounds of the strings. "He is driven onward," the voiceover continues, "through the burning crucible of desert, where holy men and prophets are cleansed and purged for God's great purpose. Until at last, at the end of human strength, beaten into the dust from which he came, the metal is ready for the maker's hand." With this text, Bernstein introduces the theme of God, inflected so that it blends more easily with the Dorian/Aeolian harmonies of the Moses theme. When Moses— at the very end of his strength—at last finds a date tree growing in a desert oasis, we hear the normal major-mode version of the theme of God, climaxing with a grand cadence.

As is the case with most other parts of the score, the underscoring for the Wilderness of Shur sequence is informed by a very straightforward semantic logic. When Moses is cast into the desert, his theme loses its connection with the Egyptian melodies (such as the slavery motive and the Nile theme) and moves instead into a new thematic environment. Chief among the melodies that constitute this environment, of course, is the theme of God. But in subsequent scenes, as Moses is integrated into the society of the Bedouin chief Jethro, Bernstein introduces another important theme. This music is associated with Sephora— the eldest of Jethro's seven daughters—and, in particular, with her relationship with Moses. This relationship develops essentially in the two scenes in which Moses and Sephora appear alone together, scenes that take place—significantly— against the background of Mt. Sinai: the mountain of God.

The first of these (beginning at 1:53:04) starts essentially as a theological discussion about the nature of God and his relationship to the holy mountain. The God theme and a variant of the Moses theme are prominent in the underscoring here. Sephora then turns the discussion to Moses himself: to his escape from Egypt and his possible destiny in the lands of Jethro: "My father has many flocks," she says, "and no son to tend them. There would be peace of spirit for you, Moses, in our tents beneath the holy mountain." With this line, Bernstein introduces the opening phrase of a new melody in the oboe and then taken up by the strings, a melody that he will develop into an expansive theme during the subsequent Moses/Sephora scene. At this point in the narrative, however, the theme remains fragmentary, just as the relationship between Moses and Sephora remains undeveloped. The next scene shows the daughters of Jethro preparing to dance before the sheikhs, supposedly so that Moses may choose one of them to be his wife. The six youngest daughters embrace this opportunity, but Sephora refuses "to be displayed like a caravan's wares." Despite the rhythmicized allure of the dancing daughters, Moses defers his choice and instead walks out into the desert night (1:59:41). He finds Sephora sitting on a rock while Mt. Sinai rumbles in the distance.

Unlike her sisters, Sephora understands that Moses is still haunted by memories of Nefretiri. At this point in the narrative, of course, Nefretiri no longer

Example 5.4. Moses/Sephora theme (beginning).

functions as the domestic woman in the two-woman plot archetype. Once Moses casts off his false Egyptian identity, it is she (and not the Ethiopian princess) who represents the forbidden woman whose sexuality the hero must resist. Although Sephora has never seen Nefretiri, she nevertheless conjures a poetic image of Moses' previous love: "Her skin was white as curd, her eyes green as the cedars of Lebanon, her lips tamarisk honey. Like the breast of a dove, her arms were soft, and the wine of desire was in her veins."

Sephora continues by articulating all the ways in which life among her people contrasts with the luxurious sensuality represented by the Egyptian princess:

> Our hands are not so soft, but they can serve. Our bodies are not so white, but they are strong. Our lips are not perfumed, but they speak the truth. Love is not an art to us, it's life to us. We are not dressed in gold and fine linen. Strength and honor are our clothing. Our tents are not the columned halls of Egypt, but our children play happily before them. We can offer you little, but we offer all that we have.

Sephora, of course, is offering Moses a great deal: strength, truth, honor, and, above all, tribal affiliation. She is the true domestic woman of the plot, and by marrying her Moses will confirm his authentic identity. It is significant in this regard that Sephora's comparative list quoted above is cast in the plural: "*our* hands are not so soft" rather than "*my* hands are not so soft." Indeed, her identity is largely subsumed into that of the community.

The extensive (or excessive) binarisms that Sephora lays out in this dialogue are reinforced by other aspects of the film. Unlike Nefretiri, who is often seen preening and adjusting various elements of her luxurious costumes, Sephora appears in a plain white dress. Like Miriam in *Samson and Delilah,* she is quite directly associated with housekeeping and other domestic tasks. In *The Ten Commandments,* Sephora first appears herding sheep with a crook, and in the next scene she serves food to Moses and Jethro. In the first of the two private conversations between Moses and Sephora, she carries a waterskin and a basket of food, and in the desert scene that I described above Sephora is carding wool. It is therefore hardly surprising that the opposition between her and Nefretiri should also find expression in music. As we might expect, Bernstein uses the Nefretiri motive to underscore Sephora's erotic description of the Egyptian princess ("her skin was white as curd . . . and the wine of desire was in her veins"). During Sephora's subsequent series of binarisms, however ("our hands are not so soft, but they can serve . . ."), he shifts to music that I call the Moses/Sephora theme (see Example 5.4). Fragments of this theme have already accompanied Sephora in earlier scenes, but now the theme appears in its full, expanded version. By casting the Moses/Sephora theme in a Dorian/Aeolian mode and eschewing the slippery chromaticism of the Nefretiri theme, Bernstein is following the semantic logic of musical storytelling. The contrast between the two themes clearly expresses the difference between the sensual delights offered by the Egyptian princess and the peace of the spirit that an alliance with Sephora offers. It forms, in short, a musicalization of the two-woman plot archetype.

The musical dramaturgy here is very similar to that which informs *Samson and Delilah*. In this context, it is interesting to compare the Moses/Sephora theme to the motive that Young wrote for the Miriam character in DeMille's 1949 epic. Saturated with ethnic topoi such as the augmented fourth scale degree and the sobbing dyadic figures, Young's Miriam motive—as I pointed out in chapter 1—functions as a musical marker for the character's Jewish identity.[21] Bernstein's Moses/Sephora motive would seem to be quite distant from Young's music. It contains none of the augmented seconds or augmented fourths that are so prominent in the Miriam motive, and the distinctive sobbing double dyads are also absent. It is certainly possible to understand these musical differences in terms of the plot differences between the two films. Sephora, after all, is a Midianite and not (at least at this point in the film) a Hebrew. It's possible that Bernstein and/or DeMille would therefore have felt that the kinds of ethnic topoi that are to be found in the Miriam motive would have been inappropriate for music associated with an Ishmaelite character. I would like, however, to suggest a different context for the Moses/Sephora theme: not the traditional ethnic topoi typified by the Miriam motive from *Samson and Delilah*, but rather a new, specifically postwar cluster of musical signifiers for a certain kind of Jewishness, a cluster that I call "epic Judaica."

The historical context for epic Judaica was shaped by the special relationship that developed between Israel and the United States during the period between the founding of the State of Israel in 1948 and the 1967 Six Day War. A full exploration of this relationship, of course, is beyond the scope of this book, and generalizations—particularly about this subject—are dangerous to make. It is nevertheless important to point out that this epic Judaica music in the biblical epics and in other films emerged during a period in which Jewish culture and Jewish identity were being much more fully integrated into mainstream America. In

Example 5.5. *Exodus* theme (beginning).

her widely read book from the late 1990s, *How Jews Became White Folks,* Karen Brodkin speaks about this process. "By the late 1940s," she writes, "not only did economic and social barriers to Jewish aspirations fall away but the United States, perhaps in part from guilt about having barred Jews fleeing the Nazis, perhaps in part from a more general horror of the Holocaust, became positively philo-Semitic in its embrace of Jewish culture."[22]

It is certainly possible to understand the popularity of the biblical epics during the postwar period as part of this "embrace of Jewish culture": an embrace that took the form of a fascination with Jewish history. In their book on the biblical epics, Babington and Evans discuss the ways in which the films reflected a fascination with the recent and not merely the ancient past. "The Cold War motif," they write, "spreads across the whole genre. Central, however, to the Old Testament sub-genre is a second parallelism, between ancient and modern Israel, though again largely in de-ethnicised terms, with questions of Jewishness secondary to the idea of the small quasi-Western democratic state surrounded by aggressive Arab absolutism."[23] This parallelism finds its most direct expression, perhaps, in the voiceover prologue to the 1959 film *Solomon and Sheba.* "This is the borderland," the prologue begins, "that lies between the countries of Egypt and Israel. As it is today, so it was a thousand years before the birth of Jesus of Nazareth. Even then, these lands were kept ablaze with the fires of hatred and conflict." The resonance between ancient and modern Jewish history, I would argue, became especially important during the postwar period. As America assumed the role of global hegemon, Americans needed a way to distinguish their postwar imperium from the colonial empires that preceded it. The American empire—to put this in terms of the voiceover prologue to *Samson and Delilah*—needed to be on the side of the "unquenchable will for freedom" and not part of the forces of tyranny. In the immediate postwar period, British resistance to Zionist aspirations could be understood as a legacy of an outdated and repressive colonialism. For many postwar Americans, an emotional identification with Israel could help to separate the new American empire from the old British or French system of mandates and spheres of influence. The old empires were about exploitation and control; the American empire was the fulfillment of historical destiny. To some degree, then, the Zionist narrative could be imaginatively adopted by mainstream America.

In this sense, the fascination with recent Jewish history is to a greater or lesser extent a feature of the entire genre of the biblical epic. But it finds its most direct

Example 5.6a. The opening of the Moses/Sephora theme (transposed to D Dorian), with chordal structure indicated.

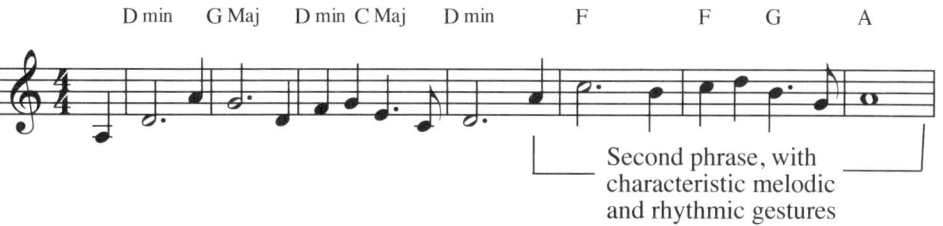

Second phrase, with characteristic melodic and rhythmic gestures

Example 5.6b. The opening of the *Exodus* theme, with chords and annotations.

cinematic expression, perhaps, in the film *Exodus* from 1960 (in which, it should be noted, the role of the British is highly ambivalent). Based on a novel by Leon Uris, *Exodus* dramatizes events surrounding the creation of the state of Israel in 1947 and 1948, and features an Academy Award–winning score by Ernest Gold (see Example 5.5). The main theme from the movie was enormously popular during the 1960s and 1970s. With words by Pat Boone, it became a best-selling song. Within the film itself, the theme is strongly associated not only with the hero Ari, but also more generally with historical—dare we say "epic"—claims of the Jewish people to Palestine. It appears prominently, for instance, during a scene in which Ari and his American love interest Kitty Fremont look out over the Valley of Jezreel (1:52:00). "3,200 years ago," Ari tells Kitty, "that's when the Jews first came to this valley. It wasn't yesterday, or the day before. . . . I just wanted you to know that I am a Jew, that this is my country."

The score was endlessly re-recorded and parodied and was an important musical signifier for Israel during the 1960s. But Gold's music has little in common with the ethnic topoi of Victor Young's Miriam motive. In place of augmented fourths and seconds, Gold uses a different cluster of melodic gestures for his archetypical Jewish music. Foremost among these are the $\hat{1}$-$\hat{5}$-$\hat{4}$ and the $\hat{1}$-$\hat{3}$-$\hat{4}$-$\hat{2}$-$\flat\hat{7}$-$\hat{1}$ melodic cells that he uses to construct the first phrase of the theme. The second phrase of the theme (beginning with the last beat of the fourth measure) is essentially a variation or expansion of the second of these gestures, oriented around the dominant rather than the tonic. Its similarity to the first phrase of the Moses/Sephora theme is striking. In addition to these melodic affinities, the two themes

Example 5.7. Esther theme from *Ben-Hur*.

are typically harmonized in much the same way, and employ nearly identical rhythmic gestures. I have illustrated these relationships with Examples 5.6a and 5.6b, reproducing the Moses/Sephora theme (here transposed down to D Dorian) and the theme from *Exodus* with chord symbols and annotations. These musical relationships encourage us to understand Sephora as a prototype—if not of the Ari character, then at least of the intrepid, colonizing spirit of the Jewish people. The process to which Ari refers—namely, the partial conquest and colonization of Canaan after the Exodus—is, after all, prefigured in the final sequence from *The Ten Commandments*. In a similar manner, Sephora's description of her people's strong hands and serving bodies recalls descriptions of twentieth-century Jewish immigrants to Palestine. In this context, the similarity between Sephora's music and the theme from *Exodus* articulates a more general resonance between Old Testament and modern narratives of epic Jewish heroism.

Both the theme from *Exodus* and the Moses/Sephora theme from *The Ten Commandments* share many commonalities with the music that Miklós Rózsa wrote for Esther, the domestic woman in *Ben-Hur* (see Example 5.7). In the next chapter, I discuss in more detail the musico-dramatic function of this theme. My purpose here is to show the ways in which it participates in the epic Judaica topos. Unlike the Moses/Sephora theme, the Esther theme from *Ben-Hur* features a characteristic mordent arabesque. In Ernest Gold's melody, this figure is, so to speak, displaced onto the bridge section, and in the Pat Boone version of the song it appears only as a quasi-contrapuntal ornament. Its prominence in the *Ben-Hur* theme tends to mask the many ways in which this music is similar to the theme from *Exodus*. Both themes share, for example, the same characteristic melodic cells: the $\hat{1}$-$\hat{5}$-$\hat{4}$ opening gesture and the $\hat{3}$-$\hat{4}$-$\hat{2}$-$\flat\hat{7}$-$\hat{1}$ closing figure. A further similarity between the two themes may be found at the medium-range level of what we might call melodic ambitus. After establishing the tonic, both themes rise to the fourth and fifth scale degrees, then stretch upward to the minor seventh and on to octave.[24]

No one—at least to my knowledge—has claimed that Ernest Gold used either *The Ten Commandments* or *Ben-Hur* as a source for his *Exodus* theme, and I make no such claim here. It is more accurate to understand Gold, Rózsa, Bernstein, and other composers drawing from and contributing to a musico-dramatic topos whose contours were continually changing. In this sense, epic Judaica is akin to what Philip Tagg has called the "High Plains Mixolydian" that informed the scores to postwar westerns, or the "evil medieval" topos that Jim Deaville has traced in the *Omen* films.[25] All these topoi are—almost by definition—chronologically bounded by the same processes of crystallization and disintegration that inform the life cycles of the genres with which they are associated. New topoi are continually coming together even as older topoi fall apart.

The disintegration of the epic Judaica topos seemed to have happened fairly quickly during the middle and late 1960s. The title track to John Huston's 1966 film *The Bible: In the Beginning* might be regarded as a late example of epic Judaica, but by this time the topos had lost much of its cultural currency. Many factors account for this collapse. For reasons that I explore in more detail in the following chapters, the biblical epics with which the topos was so closely bound quickly fell out of favor. After the Six Day War, moreover, and especially with the establishment of Jewish settlements in the occupied territories, the status of Israel in the American imagination became much more ambivalent. Israel emerged from the Six Day War as an occupying power with an intractable minority problem, a quasi-imperial state that seemed—at least to some—to be "grinding the human spirit beneath the conqueror's heel." The Zionist narrative seemed less and less like a chapter in the eternal struggle between the forces of freedom and the forces of tyranny, and more and more like an intractable political morass. After 1967, then, heroicized versions of Jewish history for the most part passed out of mainstream Hollywood.

Generic Cross-Fertilization:
The Ten Commandments and the Western

Heroic Jews, of course, have no special claim to rising fifths, turning arabesques, or the Dorian mode. In the epilogue, I take up ways in which the specific signifiers of the epic Judaica topos may have passed into other signifying realms after shedding their specific postwar Zionist (or quasi-Zionist) associations. Before leaving the topic of epic Judaica, however, I would like to place the Exodus story narrated in *The Ten Commandments* in a different context, namely, the idea (articulated by Wood as part of his characterization of the epics in terms of the "myth of excess") that America enjoyed a special covenant with God. In the history of the United States, the most famous appropriation of the Exodus story surely comes in the context of the long African American struggle for freedom and justice. But the Exodus narrative—of a heroic people reclaiming a harsh (if beautiful) land while struggling against implacable enemies—also resonated with the westward expansion of the eighteenth and nineteenth centuries. The abundance of Old Testament place names scattered across the West and Midwest is a partial indicator of the extent to which nineteenth-century Americans in particular understood this colonizing movement in biblical terms.

The westward expansion, of course, forms an essential part of the historical background for western films. In this context, it is highly significant that this cinematic genre was flourishing precisely during the period in which the biblical epics were enjoying their greatest popularity. Many of the most successful and influential westerns—films such as *Red River* (1948), *High Noon* (1952), *Shane* (1953), *The Searchers* (1956), *Giant* (1956), and *The Alamo* (1960)—were produced during this period. It is therefore hardly surprising that there should be a certain amount of interchange between the two genres. *Giant* and *The Alamo*—along with the much less successful film *Cimarron* from 1960—are sometimes cited as examples of generic hybridity: of western films that incorporate certain aspects of the epic style. But this process also operated in the opposite direction. Both genres, for instance, frequently unfolded in a desert landscape, and we might trace some of the cinematography in the biblical epics to certain styles that were pioneered in westerns. This cinematographic connection is perhaps most overt in George Stevens's *The Greatest Story Ever Told,* but it may also be found in DeMille's last epic. The final sequence of *The Ten Commandments,* as Alan Nadel points out, in many ways replicates the iconic cinematography of the western. "The viewer," he writes, "first looks *at* [Moses] and then *with* him, over his shoulder, at the Hebrews heading for the River Jordan between two vast expanses of mountains. The scene replicates the familiar image of wagon trains taking 'civilization' to the West."[26] This scene thus suggests an ideological conflation of Jewish emigration into Palestine with the "manifest destiny" of Euro-American expansion into the West. Just as traditional Christian typology interpreted Old Testament figures and events as a prefiguration of narratives or parables in the New Testament, so too could the Old Testament epic present chapters from the history of ancient Israel as an adumbration of the history of the United States.

A possible musical analogue to these kinds of cinematographic and narrative links between the western and the biblical epic might be found not in the underscoring to the scene that Nadel describes, but rather somewhat earlier in the film: in the underscoring to the famous Red Sea sequence.[27] Grieving for his dead son and goaded by Nefretiri, Rameses decides to renege on his promise to let Moses and the Hebrews depart in peace from the land of Egypt. Instead, he calls for his armor and vows to build a magnificent tomb for his son on the bones of the vanquished former slaves. As Rameses completes his preparations for battle (disc 2, 58:09), we hear fragments of a theme that Bernstein first used for a brief march-like section of the main title music. Its presence in this main title music suggests that it might play a central role in the musical dramaturgy of the film. For most

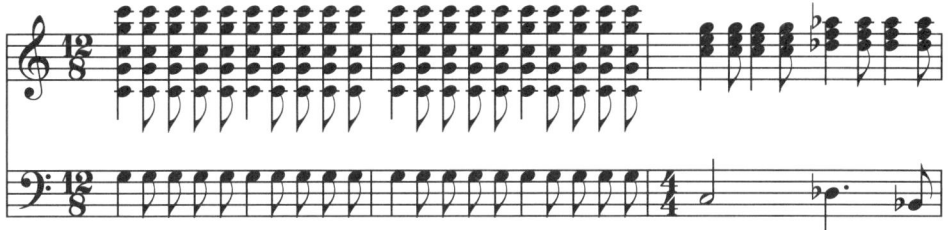

Example 5.8. Mission of Vengeance cue (part of the beginning).

of narrative, however, it stays very much in the background. It does appear during the scene in which the Nile is turned to blood, as Rameses ineffectually calls upon the gods of Egypt to purify the river. Nevertheless, it is far less prominent in the score than the Moses theme or the theme of God. Insofar as it has a distinct semantic identity, it is associated with the military glory of Egypt and more specifically with Rameses himself.

During the preparatory scene, the Egypt/Rameses theme appears only in fragments. It comes into its own only in the sequence that follows. After a brief trumpet fanfare, we see the Egyptian chariots pouring out of the palace complex and out into the desert sands (see Example 5.8).[28] In the underscoring we now hear a full statement of the Egypt/Rameses theme unfolding in an antecedent and consequent phrase. Bernstein adds a characteristic rhythmic counterpoint to this theme, so that it comes to dominate the soundscape in a way that has hardly been heard since the section of the main title music to which I referred above. The cue sheet refers to this music as "Mission of Vengeance" (that is to say, Rameses' mission to take vengeance on Moses and the rest of the Hebrews).

The dotted rhythms and ostinato patterns of this rhythmic counterpoint represent or imitate the sounds of galloping horses and are clearly a part of a long tradition of film music semantics. Similar kinds of music might be found accompanying shots of galloping horses in any number of other films, and it is hardly

Example 5.9. Title theme from *The Magnificent Seven*.

surprising to find analogous galloping music in westerns. Taken by itself, the presence of such music in *The Ten Commandments* would have more to do with functionality than with generic hybridity. The relationship between the underscoring of this sequence and the music for western films becomes more interesting when we consider the ways in which Bernstein combines this galloping music with the main Egypt/Rameses melody. The relationship between this theme and its accompanimental pattern, I would like to suggest, adumbrates a technique that Bernstein would later use to great effect in some of his western scores: most notably in the main title music for *The Magnificent Seven* (see Example 5.9). In an unpublished manuscript exploring Bernstein's music for western films, musicologist and composer Donald Meyer describes what he calls a "two-tactus" rhythmic structure that typifies Bernstein's western style. In passages characterized by this two-tactus rhythmic structure, interest is focused on two planes, so to speak: a sweeping western melody and a distinctive accompanimental pattern: block chords that articulate another galloping ostinato as well as the fundamental harmonic sequence. The tactus of this accompanimental pattern seems to be twice as fast as that of the sweeping melody. Expressing this in terms of time signatures, we could say that the main melody seems to move in $\frac{2}{2}$, while the accompanimental pattern moves in $\frac{4}{4}$.[29] While I would be reluctant to claim Bernstein's music for the Red Sea sequence as an early example of this characteristic two-tactus technique, I would like to highlight features that it shares with passages such as this famous example of Bernstein's two-tactus western style.[30] The tactus of the Egypt/Rameses theme in the Red Sea sequence, admittedly, is not so clearly differentiated from that of the accompanimental pattern. Nevertheless, the melody in the bass seems to follow a different rhythmic organization, a fact that Bernstein indicates by using a $\frac{4}{4}$ time signature for the melody while the block-chord accompanimental pattern remains in $\frac{12}{8}$. The first phrase of both melodies, more-

Ja - cob che - rished   his son Jo - seph,   ma - ny co-lors was his   coat.

God of   A - br'am,   I - saac, Ja - cob,   e - ver bless us with Thy   hand.

God of   A - br'am,   I - saac, Ja - cob,

Example 5.10. Song of Joseph.

over, ends with the same melodic gesture: an upward leap of a major fifth articulating a short-long rhythmic pattern, giving each of them a similar kind of epic sweep. And while the accompanimental pattern of *The Magnificent Seven* title music is far more distinctive and characteristic than that of the music for the Mission of Vengeance cue, its kinship with this earlier music is very strong. Both are instances of the galloping music topos, combining block chords with a fast-moving, repetitive rhythmic pattern. In this sense, the relationship between the Mission of Vengeance cue and Bernstein's two-tactus western style is similar to that which obtains between the typical western long-shot and the scene of *The Ten Commandments* that Nadel references, in which we see the long trail of emigrant Hebrews snaking through the desert mountains.

But if the Mission of Vengeance cue is related to music such as the main title theme from *The Magnificent Seven*, its ideological or narrative associations are quite different. In *The Magnificent Seven,* the two-tactus title music is associated with the flawed heroes and, more generally, with the white expansion into the open spaces of the West. Its counterpart in *The Ten Commandments,* by contrast, is associated with the villains. In *The Magnificent Seven,* Bernstein juxtaposes the main title music with "ethnically marked" music for the Mexican villagers. This too is typical of western films, in which white colonizers are frequently placed in musical opposition to stereotyped ethnic Others: Mexicans and/or Native Americans. But in *The Ten Commandments,* it is the Hebrews who are musically exoticized. As they make their way across the miraculously revealed floor of the Red Sea, they carry the bones of their ancestor Joseph. Bernstein includes special music for this part of the narrative, which in the cue sheet for the film is titled "The Song of Joseph" (see Example 5.10).

Bernstein uses parts of this theme in the underscoring for the Red Sea sequence, but its most memorable appearance comes as diegetic music: when it is sung in parallel octaves by the men who are bearing Joseph's primitive sarcophagus. It is perhaps the most archaic-sounding section of the score, the section in which Bernstein comes closest to the aesthetics of authenticity that inform so much of the music in *Quo Vadis*. While it is too much to say that this music undermines the fundamental identification (that scholars such as Nadel discuss) between emigrating Hebrews and the participants in the westward expansion, it does serve as a reminder of difference. The (predominantly white) emigrants in the typical western represent the future: the rhythmic drive of Bernstein's two-tactus themes captures and expresses their dynamic energy.

"The Song of Joseph," on the other hand, links the emigrants with the past. Their musical location, so to speak, has more in common with the exoticized Mexicans and Native Americans of the typical western than with the white emigrants who are bringing civilization to the wilderness. Despite the technical similarities between certain parts of the music for the Red Sea sequence (namely, the Mission of Vengeance cue) and Bernstein's western style, then, the musical semantics of *The Ten Commandments* are ultimately very different from those of films such as *The Magnificent Seven*.

It is hard to imagine a film more devoid of self-reflective irony than *The Ten Commandments,* or a director who was more confident about his vision than Cecil B. DeMille. Bernstein's task was to support that vision, and it would be a mistake to interpret the underscoring to the Red Sea sequence as evidence of a desire on his part to subvert the fundamental ideology of DeMille's epic. As with the Ethiopian drumming, the Land of Goshen sequence, and the music of epic Judaica that he wrote for the Moses/Sephora scenes, Bernstein here was simply following the demands of musical storytelling as he and DeMille interpreted them. The music, to put this another way, cuts with the grain of the story rather than against it. If—as I have suggested here—the music creates a sense of irony, it does so not because it articulates some kind of alternative semantic structure, but rather precisely because it so earnestly buttresses the narrative of the film. The music does not so much create paradox as expose the paradoxes inherent in DeMille's film. These paradoxes are nothing more and nothing less than the paradoxes of the American postwar historical/imperial vision. They thus emerge not from an analysis of Bernstein's compositional technique, but rather from a consideration of the cultural assumptions that the film—together with its music—so powerfully articulates.

The legacy of *The Ten Commandments* has to do precisely with this articulation. No other film so confidently expresses the idea of world history as a Manichaean struggle between freedom and tyranny, and the belief that contemporary (white) America has inherited the role of the ancient Israelites as the community of the spirit fighting against the evil empire. Needless to say, the relationship between spirit and empire was and always has been far more complex. In the years that followed the premiere of *The Ten Commandments,* these complexities became more and more apparent. As suggested by the quotation from Wood at the start of this chapter, the film became for many Americans the embodiment of an outdated ideology that was from its origins flawed and illusory. In this context, Bernstein's score commands our interest not merely because of its sweeping grandeur and the compositional skill that it exemplifies, but also because of the ways in which it exposes the conflicts and contradictions implicit in the myth of excess which was such a central part of postwar American culture.

6   The Law of Genre
and the Music for *Ben-Hur*

In 1981, Jacques Derrida published an influential essay entitled "The Law of Genre"—an essay that begins with a gesture at once provocative and ludic.[1] "Genres are not to be mixed," Derrida writes. "I will not mix genres. I repeat: genres are not to be mixed. I will not mix them." Derrida's rhetorical strategy is to trace the various contradictory resonances of this doubled prohibition in order to arrive—several pages later—at what he calls "the law of the law of genre." This "law of the law," he writes,

> is precisely a principle of contamination, a law of impurity, a parasitical economy. In the code of set theories, if I may use it at least figuratively, I would speak of a sort of participation without belonging—a taking part in without being part of, without having membership in a set. With the inevitable dividing of the trait that marks membership, the boundary of the set comes to form, by invagination, an internal pocket larger than the whole; and the outcome of this division and of this abounding remains as singular as it is limitless.[2]

Derrida's diction in this passage—"participation without belonging . . . taking part in without being part of"—is an eloquent distillation of some of the tax-onomical problems that I touched upon in the introduction. But what is interesting about his formulation is not simply the observation that no individual cultural expression is completely described or determined by the generic set to which it ostensibly belongs. The ways in which an individual work participates in a genre—or in multiple genres—is certainly one of the central issues of genre theory, and Derrida was neither the first nor the last scholar or critic to engage with it. What sets this passage apart is rather the allusive metaphorical description with which it ends. The term "invagination" is used primarily in the context of botany or medicine, to describe an infolding of a sheet of cells or a membrane resulting from an organic process. To understand the relationship between the individual and the set in which it participates in terms of organic growth is relatively simple or even banal. As individual works are added to the set, its boundaries naturally grow, much as a plant might extend its branches and roots. But Derrida's metaphor points us in a different direction: toward the "internal pocket" instead of the outward extension. The boundary of the set is not so much expanded as turned inside-out.

As I wrote in the introduction to this book, the borders (or, to use Derrida's language, the "boundaries of the set") that surround the genre of the postwar biblical epic are open to contestation. Nevertheless, it is hard to imagine any definition of the postwar biblical epic that did not centralize *Ben-Hur*.[3] The film is a virtual compendium of what Rick Altman might call the "semantic" and "syntactic" markers of the genre. Filmed with overwhelming sets and grand desert landscapes, *Ben-Hur* contains nearly all of the standard scenes of the genre, including a bacchanal, a justly famous chariot race, and a triumphal procession into the seat of the empire. As in *Quo Vadis, The Robe,* and *The Ten Commandments,* the plot centers on a masculine hero who abandons his position of power within the imperial structure through a process of conversion to the true faith: a process that is supported by the love of a virtuous woman. In early versions of the *Ben-Hur* script, the foreign woman (the analogue of Delilah and Nefretiri) is a character called Iras. Judah Ben-Hur first meets her in the sheik's tent at night. The script describes her as "a girl in her twenties, wearing a gown of Egyptian style . . . lovely, with the mysterious, intense, tawny beauty which the women of her race sometimes have."[4] Iras did not survive into the final version of the film, and the foreign woman of the two-woman plot archetype is admittedly far less significant in *Ben-Hur* than in *Samson and Delilah* or *Quo Vadis.*[5] But—like Samson and Marcus Vinicius—Judah Ben-Hur is nevertheless tempted by the *luxuria* of the court culture. Like Miriam, Lygia, and Sephora (and like Abishag from *Solomon and Sheba*), the domestic woman of *Ben-Hur* represents the spiritual values that stand in opposition to the decadent materialism of the city. In a similar manner, other characters in *Ben-Hur* also recapitulate or anticipate similar roles in other biblical epics. Indeed, these roles were often played by the same actors and actresses, so that character types (and the specialist actors and actresses who portrayed them) seem to migrate from film to film. Like Moses in *The Ten Commandments,* Charlton Heston's Judah Ben-Hur epitomizes the combination of masculine vigor and earnest faith. Finlay Currie (Balthazar in *Ben-Hur*) recapitulates the role of the kind and faith-filled elder that he portrayed as Peter in *Quo Vadis,* a role that he would essentially play again as the aged King David in *Solomon and Sheba.* Frank Thring would recycle the preening decadence of his Pontius Pilate (in *Ben-Hur*) for the role of Herod Antipas in *King of Kings.*[6] By many measures, then, *Ben-Hur* seems more than any other film to typify the genre of the biblical epic.

Ben-Hur and Genre History

In the first section of his influential 1981 book *Hollywood Genres: Formulas, Filmmaking, and the Studio System,* Thomas Schatz outlines what he calls a "grammar" of cinematic genre: a theoretical apparatus that he implies can be used to categorize and analyze the entire corpus of Hollywood film. At the end of this first section, Schatz describes what he calls the "life cycle" through which (in his view) all genres must pass. Building on the work of the art historian Henri Focillon and especially on the work of Christian Metz, Schatz characterizes this life cycle in terms of "stages." A form, he writes,

> passes through an *experimental* stage, during which its conventions are isolated and established, a *classic* stage, in which the conventions reach their "equilibrium" and are mutually understood by artist and audience, an age of *refinement,* during which certain formal and stylistic details embellish the form, and finally a *baroque* (or "mannerist" or "self-reflexive") stage, when the form and its embellishments are accented to the point where they themselves become the "substance" or "content" of the work.[7]

Needless to say, this evolutionary concept of genre has been subjected to rigorous critique.[8] The model of generic evolution articulated by Schatz, Metz, Focillon, and other scholars—as many critics have noted—reproduce ideas of organicist or quasi-Hegelian notions of growth and decay that have their origins in the biological and social sciences. In his book *Film Genre: An Introduction,* for instance, Robert Stam cites Schatz directly as an example of "biologism," a set of assumptions that he identifies as one of the main problems of genre analysis. "Thomas Schatz," writes Stam, "argues that genres have a life cycle, moving from birth to maturity to parodic decline, but in fact we find parody at the very beginning of art forms (for example in Richardson's *Pamela* and Fielding's *Shamela* in the novel, or Griffith's *Intolerance* and Keaton's *The Three Ages* in film)."[9] Expanding Stam's critique, we could say that the characteristics that Schatz ascribes to various evolutionary stages—not only "parody" but also "refinement" and "self-reflexivity"—may be found at all points in the history of a genre, a history that is not bound by any deterministic law.

Clearly, the viability of Schatz's system—as well as the cogency of any critique to which it might be subjected—is bound up with the taxonomical issues that I discussed in the introduction to this book. For Schatz—as for Christian Metz and others—it is the Western that serves as the exemplary cinematic genre, and their ideas about generic history are at least to a certain extent generalizations drawn from their observations about this particular type of film. Although Schatz lavishes a great deal of attention on the western, he virtually ignores the biblical epic, sharing, no doubt, in the general disdain for the genre that was so common among critics and scholars from the 1970s and 1980s. Nevertheless, it is relatively easy to understand how the biblical epic could fit into the evolutionary paradigm that Schatz articulates. If he had chosen to analyze the biblical epic in this manner, we might imagine Schatz describing films such as the 1913 version of *Quo Vadis* directed by Enrico Guazzoni, D. W. Griffith's *Intolerance,* and Cecil B. DeMille's first version of *The Ten Commandments* as experimental works, in which various approaches to the genre were articulated and also discarded. In the classic period, we might place epics from the 1930s such as DeMille's *The Sign of the Cross*. The first of the hugely successful postwar epics—*Samson and Delilah, David and Bathsheba,* and *Quo Vadis*—could be understood as an extension of this classic stage or, alternatively, as the beginning of the age of refinement. The climax of the genre, by most measures, comes with *The Ten Commandments* and *Ben-Hur*. As Babington and Evans note, 1959 marked the peak of production for the biblical epics (both *Solomon and Sheba* and *The Big Fisherman* were also released in that year), and *Ben-Hur* was the last of the biblical epics to be an unqualified success. The winner of eleven Academy Awards, with an enormous budget and a gigantic cast, *Ben-Hur* was one of the most popular and influential films of the postwar period. *Ben-Hur* was also the greatest box-office draw of the 1950s, surpassing even *The Ten Commandments* (which was second) and *The Robe* (which was fourth).[10] But despite these and other films such as *King of Kings, The Greatest Story Ever Told,* and *The Bible: In the Beginning,* Hollywood largely turned away from biblical themes in the 1960s. The early 1960s saw the production of a number of large-scale epic films set in the ancient world which—although they did not use plot material drawn from the Bible—resembled the biblical epic both in terms of their spectacular cinematic style and their plot structures (what Altman would call their "semantic and syntactic markers"). These films—*Spartacus* (1960), *Cleopatra* (1963), and *The Fall of the Roman Empire* (1964)—were enormously expensive, but only *Spartacus* can be regarded as a box office success. By the mid-1960s, large-scale historical epic films seemed to be a thing of the past. Following Schatz's paradigm we could say that the biblical epic—and perhaps the historical epic more generally—entered a late stage, characterized by mannerism (as in *The Greatest Story Ever Told*) or by parody (as in *Life of Brian*).

The process of generic growth and decay that Schatz describes is completely self-contained; it seems to be driven by its own internal logic. Yet even the most cursory glance at the history of film reveals ways in which specific genres responded to external events. Leaving aside the most obvious examples (World War II or the collapse of the studio system), we might consider the ways in which the western responded to the quincentennial anniversary of Columbus's landing in the New World. In the years around 1992, films such as *Dances with Wolves, Black Robe,* and *The Last of the Mohicans* reconsidered the confrontation between Euro-American and Native American that is central to the western, transforming or even inverting some of what Altman might call the "syntactic markers" of the genre. In a similar way, the turn away from the biblical epic reflected the waning of what Cohan and others have called the "religious boom" of the 1950s. But the development of the biblical epic—and the historical epic more generally—also seemed to be driven by a unique logic, or at least one that pertained to the epic in special sorts of ways. Extending Michael Wood's language, we could say that this logic was determined by the myth of exceeding: the idea that each of the epics should be greater than its predecessor. We may read this myth of exceeding in one of the most common (and most commonly parodied) features of American cinema during the 1950s: namely, the hyperbolic rhetoric through which the major Hollywood studios advertised their epic films. This kind of rhetoric, of course, is to some extent a general feature of the Hollywood film industry (and other film industries as well). But it seems to have played a particularly important role for the postwar biblical epics. Superlatives cling with extraordinary tenacity to nearly every film considered in this book. In addition to being billed as a "modern miracle," for example, advertising copy described *The Robe* as "the greatest story of love and faith the world has ever known."[11] *Quo Vadis* was simply "the big one" and "the most colossal ever."[12] Even more hyperbolic was the description of *The Ten Commandments* as "the greatest event in motion picture history."[13] *Ben-Hur* was "the entertainment experience of a lifetime," and, with *The Greatest Story Ever Told*, hyperbole colonized the title.[14]

One would be tempted to dismiss this inflated language as a mere quirk of studio publicity departments were it not for the ways in which it reflected actual production values. As I noted in the introduction, each blockbuster epic film tended to be longer than the one that preceded it; with bigger sets, more elaborate costumes, and more expensive stars. The myth of exceeding, in other words, did not merely describe the postwar epics, but also fostered an aesthetic of the superlative: shaping the creative processes through which they were made. For obvious reasons, this historical process had an unavoidable endpoint. During the 1950s and 1960s—as many scholars have noted—the American film industry was under intense financial pressure, and the aesthetic of the superlative was ultimately unsustainable.[15] The $15 million that MGM spent to produce *Ben-Hur* made it at the time the costliest film in cinematic history, and while this extraordinary financial gamble paid off, these kinds of escalating expenses could not be continued forever.[16] In *Ben-Hur,* we might say, the generic formulae of the postwar biblical epic seem in many ways to have reached their apogee, before the myth of exceeding began to drive the genre to its inevitable collapse.

On the most basic level, the aesthetic of the superlative simply promises an amplification and intensification of these familiar generic formulae. But it may also manifest itself in an impulse to make a movie not simply quantitatively but also qualitatively different from all the preceding films in the genre. We may detect this impulse at work in many different films and in many different genres, but—as I argue below—it was particularly pronounced in *Ben-Hur*. As a result, the film occupies a unique position: at the apogee of the biblical epic and yet also standing apart from the rest of the genre. It is both exemplar and exception, at once the most generic of the biblical epics and the most distinctive. To adopt the Derridean language with which I opened this chapter, we could say that the "law of the law of genre" thus operates with particular force with regard to *Ben-Hur*. In this film, the manipulation of the "traits that mark membership" opens up an "inner space" so that the boundaries of the set—in this case, the genre of the biblical epic—are transformed.

The Epic Frame

In the postwar biblical epics, as in the epic style more generally, the aesthetic of the superlative is typically apparent at the very beginning of the film, in what we might call the framing materials that precede (and follow) the main diegesis. I have already touched upon the conventions for these framing materials in my discussion of *Samson and Delilah* and *The Robe*. Much of this material, of course, is highly variable. In a movie theater, the film may be preceded by newsreels, trailers, or other materials; in DVD releases designed for home viewing there may be anti-piracy warnings, advertisements, or various menu screens. These materials must necessarily fall outside our purview. For our purposes here, the frame proper begins (at least in typical mid-century Hollywood style) with the projection of the studio logo. It is hardly accidental that these logos—the MGM lion, the statue of Columbia with her lighted torch, Paramount's image of a mountain peak—are frequently accompanied by a striking musical or sonic gesture such as the roar of the lion or the fanfare at the beginning of many Twentieth Century–Fox films. These aural signatures, of course, help to establish the studio brand. But they are also calls to attention, marking the beginning of a temporal span. In the period of classical Hollywood films, the studio logos are typically followed by the opening credits, accompanied by music that usually lays out the most important musical themes for the filmic diegesis that is to follow. In the biblical epics—as in some other films from the period—the final section of the cinematic frame is a narrative voiceover (as in *Samson and Delilah* or *Casablanca*) or a scrolling text (as in *David and Bathsheba* or *The Adventures of Robin Hood*). We may illustrate this pattern in the following manner:

Studio logo
Opening credits
Narrative voiceover; scrolling or projected text

As James Buhler, Rob Deemer, and David Neumeyer point out, these introductory sequences function as "buffers between the outside world and the diegetic world (time, space) of the film."[17] Like the famous multiple proscenia of the Bayreuth Festspielhaus, they serve both to frame the action and to immerse the viewer into the cinematic narrative, forming a transition between external reality and the imaginary world of the film.

The complexity and length of this introductory material is a kind of index: first of the film's pretensions, and also of the emotional distance that separates the filmic diegesis from the quotidian world. It is therefore hardly surprising that it should figure so prominently in those films that aspire to epic status. In most of the films under consideration in this book (as well as grand historical films such as *Gone with the Wind* or *Cleopatra*), the complex filmic diegesis of the epic seemed to demand expansive musical cues for both the main title (or opening credit music) and the narrative voiceover. Indeed, in some of the postwar biblical epics, the triple frame—studio logo, opening credits, and narrative voiceover (or projected script)—is also augmented by an additional section or sections. *Quo Vadis, Ben-Hur,* and *The Ten Commandments,* for example, all include a self-proclaimed overture. As Buhler, Deemer, and Neumeyer point out, more complex variants of the opening sequence became increasingly common in the widescreen spectacles of the 1950s and 1960s.[18] Overtures (such as those in *Quo Vadis, The Ten Commandments,* and *Ben-Hur*) are typically found in films such as *The Music Man* that in some way mimic the stage reality of the theatrical experience, or else in epic films (such as *Gone with the Wind* or *Spartacus*) which in their length and grandeur aspire to the prestige of grand opera. In mid-century Hollywood, overtures, entr'actes, and exit music were generally reserved for films that were exhibited as road shows—traveling from city to city for exclusive engagements in grand and expensive cinema houses. The overture typically precedes the music for the studio logo, which in turn forms a single unit with the music for the opening credits. *Quo Vadis* may serve as an example of this expanded pattern:

Overture
Studio logo
Opening credits
Narrative voiceover

The framing materials for *The Ten Commandments* are even more expansive. In this film, as I discussed in the previous chapter, the overture is followed by what amounts to an additional introduction: the prologue in which Cecil B. DeMille addresses the audience directly:

Overture
Spoken prologue
Studio logo
Opening credits
Narrative voiceover

The pattern at the beginning of *Ben-Hur* is, if anything, even more complex (or at least more culturally pretentious). These pretensions are clearly evident in the title card for the overture—the background of which is a detail from Michelangelo's Sistine Chapel ceiling. The subject matter of the fresco—the moment in which God endows Adam with life—has very little to do with the plot of *Ben-Hur.* Instead, it serves to reinforce the film's claim to religious and cultural authority. As in *Quo Vadis,* the overture to *Ben-Hur* is followed immediately by the studio logo (in which the MGM lion is famously silent, supposedly in deference to the religious significance of the film). The studio logo in *Ben-Hur,* however, is followed not by the expected opening credits, but rather by the voiceover, a voiceover that leads seamlessly into the cinematic narrative of the birth of Christ.

The opening credits come only after this cinematic prologue is complete, nearly twelve minutes after the beginning of the overture.

Overture
Studio logo
Narrative voiceover
Cinematic prologue (the Nativity sequence)
Opening credits

To some extent, the idea of displacing the opening credits for the film reproduces the form of the Lew Wallace novel upon which *Ben-Hur* is based. Like the film, Wallace's novel begins with a prologue that narrates the events of the nativity (with special emphasis on the visit of the Magi). The structure of *Ben-Hur* also adumbrates the pattern that was to become increasingly common in the late twentieth and early twenty-first centuries, in which the title image for the film appears only after a narrative prologue and/or introductory sequence.[19] The most famous examples of pre-title sequences from the latter part of the twentieth century are probably those that begin the *James Bond* films, and the practice seems to have become more common during the 1990s. But however much the structure of this epic frame might reproduce nineteenth-century novelistic patterns or anticipate those of later films, its principal purpose in 1959 was to function as part of the aesthetics of the superlative.

As I suggested above, its effectiveness in this regard depended at least in part on the ways in which it (and other framing music) emulated the patterns of grand opera. Although the cultural prestige of this operatic heritage was arguably waning in postwar America, it still served as a touchstone for directors and composers who wanted to augment the grandeur of epic film. It is hardly surprising that the mammoth works of Richard Wagner should be particularly important in this regard. Wagner seems to have played an especially large role in DeMille's cinematic imagination. In the memo from Roy Fjastad quoted in the previous chapter, Fjastad assured DeMille that Elmer Bernstein would be an appropriate choice for *The Ten Commandments* score precisely because he could "compose like Wagner." This invocation is only one of many. References to Wagner and to specific Wagnerian works run through the copious notes and minutes that document the production of *The Ten Commandments* like a red thread. A memo from May 26, 1955, for instance, documents a discussion between DeMille and choreographer LeRoy Prinz in which the director mentions the "motif of the Flying Dutchman" in connection to the storm that accompanies the crossing of the Red Sea.[20] A more extensive typescript documents DeMille's reel-by-reel instructions to Bernstein concerning the scoring for the film. "When you see the Mountain," DeMille wrote in connection with the Moses/Sephora scenes that I described in the previous chapter, "it's not just an ordinary mountain. . . . There's an atmosphere about it—like Wotan going up to the mountain where Brunhilde [*sic*] is surrounded by fire." Concerning the scene a couple of reels further into the film, in which Moses descends from the mountain, DeMille simply noted, "Parsifal. . . . Then you come back to Joshua, who says 'Look at his face'—and Sephora says 'He has seen God'—that is your climax of the Parsifal theme there." DeMille's Wagnerian analogies, to be sure, are not particularly exact. The storm music from *The Flying Dutchman* would be a more logical choice for the Exodus scene than the open fifths and fourths of the Dutchman's motive, and in later memos DeMille referred to *Lohengrin* rather than *Parsifal* in the context of the scene in which Moses comes down from Mt. Sinai. It is nevertheless clear, however, that (at least for DeMille) Wagner was a key part of the "epic imagination."[21]

In *Ben-Hur*, his second foray into the genre of the biblical epic, Rózsa eschewed the kinds of direct references that we may hear in *The Ten Commandments*. The Wagnerism of his *Ben-Hur* score is of a different order. What interests us here is not the issue of direct or indirect quotation, but rather the ways in which the musical logic behind the *Ben-Hur* score resembles that which informs Wagner's work. The quasi-Wagnerian musical semantics of Rózsa's score, I maintain, distinguish it from the music for the other biblical epics—and indeed, from postwar film scores more generally. In addition to the countless ways in which it enriches the drama of the film, Rózsa's musical semantics may be understood as yet another attempt to enhance the grandeur of *Ben-Hur:* to bring the film closer to the cultural position of classical opera and concert music. In this sense, the score manifests the qualitative as well as the quantitative aspects of the aesthetic of the superlative. It is longer and grander than any of the other biblical epic scores, but—by virtue of its quasi-operatic construction and semantic density—it also lays claim to a different kind of musical sophistication.

Motive and Leitmotif

The idea that Wagner's musical semantics could serve as what William Darby and Jack Du Bois called an "embryonic model" for film composers, of course, goes back to the very beginnings of the craft.[22] At the center of this discourse, needless to say, is the relationship between Wagner's leitmotivic technique and twentieth-century film scoring practices. What we might call classic Hollywood film scoring technique—in which particular themes and motives are associated with specific characters or (less commonly) dramatic themes and ideas—is frequently understood as a direct historical development of Wagner's leitmotivic technique. Although this idea is perhaps most closely associated with Max Steiner, it seems to have lost little of its currency. In the introductory chapter of his film music history textbook *Reel Music: Exploring 100 Years of Film Music,* for example, Roger Hickman provides a brief synopsis of Wagner's leitmotivic technique, explicitly positioning Wagner's works as the precursors to cinema.[23] The recently published volume of collected essays entitled *Wagner and Cinema* might be taken as another index of the enduring interest in this connection. In her introduction to this volume, Jeongwon Joe includes a long list of twenty-first century artists, directors, and scholars who in one way or another link Wagner's techniques to cinematic practice.[24]

But if the Wagnerian connection has been a prominent part of film music discourse since its earliest decades, its relevance has by no means been universally accepted. Many scholars and critics have questioned the extent to which Wagner's music dramas—and more specifically, the leitmotivic technique that he uses in them—are models for film music scoring.[25] Indeed, the recognition that leitmotivic practice in film scoring differs from the Wagnerian model is nearly as old as the assertion of a Wagnerian antecedent for the craft. In the 1927 edition of the *Handbuch der Film-Musik,* for instance, Hans Erdmann writes:

> The deeper effectiveness of the leitmotivic technique does not lie on the surface, but rather belongs to a more genuine knowledge of the specific work, which can only be instilled through repeated listening. From this perspective, the temporary and ephemeral nature of film is very decisive; one might even say that it is not exactly "leitmotif-friendly." . . . One must be emphatically warned against going too far in this area. To be sure, in the "Ring," Wagner built up an entire leitmotivic system. This, however, remains the brilliant achievement of an individual genius.[26]

Erdmann was concerned that by applying the term "leitmotif" to any recurring motive in a film score, critics would dilute its (more specifically Wagnerian) meaning.

Royal S. Brown, in contrast (and to take a more recent example), objects to the potentially reductive nature of leitmotivic analysis. In his keynote address for the inaugural "Music and the Moving Image" conference at New York University in May 2007, Brown described one of his recent articles entitled "Music and/as Cine-Narrative; or *Ceci n'est pas un leitmotif.*" The article's subtitle, he explained,

> is aimed at a particular type of film-music analysis that tends to be what I described as "an almost purely descriptive catalogue of all of the various themes and motifs in a given score and their tie-ins to various characters, situations, and places that turn up in the film, with little or no thought given as to why, just for starters, the filmic text needs these non-visual doublings."[27]

Perhaps the most famous discussion of the relationship between film scoring practice and Wagner's leitmotivic technique comes near the beginning of Eisler and Adorno's *Composing for the Films,* first published in 1947. "The fundamental character of the leitmotif," they write, echoing the comments from Erdmann quoted above,

> —its salience and brevity—was related to the gigantic dimensions of the Wagnerian and post-Wagnerian music dramas. Just because the leitmotif as such is musically

rudimentary, it requires a large musical canvas if it is to take on a structural meaning beyond that of a signpost. The atomization of the musical element is paralleled by the heroic dimensions of the composition as a whole. This relation is entirely absent in the motion picture, which requires continual interruption of one element by another rather than continuity.[28]

For Eisler and Adorno, the use of the leitmotif in film scoring is symptomatic of broader "regression of listening": a decline, as Graham McCann writes in his introduction to *Composing for the Films*, "in the ability of the listener to concentrate on anything more than the most truncated aspects of a composition."[29] The leitmotif, to quote Eisler and Adorno once again, is "drummed into the listener's ear by persistent repetition, often with scarcely any variation, very much as a new song is plugged or as a motion-picture actress is popularized by her hair-do."[30] The "atomization of the musical element" represented by the leitmotif, in other words, enables the processes of standardization and duplication by which film music may be fully integrated into the culture industry of American capitalism.

In relation to film music, then, the leitmotif thus occupied a curious position. In actual practice, film-scoring technique may have had little to do with Wagner's procedures. The idea of the leitmotif nevertheless could—at least for some audiences—help to associate film music with the prestigious art of the music drama and the grand operatic tradition of which it was a part. As David Neumeyer points out in his discussion of Steiner's relationship to the Wagnerian tradition, invoking the leitmotif was a way for film music—and by extension, the medium of film itself—to establish its cultural legitimacy.[31] And yet, both as a compositional technique and as an analytical tool, the idea of the leitmotif could also be disparaged as a symptom of a particularly middlebrow variety of reductionism (à la Brown), or—as in Adorno and Eisler—as a typical product and/or tool of debased popular culture.

Obviously, a full account of the use of the term "leitmotif" in film music analysis is beyond the scope of this chapter, and I take it as self-evident that leitmotivic technique has widely varying relevance for film scoring. What interests me here is not the extent to which Wagner's thematic practice served as an "embryonic model" for Rózsa (or any other film music composer, for that matter), or the potential procedural or theoretical links between film scores and specific Wagnerian works—works that after all manifest quite different practices of thematic transformation and development. Instead, my focus is on the cultural resonance of leitmotivic technique, and, more specifically, in Rózsa's use of this technique in the score to *Ben-Hur*. What is at stake here, then, is the extent to which this cultural resonance sets *Ben-Hur* apart from the other biblical epics, the extent—to return to the Derrida quotation with which I began this chapter—to which it contributes to a process of "invagination" whereby the contours of the genre are reshaped.

Ben-Hur and the Leitmotif

As a well-educated mid-century European composer, Rózsa was surely quite familiar with Wagner's works, and in his autobiography he describes a visit to the Bayreuth Festival in 1930 as "one of the most memorable and moving experiences of my life."[32] There is little if any evidence, however, that Rózsa conceived of the *Ben-Hur* score, or any of his other film music, for that matter, as a direct imitation of Wagner's music-dramas. In contrast to Steiner, Rózsa does not refer to Wagner as a model for his own practice, and much of the music in *Ben-Hur* sounds far more similar to that of the other postwar biblical epics (and other films as well) than anything that Wagner wrote. As I noted in the previous chapter, for example, the Esther theme from *Ben-Hur* is closely related to music from other films that feature noble and sympathetic Jewish characters. In musical as well as dramatic terms, Esther has far more to do with Rachel (from the *Ivanhoe* film) or Sephora (from *The Ten Commandments*) than she does with Brünnhilde or Isolde. It is hardly surprising that the music for *Ben-Hur* should bear a particularly close relationship to that which Rózsa wrote for *Quo Vadis*. The sense that the score to *Ben-Hur* was essentially recycling elements of earlier epics is perhaps most apparent when we compare the imperial Roman music in the two films. In both *Quo Vadis* and *Ben-Hur*, Rózsa uses a particular kind of modal parallelism to conjure the world of ancient Rome.[33] The fundamental qualities of this imperial Roman style are apparent in the themes with which the two films begin: the Quo Vadis Domine motive from *Quo Vadis* and the theme from *Ben-Hur* that Roger Hickman (following Rózsa himself) calls the Anno Domini motive (see Examples 6.1a and 6.1b). Both these themes center around scale degrees $\hat{1}$, $\flat\hat{7}$ and $\flat\hat{3}$, suggesting the Dorian mode. Both themes employ block-like parallel harmonies, hinting, perhaps at the convention of using parallel organum as a marker for antiquity and/or the Middle Ages. Apart from the very first measure of the Anno Domini theme (which could just as easily be rewritten as in duple meter with a pick-up measure), each is cast in moderate duple meter and uses a fairly small number of rhythmic values. Although to describe the themes as interchangeable would be an exaggeration, they are certainly expressions of the same musical topos.

In both films, the expression of Roman power reaches its apogee in the so-called Roman marches: Vinicius's triumph and the Hail Galba cue from *Quo Vadis* and the five marches in the *Ben-Hur* score. It is hardly surprising that the marches from the latter film should closely resemble those from Rózsa's first foray into the Roman style. Indeed, as Hickman has pointed out in his film score guide to *Ben-Hur*, the latter movie even incorporates a cue—"Panem et Circenses"—that Rózsa originally wrote for the 1951 film.[34] The other marches in *Ben-Hur*—even thought they are not borrowed directly from *Quo Vadis*—are nevertheless quite similar to those from the earlier film. Indeed, the cues share not only the same basic rhythmic structure (as we would expect) and harmonic-melodic lan-

Example 6.1a. Quo Vadis Domine motive from *Quo Vadis*.

Example 6.1b. Anno Domini motive from *Ben-Hur*.

guage (e.g., parallel chords in the Dorian or Mixolydian mode) but many formal/structural patterns as well. These shared formal patterns are evident, for example, in the well-known "Parade of the Charioteers."[35] This cue—which precedes the famous chariot race—is the most fully developed of all Rózsa's Roman marches. As in Vinicius's Triumph from *Quo Vadis*, Rózsa uses a fanfare-like trumpet motif as a prelude to his main melody (see Example 6.2). Just as Marcus Vinicius's motive forms the theme for the middle section of the *Quo Vadis* cue, so too in the Parade of the Charioteers Rózsa uses the hero's motive as the main theme of what we might call the second trio of the Parade of the Charioteers. Both in terms of harmonic/melodic materials and in terms of structure, then, it seems (at least with respect to the Roman music) as if Rózsa was sometimes doing little more than dusting off—in a literal and a figurative sense—the replicas of trumpets and *cornua* that he had asked to be built for the earlier film.[36]

Ironically, it is precisely the kinship between the Roman music in these two films that throws into relief the subtle and yet essential ways in which the music

Judah Ben-Hur theme

Example 6.2. Excerpt from the middle section of Parade of the Charioteers cue, showing the Judah Ben-Hur motive with trumpet counterpoint.

for *Ben-Hur* differs from that of *Quo Vadis*. As with other aspects of the production, there is a relatively straightforward quantitative distinction between the Roman marches in the two films. Apart from the fact that *Ben-Hur* contains more of these marches than *Quo Vadis* does, none of the marches in the earlier film approaches the length of the massive Parade of the Charioteers cue. With two trio sections instead of one, this latter march is also more structurally complex than the Roman marches in *Quo Vadis*. Yet it is in the principal theme of the Parade of the Charioteers cue that the distinction between the music of *Quo Vadis* and *Ben-Hur* is most striking. As earlier commentators on the *Ben-Hur* score have noted, this principal theme is a variant of a motive that is heard frequently in other sections of the score: a motive that is associated with Judah Ben-Hur's hatred for his

Example 6.3. Hatred motive.

former friend Messala and, by extension, for the Roman imperium of which he is a part.[37] I follow Hickman's practice by referring to this music as the Hatred motive (see Example 6.3). As Hickman points out, the Hatred theme is structured around the tritone (E to B♭ in the iteration of the motive that I have transcribed above). In melodic/harmonic terms, the main theme of the Parade of the Charioteers cue represents a diatonicization of this tritone dissonance, an alteration that moves the theme into the orbit of the imperial style. But it also brings the Hatred theme into association with the Judah Ben-Hur music that Rózsa—as I noted above—uses for the second trio of the Parade of the Charioteers. On one level, this association reflects the fact that despite the fact that there are six other competitors in the chariot race that is to follow the parade, the competition is essentially a contest between Judah Ben-Hur and Messala. But these musical affinities might also be understood in other, more symbolic ways. We might, for example, read the main theme of the Parade of the Charioteers cue as a reflection of Judah Ben-Hur's emotional state: his desire for victory in the race, after all, is essentially motivated by his hatred for Messala. More suggestively, we might understand these musical relationships as a reflection of Judah Ben-Hur's own transformation: of the ways (to paraphrase Esther's comments later in the film) that he has become like his enemy.

The musico-dramatic associations of the Parade of the Charioteers cue become more interesting when we consider the evolution of the Hatred motive from which the main theme of the march is derived. The Hatred motive itself can be understood as a close relative of a theme heard earlier in the score that is associated with the boyhood friendship between Judah Ben-Hur and Messala (see Example 6.4). The tritone in this Friendship theme appears in two different intervallic spaces (F to B♮ and G to C♯ in this iteration). Just as the tritones of the Hatred

Example 6.4. Friendship motive (original tritone version and later diatonicized version).

Example 6.5. Land of Judah motive.

theme are diatonicized in the Parade of the Charioteers cue, so too are the dissonances of the Friendship motive eventually transformed into consonant intervals in the last parts of the film.

These kinds of musical relationships may be found throughout the *Ben-Hur* score. The so-called Rowing theme that is heard prominently in the famous naval battle scene, for example, features the same tritone leap that characterizes both the Hatred and the early iterations of the Friendship theme. In a similar manner, the Land of Judah theme, first heard in the overture (transcribed as Example 6.5), is linked to the Esther theme that I discussed in the previous chapter (see Example 5.7) through turning arabesque motives and melodic leaps of fourths and fifths. Just as the musical relationships among the Hatred, Friendship, and Judah Ben-Hur motives might be understood in terms of dramatic symbolism, so too can we hear the connection between the Esther and the Land of Judah motives in terms of the heroine's broader function within the *Ben-Hur* story. As I pointed out in the previous chapter, Esther is another example of the domestic woman in the two-woman plot archetype: a woman of the tribe with symbolic links to the land. The musical affinities between these two themes make these links audible.

Of course, *Ben-Hur* is hardly the only film in which harmonic/melodic transformation takes on dramatic significance. The diatonicization of the Hatred theme in the Parade of the Charioteers cue is in a certain sense no different from those moments in *Casablanca* in which Max Steiner presents a dissonant version of the Marseillaise in order to represent internal or external threats to French national sovereignty; or the moment in *The Return of the Jedi* in which composer John Williams presents Darth Vader's theme in the major mode in order to reflect the villain's dying expression of fatherly love. What distinguishes Rózsa's score from these and countless other examples is not the technique of motivic transformation per se, but rather the extent to which this technique seems to inform nearly every part of the film. It is therefore hardly surprising that the kinds of musical observations that I have made are central to the scholarly reception of the *Ben-Hur* score. In his analysis of Rózsa's music, for example, Steven Wescott groups the various motives of the score into different spheres (e.g., the Roman sphere, the Judean sphere) whose essential melodic/harmonic materials are opposed to one another.[38] Hickman takes a less comprehensive approach, preferring instead to show the melodic and harmonic links between individual motives. Both scholars recognize (as I do) Rózsa's extraordinary craft, and the great care that he took with every cue in the score.

An "Entire Leitmotivic System"?

What we might call the exceptional motivic saturation of the *Ben-Hur* score leads us to consider Rózsa's achievement in light of the "critique of the cinematic leitmotif" that I outlined above. What is arguably the most telling crystallization of this critique comes at the end of the section on the leitmotif in *Composing for the Films,* in a passage that is worth quoting at some length. "The Wagnerian leitmotif," Adorno and Eisler write,

> is inseparably connected with the symbolic nature of the music drama. The leitmotif is not supposed merely to characterize persons, emotions, or things, although this is the prevalent conception. Wagner conceived its purpose as the endowment of the dramatic events with metaphysical significance. When in the *Ring* the tubas blare the Valhalla motif, it is not merely to indicate the dwelling place of Wotan. Wagner meant also to connote the sphere of sublimity, the cosmic will, and the primal principle. The leitmotif was invented essentially for this kind of symbolism. There is no place for it in the motion picture, which seeks to depict reality. Here the function of the leitmotif has been reduced to the level of a musical lackey, who announces his master with an important air even though the eminent personage is clearly recognizable to everyone. The effective technique of the past thus becomes a mere duplication, ineffective and uneconomical. At the same time, since it cannot be developed to its full musical significance in the motion picture, its use leads to extreme poverty of composition.[39]

Clearly, Rózsa's treatment of motives in the *Ben-Hur* score resists this kind of curt dismissal. His work in this regard seems rather to correspond more closely to Adorno and Eisler's description of the Wagnerian leitmotif. While it might be too much to say that Rózsa's underscoring for the Parade of the Charioteers cue endows the dramatic events of the film with metaphysical significance, the ways in which the Judah Ben-Hur motive is contextualized (to take just one example) certainly give the music rich significance. To paraphrase Adorno and Eisler, it does not merely indicate the presence of the hero, but it also suggests key elements of his emotional condition. More broadly, the relationships among the various motives might connote the power of hatred to corrupt even the most noble of human spirits.

In the score to *Ben-Hur,* as in Wagner's *Ring,* the motives are related to one another through processes of melodic-harmonic transformation and contrapuntal elaboration. And though to describe these processes as part of what Erdmann calls an "entire leitmotivic system" might be an exaggeration, it is nevertheless clear that Rózsa conceived the score along these lines. Indeed, it is possible to understand some of Rózsa's procedures as distant echoes of some famous motivic relationships in the *Ring* operas. The similarity between the Esther and the Land of Judah motives, for example, recalls a similar symbolic and musical relationship between the opening arpeggio figures with which *Das Rheingold* begins and the C♯ minor arpeggios that accompany the appearance of Erda. To regard Esther as an allegorical embodiment of the land of Judah (as Erda is a personification of the earth itself) would be to exaggerate the mythological resonance of her character. Nevertheless, the musical relationships in Rózsa's score certainly endow the figure of Esther with greater symbolic meaning. In a similar manner, we might hear the transformation of the Hatred motive into the march theme of the Parade of the Charioteers cue as an echo of the famous passage between scenes one and two of *Das Rheingold,* in which the Ring motive is progressively diatonicized so that it leads seamlessly into the Valhalla motive. Just as this musical relationship in Wagner's score suggests a symbolic link between Alberich's theft of the Rhinegold and Wotan's desire for power, so too do the musical relationships among the motives in the Parade of the Charioteers cue suggest a symbolic link between Judah Ben-Hur and the Roman Messala.

My brief description of the relationships among selected motives is little more than a suggestion of the kinds of analyses that might be applied to the *Ben-Hur* score. Both Hickman and Erkelenz have given much fuller accounts of the kinds of motivic connections that may be found throughout the film.[40] It is hardly surprising that their work (especially Hickman's) should so closely resemble classic analyses of Wagnerian operas such as Robert Donington's *Wagner's Ring and Its Symbols.*[41] The motivic density of Rózsa's score seems to call for this kind of quasi-Wagnerian analytical approach. Hickman's *Film Score Guide,* in particular, provides more than a simple "descriptive catalogue of all of the various themes and motifs in a given score and their tie-ins to various characters, situations, and places that turn up in the film" (to repeat the words of Royal Brown). It also shows how Rózsa's music enriches the filmic narrative and contributes to the metaphysical or spiritual meaning of the cinematic text. What lies beyond the purview of these kinds of analyses are questions about the phenomenology and ontology of this leitmotivic technique, and its meaning within the meta-narrative of the biblical epic genre (and not simply within the specific narrative of the film).

In order to probe some of these questions, I would like to take a more detailed look at materials concerning a single cue from the *Ben-Hur* score entitled "Aftermath." This cue comes in the second half of the film, after Judah Ben-Hur has won the famous chariot race. Messala—Judah's principal opponent in the race—has just met a gruesome death, but not before telling the Jewish hero that his wife and sister are lepers. As Erkelenz points out in his description of the *Ben-Hur* score, the cue underwent numerous revisions between June and October 1959. Indeed, there are at least four extant written versions of the cue, none of which actually corresponds to the music that is heard on the final cut of the film. To further complicate matters, the music (apparently without Rózsa's prior approval) was also used for the Golgotha sequence later in the film.[42] In the following discussion, I focus on an inked conductor's score dated from June 1959. Rózsa seems subsequently to have returned to this cue, adding some percussion instruments and (more significantly) replacing the final page with new music. On

Figure 6.1. The final page of the Aftermath cue from Rózsa's June version of the *Ben-Hur* score, showing the antiphonal trumpet fanfare. Miklós Rózsa Papers, Special Collections Research Center, Syracuse University Library.

the score, Rózsa has written "Revised July 1959," indicating when these revisions took place. The cue—especially in the June version—is built around the same Hatred and Friendship motives whose relationship Hickman describes. Indeed, in this cue Rózsa accentuates the musico-dramatic relationship between these two themes by beginning each of them on the same pitch. What we might call the leitmotivic logic of the cue is (in this version) fairly straightforward; it is natural that the final confrontation between Judah Ben-Hur and Messala should focus on the themes that—in musical terms—have defined their relationship.

In the last section of Aftermath, as Judah Ben-Hur walks out into the empty arena, Rózsa reiterates the trumpet fanfare motif from the Parade of the Charioteers cue. In the June version of this cue (as we can see from the selection of the conductor's score reproduced as Figure 6.1) Rózsa calls for an antiphonal iteration of this fanfare idea. Not coincidentally, the two statements are a tritone apart, beginning on the same pitches (E♭ and A♮) that formed this interval in the Hatred motive at the beginning of the cue. In musical terms, all the main musical materials of the cue (the Hatred motive, the Friendship motive, and the trumpet fanfare) thus revolve around the same E♭ to A♮ tritone axis. The June version of the Aftermath cue is an excellent example of the kind of motivic saturation that Rózsa applied with such consummate skill in the *Ben-Hur* score. If it is perhaps too much to say that his motives endow the film's narrative with metaphysical significance, it is nevertheless clear that the relationships among the three motives deepen and enrich the dramatic ironies of the scene. In the June version of the cue, we might say, the E♭ to A♮ tritone symbolizes the corruption of the Judah

Ben-Hur/Messala relationship, a corruption that in turn hollows out the trumpet fanfare so that it becomes a bitter mockery of the hero's triumph.

In speaking of *Ben-Hur* in this manner, of course, I am treating the film very much as if it were a Wagnerian music drama. Such a flowery analysis, however, ignores the simple fact that the June version of the cue was unrealized. In the final cut for the film, the underscoring begins with the transitional passage at the top of the second page of the cue. As in the June version of the cue, the final version of this scene ends with the trumpet fanfare from the Parade of the Charioteers. But its tritone antiphonal answer is absent. The melodic/harmonic similarities that in the June version of the *Ben-Hur* score link the Hatred motive, the Friendship motive, and the fanfare from the Parade of the Charioteers, in short, did not survive into the final cut of the film. The cue is still oriented around motives, to be sure, but the organic and transformational relationships among these motives—in other words, those qualities that make the score more Wagnerian—have been attenuated.

"De-Wagnerization"?

I have not been able to find references to this cue or to its revisions in the Rózsa correspondence that I have examined, and it is idle to speculate about his attitude regarding the ways in which this cue was cut in the final version of the film.[43] Some interesting context may be provided, however, by comments that Rózsa made in his autobiography concerning the final cut for *Quo Vadis*. Rózsa was very disappointed in the way that the film turned out. "I was sure," he writes, "that the music of *Quo Vadis* was going to be interesting not only to the audience but also to musicologists, on account of its authenticity. Unfortunately this did not turn out to be the case. . . . After all the trouble I went to, much of my work was swamped by sound effects, or played at such a low level as to be indistinguishable."[44] Rózsa is hardly the only film composer, of course, to have his or her work manipulated during the final stages of the editing process. Indeed, given the length and complexity of the score, Rózsa's music for *Ben-Hur* seems to have passed remarkably intact into the version of the film that was eventually screened. The editing process for *Ben-Hur*, after all, did not swamp Rózsa's music by sound effects or unravel the network of leitmotifs through which it was organized. But my glance at the Aftermath cue does suggest that with *Ben-Hur*, as with *Quo Vadis*, Rózsa's musical/musicological ambitions were not completely realized in the final cut of the film. What I would like to suggest is that the complex, quasi-Wagnerian leitmotivic technique that Rózsa employed in the *Ben-Hur* score was—at least in part—analogous to the ideals of musical authenticity that informed *Quo Vadis*. If the use of historically accurate source material in this earlier film could—at least potentially—generate genuine musicological interest, so too might the elaborate leitmotivic logic of the *Ben-Hur* score help to move the film from the sphere of mass entertainment into the realm of the music drama.

In each case, we might understand the score as a refraction of Rózsa's complex relationship to various traditions of serious music composition and music scholarship.[45] Indeed, the hope that film music might partake of the more elevated or intellectual conventions of art music runs like a red thread through many of Rózsa's scores from the postwar period. Like the music for *Quo Vadis, El Cid,* or even less pretentious films such as *Ivanhoe* or *Knights of the Round Table,* the *Ben-Hur* score thus reflects the tensions inherent in what Rózsa himself called his "double life": the tensions between "pure" musical composition and the conditional, commercial work of the film music composer.

Rózsa was by no means a subscriber to the ideas put forward by Adorno and Eisler in *Composing for the Films* (indeed, there is little evidence that he was even aware of the book). In the tension between the two sides of Rózsa's "double life," however, we may nevertheless read a simplified version of the critique of mass culture that Adorno and others were to develop so brilliantly during the middle years of the twentieth century. It is tempting, therefore, to understand the changes made to the Aftermath cue in terms of the critique of the leitmotif that I outlined above. In this reading, what we might call the "de-Wagnerization" of Rózsa's musical ideas undermines the coherence of the "entire leitmotivic system" and the potential for the score to endow the dramatic events with metaphysical significance. The changes to the Aftermath cue, we might say, move the score of *Ben-Hur* back toward the mainstream of film music scoring practice— toward the Steineresque aesthetic that Eisler and Adorno understand as a manifestation of the late-capitalist debasement of listening.

Such a reading, however, would ignore the significant ways in which the cultural resonance of the leitmotif was changing during the postwar period. This cultural resonance, admittedly, cannot be quantified in any specific manner. Nevertheless, the kind of discourse that I outlined above, in which film scoring technique was positioned either as an extension of Wagner's practices (as in Steiner) or else in opposition to them (as in Eisler/Adorno or Erdmann), seems to typify the prewar and immediate postwar periods. In the context of the 1950s, direct invocations of Wagner in the context of film music begin to seem anachronistic. DeMille's habit of referencing Wagner whenever he wanted a grand or particularly meaningful musical effect in *The Ten Commandments,* for example, probably marked him as belonging to an earlier generation of filmmakers. For modernist scholars writing in the tradition of Adorno, the tremendous expansion of television and of new styles of popular music seemed more important objects of critique than the use of the leitmotif in film music. As I pointed out in the introduction to this book, moreover, the 1950s witnessed many new kinds of approaches to the use of sound and music in film. When films were typically accompanied by large-scale symphonic scores (such as those typically found in the biblical epics or in most films of the so-called golden age of Hollywood), questions about the relationship between Wagnerian opera and film music loomed large. But as new styles of music and new scoring practices found their way into Hollywood films, these questions inevitably became less important. What is being de-Wagnerized in the course of the postwar biblical epic, then, is not simply the Aftermath cue, nor even a broader aspect of Rózsa's *Ben-Hur* score, but rather the discourse surrounding film music scoring itself.

At the end of his *Film Score Guide to Ben-Hur,* Hickman strikes an elegiac tone. "The music for *Ben-Hur,*" he writes,

> is Rózsa's most celebrated artistic achievement. In many ways, Rózsa's music stands as the last major symphonic score of the opulent Golden Age; it received both critical and popular acclaim, a feat that was becoming increasingly rare during the 1950s. While numerous orchestral film scores appear in succeeding generations, notably after 1977, few have received similar dual recognition, and all have benefitted from Rózsa's model. Over fifty years after its inception, the music for *Ben-Hur* still stands as one of Hollywood's greatest musical achievements.[46]

One might take issue with the idea that *Ben-Hur* was the last of the great symphonic film scores. Films such as *El Cid* (for which Rózsa wrote a score nearly as elaborate), *Cleopatra* (with a score by Alex North), and *The Fall of the Roman Empire* (music by Dmitri Tiomkin) continued the tradition of grand orchestral underscoring into the 1960s. But even if the position of *Ben-Hur* as the last instantiation of a grand tradition is open to question, it nevertheless occupies a uniquely important position in the history of the epic and in the history of cinema more generally, a position that is deeply ironic. The last of the biblical epics to be an unqualified financial success, it also features the longest and most complex musical score. No other film more closely approximates the musical semantics (if not the harmonic-melodic vocabulary) of Wagner's music-dramas. Yet this (arguably) most Wagnerian of film scores appeared precisely during the period in which Wagner's cultural resonance—particularly with regard to film— was fading.

A Past and Future *Ben-Hur*

In terms of Derrida's "law of the law of genre," we might speak of this irony initiating a "process of invagination" with regard to the *Ben-Hur* score. In Rózsa's music, the characteristic features of the epic genre—the framing materials, the imperial Roman style, and, above all, a musical semantics that centers on the motive—are intensified to the point that they begin to turn back in against themselves, to the point, in other words, that they begin to take on a different shape. In this light (to use Derrida's words again), the complexity of the *Ben-Hur* score appears as a kind of "impurity," or even as a "contamination" stemming from the ultimately alien semantics of the music drama. The apogee of the biblical epic, the *Ben-Hur* score thus seems somehow nostalgic, as if it were fulfilling the cultural ambitions of the past rather than anticipating those of the future. As the passage from Hickman that I quoted above suggests, Rózsa's music is more often understood as the end of an era than the beginning of a new one.

From the perspective of the late 1960s and early 1970s, the score to *Ben-Hur* must indeed have seemed like the last monument of a dying age. But the scoring practices for the blockbuster epics of the latter part of the twentieth century surely made it more difficult to consign Rózsa's music to the dustbin of history. John Williams's scores for the *Star Wars* films—to take only the most prominent example—are as deeply informed by the semantics of the leitmotif as that to *Ben-Hur*. In the epilogue to this book, I explore the legacy of the biblical epic scores more fully. With regard to *Ben-Hur*, it is enough to draw attention to a small detail in the conductor's score for the Aftermath cue (reproduced in Figure 6.1 above). In the score, we can read "microphone right" and "microphone left" above the two entrances of the antiphonal trumpet fanfare that ends the cue. As Erkelenz points out, this is the only point in the entire score that contains these kinds of instructions, that have to do not simply with the production of the music but with the way it should be recorded. One cannot be sure, of course, that these instructions came from Rózsa himself. They are just as likely to have been inserted by a music editor or recording engineer. Nevertheless, their presence reminds us of one of the most advanced aspects of the biblical epics, namely, the ways in which they used new sound recording and reproduction technologies (e.g., magnetic tape recording, stereo sound) to control and manipulate the aural environment. In this sense, the Aftermath cue looks like an adumbration of what we might call the blockbuster style of the late twentieth century, in which a motivically saturated orchestral score is combined with increasingly sophisticated sound engineering.

It is tempting to see in this particular combination yet another manifestation of Wagner's legacy. The desire to manipulate the aural environment, after all, burned as brightly for Wagner as for any late twentieth-century sound engineer; it informs the construction of the Festspielhaus in Bayreuth just as surely as it does the production of any blockbuster film. And what are the antiphonal trumpet motives at the end of the Aftermath cue but a distant echo of the orchestral prelude that introduces the final scene of *Lohengrin,* in which groups of trumpets, playing in different keys, announce the arrival of the Brabantine warriors from different parts of the stage? The process of reflecting upon the score to *Ben-Hur* continues to generate new ironies, new ways of understanding the history of cinematic music: new interior spaces.

7 *King of Kings* and the Problem of Repetition

Among the many markers of the aesthetics of the superlative was a distinctive visual style that was used to market the biblical epics and the ephemera with which they were associated. We may see this specific visual style, for example, in the sheet music covers for *Ben-Hur* arrangements that were published in the early 1960s (see Figure 7.1a). On these covers, the visual field is dominated by the title of the film, which appears in block capitals as if it were part of a gigantic stone edifice. This edifice is oriented with its corner toward the viewer, so that the gigantic letters appear foreshortened by perspective. Around these monumental letters are vignettes from the chariot race (which had quickly become the most famous scene in the film). This visual style finds interesting analogues in some of the *Quo Vadis* posters, but it is most closely connected to the promotional materials for *King of Kings* (see Figure 7.1b). In these images, we see the same kind of block letters, foreshortened so that they appear to be a part of some monumental construction. Instead of the chariot race, the title is surrounded by a legionnaire's helmet and a visual allusion to the Sermon on the Mount scene—a scene that (in terms of spectacle, if not of content) was marketed as the successor to the chariot race in *Ben-Hur.*

Although this style was in truth mainly associated with the MGM epics, it came by extension to represent the pretensions of the entire postwar biblical epic genre. Indeed, when Monty Python satirized these pretensions in the 1979 film *Life of Brian,* they used just this kind of hyperbolic visual style to parodic effect. Indeed, the visual style is so easily mocked that its original meanings have arguably been inverted: the monumental has been transformed into the merely comic. Yet this comic effect suggests a deeper problem that emerged precisely at this historical moment, in the wake (so to speak) of *Ben-Hur;* namely, the problem of what to do next.

One does not need to subscribe to the deterministic paradigm of scholars such as Schatz in order to understand how this problem drives the evolution (or devolution) of cinematic genres. And yet this problem was perhaps extraordinarily acute with regard to the biblical epic in the early 1960s. The enormous success of *Ben-Hur* seemed to have saved MGM from financial catastrophe, and it was

Figure 7.1a. Sheet music cover for *Ben-Hur*. Miklós Rózsa Papers, Special Collections Research Center, Syracuse University Library.

hardly surprising that Hollywood executives would want to produce another blockbuster biblical epic. And yet the complex, studio-based production methods that created the film were becoming increasingly difficult to sustain. The creative and aesthetic problems associated with replicating a blockbuster are perhaps less easy to document, but they are no less important. Indeed, the *King of Kings* poster may have been the work of a marketing department that—by the early 1960s—had simply run out of new ideas with regard to the biblical epic genre.

It is precisely these creative and aesthetic problems that figure so prominently in Miklós Rózsa's comments about his work on *King of Kings*. "My main problem" with *King of Kings,* he wrote in his autobiography, "was to write new music to exactly the same themes and scenes as those in *Ben-Hur*—the Nativity, the Way of the Cross, Golgotha, the Resurrection."[1] In a BBC interview after the release of *King of Kings*, Rózsa employed more metaphorical language to speak about the same issue. "There were all the great scenes which I had to do again," he said, "and obviously, differently. I have no intention to compare myself with Michelan-

Figure 7.1b. Sheet music cover for *King of Kings*. Miklós Rózsa Papers, Special Collections Research Center, Syracuse University Library.

gelo, but imagine that after Michelangelo had worked years and years on the Last Judgment in the Sistine Chapel, the Pope would have asked him to decorate another chapel, also with a same theme but entirely differently."[2]

Although the specific scenes that Rózsa enumerates (e.g, the Nativity and the Way of the Cross) are in some sense present in both *Ben-Hur* and *King of Kings,* they are handled much differently in the latter film. Indeed, if we were to conduct a detailed semantic/syntactic analysis of the three MGM biblical epics that Rózsa scored during this period (*Quo Vadis, Ben-Hur,* and *King of Kings*), we would certainly find that *Quo Vadis* and *Ben-Hur* are more closely related than either film is to *King of Kings*. But when Rózsa began to write the music for *Ben-Hur,* the ways in which it recapitulated the drama of *Quo Vadis* (some of which I have already described in the previous chapter) do not seem to have caused him undue anxiety. On the contrary, Rózsa seems to have seen the generic similarity between the two films in a positive light. "I had no difficulty conceiving the music [for *Ben-Hur*] stylistically," he writes. "This time I didn't go to first-century sources, but simply developed the 'Roman' style I had already established in *Quo Vadis* to create an archaic feeling."[3] Rózsa seems to have had no compunction about recycling the Hail Galba cue from the earlier film for use in *Ben-Hur* (to take the most obvious example of this kind of borrowing). Nor, we must assume, was it particularly difficult for him to generate new music for the banquet scene in *Ben-Hur* even though—at least in terms of its dramatic function—it is quite similar to the banquet scene in *Quo Vadis*. Indeed, if the problem of repetition had been a persistent difficulty for Rózsa, he could not have had such a successful career. Like other Hollywood film composers, Rózsa needed to be able to work quickly and in a generic manner: applying similar kinds of music to similar kinds of scenes in similar kinds of films. Why, then, did the dramatic similarities between *Ben-Hur* and *King of Kings* create an aesthetic problem?

Although Rózsa himself does not expand upon his comments, I would like to suggest two interlocking answers to this question. The first has to do with the special status of the *Ben-Hur* music as the epitome and exemplar of the biblical epic score. As I discussed in the previous chapter, Rózsa felt that the *Ben-Hur* score—of all his works—"lay closest to his heart," and after its premiere it may have been difficult to return in any sense to the biblical epic genre. Seen in this light, the specific scenes that Rózsa enumerates—the nativity, the way of the cross, the crucifixion, and others—are simply the points at which *King of Kings* and *Ben-Hur* intersected. But it could also be that Rózsa had a more specific problem with the fact that these scenes were at the very heart of the Christian message. In this sense, Rózsa may have been sharing a more widespread ambivalence about depicting Christ on the silver screen. Although the life of Jesus has been a cinematic subject since the very earliest days of the art form, many found the appearance of Christ on film to be disturbing or even potentially blasphemous.[4] As Peter Malone points out, "*King of Kings* was the first film in thirty-five years to use an actor to portray Jesus as a fully developed character in the Gospel drama, a Jesus who is seen face-on and in wide-screen color."[5] In *Ben-Hur*, we must remember, Christ's face is never seen; he never speaks, and is typically viewed only from behind. Rózsa would not have needed to have been particularly devout in order to feel some discomfort with treating the story of Christ as if it were simply another generic narrative.

Such a hypothesis (and a hypothesis is all that it is) would cast Rózsa's comments about the problems of repetition in a somewhat ironic light. The decision to produce a Christ biopic, after all, can be understood as a response to the very same problem of repetition that Rózsa faced in a musico-dramatic sense. In terms of epic grandeur, sheer expense, and perhaps of cultural pretension, *Ben-Hur* had stretched the genre to the limits of sustainability. Creating a fully Christ-centered film, we might say, was a means of going beyond *Ben-Hur*, of extending the aesthetics of the superlative. *King of Kings*, in this sense, represented an important development in the history of the postwar biblical epic—a shift that we can clarify by once again invoking Babington and Evans's tripartite division of the genre. Although there were Christ films during the prewar period (most notably DeMille's 1927 silent epic *The King of Kings*), biblical films of the postwar period—at least before 1961—fell into the other two subtypes of the genre: the Old Testament epic and the Roman/Christian epic. The Christ film was the last of the three subgenres to be revived. Indeed, the 1961 *King of Kings* inaugurates what we might almost call a cycle of Jesus films that stretch from *The Greatest Story Ever Told* to films such as Pasolini's *The Gospel According to St. Matthew* (1964) and *Jesus Christ Superstar* (1973) that essentially lie outside of the Hollywood biblical epic genre. Seen in this light, we might understand the Christ film as the successor to the postwar biblical epic, rather than as a symptom of its decline.

We can easily imagine scriptwriters, costume designers, and cinematographers feeling much as Rózsa did in 1961: wondering how they might find new ways of capturing the "same themes and scenes." Their problem, we might say, was one of finding new forms through which to express the same dramatic or thematic content. But if we think of *King of Kings* as part of a new cycle (if not a new genre) of the postwar Christ film, then these fundamental aesthetic problems are all inverted. The question now is the extent to which the old aesthetic forms— costumes, camera shots, stock scenes and characters, musical underscoring, and so on—can be used to express the new dramatic content, the new character, of the Christ film in the postwar era. The problem of repetition that Rózsa articulates, in other words, can cut in both ways. In what follows, then, I am interested not only in how Rózsa responds to the "same themes and scenes," but also in the extent to which the old musical approaches of his historico-biblical style might respond (or fail to respond) to the new demands of the postwar Christ film.

Adapting Generic Conventions

The process whereby a screenplay moves through various drafts and revisions to some kind of (at least provisionally) final state, of course, is often quite complex, but it seems to have been particularly tortuous with regard to *King of Kings*. One version of the *King of Kings* script features a character named David, a merchant prince who is the son of a Temple elder and a former lover of Mary Magdalene. He is accompanied by Abdul, who is variously described as an "oriental," a "Persian," and a "follower of Islam" in different versions of the script.[6] These two characters were initially imagined to wander through the temptation scene that I describe below, and were featured in other sections of the film as well. The elimination of David and Abdul—along with other subplots and characters—seems to have been part of an effort to focus the film more directly on the life of Jesus. But this effort was only partially successful. Although many critics were positive, others complained about the film's confusing narrative and its lack of dramatic power. Bosley Crowther's 1961 review of the film is typical in this regard. "The drama of Jesus," he wrote, "is strangely lost or confused or omitted in this peculiarly impersonal film that constructs a great deal of random action around Jesus and does very little to construct a living personality for Him."[7] Indeed, the individual scenes often seem disconnected from one another, and one

Example 7.1. Nativity scene music from *Ben-Hur*.

has the impression that the director (Nicholas Ray) had difficulty linking them together in a coherent way.

The disjointed structure of *King of Kings* is particularly apparent in the first section of the film. After a suitably expansive overture (much in the style of *Ben-Hur*), the main diegesis begins with images of marching legions and a voiceover narration. By the time of *King of Kings,* these kinds of scenes had become the stock in trade (or perhaps a cliché) of the epic style. *Quo Vadis* begins in exactly the same manner, and the first scene of *The Robe* is what we might call a close relative of this gesture, in which gladiators occupy the semantic position of the legionnaires. In *Ben-Hur,* the marching legions and voiceover narration are delayed until after the prologue, but the cinematic effect is much the same. As we might expect, Rózsa provides a typical *marcia romana* to accompany this scene. The Roman march in *King of Kings* is admittedly somewhat more dissonant than its analogues in *Quo Vadis* and *Ben-Hur,* but it is still a clear example of the topos. But although the marching legions in *King of Kings* recapitulate those in earlier films, the scene doesn't seem to have contributed to the problem of repetition that Rózsa identified as his central difficulty with the film score. Instead, Rózsa draws attention to the nativity scene, which occurs in *King of Kings* at 14:40. In both narrative and cinematic terms, it is quite similar to the nativity scene in *Ben-Hur* (see Example 7.1). With its clear D-major tonality and straightforward symmetrical phrase structure, the underscoring that Rózsa provided for this earlier iteration of the nativity forms a strong musical contrast with other kinds of styles and gestures in the *Ben-Hur* score. Rózsa isn't quoting any specific melody, but his nativity music does seem (in a general way) to allude to the style of a Christmas carol: a common-time version, perhaps, of "Bring a Torch, Jeannette Isabella." Not surprisingly, Rózsa's underscoring also reinforces the pastoral images that are so prominent in this scene. The composer punctuates each phrase of his D-major melody with brief accompanimental figures that allude to the braying of donkeys and the lowing of cattle. These gestures stop just short of "Mickey-Mousing,"[8] but they nevertheless express the idea of the pastoral in a very direct way.

The pastoral also seems to be the point of departure for the nativity music of *King of Kings* (see Example 7.2). But instead of alluding to animal sounds, Rózsa's underscoring in this later iteration of the nativity employs less directly imitative pastoral topoi from the European concert repertoire: parallel fifths and drones; siciliano rhythms; and an orchestral texture that foregrounds flutes and double-reed instruments. If "Bring a Torch, Jeannette Isabella" seems to hover in the

Example 7.2. Nativity scene music from *King of Kings*.

background of the *Ben-Hur* nativity music, the reference in this latter film might be to Pietro Yon's "Gesù Bambino." Comparing the nativity scene underscoring from these two films gives insight into the ways in which Rózsa grappled with the problem of repetition. In the most general sense, Rózsa uses the same aesthetic strategy in both *Ben-Hur* and in *King of Kings* (and also in *Quo Vadis,* for that matter). In both of these films, the pastoral qualities of the nativity music contrast sharply with the imperial style. Each melody helps to evoke both the humbleness of Christ's birth and the sense of hope and expectation that it brings. At the more granular level, however, Rózsa does seem to be concerned with creating distinction between the two scores. Both scenes are in the broadest sense pastoral, but for the *King of Kings* nativity scene, Rózsa employs precisely those components of the musical topos that he did not use for the analogous sequence in *Ben-Hur.* Here, perhaps, is a direct example of Rózsa's desire (as he said) to find a way to treat the same theme entirely differently.

A more complex—and perhaps more problematic—example of the oblique relationship between the *King of Kings* music and Rózsa's earlier biblical epic scores has to do with the title theme (see Example 7.3). This music functions as the principal theme of the overture, and in the course of the cinematic narrative it will come to be associated with the character of Jesus himself. As I noted above, the figure of Christ is treated very differently in *King of Kings* than in *Ben-Hur.* Bosley Crowther and other critics might complain about the strangely impersonal way in which Jesus is depicted in the latter film, but they certainly could not deny

Example 7.3. *King of Kings* title theme.

that he is the central figure of the movie. It is therefore hardly surprising that the title theme for *King of Kings* should bear little resemblance to the shimmering string chords that function as the Christ theme in the *Ben-Hur* score. Indeed, if the title theme from *King of Kings* resembles any music from *Ben-Hur,* it is probably closest to the motive that Rózsa uses for Judah Ben-Hur (see Example 6.2). A closer analogue may be found in the Marcus Vinicius music from *Quo Vadis* (see Example 3.1). All these themes have a strongly modal character and contain similar kinds of melodic gestures. The first phrases of both the title theme from *King of Kings* and the Marcus Vinicius motive, for example, employ scale degrees 1̂, 5̂,♭7̂, and 2̂: a pentatonic collection that may imply either the Dorian or the Mixolydian mode. Another gesture typical of Rózsa's hero themes is the leap up to the fifth above the tonic: this may be found in both the second phrase of the *King of Kings* title music and the first phrase of the Judah Ben-Hur motive. The *King of Kings* title theme, to be sure, is far from being a recapitulation of either the Judah Ben-Hur motive or the music for Marcus Vinicius. It is cast in triple rather than duple meter, and many of the rhythmic gestures that characterize the hero music of *Ben-Hur* and *Quo Vadis*—such as the quarter-note triplets and the two sixteenth-note, eighth-note pattern—are absent. But although these differences make the *King of Kings* music much less military or march-like than either the Marcus Vinicius or the Judah Ben-Hur themes, Rózsa's music for the central figure of *King of Kings* is nevertheless closely related to the hero motives from his earlier epic scores. Like the nativity music that I described above, then, the title theme from *King of Kings* evinces what we might call an oblique relationship to the musical topoi of these earlier films.

The Dodecaphonic Devil

In narrative terms, of course, Jesus cannot act like the typical hero of a postwar biblical epic. He cannot wield sword or spear, and he certainly cannot compete in any chariot race. Although the figure of Mary Magdalene in *King of Kings* to some extent resonates with the love interests in other ancient epics, her relationship with Jesus must of course eschew the passion of Marcus and Lygia or the master/slave tension between Judah Ben-Hur and Esther. In *King of Kings,* the typical features of the hero are to some extent taken over by other characters. Barabbas (and not Jesus) is the military leader fighting for the freedom of his people; the Roman centurion Lucius undergoes the conversion experience; and Robert Ryan's portrayal of John the Baptist partakes of the same kind of rugged masculinity that made Charlton Heston so successful. But if the Jesus of *King of Kings* does not in most senses fit the mold of the epic hero, there are nevertheless certain sequences from the film that repeat the narrative semantics of earlier biblical films. Particularly interesting in this regard is the sequence that narrates Christ's forty days in the wilderness.[9]

In many ways, we might understand the biblical account of the forty days in the wilderness as an instantiation (albeit a very singular one) of a broadly distributed archetypal myth concerning the solitary hero wandering through a rugged landscape in which he is emotionally and/or physically tested and shaped for the destiny that awaits him. The Mt. Gilboa scene from *David and Bathsheba* that I examined in chapter 2 is also an example of this archetype, but the sequence from *The Ten Commandments* in which Moses wanders through the desert before collapsing near the well tended by Jethro's daughters is a closer analogue to the Gospel narrative. Although the underlying mythic structure of these scenes is similar, their cinematic manifestation is not. The Mt. Gilboa sequence—as we saw in chapter 2—is accompanied by auditory hallucinations. In *The Ten Commandments,* by contrast, images of Moses wandering across the burning wastes of Shur are accompanied by both underscoring and a narrative voiceover. The soundscape for the wandering scenes in *The Greatest Story Ever Told* is different still. In this film, Jesus' forty days in the wilderness is imagined as a rigorous climb to the top of a stony mountain. As in *David and Bathsheba* and *The Ten Commandments,* the hero's journey is accompanied by underscoring, but in *The Greatest Story Ever Told* it is mixed at a very low volume. The most prominent component of the cinematic soundscape is the voice of John the Baptist (memorably played by Charlton Heston) calling for repentance and echoing through the stony landscape (or perhaps simply in the mind of Jesus). In *The Greatest Story Ever Told,* then, the *voix acousmatique* belongs to John and not (as it does in *The*

Ten Commandments) to an omniscient narrator. Each of these films, therefore, employs what we might call a distinct sonic strategy in order to help narrate a mythic archetype that they hold in common.

Like the desert wandering sequence in *The Ten Commandments* and its analogue in *The Greatest Story Ever Told,* the soundscape that accompanies Jesus' forty days in the wilderness in *King of Kings* (beginning at 36:54) mixes underscoring with a *voix acousmatique.* But the combination of these elements takes a very different form. The beginning of Jesus' wandering is marked with a special statement of the main title theme, chromaticized in order to represent the hero's spiritual and physical pain. As in *The Ten Commandments,* a narrative voiceover tells of his travails. In the middle section of this sequence, however, this voiceover is replaced, so to speak, by a different *acousmetre:* the voice of the Devil himself. The Devil tempts Jesus three times: first by suggesting that he transform stone into bread, then by offering him dominion over all the kingdoms of the earth in exchange for his worship, and finally by suggesting that he throw himself from the top of the Temple to test God's willingness and power to save his life. In each of these instances, the voice of the Devil is accompanied by a distinctive theme. Rózsa describes his compositional logic for this scene in the following manner: "I did my best to explain [the scene] musically, and in spite of (or rather because of) my disbelief in Schoenberg's twelve-tone system, I wrote the only twelve-tone theme of my career for the Devil. For me twelve-tone music is a stillborn idea and thus naturally and admirably suited to the Devil, the 'Spirit of Negation,' the 'Father of Lies.'"[10] Rózsa's decision to use a twelve-tone row in this particular context, of course, carries heavy ideological freight. Before we examine some of these ideological questions, however, we must first address issues of semantics, and the numerous slippages among various interrelated terms. In the quotation above, Rózsa refers to twelve-tone music (a term that I take to be essentially equivalent to dodecaphonic music), and not to the serial style. The terms are not interchangeable. One may, of course, use serial techniques to manipulate rows of less (or more) than twelve pitches; one may also (as in the integral serialism of Babbitt and others) adapt these techniques to different parameters of music. In practice, dodecaphonic and/or serial music in films was usually characterized by a cluster of gestures—angular melodies, irregular rhythms, and certain types of textures—that were not a part of the definition for either term. In this sense, "dodecaphonic music" and "serialism" also overlapped with other terms such as (Viennese) "expressionism" or (more broadly) "modernism." The slippages among these terms, we might say, reveal ways in which a specific *technique* (serialism) became associated with a particular musical *style.*

The slippage between a specific style and a specific technique is readily apparent when we look more closely at Rózsa's dodecaphonic Devil music (see Example 7.4). In terms of functionality, the most important tonal aspect of the Devil motive is not the fact that it contains all twelve chromatic pitches, but rather its extreme dissonance. A closer look at the row itself shows how Rózsa studiously

Example 7.4. Violin music for the Devil.

avoids nearly all consonant melodic intervals in order to create a highly distinctive melody, comprising mainly semitones and large seventh leaps. Highly irregular rhythmic values add to the sense of spiky angularity. All these features combine to set the Devil music at the extreme end of a continuum between diatonic and chromatic, a continuum that Rózsa uses in a conventional way to register various degrees of spiritual or emotional agitation. As Jesus is tempted, we might say, his music partakes of the Devil's dissonant soundscape—hence the chromaticized version of the title theme with which the sequence begins. His victory over the Devil at the end of this sequence is accompanied by a triumphal restatement of his motive, now purged of any chromatic turmoil. In the context of *King of Kings*—and speaking of course primarily in musical terms—the Devil is not so much the "Father of Lies" as the exemplar of extreme chromaticism. The re-diatonicization of Jesus' motive at the end of the scene is the unambiguous musical marker of his resistance to and ultimate victory over Satan. Despite the fact that it happens to contain a twelve-tone theme, therefore, the underscoring essentially follows the same kind of semantic logic that we might find in *Quo Vadis* or *Ben-Hur*.

That is not to say, however, that the dodecaphonic structure of the Devil music carries no meaning. The temptation sequence in *King of Kings* may contain the first use of dodecaphonic music in the postwar biblical epic, but by 1961 serial techniques were already a well-established part of film scoring. Indeed, Schoenberg himself may be said to have inaugurated the subgenre of serial film music with his *Begleitungsmusik zu einer Lichtspielszene,* op. 34 (1929–30).[11] By the 1950s and 1960s, a number of other film music composers had incorporated serial music into their scores. The music that Leonard Rosenmann wrote for *The Cobweb* (1955) appears to be the first fully serial score for a full-length film, but the most famous example of this subgenre is probably the serial score that Jerry Goldsmith wrote for the 1962 film *Freud.*[12] Goldsmith would also use serial techniques extensively in his score for *Planet of the Apes* (1968). As the titles of these films suggest, serial techniques were most prominent in the scores to horror/science fiction films and those that explored intense or abnormal psychological states: what Rózsa in his autobiography called "psychological thrillers." Although Rózsa was a relative latecomer to the idea of using dodecaphonic music in film, he was one of the most accomplished composers for just these kinds of psychological films. Indeed, Rózsa won his first two Academy Awards for films of this type: Alfred Hitchcock's *Spellbound* (1945) and George Cukor's *A Double Life* (1947).

In early versions of the wilderness sequence from *King of Kings,* it seems that the Devil was intended to appear as an onscreen character. In his autobiography, Rózsa describes the scene as a confrontation between Jesus and "an Arab in a burnous."[13] The assumption that this figure represents the Devil is supported by annotations in the conductor's score for the film (such as "Devil Appears"). Red pencil slashes through these sections indicate that this idea was ultimately cut. In the final version of the film, however, the Devil is never seen: he *is aurally but not visually* present. It is possible, then, to see the Jesus of *King of Kings* as a man— like Anthony John in *A Double Life* or John Ballantine in *Spellbound*—who is tormented by inner rather than external demons. In this sense, we might perhaps understand the temptation scene in *King of Kings* as another example of generic hybridity in the biblical epic. Just as *David and Bathsheba* employs certain elements of the woman's film, and *The Ten Commandments* employs—at least in certain scenes—the conventions of the western, so too might we understand the temptation scene as a point of intersection between the biblical epic and the psychological thrillers from the 1940s and 1950s. This similarity is perhaps more pronounced in the film score than in cinematography, for in many ways Rózsa's approach to the temptation scenes from *King of Kings* recapitulates that which he follows in his psychological films from the 1940s. In all these films, Rózsa follows typical underscoring practice by associating abnormal or hallucinatory psychological states with specific textures. In *Spellbound,* for example, Rózsa reserves a particular combination of instruments—the vibraphone, the novachord (a kind of early synthesizer), and the theremin—for dreams and/or hallucinations. Jesus' hallucinations (if we may call them that) in *King of Kings* are linked with a similarly uncanny musical texture: scurrying violins playing thirty-second-note partial chromatic scales in contrary motion, lower strings playing tremolando and pizzicato parallel fifths and octaves, along with vibes, gong, and cymbals. In the aural world of *King of Kings,* we might read this specific soundscape as a textural marker for psychosis.

Such a reading, however, ignores ways in which the music for the temptation scene intersects with traditional musical topoi for the Devil. The dissonant, scurrying violin sounds in this scene certainly evoke one of these topoi, namely, the association of the Devil with manic fiddling. In the world of Hollywood, the clearest manifestation of this association is probably the dancing scene from the 1941 film *The Devil and Daniel Webster,* with music by Bernard Herrmann. In this scene, the Devil (disguised as "Mr. Scratch") whips the dancers into a frenzy with his fiddle by playing ever more distorted variations on "Pop Goes the Weasel." This scene, of course, builds on associations that stretch back before the era of sound film, to pieces such as Saint-Säens's *Danse Macabre* or to the figure of Paganini.[14] Even without a diegetic visual cue, I would argue, the prominent violin textures (and perhaps the related sound of the solo cello that plays the twelve-tone theme itself) reference this tradition of the satanic fiddler.

Herrmann's music for *The Devil and Daniel Webster* engages yet another trope in the musical semantics of satanic representation—the idea that the Devil proceeds only by twisting and perverting the aspirations of his victims. At the beginning of the temptation scene in *King of Kings,* it might appear that Rózsa's underscoring might also adhere to this convention. In this interpretation, the chromaticized motive with which the sequence begins seems to be the work of a modernist Mephistopheles attempting to subvert a diatonic (or at least modal) Faustian Jesus. Through his chromatic mockery, we might say, the Devil threatens to expose the logical contradictions in Jesus' position: that he is both one of the persons of a triune God and also a man who must suffer and die. This interpretation follows a clear logic, but the concrete musical semantics of Rózsa's music seem to lead in another direction. The dodecaphonic Devil music, after all, is not a perversion of any specific motive from the rest of *King of Kings;* in this sense it is not analogous to the "Mephistopheles" movement from Liszt's *Faust Symphony.* Indeed, it bears little relation to any other section of the score, and it never appears again, even in those parts of the narrative when we might perceive the Devil's influence to be at work.

Instead, Rózsa's music (as the composer notes) follows a more modern and more specific semantic connection that associates dodecaphonic music with the figure of the Devil. The most famous articulation of this connection, of course, comes in Thomas Mann's 1947 novel *Doktor Faustus*. I have found no evidence that Rózsa's procedure for the temptation scene was directly influenced by Thomas Mann's novel, or even that Rózsa himself was familiar with the work. Nevertheless, the logic behind the Devil/dodecaphonic music association in *King of Kings* is in some ways similar (although far less fully developed) than that which informs Mann's novel. Rózsa's characterization of twelve-tone music as a "stillborn idea," moreover, echoes the sense of sterility that attends the descriptions of serial works in *Doktor Faustus*. Despite these similarities, the association between the Devil and dodecaphonic music in *King of Kings* and in *Doktor Faustus* are different in at least one crucial respect. In his descriptions of Adrian Leverkühn's serial technique, Thomas Mann typically emphasizes not merely the dissonant surface of the music, but also those procedures (inversion, transposition, retrograde, and so on; along with various forms of contrapuntal combination) that are so central to the serial music of the Second Viennese School composers. In *King of Kings,* by contrast, Rózsa subjects his tone row (which appears as the third staff in my transcription) to only a single transposition. The row, moreover, maintains a consistent rhythmic profile, and is always voiced by the solo cello. Indeed, in terms of harmonization, intervallic content, register, and texture it is far more stable than any of the other motives that Rózsa uses in *King of Kings*. Insofar as none of the twelve chromatic pitches that make up the Devil's motive repeats, the tone row exemplifies the serial style of Schoenberg and his various followers. In every other respect, however, Rózsa's procedures have nothing to do with those of these composers. His music, we might say, is dodecaphonic but not serial.

Miracles False and True

If Adrian Leverkühn's (imaginary) use of the twelve-tone technique has little in common with Rózsa's dodecaphonic Devil music, there is nevertheless another important point of connection between novel and film: namely, the close association that both works draw between twelve-tone music and false promises or deception. In *King of Kings,* this motif of deception is reinforced by the film's only clear manifestation of visual special effects, which occurs as part of the second temptation. As the Devil offers to give Jesus sovereignty over all the kingdoms of the earth, we see a mirage-like vision of a quasi-Arabian city glimmering on the screen, its blue and white buildings capped by domes and spires. The artificiality of this vision is readily apparent, particularly in the context of the relentless realism that informs the rest of the film's cinematography. There is in this sense a happy congruence between our distrust of the camera and Jesus' distrust of the Devil: in both cases the cheesiness of the special effects undermines the suspension of disbelief. But while the congruence between satanic and cinematic illusion might function effectively in the local context of the temptation scene, it engages a more fundamental problem with the biblical epic: namely, the problem of the miracle that I addressed in chapter 4. Unlike the Devil's illusions, Christ's miracles must seem to be real.

The Devil's "cinematic tricks" (if I may temporarily appropriate Forshey's language) are strongly contrasted with the cinematic treatment of Jesus' miracles. Director Nicholas Ray chose to include three of these as part of the filmic diegesis, perhaps in order to form a counterpoint to the Devil's three temptations. In a sequence beginning at 52:03, Jesus causes a crippled child to walk again and then restores vision to a blind man. After several intervening scenes, we see Jesus enter a courtyard in which a madman is violently attacking other people. Jesus stills his manic behavior, presumably by healing his troubled soul. In cinematic terms, each of the scenes follows a similar trajectory. Ray relies primarily on camera work and on music to tell the story; the three scenes unfold essentially without dialogue. In contrast to the long shots that show the Devil's illusory promises, Ray favors close-ups for each of the genuine miracles, using the camera to probe the transformation wrought by the Holy Spirit. In the first of these scenes (the healing of the crippled child), the camera focuses with almost clinical clarity on the coiled hands and feet of the boy, which begin to quiver and unfurl. Jesus' presence is indicated only by a shadow on the wall behind the boy. Ray follows a similar cinematographic strategy for the second miracle scene. Here, too, the focus is securely on the transformative effects of the spirit rather than on Jesus himself. And if Jesus appears more prominently in the third miracle (the healing of the madman), his physical actions are in no sense extraordinary: he simply holds the madman still for a moment while the miracle takes place.

Rózsa's score plays a particularly important role in each of these scenes: articulating the precise moment in which the miracle takes place and investing it with emotional power. The composer's strategy for the first miracle may serve here as a representative example. Rózsa's music for this scene is tense and agitated: its sequentially rising motives and increasing volume press inexorably toward a climactic point of arrival. As we might expect, this is a sweeping iteration of the Jesus motive, which occurs just as Jesus (his presence implied only by the shadow that he casts on the wall) withdraws his hands from above the boy. The former cripple, his face beaming with joy, begins to rise from his bed. As he walks toward his parents and his friends, Rózsa's Jesus motive spins out in the underscoring. The boy stumbles, and the underscoring articulates this momentary setback by a strategically placed minor chord. When the boy rises to his feet again, the motive returns, now transfigured by bells and a wordless choir.

The idea of using music to mark the transcendental moment in which the miracle takes place, of course, was a common strategy in the biblical epics, and in many ways we can understand Rózsa's procedure here as an extension of the underscoring practices that we have already seen at work in Newman's score for *The Robe* (and many other films as well). What distinguishes Rózsa's practice from that of Newman in *The Robe* is the intensity of the musical opposition between true miracles and false ones. In this respect, what we might call the non-progressive nature of the Devil music is of central importance. Rózsa's underscoring for the genuine miracles follows a clear narrative trajectory: building tension that is discharged at the moment of transcendence by a reiteration of the film's title theme. This pattern of tension and release is absent from the Devil music. In its place, we have what we might call (with apologies to Schoenberg) a pan-dissonant harmonic space. The scurrying violin accompanimental pattern is nothing but a chromatic ostinato, and the principal theme itself moves in a melodic circle. Adapting Rózsa's own description of the Devil music, we could say that it is "stillborn," not simply because it cannot serve as the basis for a new musical style (an arguable point), but because it has no possibility of genuine transformation or development.

A Message to the Avant-Garde?

Within the sound world of *King of Kings,* the dodecaphonic Devil motive thus has a relatively straightforward purpose. But Rózsa seems also to have wanted the motive to function outside the immediate context of the film. In his autobiography, Rózsa follows the passage about the twelve-tone row with some telling comments about the possible reception of his music. The use of the row, he writes, "was an 'in-joke'; I didn't expect a cinema audience to get the message but thought it might rehabilitate me with the avant-garde. No such luck."[15] The quotation is strange on at least two counts. In order for Rózsa's rehabilitation fantasy to have become reality, of course, members of the avant-garde would have had to engage seriously with *King of Kings*. Even in its heyday, however, the biblical epic was aimed squarely at a middlebrow cinematic audience, and by the early 1960s its cultural cachet (along with its financial viability) was already in decline. For critics of the early 1960s, it is fair to say, the idea of an avant-garde biblical epic would have seemed at best oxymoronic. The fate of *Barabbas* (to which we turn in the next chapter), in which the generic conventions of the biblical epic were to some extent infused with the highbrow aesthetic of the European art film, is a case in point. The film essentially fell in between two different generic categories (art film and blockbuster epic) that, at least for audiences in the early 1960s, were diametrically opposed to one another. And even if we allow that Rózsa's dodecaphonic Devil music might have had some distinct identity independent from its function in the film, it is—as we have seen—a rather poor example of serial technique. Although it is difficult to know exactly whom Rózsa had in mind as exemplars of the avant-garde, the music for the temptation scene in *King of Kings* seems quite distant from works that composers such as Stockhausen, Boulez, or

Babbitt were writing during the late 1950s and early 1960s. Rózsa was a consummate musical craftsman, and if he had genuinely intended to write music approximating the style of the serialist avant-garde, I am confident that he would have done a better job. Rózsa's dodecaphonic Devil music, in other words, reads more like a parody of serial technique than as a model, and is better understood as a critique than as an effort at ingratiation. In both practical and technical terms, then, it is difficult to imagine any way in which this music might have rehabilitated Rózsa's reputation as a modernist composer.

It's highly unlikely that Rózsa himself gave much thought to these issues, and I personally doubt that he seriously imagined that his dodecaphonic Devil music would change his compositional status. It is probably more fruitful to read his comments as symptomatic of his own ambivalent relationship to the world of concert music. Indeed, this ambivalence runs like a scarlet thread through his entire autobiography, and not simply the sections that concern *King of Kings*. The title that Rózsa uses for this work—*Double Life*—references the 1947 picture for which he won his second Academy Award. But as Rózsa himself makes clear, it also alludes to the split between his work as one of the most famous film composers of the postwar period and a much less prominent career as a creator of serious concert music. Rózsa fell into film composition almost by accident, and during the first part of his career he seems to have thought of cinematic work essentially as a supplement to his real vocation. As film composition absorbed more of his time and energy, he seems to have searched for ways to link the two parts of his "double life." The 1946 *Spellbound* Concerto may be seen very much in this light: as an attempt to adapt his Academy Award–winning film score to the concert stage. Dedicated to the pianist Leonard Pennario, the *Spellbound* Concerto was indeed programmed by symphony orchestras (although probably not as often as Rózsa would have liked) and occasionally recorded. But with the addition of romantic lyrics by Mack David, Rózsa's *Spellbound* music (or at least the compelling love theme from the movie) was also transformed into a popular song. The *Spellbound* music could thus occupy both high and low segments of the cultural hierarchy. We can get a sense of this range by comparing the sheet music covers for the *Spellbound* Concerto and the popular song "Spellbound," both of which, incidentally, were published by the Chappell Company. Both covers, as we might expect, reference the film quite directly, but they do so in different ways. The abstract wavelike patterns on the cover to the *Spellbound* Concerto score allude to the most distinctive visual aspect of the film, the famous surrealist dream sequences designed by Salvador Dali. The image conveys a strong message that the *Spellbound* Concerto is art music derived from an art film. The cover for the "Spellbound" song, on the other hand, trades on the star power of Gregory Peck and Ingrid Bergman. The dreamy passion of their romantic clutch anchors the song—and by extension its composer—firmly in the field of popular music (see Figures 7.2a and 7.2b).

Like his music for *Spellbound*, Rózsa's great epic film scores from the 1950s and early 1960s—*Quo Vadis, Ben-Hur, King of Kings, El Cid* (among others)—

Figure 7.2a. Sheet music cover for the *Spellbound* Concerto. Miklós Rózsa Papers, Special Collections Research Center, Syracuse University Library.

Figure 7.2b. Sheet music cover for "Spellbound" (popular song). Miklós Rózsa Papers, Special Collections Research Center, Syracuse University Library.

had an important second life in arrangements for orchestra, symphonic band, choirs, and so forth. But the position of this music within the cultural hierarchy of American concert music had shifted. Orchestral suites on the music from *Ben-Hur* or *King of Kings* could hold their place in the field of light classics—in performances from the Hollywood Bowl or by the Boston Pops, but they could no longer be said to represent musical modernism. A new avant-garde had come to prominence, a group of composers with whom Rózsa had little in common. And if what Rózsa called his "historico-biblical" style had little currency with avant-garde modes of concert music, neither was it well adapted to new styles of popular song. Instead, Rózsa's music for the great biblical epics found a flourishing double life (pun intended) in other fields of American culture: in arrangements for church choirs and school bands, in concerts of light classical music, and perhaps above all in the field of recorded sound.

Authenticity Revisited: "Victimae Paschali Laudes"

As I have already discussed in chapters 3 and 6, Rózsa was profoundly ambivalent about the middlebrow status of his music. In this respect, his specific comments about dodecaphonic music in *King of Kings* and the compositional avant-garde might be understood—to use a musical metaphor—simply as another repetition of the *cantus firmus* of his autobiography. This interpretation, however, ignores the ways in which Rózsa's attitudes were shifting over time, and, more importantly, how these shifts informed his approach to the biblical epic. We gain insight into these shifts by returning to a topic foregrounded in chapter 3, namely, the idea of historical authenticity. With *Quo Vadis*, as we have already seen, Rózsa attempted to make this idea a cornerstone of his score, by using authentic sources in order to generate the diegetic music for the film. Rózsa wanted his work to be taken seriously, and, as I pointed out in chapter 3, it may be understood as manifestation of his desire to elevate the cultural status of his film music more generally (his comments on the Devil music in *King of Kings* are informed by the same impulse). For his later biblical epic scores, however, Rózsa seems to have turned away from the goal of historical authenticity. As Rózsa himself wrote (see note 33 of the previous chapter), he did not use historical sources for his *Ben-Hur* music, and the idea of musical authenticity would seem to play an even smaller role in *King of Kings*. And yet, his score for this latter film contains at least two possible points of intersection with the idea of musical authenticity. The first of these concerns the theme that throughout the film is associated with Mary, the mother of Jesus. Featured prominently in many parts of the score, this Mary theme first appears as the second theme in the title music for the film. As the following transcription makes clear, the Mary theme (especially its first phrase) is quite similar to the medieval sequence "Victimae paschali laudes" (see Example 7.5).[16] Along with the "Dies irae, dies illa" sequence, the melody for "Victimae paschali laudes" was one of the most frequently referenced and para-

Victimae paschali laudes

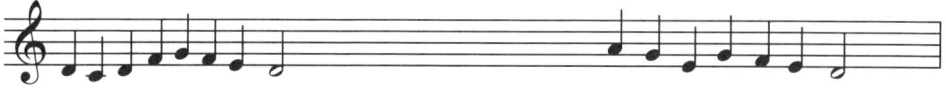

"Mary" theme from *King of Kings*

Example 7.5. Mary theme from *King of Kings* compared to "Victimae paschali laudes."

phrased parts of the monophonic liturgical chant repertoire. It appeared in many twentieth-century hymnals under titles such as "Christians, to the paschal victim," and although it's possible to understand the Mary theme as a kind of subconscious invocation of the medieval sequence, it is hard to believe that Rózsa would not have been quite familiar with the melody. The fact that the sequence is part of the liturgy for Easter may also have suggested it to Rózsa for use in *King of Kings.*

In purely musical terms, we might say that the relationship between the Mary theme from *King of Kings* and "Victimae paschali laudes" is similar to that which obtains between Nero's song "O lambent flames" from *Quo Vadis* and the Epitaph of Seikolos. If Rózsa inserted a few notes into "Victimae paschali laudes" in order to generate his Mary theme, so too did he embellish the Epitaph of Seikolos by placing the original sequence of pitches into a particular metric structure. The association between a medieval sequence and a first-century character is anachronistic, yet Rózsa had already countenanced a similar anachronism in *Quo Vadis* when he put the presumably fourth-century Ambrosian hymn "Aeterna rerum conditor" into the mouths of his first-century Christians.

A key difference between the examples from *Quo Vadis* and the Mary theme in *King of Kings,* of course, is that the latter never appears diegetically in the film. It could be that, at least for Rózsa, the idea of historical authenticity pertained only to diegetic music, and could not properly be applied to underscoring. More significant, however, is that the idea of historical authenticity had simply lost much of its importance for Rózsa, at least with regard to his film music. In this sense, the musical differences between the Mary theme and the historicist examples from *Quo Vadis* are less important than the differences in the ways in which the two scores were framed and presented. The historicist music in *Quo Vadis* is meant to be recognized as such; its meaning, we might say, is bound up with its historical verisimilitude. Even if we regard the Mary theme as a paraphrase of "Victimae paschali laudes," by contrast, it is not historical, or at least not historical in the same sense. To find analogies for the Mary theme, therefore, we must turn not to *Quo Vadis*, but rather to the allusive techniques of Alfred Newman. The relationship between Rózsa's Mary theme and "Victimae paschali laudes," in this sense, is like that between the title theme for *The Robe* and the monks' music in Meyerbeer's *Les Huguenots*, or between Newman's *Street Scene* and Gershwin's *Rhapsody in Blue*. Given the hegemonic position of Christianity in American culture during the postwar period, it seems possible that some members of the audience may have recognized the relationship between these two melodies. For most of the audience, however, this connection was at least consciously unnoticed. Like so many other aspects of cinematic underscoring, the allusion to "Victimae paschali laudes" operated subliminally to give the figure of Mary (and, more generally, the film as a whole) a special aura of the sacred. For the Mary theme, we might say the aesthetics of authenticity have been replaced by the aesthetics of appropriation.

The Last Supper

A second point of intersection between the idea of musical authenticity and the *King of Kings* score comes in the Last Supper sequence toward the end of the film. The Last Supper, of course, does not appear in either *Quo Vadis* or in *Ben-Hur*, and is consequently not one of the scenes listed by Rózsa in his discussion of the problem of repetition that I quoted above. The historical freight with which this scene is weighted is visual rather than musical. For audiences in the early 1960s (and probably for contemporary audiences as well) the primary image associated with the Last Supper was surely da Vinci's famous mural painting of the same name. The "widescreen" format of this image made it especially apt for the new aspect ratio in which most of the postwar biblical epics were filmed. Indeed, when George Stevens filmed the Last Supper scene for *The Greatest Story Ever Told*, he essentially recreated da Vinci's mural painting in cinematic terms (see Figure 9.1). In *King of Kings*, on the other hand, Nicholas Ray found an interesting way to cut across the grain of these visual conventions. Rather than placing Jesus at the center of a long table, he instead imagines a table in the shape of a "Y," with Jesus at the juncture of the two arms (see Figure 7.3). Jesus is still at the center; the disciples still look at him with bewilderment and consternation, but the visual structure of the scene has been reconfigured.

The underscoring for this scene might be understood in a similar way: as a reconfiguration of conventional elements. Rózsa uses familiar leitmotif scoring techniques for the first part of the sequence (beginning at 2:02:59). Since the drama of this section centers on the confrontation between Judas and Jesus, Rózsa's underscoring combines the title theme of the film (the Jesus motive) with a dissonant motive associated throughout the movie with the disciple who must betray him. After Judas leaves, Jesus leads the remaining disciples in an abbreviated and modified Passover feast. This section climaxes with the words "For you

Figure 7.3. The Last Supper scene from *King of Kings*. From the core collection production files of the Margaret Herrick Library, Academy of Motion Picture Arts and Sciences.

believe in me, and in him, from whom I was sent," accompanied, quite naturally, by another statement of the title theme from the film. The final section of the scene—and the most interesting for my purposes—is the breaking of the bread. The underscoring is a haunting chant in the Aeolian or Hypodorian mode, sung unaccompanied in unison octaves (see Example 7.6).

The process whereby this music came to be placed into the sound track at this point is admittedly opaque. As we might imagine, the conductor's score for this cue breaks off at the end of the orchestral underscoring: in other words, at the moment when the chant begins. Part of the last page of the cue, however, has been cut away—suggesting that there may originally have been orchestral underscoring for the breaking of the bread. At the beginning of the cue, Rózsa has penciled a brief annotation: "Babylonian p. 90, no. 4," indicating, perhaps, a possible source for the chant melody that follows the orchestral cue. Given Rózsa's musicological predilections, a logical place to look for such a source would be A. Z. Idelsohn's eight-volume *Hebräisch-orientalischer Melodienschatz*, volume 2 of which is dedicated to the music of the Babylonian Jews.[17] The melody is not found on page 90 of this second volume, but Idelsohn does include it as one of the Pass-

Example 7.6. Chant underscoring for the breaking of the bread.

over chants in volume 1 of his collection *Songs of the Yemenite Jews*.[18] Since Rózsa never mentions this chant in published material or in the correspondence that seems to have survived, we cannot be sure that he was responsible for the decision to insert the chant at this point in the film. It seems likely, however, that Rózsa's annotation is either a memory slip or else a reference to another source that contains this same melody.

My supposition is supported by the example of *Quo Vadis*, in which (as we have seen) Rózsa assiduously based so much of his score on historical sources (e.g., the Ode of Pindar, the Epitaph of Seikolos). Like other isolated communities, the Jews of Yemen and Babylonia were generally understood to have preserved ancient liturgies and other religious practices. Of the Yemenite Jews, for example, Idelsohn writes the following: "Owing to their very long seclusion a characteristic Jewish life with all its cultural attributes developed among them, and consequently some old spiritual values were preserved in their midst which might prove of great consequence in an investigation of the Oriental-Jewish and especially the ancient Hebrew culture."[19] Inserting Jewish music for the Passover feast (be it Yemenite or Babylonian) at this point might be understood as another gesture toward musical authenticity, akin to Rózsa's decision to use the Ambrosian chant as the third Christian hymn in *Quo Vadis*. But despite the fact that the Yemenite chant is liturgically appropriate to the Passover feast that the disciples are celebrating, and despite the fact that it is presented without orchestral accompaniment, the disciples themselves are not singing. The Yemenite chant, in other words, could function as diegetic music, but it does not. Even though it is not a part of the conductor's score, then, the chant thus serves as part of the underscoring. As with the paraphrase of "Victimae paschali laudes," therefore, the function of the Yemenite music in *King of Kings* is ultimately quite distinct from its analogues in *Quo Vadis* or *The Robe*. Despite its superficial resemblance to other music from earlier biblical epics, the Yemenite chant thus creates a very different effect.

Much of this effect comes from the particular melodic structure of the chant itself. Like most of the other material that Idelsohn collected—and indeed, like some analogous examples from Christian psalmody and other traditions—the Yemenite chant in *King of Kings* is built up from a relatively limited group of melodic cells: the $\hat{1}$-$\hat{3}$-$\hat{2}$-$\hat{1}$ figure that occurs near the opening of the chant, a $\hat{1}$-$\hat{2}$-$\hat{1}$-$\hat{2}$-$\flat\hat{7}$-$\hat{5}$ figure; the triplet idea that becomes more common in its final phrases, and so on. But the overall structure of the chant is non-periodic, with irregular phrase lengths and rhythmic stresses. Repetition and unpredictability are thus paradoxically combined, creating a sense, perhaps, that time itself has been suspended. Equally striking—at least in the context of an MGM epic film—is the way in which the scene departs from certain hallmarks of classical underscoring technique. There are no synch points, and none of the kind of leitmotivic manipulation that is so prominent in *Ben-Hur* or *Quo Vadis*. In terms of its function (if not its sound), the Yemenite chant is unlike anything else either in *King of Kings* or the other epics that Rózsa scored.

The use of this Yemenite chant as underscoring for what is arguably the most emotionally intense scene of the entire film exemplifies the particular position of *King of Kings* in the history of the postwar biblical epic—or, to put this in terms of the idea with which I have framed this chapter, the ambiguous response of its creators (Rózsa included) to the problem of repetition. Like so many other aspects of the film, much of the score seems to look backward to the traditions of the earlier postwar biblical epics. Yet other sections of the score seem more experimental in nature. Some of these sections—most notably, the temptation sequence—seem to present dead ends (at least in terms of the stylistic development of the genre). But in others, the music seems to grope toward a new aesthetic: a different way in which biblical stories might intersect with the cinematic imagination. In the chapters that remain, I examine two additional films that occupy a similarly enigmatic position between the traditions of the past and the emerging spiritual and cultural climate of the 1960s.

8 Suoni Nuovi, Suoni Antichi:
The Soundscapes of *Barabbas*

The popularity of the biblical epic, as I have already noted, was closely associated with the "fourth great awakening" that filled the pews of churches during the postwar period. The crest of this religious wave is of course impossible to mark with specificity, but we might use church attendance as a rough measure of the centrality of Christianity in American life during this period. Self-reported church attendance reached its all-time high in the United States in 1955 and 1958: years which correspond almost exactly to the release dates of the two films that probably mark the high water point of the genre (*The Ten Commandments* and *Ben-Hur,* respectively). The association between the postwar biblical epic and the postwar Christian church, moreover, was not merely a matter of statistics. Cinematic representations of biblical narratives found their way into the fabric of American religious life, not least through musical adaptions. Selections from Miklós Rózsa's scores for *King of Kings* and for *Ben-Hur* were arranged for church choir, while *The Ten Commandments*—especially after it began to appear on television in 1973—attained a special, quasi-sacramental position as a special Easter program. The monumental scale of these films, their centrist theological stance and optimistic messages, position them as cinematic analogues of the expansionist, self-confident mainline Christianity of the 1950s. The postwar biblical epics, in other words, were both participants in and expressions of the "fourth great awakening" of American religious life.

By the early 1960s, however, the postwar wave of religious enthusiasm had begun to ebb. In his book *The Sixties Spiritual Awakening,* Robert S. Ellwood captures this shifting cultural climate by comparing cover stories for two Easter issues of *Time* magazine. The *Time* cover portrait for April 18, 1960, Ellwood notes,

> was of St. Paul, and the story was on Christian missionaries: "From St. Paul to 1960." The article described the life and times of the great missionary apostle, then, with the help of vividly colored photographs, it surveyed the work of missionaries in the world of 1960.
>
> The generally upbeat, laudatory tone, the obvious favoritism toward Christianity and its American mainline denominations, the unobtrusive but respectable

academic scholarship behind its portrayal of the first century, all make the *Time* article . . . a kind of capstone and epitaph for Fifties-style, public, self-assured, modernist religion, confidently working out of unquestioned great traditions and, like America generally, thought to be doing good on a global scale. It was much in contrast to other famous *Time* cover pieces on religion that were to appear only a few years later, such as the "Is God Dead?" of Easter 1966.[1]

Although Ellwood does not make the connection between the 1960 article and the style of the typical postwar biblical epic, his description of the "From St. Paul to 1960" story could in many respects apply to films such as *The Ten Commandments* and *Ben-Hur*. The decline of this self-assured, Christian-centered religious culture, then, posed real problems for the biblical epic, and in the emerging climate of the 1960s, the genre risked becoming a cultural relic.

The challenges to the biblical epic posed by these religious and cultural changes unfolded alongside other difficulties inherent within the production/marketing logic of the genre itself. As I discussed in chapter 6, the aesthetics of the superlative that characterized the biblical epic throughout the 1950s seemed to reach its apogee with *Ben-Hur*. In the wake of this colossal film, the demand that each new blockbuster epic should be more impressive and more grandiose than its predecessor became increasingly difficult, if not impossible, to satisfy. Budgets for epic films produced in the early 1960s tended to spiral out of control precisely at the moment in which the religious environment for the biblical epic—at least as it was imagined during the heyday of the genre—was becoming more inhospitable.

Beginning "Where the Other Big Ones Leave Off"

Nowhere are the specific qualities of this cultural moment in the history of the biblical epic more clearly expressed than in *Barabbas*, a Dino De Laurentiis–produced film released in Italy during the final weeks of 1961 and in the United States in October 1962. Directed by Richard Fleischer and starring Anthony Quinn in the title role, the film opened to mixed reviews and never came close to rivaling the popularity of *The Ten Commandments, Ben-Hur,* or even *King of Kings*. The film's importance for my purposes lies not so much with its influence on subsequent movies, but rather for the ways in which it exemplifies the transformation (we might go so far as to say the disintegration) of the biblical epic. This transformation is perhaps not immediately clear, for in many ways *Barabbas* recapitulates the typical features of earlier biblical epic films. There are gladiatorial combat scenes reminiscent of those in *Demetrius and the Gladiators;* there is a spectacular burning of Rome sequence similar to the one in *Quo Vadis;* and, like both *Ben-Hur* and *The Robe,* the film also foregrounds the atmospheric/meteorological effects associated with Christ's crucifixion. But *Barabbas* also departs from the conventions of the genre, most notably in its portrayal of the doubt-filled, tortured character at its center. Barabbas is in many ways an inversion of the typical biblical epic hero: an ignoble thief and murderer unwilling or unable to understand the message of Christ, whose conversion is at best provisional and incomplete. The self-confident or even triumphalist ethos that suffuses the biblical epics of the previous decade is absent from *Barabbas,* as are many key elements of the epic style. The film, in short, seems both to invoke the past and to anticipate an uncertain future.

Indeed, what we might call the ambivalent relationship of *Barabbas* to earlier biblical epics seems to have been a part of the marketing strategy for the film. The theatrical trailer for *Barabbas* begins with a scrolling text against a background clip of what is probably the most famous scene of the movie: a representation of Christ's crucifixion filmed during an actual solar eclipse. The text features the hyperbolic language that is so typical in the marketing of the postwar biblical epics. "Soon you will experience a motion picture of unparalleled inspiration and unprecedented magnificence," the text promises, "a motion picture for all time." Similar promises, of course, were made for most of the other blockbuster biblical epics, and the words could easily have been used to advertise *Quo Vadis, The Ten Commandments,* or *Ben-Hur.* But the scrolling text ends with an unusual phrase: one that also appears on posters and in other promotional material for the film. "It begins here," the text reads, "where the other big ones leave off." The fact that we see these words in front of an image of the crucifixion, of course, encourages us to understand the sentence in terms of plot chronology. The "other big ones" in this sense are probably *Ben-Hur* and *King of Kings,* both of which (apart from their epilogue-like closing scenes) end with the crucifixion. *Barabbas* might be said to "begin where the other big ones leave off" because Christ's crucifixion takes place near the start of the film rather than near its end.

The remainder of the trailer follows the familiar practice whereby a narrative voiceover describes the film as we see a sequence of highlights. The voiceover ends by recapitulating the final sentence of the opening scrolling text. Here, however, the text appears not against the background of the crucifixion, but rather with a brief shot from the scene in which Barabbas is sentenced to slavery in the sulfur mines of Sicily (a scene that I examine in more detail below). The repetition, I would argue, gives a different inflection to the idea that *Barabbas* "begins where the other big ones leave off." The voiceover now seems to be promising not simply a chronological continuation of the biblical story, but rather some kind of stylistic or spiritual extension of the biblical epic. *Barabbas,* it implies, will be something altogether new. Something of this spirit informs De Laurentiis's comments concerning his motivations for making the film. The challenge and risk of producing *Barabbas,* he writes, "was the modern significance of Barabbas' story; that is, the opportunity of rendering understandable and acceptable to the vast cinema-going public the creature of fantasy who epitomizes the doubts and torments of modern man, with his spiritual conflicts, and his struggle with the problem of the supernatural."[2] This story, he tells us, demanded a biblical film unlike any that had been previously made: an historical film with a modernist aesthetic, an intimate spectacle, a biblical epic with an existentialist heart.

The new spiritual climate of the film, and its corresponding distance from the biblical epics of the 1950s, is to a large degree predicated on the special character of its source material. *Barabbas* is based on a 1950 novel of the same name by the Swedish author Pär Lagerqvist.[3] Greatly admired by international literati such as André Gide, the novel's success helped Lagerqvist win the Nobel Prize for literature. In the most direct sense, Lagerqvist's work belongs to a literary subgenre that was enormously popular during the 1940s and 1950s, a subgenre that I described in chapter 4. Like Thomas B. Costain's *The Silver Chalice* or Lloyd Douglas's *The Robe* and *The Big Fisherman*, Lagerqvist's *Barabbas* is a fictional tale spun out from the narratives contained in the New Testament. These twentieth-century works, of course, built upon the success of nineteenth-century exemplars such as *Quo Vadis?* and *Ben-Hur*. But despite the structural similarity between Lagerqvist's novel and these other works, its style (as well as its theological stance) is completely different. Although Fleischer's movie is far from being a straightforward adaptation of Lagerqvist's work, much of this distinctive style found its way into the film.

We may get a sense of this distinctive style (and the distance between Lagerqvist's work and other biblico-historical novels) by examining two passages that occupy the same structural position in their respective narratives: namely, the moment in which the hero is first introduced. The reader of Lew Wallace's *Ben Hur: A Tale of the Christ* must wait nearly a hundred pages for this moment. As in the 1959 film, Judah Ben-Hur first appears in the company of his boyhood friend Messala. Wallace makes a great deal of the contrast between the two young men. Beginning with the young Roman, he describes details of dress, physiognomy, and bearing that reveal the essential qualities of his character. He next turns his attention to Judah Ben-Hur. "The associate of the Messala," he writes,

> was slighter in form, and his garments were of fine white linen and of the prevalent style in Jerusalem; a cloth covered his head, held by a yellow cord, and arranged so as to fall away from the forehead down low over the back of the neck. An observer skilled in the distinctions of race, and studying his features more than his costume, would have soon discovered him to be of Jewish descent. The forehead of the Roman was high and narrow, his nose sharp and aquiline, while his lips were thin and straight, and his eyes cold and close under the brows. The front of the Israelite, on the other hand, was low and broad; his nose long, with expanded nostrils; his upper lip, slightly shading the lower one, short and curving to the dimpled corners, like a Cupid's bow; points which, in connection with the round chin, full eyes, and oval cheeks reddened with a wine-like glow, gave his face the softness, strength, and beauty peculiar to his race. The comeliness of the Roman was severe and chaste, that of the Jew rich and voluptuous.[4]

Although lengthy descriptive passages such as these are typical of many nineteenth-century novels, Wallace's expansiveness is remarkable. He displays what I am tempted to call (anachronistically, of course) a cinematic imagination, and it is easy to see how his work—and others like it—may have stimulated the stylistic development of the biblical epic. Wallace's elaborate descriptions find a cinematic analogue in the extraordinary attention to detail that characterizes postwar epic film: its visual magnificence, its emphasis on splendor and spectacle.

Wallace's description may be compared to the passage from *Barabbas* in which Lagerqvist introduces his main character, a passage that occurs only a few paragraphs from the beginning of the novel: "He was about thirty, powerfully built, with a sallow complexion, a reddish beard and black hair. His eyebrows also were black, his eyes too deep-set, as though they wanted to hide. Under one of them he had a deep scar that was lost to sight in his beard. But a man's appearance is of little consequence."[5] By disavowing the descriptive ebullience of works such as *Ben-Hur* (or the more contemporary novels of Costain and Douglas), Lagerqvist is articulating a distinctive style for the biblico-historical novel. Sparse and austere, this style clearly reflects a more broadly disseminated mid-century modernist aesthetic, and may be found (among other places) in novels such as Albert Camus' *L'Étranger* and Max Frisch's *Homo Faber*. But it also resonates with the central theological question of Lagerqvist's novel: namely, how it is possible to live with the knowledge that someone has given up his life in place of yours. Like the biblico-historical novels of the late nineteenth century, works such as *The Robe* and *The Silver Chalice* approach the crucifixion through the stance of the Christian convert. The heroes of these novels—Judah Ben-Hur and Marcellus and analogous characters such as Basil in *The Silver Chalice*—come to understand Christ's sacrifice as central to their new faith, as the vehicle of a redemption that is both potentially universal and essentially spiritual. For Barabbas, by contrast, Christ's sacrifice is direct, literal, and intensely personal. Lagerqvist's stylistic simplicity brings the reader directly into Barabbas's spiritual condition, in which the meaning of Christ's sacrifice—and perhaps, by extension, the meaning of human existence—can never be understood.

To use Lagerqvist's novel as the source material for an epic film was therefore to invite a certain dissonance between form and content. It is this dissonance that accounts for at least some of the awkwardness of the screenplay (generally credited to Christopher Fry). Many scenes in the movie—most notably the extensive sequences that concern Barabbas's career as a gladiator—have no counterpart in the novel, and seem to have been added mainly in order to bring the plot closer to the surge and splendor of the typical postwar epic film. And yet, paradoxically, it was the very distance between Lagerqvist's novel and the conventions of the biblical epic that may have made it attractive to those responsible for the film's production. Indeed, by disavowing the spiritual certainty of films such as *The Ten Commandments* and *Ben-Hur*, *Barabbas* could—at least potentially—stake out a new theological space for the biblical epic, one that would be more in accord with the changing religious climate of the early 1960s. One of the principal ways in which the film articulates this new theological space is through its music.

Nascimbene and the Epic Style: Persistence and Resistance

As I noted in the introduction to this book, the postwar biblical epics were not always exclusively American enterprises. Much of *The Ten Commandments*, for example, was shot on location in Egypt, and various Spanish locations were used for *King of Kings*. Both *Quo Vadis* and *Ben-Hur* were largely produced at the famous Cinecittà studios in Rome. For *Barabbas*, De Laurentiis used the resources of the Italian film industry even more extensively. Like the famous spaghetti westerns that were to become so important in the wake of Sergio Leone's "Dollars" trilogy (*A Fistful of Dollars*, 1964; *For a Few Dollars More*, 1965; and *The Good, the Bad and the Ugly*, 1966), *Barabbas* was thus very much an international co-production.[6] Mario Nascimbene—who wrote the score for *Barabbas*—was well suited to work in this environment. One of the best known and successful Italian film music composers of the postwar period, Nascimbene worked extensively with both Italian and American film directors during the 1950s, scoring films such as *Roma ore 11* (Giuseppe de Santis, 1952) and *The Barefoot Contessa* (Joseph Mankiewicz, 1954). Nascimbene also had experience with epic films, creating the music for *Solomon and Sheba* (1959) as well as *Alexander the Great* (1956). His best-known effort in this genre was the enormously successful Kirk Douglas film *The Vikings* (1958). The director of *The Vikings*, Richard Fleischer, was also tapped for *Barabbas;* the latter film therefore represented the second collaboration between composer and director.

Nascimbene's work for these earlier films showed his mastery of postwar epic-historical film scoring styles. For *Solomon and Sheba*—to cite the example that is most relevant here—Nascimbene created music similar, at least in some ways, to the epic scores of Rózsa and Elmer Bernstein. The leitmotifs in *Solomon and Sheba* employ familiar musical topoi, and although they are neither as numerous nor as highly developed as those in *Ben-Hur*, they nevertheless determine the basic structure of the score. Nascimbene's music for the foreign woman of the two-woman plot archetype (in this instance, the Queen of Sheba) has much in common with the sinuous, slippery melodies associated with analogous characters in *The Ten Commandments*, *Samson and Delilah*, and *David and Bathsheba*. As in these other films, it figures prominently in the opening credits to *Solomon and Sheba*, where it is accompanied by open fifths and octaves moving by major seconds. As I pointed out in my discussion of *Quo Vadis* and *Ben-Hur*, such gestures were a central part of Rózsa's imperial Roman style (see Example 8.1). Like *Samson and Delilah*, *The Ten Commandments*, and *Ben-Hur*, *Solomon and Sheba* also features a devout woman of the tribe—Abishag, the daughter of Ahab. Rival of the Queen of Sheba, and (for most of the film) her moral antipode, Abishag is the domestic woman of the two-woman plot archetype that is so important to the biblical epic genre. Like Miriam in *Samson and Delilah* or Sephora in *The Ten Commandments*, Abishag is ethnically marked by the stereotypically Jewish

Example 8.1. Queen of Sheba theme from *Solomon and Sheba* (as it appears in the opening credit music).

music with which she is continually associated. This association reaches its climax in the music for her funeral, an adaptation of an Ashkenazi cantillation for "El malei rachamim" ("God full of mercy," said for the deceased at a funeral or as a commemoration on a death anniversary).[7] In addition to these common semantic markers, the music for *Solomon and Sheba* also features certain set pieces similar to those in the other biblical epics. The famous orgy scene, in which the Queen of Sheba performs a lascivious dance in front of the pagan god of fertility, finds analogues in scenes such as the Golden Calf sequence from *The Ten Commandments* or (more distantly, to be sure) the banquet scene from *Ben-Hur*. Like other aspects of the film, then, Nascimbene's work in *Solomon and Sheba* is fairly conservative and conventional.

The existentialist aesthetic of *Barabbas,* however, clearly inspired Nascimbene to strike out in a new direction. "When I saw the first rough-cut of *Barabbas,*" the composer wrote,

> I felt at once that this film, although based on a "historical" theme, was decidedly modern in its conception and presentation. As a result, I was presented with the opportunity to create a musical commentary that was quite different from those used so often for historical "spectacle" pictures: large orchestras, seas of stringed instruments, violins taut and relaxed during the usual dominating motif, "cantabile e tanto melodico," heavenly choirs, dramatic drum rolls over fire-red sunsets, and the inevitable brass fanfares booming forth from the screen to accompany the armies marching alongside the inevitable river.[8]

Although we cannot know precisely which scenes Nascimbene had in his mind when he wrote of fire-red sunsets and seas of strings instruments, many elements of his description would apply quite well to some of the scores I have already examined (in particular, those to *Samson and Delilah, The Robe, Quo Vadis,* and *The Ten Commandments*). Nascimbene seems determined to position his *Barabbas* music in opposition to earlier examples of the epic style (including, perhaps, his own scores to films such as *The Vikings* and *Solomon and Sheba*).

Example 8.2. Roman fanfare motive from *Barabbas*.

Nascimbene's music for the opening scene of *Barabbas* would in some ways seem to belie his stated ambition to create a new kind of "musical commentary" for the epic. The film begins with Pilate on the steps of what we take to be an official Roman building, passing judgment on condemned prisoners. Nascimbene's underscoring for this scene features a fanfare-like trumpet motive similar in many ways to the fanfares in *Quo Vadis, The Robe,* or *Ben-Hur* (see Example 8.2). Throughout the film, this motive is associated with Rome and its imperial power. It figures prominently, as we might expect, in the latter part of the film, in which Barabbas becomes a gladiator in the imperial city. In these arena scenes (for example, at 1:23:09), the fanfare occasionally migrates from the underscoring to become diegetic music, just as it does in *Quo Vadis* and *The Robe*.

A more ambiguous example of the persistence of the epic style comes with regard to the music that Nascimbene calls variously the "fundamental theme" of the film, or (in other contexts) the "Christ theme" (see Example 8.3). It first appears as underscoring at the beginning of the opening credit sequence. In an image that evokes, perhaps, the famous painting *The Prisoner's Dream* by Moritz von Schwind, we see Barabbas awakening from the floor of his prison cell. Light streams through a barred window, and we hear Nascimbene's theme played by the strings in unison at the octave. Nascimbene tells us little about his source for this melody, aside from the fact that it is "Gregorian" (see the quotation below). It seems that he either consciously or subconsciously modeled it on the first two phrases of a first-mode Kyrie that appears in the *Liber usualis* as "Kyrie X." Needless to say, Nascimbene was hardly the only film composer to use chant in order to symbolize Christ or early Christianity. Rózsa's music for the Christian captives in *Quo Vadis*—as we have already seen—was a particularly fully developed instantiation of this idea, but it was hardly the only one. The "Song of Miriam" in *The Robe* is less directly modeled on ancient or medieval sources, but it also features the rhythmic freedom and modally inflected melodies that cinematic audiences of the postwar period associated with the simplicity and earnestness of the early Church. In contrast to these examples, however, Nascimbene's Christ

Example 8.3. Christ theme from *Barabbas*.

theme never appears diegetically. In this sense, it seems related to the paraphrase of "Victimae paschali laudes" that Rózsa used for the Mary theme in *King of Kings,* or—even more directly—to the Yemenite chant that accompanies part of the Last Supper sequence in Nicholas Ray's film.

Nascimbene's *Suoni Nuovi*

What distinguishes Nascimbene's practice from that of composers such as Rózsa and Newman, in any case, is not so much the nature of his individual themes, but rather the ways in which he combines conventional underscoring with what he calls the *suoni nuovi:* new sounds that seem to inhabit a space between sound effects and underscoring. Although Nascimbene first speaks of the *suoni nuovi* in connection to *Barabbas*, his practice for this film is in many ways prefigured in some of his earlier film scores in which sound and music are commingled in various and interesting ways. In his biography of the composer, Luca Bandirali traces this aspect of Nascimbene's compositional practice back to Enzo Masetti, one of Nascimbene's early teachers and a pioneering figure in the development of Italian cinematic music. For Masetti, "one of the greatest peculiarities of film music is that of transfiguring sound into music and music into sound."[9] Nascimbene's scores contain many examples of these twin transfigurations. In the score to *Alexander the Great*, for instance, Nascimbene uses percussion sounds in a quasi-representational manner to accompany the cavalry charge scene, a practice that recalls the "Mickey-Mousing" that was such a prominent feature of music for animated cartoons. More interesting are the ways in which non-musical sound (such as the noise of the typewriter in *Roma ore 11* or the sound of the rain in *The Barefoot Contessa*) takes on musical characteristics.[10] Nascimbene, of course, was hardly the only film composer interested in these kinds of effects during the postwar period. We may find similar instances of this transfiguration of music and sound in Ennio Morricone's scores for the "Dollars" trilogy, or even in Dmitri Tiomkin's score for *High Noon*. Nascimbene's *suoni nuovi*, however, represent a far more intentional and fully developed contestation of the border between sound and music.

Nascimbene generated the *suoni nuovi* by subjecting electronic tape recordings—oftentimes of orchestral instruments and other traditional sounds—to various kinds of manipulation. A striking example of this practice comes in the flagellation of Christ sequence that follows almost immediately after the opening credits (3:36ff.). The Christ theme is preceded by *suoni nuovi* that the composer describes in the following manner:

> In [the scene that depicts] the scourging of Christ, the frustation of the crowd mutates into a sonic timbre obtained by recording a wooden block scraping along the low strings of a piano. This recording is then reproduced at double speed and in reverse. A surreal wind—created by the pedals of the organ—and the haunting screams of the chorus complete the sonic framework ["il quadro sonoro"] from which rises, majestically, the fundamental theme of the movie inspired by Gregorian chant.[11]

In the music for this sequence, each phrase of the Gregorian theme is punctuated by a percussive sound that Nascimbene created by manipulating and recombining recordings of a cymbal and a gong. This combinatorial textural gesture will return at various points of the film, almost in the manner of a leitmotif. While the *suoni nuovi* bear some similarity to the sound/music combinations in other films, and although they might be prefigured by examples from Nascimbene's earlier film scores, they thus assume in *Barabbas* a new kind of structural importance.

That is not to say, of course, that the *suoni nuovi* stand apart from other currents in postwar music. They must be placed in a broader context that includes work in northern European centers such as London, Paris, and Darmstadt, the experimental magnetic tape compositions of Ussachevsky and Luening in the United States, and the work of composers such as Maderna and Berio at the Studio di Fonologia in Milan. And yet, as Maurizio Corbella points out, the environment for the development of electro-acoustic music in Rome was in several important ways distinct from that which obtained in other European centers. Making a direct comparison between Rome and Milan, Corbella describes how electro-acoustic music in the northern Italian city was fostered by a fortunate "convergence of interests" between the composers on one hand and the administrative apparatus of the Studio di Fonologia on the other. For Berio and Maderna, he continues, the compositional activity associated with the radio drama was a field of professional "compromise." Focusing on the contributions of the composer Gino Marinuzzi Jr. and the technician Paolo Ketoff, Corbella then turns his attention to Rome. "In Rome," he writes,

> the situation can be said to be reversed. Here it was the cinematic activity of Gino Marinuzzi Jr. (which began at the end of the forties) that dictated how and when experimental research took place (and who knows, maybe even generated the initial spark for its development). Paolo Ketoff developed his inventive genius within the conventions of film post-production, and landed in avant-garde circles only after amassing a wealth of practical experience. To put it more succinctly, in Milan composers glimpsed in the radio the ideal tool for their research, while in Rome it was the sonic requirements of the cinematic environment that provided fertile soil for the interdependent experimentation of a composer and a technician.[12]

Ketoff was a recording technician at the Fonolux studio for film sound at Cinecittà in Rome, which became during this period an important center not only for film production, but also for developments in electro-acoustic music per se. It was in the Fonolux studio that Nascimbene developed the *suoni nuovi* that were to be so central to the aesthetic of *Barabbas*. In order to facilitate his work in this area, Nascimbene developed a special machine that he called the "mixerama." In a 1986 interview with Claudio Fuiano, Nascimbene described the machine in the following manner:

> The "Mixerama" is an instrument which contains 12 stereo cassette tapes, so you can get 24 different sounds. I have more than 1,000 cassettes like that. I have recorded all the possible sounds the musicians in an orchestra can make, from the piccolo to the contrabass, male and female voices, the strings (now sharp, then soft, then trilling or pizzicato . . .) on all the notes of the musical scale.
>
> When I had all the sounds separately, I recorded the high and low ranges of every single note, and then recorded them separately onto the stereo cassette tapes. So in the end I had truly infinite possibilities of a mixture of sound. Each note had its own sound, but three or four used together change that sound. It's all pulsating, creative, "living" sound. Unlike modern computer keyboards, the "Mixerama" uses pure sound treated in a human way.[13]

Although the Mixerama was not—as far as I know—adopted by other film music composers, it was similar to machines such as the Mellotron and (more distantly) to the Fonosynth that Marinuzzi, Ketoff, and Giuliano Strini were developing in Rome during these same years. For my purposes here, its mechanical and technical properties are less important than the aesthetic purposes for which it was used. These aesthetic purposes are most clearly exemplified, perhaps, in the underscoring for the crucifixion sequence. Filmed during a total eclipse of the sun, this was the most famous scene from the movie. The sequence begins (13:24) inside of a tavern in which Barabbas and some villagers have been carousing. Barabbas has retired upstairs with his erstwhile lover Rachel (who has become a Christian), while in the main room of the tavern the innkeeper notices a strange darkness. The villagers cluster in the doorway, frightened by the unnatural appearance of the sky. The camera then cuts away to an image of Jesus on the cross: a shadowy silhouette against the nearly black sky, illuminated only by a thin rim of the sun.

Nascimbene's discussion of *Barabbas* in his autobiography shows the special importance that he attached to this scene:

> I spent days and days thinking about how I could put music to the sequence of the eclipse, one of the most important in the film. Finally the idea came to me: take out all the realistic effects and simply comment on the "psychological" tension of the moment. [I used] a dissonant D-sharp/E pedal performed by violins, with sopranos and altos an octave lower. A recording of the reverberation of a tom-tom played at half speed "cemented" the indecipherable and inexorable semitone. For the total eclipse, [I created] a chord consisting of piano, timpani, vibraphone, xylophone and bells played at half speed (i.e. an octave below the lowest sound of the orchestra, a sound that does not really exist in the traditional scale) in order to create an "almost unbearable" emotion.[14]

As this quotation indicates, the semitone dissonance functions as a pedal throughout the entire sequence (it is sustained for nearly five minutes of the film). As in the opening sequence, Nascimbene uses the unusually voiced chords to punctuate each phrase of this melody. Insofar as we may speak of such a thing, this must qualify as a virtuoso performance of tape manipulation and re-recording technique.

Underscoring Blindness

As striking as it is, Nascimbene's underscoring for the eclipse sequence clearly intersects with more broadly disseminated trends in the history of cinematic sound. The high-pitched dissonant pedal in the eclipse scene, for example, can be understood as a descendant of the electronic sounds (generated by the theremin and other instruments) that were frequently used to signify emotional distress in the psychological thrillers and film noirs of the 1940s. Electronically generated sounds were even more important in the science fiction films of the 1950s. Indeed, *Barabbas* was not even the first of the postwar biblical epics to use electro-acoustic sounds: the plague scenes of *The Ten Commandments* employ the theremin as a kind of indicator for supernatural menace. Despite the rhetoric that surrounds them, then, Nascimbene's *suoni nuovi* are not exactly revolutionary. What is remarkable about the underscoring is not so much the nature of the sounds per se, but rather the complex and multifaceted function that they play in the film. For the powerful image of Jesus on the cross is not—at least in narrative terms—the only focus of the sequence. After the camera lingers on the crucifixion itself, it cuts away to the upper balcony where we see Rachel awakening Barabbas. He is bewildered and befuddled, not merely by the strong wine that he has drunk, but also by the fact that he cannot see. What Nascimbene calls the "psychological tension of the moment," then, comes not only from the crucifixion itself, but also from the effect that it has on Barabbas.

Although it is impossible to know exactly why Nascimbene struggled "for days and days" to create appropriate underscoring for this scene, it seems likely that his difficulties had to do with the complex possibilities that the introduction of what I call the "blindness motif" opens up. In a general sense, the blindness of a cinematic character sharpens the perennial semantic questions that attend nondiegetic film music. Its prominence in scenes such as this one might reflect the heightened auditory awareness of the blind, or simply the emotional or physical pain of losing one's sight. In this sense, the underscoring might belong to the blinded character (in this case, Barabbas). But if this is the case, what is its connection to those images (such as the vision of the crucifixion) that the character cannot see? In the case of this particular scene, these semantic questions are mirrored by theological ambiguities. Like Saul on the road to Damascus, Barabbas is struck blind by the reality of Christ's presence: the scene can be understood simply as a reconfiguration of a traditional Christian narrative trope (one of many such reconfigurations in the film). Barabbas's blindness, like Saul's, is a sudden physical manifestation of spiritual ignorance. And yet the scene from the film departs from its biblical prototype in several key ways. In the account from the Acts of the Apostles, Saul experiences a blinding light, while in the film Barabbas becomes blind in the context of the eclipse, in other words, in the context of darkness. Indeed, Barabbas's blindness may be nothing more than a heightened response to this eclipse. In the Acts of the Apostles, moreover, Saul hears a supernatural voice, while in the film, Jesus never speaks directly to Barabbas—in fact, Jesus never speaks at all.

One way to interpret Nascimbene's underscoring for the scene, I would like to suggest, is as a replacement for this missing divine voice. In this respect, his music represents a twentieth-century redeployment of a very old musico-dramatic strategy, in which the transcendence of the spiritual voice is expressed though its ability to speak in a gamut of different ranges and textures. The string halo that accompanies the voice of Jesus in J. S. Bach's *St. Matthew Passion* is an example of such a musical texture, but the closest parallel is probably the opening of Heinrich Schütz's motet "Saul, was verfolgst du mich" (SWV 415). The fact that this motet depicts the blinding of Saul from the Acts of the Apostles makes it a particularly interesting analogue for the crucifixion scene from *Barabbas*. In this famous piece, Schütz imagines the voice of Jesus emerging from the depths of the vocal ambitus, then carried upward from the basses through the various vocal parts and eventually into the violins. The divine voice, we might say, transcends the border between vocal and instrumental music. In a similar manner, and even more extensively than in the passages from *Roma ore 11* and *The Barefoot Contessa* to which I referred above, Nascimbene's treatment of the dissonant pedal challenges distinctions between sound and music. Like the opening of "Saul, was verfolgst du mich," then, the *suoni nuovi* of the crucifixion sequence suggest the supernatural through what Nascimbene calls their "indecipherable" texture.

What makes the underscoring for the crucifixion sequence so meaningful, however, is not simply the textural qualities of the *suoni nuovi*, but also the ways in which Nascimbene juxtaposes these new sounds with the quasi-Gregorian Christ theme: music that we might think of as an example of *suoni antichi* (Nascimbene himself never uses this term). The meaning of the music, in other words, comes from the ways in which the *suoni nuovi* and the *suoni antichi* contextualize each other. The "indecipherable" and relentlessly insistent tape sounds, I would argue, partially uproot the Christ theme from its sedimented discourses, so that it is no longer simply a marker of medievalism or of Christianity. In this new context, the theme also begins to suggest the unknowable or perhaps uncanny realm of the supernatural. The dissonant pedal, of course, is associated with the psychic and perhaps even physical pain that Barabbas feels while witnessing the crucifixion. But when it is placed alongside and around the Christ theme, it might also begin to acquire new kinds of meanings. It might, for instance, suggest the light of spiritual regeneration that Barabbas is unable or unwilling to see, or perhaps even an angelic presence. The diverse elements of the soundscape, we might say, enter into a kind of open-ended dialogue with one another, from which new meanings are continually spinning out.

New Semantics, or Simply New Sounds?

Nascimbene's description of his compositional process in the passage from his autobiography that I quoted above draws our attention to another aspect of the underscoring for the crucifixion sequence: namely, the question of how his underscoring should correspond to the screen action. His statement about finding the way out of his compositional impasse by "[taking] out all the realistic effects and simply comment[ing] on the 'psychological' tension of the moment" resonates with other more general remarks that he made concerning the *Barabbas* score. "In *Barabbas*," he writes, "the music never comments on the action on the screen, but seeks only to create atmosphere. It does not, therefore, follow the psychological movements of the characters or events, but only paints the background."[15] The distinction between underscoring that comments directly on the action or the psychological development of the characters and that which "only paints the background" goes back to the era of silent film, and it was a central topic in the discourse surrounding the development of sound film in the 1930s, when composers were working to articulate different approaches to scoring. In this particular context, however, it seems that Nascimbene was positioning his practice in *Barabbas* in opposition to a particular aspect of the epic style: distinguishing his work not only against the "large orchestras, seas of stringed instruments, [and] dramatic drum rolls" of the epic films, but also against the musical semantics of these films. What stands unnamed behind his description of music that "comments on the action" and "follow[s] the psychological movements of the characters or events" is the leitmotivic practice that typifies so many of the biblical epic scores and that reaches its apogee in the music for *Ben-Hur*. The "decidedly modern" soundscape for *Barabbas*, Nascimbene implies, would not simply be created with "new sounds." It would also operate according to a new semantic logic.

It is easy to see this semantic logic at work in the crucifixion sequence that I described above. The Christ theme does not undergo any kind of leitmotivic transformation or development; the underscoring responds neither to the movement of the camera nor to the emotional responses of the characters. In other sections of the film, however, the distance between Nascimbene's underscoring and the old musical semantics of films such as *The Ten Commandments* or *Ben-Hur* is not as clear. In order to probe the semantic logic of the *Barabbas* score more deeply, I would like to turn to the sulfur mine sequence that constitutes what we might call the second act of the film (beginning at 50:51). Even after being providentially delivered from execution, and in spite of the witness of his lover Rachel, Barabbas soon returns to his life of crime. He is eventually apprehended by Roman soldiers and sentenced to spend the rest of his life toiling in the sulfur mines of Sicily as a slave of the emperor. The famous sulfur mine sequence—which narrates Barabbas's many years of toil—begins at the entrance to this infernal world. The slaves are led before the Roman authorities, who assign them numbers in place of their names and chain them together in pairs (presumably in order to hamper escape). Like Dante's *Inferno*, the remainder of the sulfur mine sequence is structured as an articulated descent. As Barabbas moves deeper and deeper into the mine, he learns more about his condition. A fellow slave on one of the upper levels tells Barabbas how the workers are moved through the mine. "They're sending us down to the next level to make room for you," he tells Barabbas. "That's how you know how long you've been here: by how deep you're down. They break you and they drag you 'til you get used to the dark." Each level of the mine, we presume, is darker than the one above it, requiring a gradual process of ocular and/or emotional adjustment. On one of these lower levels, Barabbas learns of a terrifying physical transformation that (at least potentially) accompanies this process. Dust from the sulfur ore—he learns from a blind elderly slave—eventually causes blindness. On a metaphorical level, therefore, the sulfur mine sequence recapitulates the motifs of darkness and blindness that inform the crucifixion scene.

The association between these two scenes is reinforced by certain elements of Nascimbene's underscoring. If—in narrative terms—the sulfur mine sequence represents a reconfiguration of the themes of blindness, faith, and suffering first presented in the crucifixion scene, so too might we understand Nascimbene's soundscape for the sulfur mine as a rearrangement of the various elements that he used to score the earlier scene. Like the events of the crucifixion sequence, Barabbas's descent through the levels of the mine is accompanied by an un-settling amalgam of the *suoni nuovi* and the Christ theme. But although Nascimbene uses a similar compositional approach for both of these scenes, the end result is quite different. Instead of the chord that punctuates the phrases of the Christ theme in the crucifixion sequence (the mix of piano, timpani, vibraphone, xylophone, and bells played at half speed), Nascimbene creates a new mix of timpani and various other percussion instruments: a combination that seems to echo the diegetic sounds of chisel and hammer that recur throughout the scene. For the first part of the sulfur mine sequence, Nascimbene uses only the first five or occasionally six notes of the Christ theme. It appears here not in unison or parallel octaves (as it does in the crucifixion sequence), but rather in parallel major sevenths, as a kind of dissonant organum. As Barabbas moves further down into the mine, Nascimbene presents this organum at lower and lower pitch levels, re-flecting a basic semantic association between pitch level and physical space. At various points (e.g., the moment in which Barabbas meets the blind elderly slave), Nascimbene inserts dissonant stinger chords in order to punctuate the drama. It is hard not to understand these gestures—at least to some extent—as a rever-sion to the old semantics of the earlier epics. On the other hand, the sulfur mine sequence contains many scenes in which the underscoring procedure—and not simply the quality of the sounds that Nascimbene uses—seems to depart radi-cally from earlier practices. Indeed, much of the second part of the sulfur mine sequence, in which he meets the fellow slave Sahak and reveals his identity to him, unfolds without any musical underscoring: something that would be hard to imagine in a film such as *Ben-Hur.*

Efforts to pin down the new semantics of *Barabbas,* then, are stymied by the fact that the distinction between music that comments on the screen action and underscoring that "seeks only to create atmosphere" is not as clear as the com-poser implies. We might, for example, understand the Christ theme in the man-ner (more or less) of a conventional leitmotif, as an indication that Christ's re-demptive power abides even in the infernal depths of the mine. It is here, after all, at the very limits of human endurance, that Barabbas meets Sahak. Sahak is a Christian, and he functions in the succeeding scenes as an antipode or shadow to Barabbas. Barabbas does not know how or why he is repeatedly saved from death; he is simply carried forward by the momentum of life. Sahak's faith, by contrast, gives meaning to his suffering. When Barabbas saves Sahak from the collapse of the mine, the dissonant Christ theme reappears, the downward trajectory of its tonal motion now reversed. In this reading, Nascimbene's Christ theme appears—in semantic if not in purely musical terms—as a relative of the theme of God that Elmer Bernstein weaves through *The Ten Commandments,* or even of the shimmering chords through which Rózsa suggests the presence of Christ in his score to *Ben-Hur.* Conversely, we might hear the distinct amalgam of *suoni nuovi,* dissonant organum, and hyperamplified sound effects simply as a reflection of the unique atmosphere of the infernal mine. Ultimately, these two interpretations coexist in dialogue with one another. To put this another way, the semantics of the score are a kind of mirror of its construction: a provocative juxtaposition of the old and the new.

Barabbas and the Question of Faith

After the spectacular collapse of the sulfur mine, Barabbas and Sahak are eventually sent to Rome to serve in the arena as gladiators. In the *Barabbas* screenplay, the Coliseum is dominated by the merciless Torvald (played with wicked abandon by Jack Palance). This character, it should be noted, does not appear in Lagerqvist's novel, and the gladiatorial scenes seem in many ways to be extraneous to the plot. In stylistic terms, they bring the film closer to earlier epics such as *Quo Vadis* and *Ben-Hur,* in which arena conflicts also play a prominent role. For these scenes, then, the scriptwriters seem to have abandoned the existentialist austerity of their source material for the more conventional aesthetics of spectacle that were so central to the biblical epic style. Nascimbene seems to have responded to these more conventional aesthetics by providing the most stylistically conservative music of his score. The sequence in which Barabbas and Sahak are led into the Eternal City (beginning at 1:20:20) is accompanied by one of the longest musical cues in the film, an expansive treatment of Roman fanfare motive heard at the beginning of the movie (see Example 8.1). Unlike the scene in which Pontius Pilate passes judgment, however, the fanfare music appears here without the addition of any *suoni nuovi.* With conspicuous trumpets and full percussion, Nascimbene's music is not dissimilar to the triumphal marches that figure so prominently in *Quo Vadis* or *Ben-Hur.* As in these films, the music acts to underscore (both literally and figuratively) the irony of the scene.

The gladiatorial scenes that follow the entrance into Rome are accompanied only by the diegetic versions of the fanfare motive to which I referred above. It is only in the final scenes of the film that Nascimbene's underscoring once again becomes important. After an encounter in the catacombs with a group of Christians, Barabbas experiences a kind of provisional or incomplete conversion, fraught with anxiety and confusion. Lost amid the underground passages, he calls out for guidance and help. He emerges from the secret underground chambers in order to find Rome ablaze. As in the sulfur mine sequence, diegetic sounds (in this case, the tumult of the crowd and the sound of the fire itself) are blended together with *suoni nuovi* in order to create a psychologically disturb-

Figure 8.1. Barabbas on the cross. From the core collection production files of the Margaret Herrick Library, Academy of Motion Picture Arts and Sciences.

ing soundscape. A close-up of the fire itself is accompanied by a distorted brass fanfare, recalling the music that since the earliest scenes in the film has been associated with the imperial power. Men and women are fleeing the flames, and from them Barabbas hears that the Christians are burning Rome. "They're burning away the old world," Barabbas says to himself. "The new kingdom is coming. God, you won't find me failing this time." Barabbas then picks up a torch, believing that by helping to spread the fire, he will hasten the coming of the Kingdom of God. As he does so, the Christ theme appears in the underscoring, tinged (as in the sulfur mine sequence) by dissonance and punctuated with the brass chords of the Roman fanfare motive and another of those bell-like *suoni nuovi* that are so prominent in Nascimbene's score. The Christ theme ends abruptly when Barabbas is arrested for helping to spread the flames. The centurions ask him if he is a Christian, and Barabbas proudly proclaims that he is.

Insofar as we accept the Christ theme as a kind of leitmotif, Nascimbene's underscoring for the catacombs scenes and the burning of Rome sequence appears deeply ironic. When Barabbas is literally and figuratively searching for a way out of the darkness of the catacombs, the theme is significantly absent. It appears only when Barabbas becomes an arsonist: its dissonant harmonization suggesting, perhaps, the tragic way in which Barabbas misunderstands the Christian message. When he finally proclaims his faith (an archetypical Christian act), the theme is silenced once more. Understood in terms of conventional (that is to say, leitmotivic) musical semantics, then, the treatment of the Christ theme in these sequences might be seen as a reflection of Barabbas's modern condition. For Barabbas—as perhaps for an important portion of the film's audience—Christ is perpetually just out of reach, suggesting significance without providing clear meaning. The underscoring for these sequences, in short, helps to frame Barabbas's actions (to quote De Laurentiis once again) as those of a "creature of fantasy who epitomizes the doubts and torments of modern man."

It is only after proclaiming himself to be a Christian that Barabbas becomes susceptible to death. After being apprehended by the Roman centurions, Barabbas is—ironically—condemned to suffer the same fate as the very one he has for so much of the filmic narrative so continually disavowed. If in the crucifix scene, Barabbas symbolically occupies the position of the blinded Saul, then in the final scene of the film he takes up Christ's own place on the cross (see Figure 8.1).

Like the blindness that afflicts our anti-hero during the eclipse sequence, Barabbas's penultimate words—"Darkness, I give myself into your keeping"—are a reconfiguration of New Testament narrative. They allude, of course, to Christ's own final words as recounted in Luke 23:46: "Father, into Thy hands I commend my spirit." In the screenplay, as in the novel upon which it is based, these words seem to confirm the existential doubt that informs the entire story. In terms of sentence syntax, "darkness" in Barabbas's statement replaces "Father" in the last words of Christ, suggesting an analogous metaphysical substitution of emptiness in place of an omnipotent God. But the addition of the underscoring opens up different possibilities. The recapitulation of the Christ theme, and in particular its final appearance as a trumpet melody that ends with a Picardy third, puts forward at least the possibility of an alternate interpretation of the scene, in which Barabbas's suffering and death constitute a final act of conversion to the true faith.

Nascimbene may have been under pressure to provide this kind of underscoring for the final moments of the film, of course, but from the perspective of the early twenty-first century, it might seem as if he was simply losing the courage of his convictions. There are no "seas of string instruments playing *cantabile e tanto melodico*," to be sure, but the heavenly choir is certainly present, and the final trumpet passage sounds suspiciously like the "inevitable brass fanfares" that the composer mocked in the passage that I quoted above. It is certainly possible to understand this final music as a retreat into the more traditional aesthetic of the earlier biblical epics: a retreat into the techniques of Rózsa or Elmer Bernstein. Even in the 1960s, we might say, it was still impossible *not* to end a biblical epic with a major chord. On a broader level, we might understand the gesture as an ideological retreat: from the existential alienation that figures so strongly in the Lagerqvist novel into what Ellwood might call "Fifties-style" American Christianity, in which Jesus' salvific power inevitably triumphs over all adversity. But I prefer a more generous interpretation, which seeks to understand the entire score—including this final gesture—as a reflection of a transformative historical moment, a moment in which faith and doubt were intersecting in extraordinary ways. In a still larger sense, Nascimbene's achievement in *Barabbas* may remind us of the beauty and meaning that comes from cultural forms even in—or perhaps only in—their stages of decline and disintegration.

9 Universality, Transcendence, and Collapse

Music and *The Greatest Story Ever Told*

In the new economy of the blockbuster that began to emerge in the postwar period, Hollywood studios needed to transform the premieres of their big-budget films into high-visibility cultural events. Among the many strategies that they employed along these lines was to publish books or pamphlets in conjunction with these blockbuster premieres. Noerdlinger's *Moses in Egypt*—to which I referred in chapter 5—is a somewhat anomalous example of this kind of work. More typical is a promotional book by Ray Freiman that was designed to accompany the premiere of *Ben-Hur*.[1] Unsurprisingly, the bulk of the book is dedicated to high-impact images. At the end of the book, for instance, are a series of color prints—reproductions of oil paintings depicting various scenes from *Ben-Hur*—that may be carefully torn out along conveniently placed perforated seams (the text informs us that these prints are suitable for framing). The book also includes profiles of the stars, as well as brief essays that discuss various elements of the film such as costumes, sets, and music. The emphasis in all these essays is on size, splendor, and magnificence. The promotional book for *Ben-Hur,* in short, documents and exemplifies the aesthetics of the superlative that was such an important part of the biblical epic genre.

The 1965 premiere of George Stevens's *The Greatest Story Ever Told* was accompanied by the publication of a book that was—at least in functional terms—similar to that which Freiman produced for *Ben-Hur*.[2] Like the promotional booklet for *Ben-Hur,* this book was clearly designed to stimulate interest in the film. Its content, however, was strikingly different. The *Ben-Hur* booklet focuses on the various components of the film (e.g., the stars, the set, the costumes). But the book for *The Greatest Story Ever Told* mentions none of these things. Instead, its focus is on the figure of Christ himself. The first image in the book is a still from the film, in which an enormous crowd is reaching their hands longingly toward Jesus (who at this point is offscreen). The next page of the book—containing an image of Christ on the cross—is translucent, so that the text on the following page can also be seen:

"My God, my God, why hast thou forsaken Me?" It is towards this climactic cross-roads the story of Jesus of Nazareth leads, and to which, at the final moment, it again looks back in triumphant retrospect. It is the anguishing crossroads where the eternal questions of faith and doubt become resolved.

Indeed, it is only in the final paragraph of the strikingly minimal text for this book that the film itself is mentioned. In contrast to the *Ben-Hur* booklet, there is no discussion of film production, no information about the size of the sets or the number of scholarly articles that researchers might have consulted in order to prepare its script. Instead, the text focuses on the aesthetic and spiritual effects that the film is intended to produce. "The film," it notes,

> and the portrait achieved by the represented Christ, do not so much attempt to an-swer Pilate's question "What is truth?" as to intensify each individual's desire to discover that answer for himself within his own experience, past and future. . . . The film moves to excite the imagination of the audience by rendering before it the beauty and the extraordinary nature of Him who represents many things, and one thing. To recall, or is it to challenge, one's own image of Christ—an image derived from a word, a panel of stained glass, a Gothic-lettered Christmas card, a burst of organ music, an inner exaltation, an experience. And to come as visually close as possible to giving that sense of Jesus' passage on earth as it is within the power of any medium—the word, the painting, or the film—to convey.

The rhetorical ambivalence of this text ("do not . . . attempt to answer Pi-late's question 'What is truth?'"; "to recall, or is it to challenge, one's own im-age of Christ") might be understood in terms of the spiritual awakening of the 1960s and the increasing complexity of American religious life during this pe-riod that I referenced in the preceding chapter. And yet the text still clings to the possibility of verisimilitude. It aims to come as "close as possible to giving a sense of Jesus' passage on earth" even while recognizing that Jesus represents many things. The text (and perhaps the film that it describes) thus seems to disavow in-terpretation even while clinging fast to meaning. In this sense, the text suggests the central aesthetic conundrum of the film. Like most of the other postwar bib-lical epics that I have discussed, *The Greatest Story Ever Told* was intended to be a blockbuster. Theological controversy had no place in this arena. The spiritual values that these films articulated needed to be centrist generalizations—e.g., "the triumph of freedom"; "the return to traditional values"—to which a majority of potential audience members could subscribe. But as the postwar religious con-sensus broke down, it became more and more difficult to make a non-controver-sial biblical film: particularly one that focused on the life of Jesus.

What is surely the most notable (or notorious) feature of this film, namely, its inordinate length, can be understood as a response to this challenge. Clinging to the idea that the film should be as close as possible to representing Jesus' pas-sage on earth, the script contains nearly all of the material in all four of the Gos-pels. In addition, other familiar scriptural passages are woven into the script.

When the Holy Family is in Egypt, for instance, Joseph reads the prophetic passage from Isaiah: "For unto us a child is born." The prophetic passages from Isaiah also form the bulk of John the Baptist's excoriations in the scenes that precede (and in a certain sense overlap with) the temptation sequence analogous to the one that I referenced in chapter 7. Jesus is even given familiar words from some of Paul's letters, so that the screenplay comes to resemble a compendium of familiar scriptural quotations. What we might call the universalism of the script seems designed—at least in part—to represent a Christ who could be "many things, and one thing." Following this logic, we could say that to pare down the Gospel narrative is already to interpret it; including everything, by contrast, obviates the need to decide what to take out and what to leave in.

Yet to understand the bloated screenplay as nothing but an attempt to recapture a rapidly disintegrating sense of theological consensus would be to neglect an even more important aspect of what we might call its universalist agenda. The expansiveness of the script was not just an effort to be all things to all people. It was also an extension of the aesthetics of the superlative that played such an important role in the development of the genre, an approach that I have already discussed in previous chapters of this book. For *Quo Vadis*, this aesthetic impulse manifested itself—among other places—in the verisimilitude of its sets and costumes, and in the supposed authenticity of Rózsa's diegetic music. The aesthetics of the superlative are even more predominant in *The Ten Commandments,* driven as they were by the outsized personality of Cecil B. DeMille. In *The Greatest Story Ever Told,* these aesthetics take on a different cast. While the film certainly contains its share of magnificent cinematography, it eschews the kind of spectacular set pieces that were such an important staple of the postwar biblical epic. There is no triumphal entry into Rome; there is no chariot race or sea battle with Macedonian pirates; no miraculous parting of the Red Sea. Instead, it is through the all-encompassing, universal nature of the narrative itself that *The Greatest Story Ever Told* attempts to live up to the superlatives of its title.

Indeed, the universalist agenda of *The Greatest Story Ever Told* extends beyond the screenplay into other aspects of the film. Its most famous manifestation, perhaps, is in the film's cast list, which reads almost like a roster of Hollywood's most famous actors. In addition to Max von Sydow in the title role, the film features Charlton Heston as John the Baptist, Claude Rains as Herod, José Ferrer as Herod Antipas, and Telly Savalas as Pontius Pilate. Famous personalities such as Pat Boone and John Wayne also make brief cameo appearances (as the Angel at the Tomb and the Centurion, respectively). More interesting are the ways in which the film assimilates certain iconic images and symbols from other art forms and other cinematic genres. The resonance between the biblical epic and the western that characterizes certain scenes from *The Ten Commandments*—to take the most obvious example of this kind of assimilation—becomes far more direct in the cinematography of *The Greatest Story Ever Told*. Much of the film was shot in the vicinity of Page, Arizona, during the construction of the Glen

Figure 9.1. The Last Supper scene in *The Greatest Story Ever Told*. From the core collection production files of the Margaret Herrick Library, Academy of Motion Picture Arts and Sciences.

Canyon Dam, with the Colorado River standing in for the River Jordan. Pyramid Lake in northwestern Nevada represents the Sea of Galilee. Indeed, in its treatment of these spectacular western landscapes (if not, obviously, of the robed and sandaled characters), *The Greatest Story Ever Told* appears almost as a capstone, not of the postwar biblical epic, but rather of a cinematic tradition that stretches back through Stevens's own westerns to those of John Ford and other directors. Stevens also selectively appropriates images of Christ from the history of visual arts. In the opening scene of the film, for example, the camera pans down an interior of a church cupola until it rests on what seems to be a Renaissance fresco of the risen Christ, only with the face of Max von Sydow. An even clearer example of this kind of appropriation appears in the Last Supper scene from *The Greatest Story Ever Told* (2:25:06). Unlike the analogous sequence from *King of Kings* that I discussed in chapter 7, Stevens's staging of this scene is a clear reference to da Vinci's famous painting (see Figure 9.1). If the introduction of famous actors and actresses in minor roles and the long shots of buttes and mesas that seem to reference specific scenes from previous films help to establish *The Greatest Story Ever Told* as a kind of *omnium gatherum* of Hollywood, so too does the incorporation of these images buttress the universalist stance of the film vís-à-vís the Western art historical tradition.

Allusions to these iconic images from the art historical tradition and to the cinematography of the western find an analogue in what is surely the most famous (or infamous) aspect of the musical score, namely, the use of the "Hallelujah Chorus" (from Handel's *Messiah*) and the first twenty-seven bars of Verdi's *Requiem* to underscore certain key scenes from *The Greatest Story Ever Told*. The process whereby these selections were eventually incorporated into the final cut of the film has been extensively documented by Ken Darby in his book *Hollywood Holyland*.[3] Darby was a longtime friend of Alfred Newman and was hired by Stevens to serve as assistant conductor, arranger, and general musical ombudsman for the film. In Darby's view—which was shared by Newman himself and subsequently by most critics of the film—the incorporation of these canonical works into the underscoring of the film was an aesthetic disaster. Reading his account of the process whereby the music for the film was assembled, therefore, is a bit like watching a train wreck unfold in slow motion. Darby's work is conditioned by his deep admiration for Newman both as a musician and as a human being, and he makes no claims to objectivity or impartiality. According to Darby, Newman's masterful score is wrecked primarily because Stevens was swayed by the opinions of associate producer Tony Vellani. In the pages of Darby's book, Vellani appears as a superficial poseur who knows almost nothing about the complex art of film scoring. Newman, on the other hand, emerges as a kind of tragic hero, whose creativity and genius is ultimately disregarded.

Darby's book is an invaluable resource for understanding the music for *The Greatest Story Ever Told*, but his purposes are different from mine. Although I share Darby's deep admiration for Newman's work, I want to understand the incorporation of the "Hallelujah Chorus" and the opening bars of Verdi's *Requiem* into the score of *The Greatest Story Ever Told* as more than simply a marring of Newman's original concepts. Instead, I seek to examine this gesture—and other aspects of the score as well—in terms of the film's broader universalist aesthetic. Two contexts are essential for such an examination. The first has to do with film scoring generally: with the long and complex tradition of quotation, borrowing, and allusion that has been so central to its history. The second context is more specific to the postwar biblical epic (although it is by no means limited to this genre), and has to do with the quest for music appropriate to cinematic gestures of transcendence. The collapse of the biblical epic soundscape—insofar as we may speak of such a thing—occurs in the space in which these two contexts overlap.

Using Preexisting Music

For many decades, scholars have been engaged with the question of how film scoring engages preexisting music, and the bibliography on this topic is far too extensive to discuss here in any detail. Instead, I begin with a well-known theoretical frame for this topic presented by Anahid Kassabian in her 2001 book *Hearing Film*. "There are two main approaches to film music," she writes, the composed score, a body of musical material composed specifically for the film in question; and the compiled score, a score built of songs that often (but not always) preexisted the film. Composed scores, most often associated with classical Hollywood scoring traditions, condition what I call *assimilating identifications.* Such paths are structured to draw perceivers into socially and historically unfamiliar positions, as do larger scale processes of assimilation.[4]

The compiled score, in Kassabian's view, operates quite differently. With the compiled score, she continues, perceivers

bring external associations with the songs into their engagements with the film. A score that offers assimilating identifications is much harder to construct from such songs. More often, compiled scores offer what I call *affiliating identifications,* and they operate quite differently from composed scores. These ties depend on histories forged outside the film scene, and they allow for a fair bit of mobility within it. If offers of assimilating identifications try to narrow the psychic field, then offers of affiliating identifications open it wide.[5]

As she herself states, Kassabian's primary interest is in the film music from the 1980s and 1990s. When she speaks of the compiled score in this context, what she has in mind are films such as *The Big Chill* (1983) and *American Graffiti* (1973), in which the sound track is constructed from popular music. The compiled scores of these films do indeed derive much of their meaning from "histories forged outside the film scene," and while this music may not exactly open wide the "psychic field" of cinematic meaning, it may suggest multiple semantic pathways. With regard to genres such as the biblical epic, however, her ideas are less useful.

There are two interpenetrating issues that limit the broader applicability of Kassabian's framework. The first of these has to do with the clarity of the opposition between composed and compiled scores. In the passages quoted above, Kassabian implies a clear distinction between these two approaches. When she discusses concrete examples from specific scores, however, Kassabian treats this distinction in a more flexible manner. On one hand, she acknowledges that the practice of using preexisting music in a film score entails a certain degree of intervention. At the very least, music supervisors or sound designers must decide how to insert the preexisting music; in many cases the manipulation of the source material is a great deal more extensive. The process of using preexisting music, then, is at least in some sense compositional. On the other hand, she also recognizes that "all music refers to other music": that newly composed film scores are operating within a framework established by music outside of the specific movie for which they are intended. [6]

The second issue has to do with the associations between the composed score and assimilating identifications on one hand, and the compiled score and affiliating identifications on the other. These associations might help to clarify the ways in which the popular music of scores such as *American Graffiti* and *The Big Chill* are distinguished from those for other films, but when applied to the scores of films such as the biblical epics that I have examined in this book, they are much less useful. In *American Graffiti* and *The Big Chill*, the preexisting music generates affiliating identifications because audiences presumably recognize the individual songs from which the score is constructed. As we have seen, the scores for the biblical epics—especially Rózsa's music for *Quo Vadis*—also include a certain amount of preexisting music. Little if any of this music, however, would be recognized as such by audience members of the 1950s. Obviously, it is audience perception, and not the fact that a score might use preexisting music, that potentially generates affiliating identifications. When this kind of music is used in the biblical epics, moreover, its purpose is frequently quite different. The Yemenite chant in *King of Kings* or the Ambrosian hymn in *Quo Vadis,* to cite two specific examples, serve primarily to "draw perceivers into socially and historically unfamiliar positions." Inverting Kassabian's associations, we could say that they generate assimilating (and not affiliating) identifications. Approaching the relationship between audience identification and the use of preexisting music from a different angle, it is also clear that composed music is continually referencing music from outside the filmic diegesis, or—to use Kassabian's terms—that it is at least to some extent generating affiliating identifications. Indeed, it is difficult to understand how a film score might carry meaning if it did not at least on some level reference other music.

These references, needless to say, take a wide variety of different forms and possess very different degrees of specificity. Within the genre of the biblical epic, it is perhaps only the selections from the "Hallelujah Chorus" and from Verdi's *Requiem* that Stevens inserted into *The Greatest Story Ever Told* that would meet Kassabian's definition of the compiled score. Like the popular songs that form the sound track to *The Big Chill*, these selections had a clear identity independent from their use in the film; the audience would be expected to recognize them as coming from somewhere else. Although the Yemenite chant from *King of Kings* is also—at least to some degree—a quotation from a preexisting source, it is less easily recognizable as such. The audience might be expected to hear this music as a general reference to authentic and/or ancient monophonic Hebrew liturgical song, but only a specialist would be able to identify its specific source. In opposition to these clear examples of musical borrowing is newly composed music whose frame of reference is primarily other parts of the score. But even this music—needless to say—does not operate in a semiotic vacuum. I have, for example, already discussed ways in which the themes for the foreign woman of the two-woman plot archetype belong to a particular topos, one that also includes music for other cinematic (and operatic) femmes fatales. The Roman marches that appear with such frequency in the biblical epics constitute another such category. The associations formed by these kinds of relationships are general rather than specific, and operate on a less conscious level than (for example) those formed by the excerpt from the "Hallelujah Chorus" quoted in *The Greatest Story Ever Told*. But even if they do not generate affiliating identifications—at least in the stricter sense in which Kassabian applies the term—they nevertheless suggest other points of reference (or even specific works) that are external to the film. At least with regard to the biblical epic scores, then, we must modify Kassabian's theoretical framework. The paired dichotomies of her system must be replaced by a messy continuum between compilation and original composition: a continuum to which the notions of affiliation and assimilation might apply in complex and perhaps even contradictory sorts of ways.

Of particular interest with regard to the score for *The Greatest Story Ever Told* is music whose level of referential specificity lies somewhere in the middle of this continuum, that is to say, somewhere in between quotation and participation in a general musical topos. Such music, of course, has been an important part of film since before the advent of synchronized sound in film. The various compendia of photoplay music designed for the accompaniment of films during this period contain numerous examples of what we might call compositional paraphrases of well-known works. In his *Motion Picture Moods,* to take just one example, Erno Rapée includes a G-minor "Agitato #3" by Otto Langey that spins out the triplet figuration and choral structure from the introduction to Schubert's famous "Erlkönig" into a piece "suitable for gruesome or infernal scenes, witches, etc."[7] Closer to the topic at hand are numerous examples from the other postwar biblical epic scores. We might place the *Rheingold* reference from the first part of *The Ten Commandments* in this intermediate category, alongside the paraphrase of "Victimae paschali laudes" that Rózsa uses for the Mary theme in *King of Kings,* or (although with considerably less confidence) the music that he wrote for the nativity scenes in *Ben-Hur* and *King of Kings.* As I noted in chapters 2 and 4, Newman also made extensive use of this paraphrase technique in his biblical epic scores. The monophonic tune that accompanies the Twenty-third Psalm in *David and Bathsheba*—to take one example—is not copied from any specific exemplar, but it seems nevertheless to evoke something of ancient Israel. In a similar manner, Miriam's song from *The Robe* manages to reference early Christian monophony without quoting directly from any ancient source.[8] In chapter 4, I spoke in some detail about the ways in which the title theme of *The Robe* evokes similar kinds of harmonic progressions in Verdi's *Don Carlos,* Meyerbeer's *Les Huguenots,* and Dvořák's *New World* Symphony. The score for *The Greatest Story Ever Told* contains numerous examples of this kind of technique, analogues of the music from *David and Bathsheba* and *The Robe* in which we might see Newman's mastery of the intermediate level of musical reference in full flower. But it also contains other examples—most notably, the quotations from Handel and Verdi that I referenced above—which show a loss of faith in the power of this technique, a loss of faith that suggests a more general crisis in the musical semantics of the biblical epic genre.

Newman and the "Intermediate Level" of Musical Reference

One of the many ways in which Newman's procedure in *The Greatest Story Ever Told* resembles his work for *The Robe* is the function of the title theme in the two respective films. In *The Robe*—as I discussed in chapter 4—the title theme is associated not simply with a physical object (i.e., the homespun Galilean robe that Jesus wore), but with a whole range of different dramatic situations. The title theme for *The Greatest Story Ever Told* has a similar kind of semantic breadth. In some respects, it functions like a Jesus theme—denoting the presence of the main character. But it appears in many other contexts as well: in the Egyptian scenes near the beginning (17:40ff.), for example, or in the scenes with Mary and Martha at the house of Lazarus (1:41:24). In each of the films, then, the title theme provides a kind of musico-semantic center of gravity.

The functional similarity is to some extent mirrored by certain musical resemblances between the two themes (see Example 9.1). For each, Newman employs a transformative harmonic language, using chromatic voice leading to move freely between distantly related chords. With regard to *The Greatest Story Ever Told* I would like to suggest an allusion similar to that of the title theme for *The Robe* in its aforementioned evocation of *Don Carlos, Les Huguenots,* and the *New World* Symphony, albeit of another piece: namely, Samuel Barber's *Adagio for Strings.* Adapted from the second movement of his String Quartet in B minor, Op. 11, the piece had its radio premiere under the baton of Arturo Toscanini in 1938. Although Thomas Larson's characterization of the *Adagio* as an "icon of American grief" may be an overstatement, the piece clearly had (and continues to have) powerful resonance in American culture.[9] This resonance climaxed in the period of national mourning that followed the assassination of President Kennedy in November 1963. Unlike the similarities between the title theme for *The Robe* and its nineteenth-century referents, those between Newman's title theme for *The Greatest Story Ever Told* and Barber's *Adagio* have less to do with harmony than with texture and the character of the melodic lines. Apart from the obvious fact that both themes are played *legato* and at a slow tempo, each features a melody that moves up and down primarily in stepwise motion. Each, moreover, features a kind of dialogue between melody and countermelody, a dialogue that helps to generate a sense of rising tension.

As with the title theme for *The Robe,* we cannot speak here of quotation or even paraphrase, nor am I suggesting that Newman's allusion to Barber's *Adagio* was intentional or even conscious. But when Newman was casting about for the means to express the serious reverence that the title theme for Stevens's film required, it seems likely that his imagination would turn to music of similar character that was so predominant in the public sphere during the time in which he was engaged in composition. Similarly, the audience for the film did not need to decode the resemblance between Newman's title music and Barber's *Adagio* in order for this resemblance to evoke a powerful emotional response.

Example 9.1. Title theme to *The Greatest Story Ever Told*.

Another example of the intermediate level of musical reference—and one that may have been more evident to audiences from the 1960s—occurs in a scene near the beginning of the second half of the film (2:03:38ff.) that recounts the so-called anointing of Jesus. Versions of this scene appear in each of the four Gospels, but Stevens's interpretation is clearly based on John 12:3–8.[10] John's Gospel tells how Jesus was at supper in Bethany with Mary Magdalene, Martha, Lazarus, and some (or perhaps all) of the disciples, when Mary anointed Jesus' feet with a pound of costly perfume. When she was finished, she wiped Jesus' feet with her hair, "and the house was filled with the fragrance of the ointment."[11] Judas objects to the expense, noting that the perfume could have been sold and the proceeds used to feed the poor. Jesus defends Mary. "The poor," he says to Judas, "you always have with you, but you do not always have me."[12] Stevens sets this scene in a small fire-lit room, half-darkened by slatted shades. On the sound track we hear Newman's setting of Psalm 136: a monophonic chant sung by a small group of men (see Example 9.2). In most ways, this music is quite similar to the song that Miriam sings in *The Robe*. Both melodies feature a large amount of stepwise motion, and in both instances Newman combines short melismas with mostly syllabic text declamation (perhaps in imitation of what chant scholars sometimes call "neumatic" text setting). Although neither Miriam's song nor the setting of Psalm 136 quotes a preexisting source, each clearly references the styles of ancient religious monophony.

Universality, Transcendence, and Collapse 219

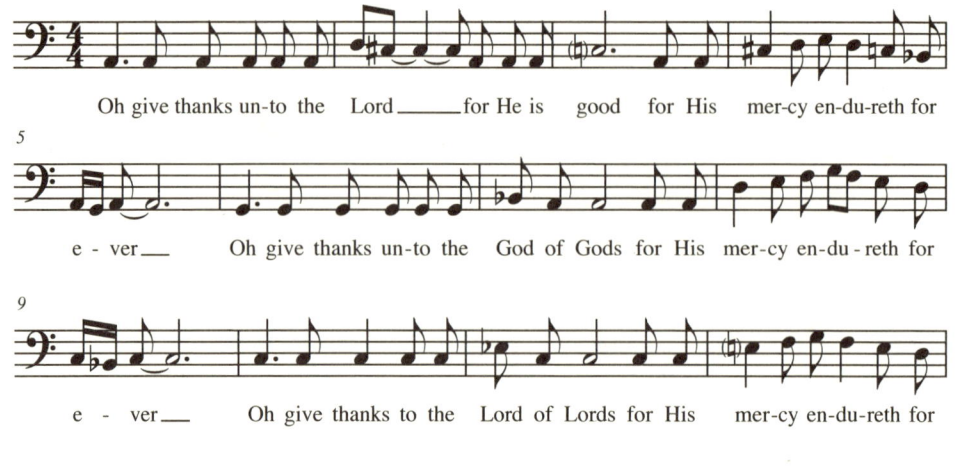

Oh give thanks un-to the Lord____ for He is good for His mer-cy en-du-reth for

e - ver____ Oh give thanks un-to the God of Gods for His mer-cy en-du-reth for

e - ver____ Oh give thanks to the Lord of Lords for His mer-cy en-du-reth for

e - ver____

Example 9.2. Psalm 136.

Despite these similarities, Newman's setting of Psalm 136 differs in several important ways from its predecessor in *The Robe*. Although Miriam's song seems to modulate freely from one mode to another, the harmonic implications of the chant in *The Greatest Story Ever Told* are more varied still. Newman's setting of Psalm 136 employs all the chromatic pitches between A and F♮, lending it an unsettling and disorienting quality that is largely absent from Miriam's song. This disorienting or unsettling quality is just one of the ways in which this example from *The Greatest Story Ever Told* differs from its predecessor in *The Robe*. For although both these examples evoke the devotional simplicity of early Christianity, their scenic function is somewhat different. The cinematography in *The Robe* clearly establishes Miriam as the source of the music. Although we presume that the disciples themselves are singing the monophonic chant in the anointing of Jesus scene from *The Greatest Story Ever Told*, we don't actually see them doing so until midway through the sequence. For reasons that will become clear as the scene unfolds, Judas does not join in the singing. When he accuses Mary of profligacy, the chant stops abruptly with what we might call a "reverse stinger" effect, in which it is sudden silence—rather than a *sforzando*—that articulates the drama (2:05:31). Only when Mary resumes her ritualistic anointing of Jesus does the chanting resume. The music thus functions to some extent as underscoring as well as source music. Its purpose is not simply to evoke the devotional simplicity of the disciples, but also to articulate Judas' alienation from the group. Here—in opposition to Miriam's song from *The Robe*—the musical reference to early Christian monophonic music thus functions at least in part in an ironic manner. This sense of irony also applies to other levels of the musical discourse as well. The screenplay at this point explicates the symbolism that in the Gospel of John is kept on the level of metaphor. "She is preparing me for my burial," Jesus tells Judas in the scene's final line. Although the text of Psalm 136 praises the goodness and mercy of God, the music in retrospect seems more closely to resemble a funeral dirge than a song of thanksgiving.

It would be a mistake to ascribe too much intentionality to these kinds of musical meanings. The production process for *The Greatest Story Ever Told* was extraordinarily complex, and many musical decisions were made at the last minute in response to cuts and other types of editing. We can get a sense of this complex production process not only from Darby's colorful descriptions in *Hollywood Holyland,* but also from various materials in the George Stevens collection housed at the Academy of Motion Picture Arts and Sciences.[13] Alongside numerous scripts, memos, and other print material, this collection includes a fascinating group of research tapes, compiled by Stevens (or at his behest) in preparation for the film. The tapes include a small number of cues from Newman's score for the film, sometimes in multiple versions. The Psalm 136 cue, for example, appears in an antiphonal setting (for soloist with choir) as well as for a unison group. It seems possible, then, that the chant was at some point intended to be presented in a different way (perhaps even completely nondiegetically). The tapes also preserve a certain amount of verbal material, including an exegesis by the biblical scholar John Fitzgerald as well as a recording of Max von Sydow reading the Sermon on the Mount. We may find various recordings of sound effects, such as an earthquake rumble and "distant and near dog howls." Much of the material, however, is quasi-ethnographic in character. Some of it, such as the recordings of various Druse songs, comes from a research trip that Stevens took to the Middle East in May 1960. The tapes also include recordings of the Inbal Dancers, a troupe of Yemenite Jews whose music Stevens was eventually to incorporate into the film (I return to this music below). But there are also tapes of unknown provenance, labeled simply "Music from Egypt and North Africa." There are recordings of Ethiopian instruments and even of an instrument that purports to be King David's harp (sent to Stevens in 1959). Closer to home, the tapes also include a Maronite Mass, sung in Arabic and Aramaic, that was recorded at Our Lady of Lebanon Church in Los Angeles. They testify to the long and complex process underlying the sound track to this film, a process whose haphazard quality may be seen not only in connection to the setting of Psalm 136, but to many other parts of the film as well.

It is difficult to make generalizations about the purpose of these research tapes. The presence of certain selections—such as Poulenc's Concerto in G Major or "Favorite Christmas Music by Jerry Fielding and his Brass Choir"—might indicate merely that Stevens was interested in using them as temp tracks for the shooting of the film. Most of the quasi-ethnographic material, however, is probably best understood as an extension of a basic impulse in the postwar biblical epic: namely, to use music in order to evoke a sense of a particular place and time. In this sense, the preparation of these research tapes resembles the careful study of music from the ancient and early medieval periods that Rózsa undertook in preparation for *Quo Vadis,* or the copious documents that Noerdlinger amassed in preparation for *The Ten Commandments.* In functional terms, then, these research tapes are predominantly analogues of the materials collected by the large research departments that supported the production of other big-budget historical films of the postwar period.

The question, of course, concerns the extent to which any of this quasi-ethnographic material might have influenced Newman in his composition of the score. In some sections of his music for *The Greatest Story Ever Told,* Newman uses solo instruments (particularly the flute) in a way that recalls some of the music on the research tapes, and the modally inflected melodies that he frequently employs might also be linked to these recordings. Yet there is little evidence that these tapes served as source material for Newman. The one exception to this observation concerns a cue that comes immediately after the anointing of Jesus scene that I described above. A dissolve connects this scene to an image of wooden doors: doors that open to reveal an expectant crowd (2:07:48). The back of Jesus' head appears in the center of the screen, letting us know that we are seeing the crowd from his point of view. In the sound track we hear an unaccompanied choir of women's voices, singing contrapuntally entwined textless melodies that lack a clear sense of metrical organization. Hyperamplification adds to the eerie quality of the soundscape. Jesus walks into the middle of the crowd and mounts a white donkey that has been led before him. Music quite similar to the choir of women's voices at the beginning of the Palm Sunday sequence may be found in the collection of research tapes that I described above. This music—entitled "Antiphonal Musical Lamentations by Alfred Newman" (#1 and #2)—appears alongside another recording entitled simply "Ancient Melodic Lamentations/Women's Voices." The source for this recording is (unfortunately) unidentified. Although Newman's music is not in any sense an arrangement of the "Ancient Melodic Lamentations," it seems clear that he was inspired by the material. With its hyperamplification and entwining dissonances, the choir of women's voices sounds radically different from the setting of Psalm 136, the title music for the film, or, indeed, the examples from *The Robe* or *Street Scene* to which I have already referred. But in compositional terms, at least, we might say that the relationship between his music and the "Ancient Melodic Lamentations" is similar to that which obtains between these examples and their various models. In all these examples, his method is best described as a creative assimilation of particular textures, rhythms, and harmonic-melodic gestures rather than any form of direct musical borrowing. As with these other selections, the end result is music of evocative beauty and emotional power.

Musical Imports: Handel, Verdi, and the Inbal Dancers

The women's choir at the beginning of the Palm Sunday sequence gives a glimpse, perhaps, of the kinds of music that Newman might have produced had he made more extensive use of the quasi-ethnographic material collected on the research tapes. We might imagine such music as the analogue of the historicist cues that Rózsa wrote for *Quo Vadis*, designed to give the film a greater degree of authenticity. Memos of various meetings that Newman had with Stevens concerning the nature of the music for the film suggest some of the composer's ideas along this line. According to meeting memos, Newman suggested that "the Sanhedrin Music could possibly incorporate some of the modes, rituals, or other material preserved from Ancient times and recorded by The Inbal Dancers (Ken Darby)."[14] A draft for press release (also included as part of the memos) originally included the following line: "Many of the musical instruments of the time of Jesus will be used in the orchestra, Newman revealed." For the most part, however, it seems that Stevens ultimately decided not to rely on Newman's score to create the desired degree of musical authenticity. The line from the press release about using musical instruments from the time of Jesus was crossed out, leading me to believe that Stevens (or someone on his staff) found it best to backtrack on claims of authenticity. And rather than following up on Newman's suggestion of incorporating or assimilating some of the modes of the Inbal music into his score, Stevens ultimately decided simply to use recordings of the Inbal Dancers themselves. Instead of using Newman's adaptations of source material, in other words, Stevens used the source material itself.

Founded in 1949 as part of the cultural revival associated with the founding of the State of Israel, the Inbal Dance Theater was a folkloric group that drew inspiration from a variety of different sources (Yemenite traditions were especially important to their repertoire). Under the musical direction of Ovadia Tuvia, the group had toured North America and Europe during the late 1950s, and it is hardly surprising that Stevens (or rather his production company) should come upon them in their search for authentic sounds "of the time of Jesus." It was just these qualities that impressed Ken Darby. In *Hollywood Holyland*, he recorded some of his initial reactions to their music. "The songs were awesomely ancient," he wrote, and "their authenticity was undeniable. They were modal, antiphonal, and definitely Hebrew, and I was impressed." The Inbal troupe seems to have made an equally strong if perhaps more complex impression on Stevens himself. "During the next musical offering [of the Inbal troupe]," Darby continued, "I kept my eyes on George Stevens's face, watching the curious interplay of expressions: paternal serenity—'I love these graceful naive children'; sharply focused interest—'this music comes straight out of racial memory'; frowning preoccupation—'how much of this documentary-type material can I ever use?'"[15] From production memos, it seems that Stevens contemplated using the Inbal music in many different sections of the film, but in the end it was essentially restricted to the scenes that take place at the court of Herod and his son Herod Antipas. In the context of the film, therefore, we might understand Stevens's decision in a variety of different ways. On one hand, it is yet another manifestation of the universalist aesthetic of the film that I described above, akin to the visual reference to da Vinci's *Last Supper* or the decision to use a roster of famous stars to cast the movie. Using the Inbal Dancers in *The Greatest Story Ever Told* might also be seen as part of a more general move toward compiled film scores in Hollywood films that would gather momentum in the latter part of the 1960s and into subsequent decades. But we can also see the inclusion of the Inbal music in terms that are more specific to the genre of the biblical epic. Like the Yemenite chant that was inserted into the score for *King of Kings,* the Inbal cues in *The Greatest Story Ever Told* to some extent take the place of earlier cues—such as the historicist music in *Quo Vadis* or the "Song of Miriam" from *The Robe*—that were designed to suggest a specific time and place. In this sense, we can see their inclusion in these late epics as evidence of an increasing loss of confidence in the ability of traditional compositional techniques to meet the demands for musical authenticity.

If the inclusion of the Inbal cues did indeed represent such a loss of confidence, there is little evidence that Newman took umbrage with Stevens's decision. When it became clear that Stevens intended to use the "Hallelujah Chorus" as part of the score for the film, however, the composer's reaction was completely different. A recording of the "Hallelujah Chorus" was transferred to one of the research tapes, and it seems that the idea of using Handel's music occurred to Stevens at some point during the shooting of the film—that is to say, well before Newman had completed his score. But Newman only became aware of Stevens's plan during a screening of a rough cut of the film, in which Stevens announced that he wanted to "try an experiment." Stevens was evidently screening the sequence that narrates the raising of Lazarus from the dead and the subsequent response of his followers. Darby's account of what transpired next forms the climax of *Hollywood Holyland*: "The picture returned to the screen, but now from the speaker issued the 'Hallelujah Chorus' from Handel's *Messiah*! Alfred and I sat transfixed to the end, not believing our ears. When the lights came on, Stevens started to speak, but Alfred was up and on his way out."[16] After Stevens asked Newman what he thought of the "experiment," Newman (at least according to Darby) said the following:

I do not now, nor will I ever presume to imply that my talent remotely compares with that of the great Handel. But in the context of this film, scored with antique modes from definite thematic sources, I think the use of the *Messiah* is vulgar and shocking, both stylistically and dramatically. It comes suddenly out of left field, totally major in mode, uprooting the audience's involvement with the film, and particularly with Christians—many of whom probably sang it in a Baptist church choir.[17]

Stevens (again according to Darby) "was stonily silent for a moment. Then he spoke abruptly. 'The fact that church choirs sing it denotes public acceptance. And I want something acceptable and familiar here. You in the music department may go now.'"[18]

Stevens stuck by his "experiment," and the scene was eventually scored with a bit of Newman's music for *The Robe* serving as a kind of introduction to Handel's music (beginning with the more subdued homophonic phrase "The kingdom of this world . . ."). Additionally, Stevens decided to use sections from the first movement of Verdi's *Requiem* during one of the final sequences of the film that depicts the Via Dolorosa: Jesus' painful march to Calvary. After Stevens ignored his protests, Newman essentially washed his hands of the score. Indeed, he felt so strongly about the negative effects of these insertions that he even attempted—without success—to have his name removed from the credits for the film. Darby took over the spade work of creating musical transitions between Newman's music and Handel's (as well as similar transitions for the Verdi insertions in the final part of the film). After *The Greatest Story Ever Told* was released to largely negative reviews, United Artists (the distributor for the film) mandated cuts that consequently necessitated a further reshuffling of the musical cues. *The Greatest Story Ever Told*, of course, is hardly the only film with a complicated production history. Film scores are nearly always the result of a process of collaboration and compromise in which a production team frequently must respond to unforeseen circumstances. With regard to Stevens's film, however, this process was especially messy and acrimonious, and it is hard to avoid the conclusion that Newman was treated rather shabbily. My purpose here, however, is not to cast judgment on Stevens's behavior, but rather to examine the consequences of the breakdown in the partnership between composer and director.

There are several things that might strike us as somewhat odd about Newman's response to the "experimental" film screening (or, at least, about Darby's memory of it). The first is his claim that the film has been scored "with antique modes from definite thematic sources." Antique modes and definite thematic sources would seem to have little relevance for much of the score; it is hard to see, for example, how this characterization would apply to the main title theme of the film. We might also remember that the score to *The Robe* includes music imported from another source (in this case, Newman's earlier score for *The Hunchback of Notre Dame*). Newman's characterization of the "Hallelujah Chorus" as "[coming] suddenly out of left field, totally major in mode" might apply equally well to the analogous moment in his earlier film score (see Example 4.6).[19] We might imagine that the fact that the *Hunchback* music came from his own pen made its inclusion *The Robe* more palatable for Newman than the analogous insertion of the "Hallelujah Chorus." And yet Newman seems to have made no complaint about the use of the Inbal music. The composer's response, it seems, was motivated by different concerns.

Newman's objections to the Handel insertion, I believe, do not have to do with the mere fact that Stevens was importing music from an external source, but rather with the effect of this imported music on the cinematic audience. Putting this in terms of the paired dichotomies of Kassabian's taxonomy that I outlined above, we could say that the aesthetic conflict between Stevens and Newman has to do not with the contrast between technique (that is to say, between compilation and composition), but rather with the question of audience identification. When Newman protests that the "Hallelujah Chorus" would "uproot the audience's involvement with the film," he is (to use Kassabian's terms) concerned that the music would no longer be able to promote assimilating identifications. He feared that the audience would instead form "affiliating identifications" with church choirs and the like. And yet it was precisely these kinds of identifications that Stevens wanted the music to create. The conflict between composer and director is therefore not simply about issues of control or credit; it also reflects a fundamental disagreement about film music aesthetics.

Transcendence

Stevens ended up using the "Hallelujah Chorus" at two different points in the film. The first of these—the screening of which provoked the confrontation that Darby described in *Hollywood Holyland*—takes place immediately before the intermission, as the climax of the first of the two acts into which the film—like other blockbuster epics from the period—was divided. Jesus has just raised Lazarus from the dead, and the "Hallelujah Chorus" accompanies the frenzied joy of Jesus' followers as they react to this news. In the context of the biblical epic, such moments of spiritual exaltation are usually accompanied by one of the most firmly established and fully developed musical topoi in the genre, namely, the celestial chorus. Typically homophonic and even hymn-like, the celestial chorus appears in nearly all of the biblical epics. It may accompany moments of redemption and triumph at any point in these films, but it is most commonly heard at the end. A classic example of the celestial chorus, for instance, accompanies the denouement of *Quo Vadis,* and similar gestures may be found at the conclusions to many of the other biblical epics as well. Newman was quite familiar with this particular topos. The "Hallelujah" music inserted into the final cue of *The Robe,* for instance, is essentially an up-tempo version of the celestial chorus. Although the choral setting of the Twenty-third Psalm that accompanies the final scene of *David and Bathsheba* is slower and less exuberant, it also represents an example of this nearly ubiquitous gesture. From Darby's book, it is clear that Newman planned a similar kind of choral cue for the sequence in which the various characters respond to the raising of Lazarus, that is to say, for the moment in the

Example 9.3. Chorale motif from the John the Baptist cue.

score in which Stevens inserted the material from the *Messiah*. Handel's music, in other words, functioned as a replacement for the celestial chorus.

It is difficult to know how the final scene of *The Greatest Story Ever Told* would have functioned with Newman's original music instead of the Handel insertion. But we may get a sense of Newman's approach to the topos of the celestial chorus in this particular film by examining another moment in which the gesture occurs. Entitled "The Highest Summit," the cue accompanies the climax to Jesus' forty days in the wilderness. In narrative terms—as I mentioned in chapter 7— this sequence is analogous to the temptation scene in *King of Kings*. And as I mentioned in my earlier discussion, Jesus' wandering in *The Greatest Story Ever Told* is accompanied by the fulminations of John the Baptist that seem to echo off the canyon walls (or, perhaps, to reverberate within Jesus' mind). But there is underscoring as well. The centerpiece of this music (which appears in the conductor's score as the John the Baptist cue) is a chorale-like phrase that modulates from major to minor (see Example 9.3).

For those audience members familiar with the traditions of European choral music, the Baptist's words that resound throughout this scene recall the biblical verses that Charles Jennens paraphrased in order to assemble the libretto for the *Messiah,* and it could be that there is some kind of oblique connection (perhaps only in the mind of the director) between the screenplay and the decision to use the "Hallelujah Chorus" so prominently in the film. Newman's music, however, recalls another work from the European choral tradition, namely, Thomas Tallis's "Third Tune." Tallis wrote the tune as a hymn (it appears in the 1982 Episcopal Hymnal as "To mock Thy reign"), but it is perhaps better known as the music that Ralph Vaughn Williams used for his 1910 *Fantasia on a Theme by Thomas Tallis.* As with the opening theme for the film, we cannot be sure that Newman was directly modeling his underscoring on this preexisting music, or indeed if the composer was even familiar with the Tallis tune or Vaughn Williams's *Fantasia*.[20] The similarities between his underscoring and the "Third Tune" may be the result of subconscious influence rather than conscious borrowing. The specifics of Newman's compositional process must remain opaque, and in any case they have little bearing on the ways in which audiences heard his music. In this regard, as with so many other aspects of Newman's music, we must speak of indirect allusion rather than of overt quotation. Although few audience members could be expected to recognize the connection between the John the Baptist cue and Tallis's "Third Tune" (or Vaughn Williams's *Fantasia*), that is not to say that it has no meaning. Indeed, one might argue that the effect of the music is heightened precisely by the fact that it operates beneath the level of conscious awareness. Like the title theme and the setting of Psalm 136, like the examples from *The Robe* or *Street Scene,* the John the Baptist cue is thus another example (as if more were needed) of the intermediate level of musical reference that was so central to Newman's style.

At the very end of the wilderness sequence (37:52), as Jesus climbs to the top of a rocky mesa, Newman transforms the John the Baptist theme. Shifting into the major mode, employing brass and a wordless choir, the somber chorale becomes what is arguably the most sophisticated iteration of the celestial chorus topos in Newman's cinematic oeuvre. In place of John the Baptist, von Sydow announces Jesus' spiritual victory as a *voix acousmatique:* "All the tribes of the earth shall see the Son of Man coming in the cloud of Heaven, with power and great glory." It is literally and figuratively a "mountaintop moment" (see Figure 9.2). In *The Greatest Story Ever Told,* therefore, the conventional expression of the celestial chorus topos coexists alongside its potential replacement—that is to say, alongside the Handel that is imported into the film in order to fulfill its function. The film—to put this another way—presents two potentially contradictory aesthetic strategies with regard to this cinematic topos. In the first—represented by The Highest Summit cue—the music derives its meaning from its connection to generic conventions (the celestial choruses of other biblical epics) and also from its links to earlier cues in the film (e.g., the John the Baptist music). In the second—represented by the "Hallelujah Chorus" and perhaps also by the Verdi insertions that come in the last part of the movie—the frame of reference is essentially external to the film. In this sense, the two iterations of the celestial chorus topos in *The Greatest Story Ever Told* represent the two poles ("assimilation" and "affiliation") of Kassabian's paradigm.

The conflict between assimilating and affiliating identifications with regard to the celestial chorus topos might best be understood by analogy with the music from the Inbal troupe that was incorporated into the film. If we can understand the decision to include the Inbal recordings as evidence of an increasing lack of confidence in the ability of traditional film scoring to create the necessary degree of musical authenticity, so too might the decision to use the "Hallelujah Chorus" instead of Newman's own music at various points in the film indicate a parallel development: namely, a lack of confidence in the ability of traditional film scoring appropriately to suggest spiritual transcendence. In this sense, we might understand the two iterations of the celestial chorus as a microcosm of the position of American Christianity in the middle of the 1960s. For if—as I

Figure 9.2. Promotional still for *The Greatest Story Ever Told*. From the core collection production files of the Margaret Herrick Library, Academy of Motion Picture Arts and Sciences.

suggested in the previous chapter—the biblical epic was a cinematic reflection of what Ellwood called "Fifties-style, public, self-assured, modernist religion, confidently working out of unquestioned great traditions and, like America generally, thought to be doing good on a global scale," then the topos of the celestial chorus is perhaps the clearest articulation of this optimistic theology. Seen in this light, the fact that *The Greatest Story Ever Told* should employ such different strategies for expressing spiritual transcendence is symptomatic of the film's historical position at the very end of the postwar cycle of blockbuster biblical epics. As the publicity booklet from which I quoted at the beginning of this chapter makes clear, *The Greatest Story Ever Told* was at least in some sense an attempt to update the monolithic theology of the earlier biblical epics, to present an image of Jesus that could be "one thing, and many things." And yet the film continually recycles the forms and patterns—not least of which are the musical conventions—of these earlier iterations of the genre.

For the modern viewer, these contradictions emerge perhaps most clearly in the final scenes of the film (3:12:15ff.). For this sequence (in contrast to the scene at the end of the first act of the film that I described above) the beginning of the insert coincides with the beginning of the "Hallelujah Chorus" as it appears in Handel's oratorio. Not all of Handel's original music is included, but the cue is nevertheless more than two minutes long: a temporal expanse that is demanded, perhaps, by the length of the narrative for which it serves as a capstone. Partway through the Handel insertion, a dissolve leads us back to the visual images with which the film began: an image of von Sydow/Jesus with arms outstretched against blue sky and fair-weather clouds. Another dissolve brings us back into the analogous image from the imitation Renaissance fresco first seen in the opening sequence of the film. In this earlier sequence, the camera moved downward across the fresco, suggesting the descent of spirit into matter (or more simply put, the Incarnation). At the end of the film, this symbolism is reversed: Jesus returns to the heavenly realm from which he came. The gesture seems intended to be transcendent in both a diegetic and meta-diegetic sense. On one hand, it simply represents Jesus' ascension into heaven: the antipode, or rather the fulfillment, of the Incarnation. On the other hand, it also reads as an effort to transcend the limits of genre by subsuming—in accordance with the universalist aesthetics that I described above—the spiritualized traditions of European art and music history (represented by the imitation fresco and by Handel's music). On both counts, this transcendent gesture depends on the capacity of Handel's music and the imitation fresco to generate affiliating identifications. But affiliation passes over all too easily into incongruence, and the audience (or at least an unacceptably large part of it) is left with the feeling that none of it—the music, the fresco, the all-star cast whose offscreen personalities are only partially hidden—really belongs. Instead of creating an apotheosis of the genre, the universalist gestures of *The Greatest Story Ever Told* collapse under the weight that they are asked to bear.

Epilogue

At the end of *The Greatest Story Ever Told*—after the Jesus image disappears and the final cadence of the Hallelujah Chorus has faded from the sound track—we hear a full reprise of Newman's title theme. At first, the screen shows an end title, reminding the audience that the film was a George Stevens production released by United Artists. But then the screen goes black, to leave the music on its own. The film ends only after Newman brings his wandering Barberesque counterpoint to a close with a stirring major-mode cadence. The idea of ending a film with a reprise of the main title music, of course, is hardly unusual, and it seems likely that Stevens intended this music to serve in a fairly conventional way as a kind of synopsis of the filmic narrative. In this reading, the major-mode cadence at the very end of the film might represent the redemption that comes as the fulfillment of Jesus' tragic suffering. But from the perspective of the early twenty-first century, it is tempting also to hear Newman's theme in a broader sense, as an elegy for the genre of the postwar biblical epic. When placed against the tremendous success of films such as *The Ten Commandments* and *Ben-Hur*, *The Greatest Story Ever Told* does indeed seem like a colossal failure. Indeed, Stevens' epic is one of the films featured in Harry and Michael Medved's 1984 book *The Hollywood Hall of Shame: The Most Expensive Flops in Movie History.*[1] In this context, organicist narratives about generic decline (such as those penned by Thomas Schatz and others to which I alluded in chapter 6) are difficult to resist.

Legacy

The notion that *The Greatest Story Ever Told* was the last stage in the decline and fall of the biblical epic, however, is undermined first of all by the fact that Hollywood continued to produce films of this type. In 1966, Dino De Laurentiis, in association with Twentieth Century–Fox, produced *The Bible: In the Beginning*. Directed by John Huston, the film is based directly on roughly the first half of the book of Genesis. Its hubristic ambition is similar to that which informs *The Greatest Story Ever Told,* and the film reproduces many of the semantic and syntactic markers of the postwar biblical epic genre that I have explored in this book. In another sense, however, *The Bible: In the Beginning* anticipates one of the more curious developments in what we might call the twentieth-century history of biblical representation, namely, the migration of biblical narratives into the medium of television. Given its subject matter, Huston's film is perhaps unavoidably episodic, and in this sense it is similar to the numerous 1970s television miniseries based on the Bible, such as *Moses the Lawgiver* (1974), *The Story of David* (1977), Franco Zeffirelli's *Jesus of Nazareth* (1977), and *Greatest Heroes of the Bible* (1978). The televised miniseries *The Bible* (produced by Roma Downey and Mark Burnett, and aired in 2013 for the History Channel) represents the latest iteration of this genre.

The success of this recent miniseries seems to have sparked a modest revival in the biblical epic genre. As I write these words, there are at least three biblical epics scheduled for release in the near future: *Son of God* (produced by Downey and Burnett), *Noah* (directed by Darren Aronofsky and starring Russell Crowe in the title role), and *Exodus* (directed by Ridley Scott and starring Christian Bale as Moses). If we may judge from movie trailers and other advance publicity, these films may display some sense of the overwhelming spectacle that was so central to their postwar counterparts. Although it seems likely that music will play an important role in these films, they must obviously remain outside of my purview. More germane to my topic here are those more isolated examples of big-budget films dealing with biblical or quasi-biblical subject matter that were produced after 1970. The most notable of these films—Andrew Lloyd Webber's *Jesus Christ Superstar* (1973); *The Last Temptation of Christ* (1988), directed by Martin Scorsese based on the 1953 novel of the same name by Nikos Kazantzakis; and Mel Gibson's *The Passion of the Christ* (2004)—deal with the life of Jesus, and in this sense continues the turn toward the Christ film that I briefly discussed in chapter 7. Each of these films—for different reasons—was extremely controversial, and in this sense they seem quite different from the Christ films of the early 1960s. As I discussed above, both *King of Kings* and *The Greatest Story Ever Told* reflected a kind of consensus Christianity which by the 1970s and 1980s was largely a thing of the past. As a filmed version of a rock opera, *Jesus Christ Superstar* would also seem in a musical sense to have little in common with the films that I have discussed in this book, and the sound tracks to both *The Last Temptation of Christ* and *The Passion of the Christ* are also quite different from those of the postwar biblical epics. Nevertheless, there are also some important continuities between the scores for these latter two films and those of earlier biblical films. Peter Gabriel's sound track to *The Last Temptation of Christ* was notable for its extensive use of world music and was justly celebrated in its time as a new approach to film scoring.[2] And yet Gabriel's work was to some degree anticipated by sequences from earlier Christ films (the Yemenite chant that accompanies the Last Supper in *King of Kings,* and the Inbal music in *The Greatest Story Every Told*) that use ethnographic or quasi-ethnographic material. In a similar manner, the hyperamplified and metadiegetic sounds that accompany the gruesome flagellation scene in *The Passion of the Christ* recall Mario Nascimbene's efforts to create similar al-most unendurable effects through his use of the *suoni nuovi* in *Barabbas*.

The music of the postwar biblical epics, I would argue, finds its most impor-tant legacy not in televised biblical miniseries or even in these later films that are concerned with biblical subject matter, but rather in more dispersed cinematic genres. For in many important ways, the successors to the postwar biblical ep-ics were not films such as Scorsese's *The Last Temptation of Christ,* Bruce Beres-ford's 1985 *King David,* or Zeffirelli's *Jesus of Nazareth,* but rather those later blockbuster films in which a sense of the epic, or, more generally, of the unfold-ing of a world-historical process, is combined with the idea of the spirit. Seen in this light, films such as the *Star Wars* trilogies or Peter Jackson's *Lord of the Rings* films are not-so-distant relatives of *Ben-Hur* and *The Ten Commandments.* The cinematographic legacy of the biblical epics is readily apparent in sequences such as the pod race from *The Phantom Menace,* which borrows extensively from the famous chariot race in *Ben-Hur.* And while it would be an overstatement to speak of the scores to *Star Wars* or *The Lord of the Rings* as homages to the music of the postwar biblical epics, there are certainly many points of similarity between the great scores of Rózsa, Newman, and Bernstein and the music of these later films. The Imperial March that John Williams created for Darth Vader (and, by exten-sion, the evil forces that he commands), for example, owes much to the Roman imperial style developed in films such as *Quo Vadis* and *Ben-Hur.* The Land of Gondor theme that figures so prominently in Howard Shore's score for *The Re-turn of the King* (to take another example) begins with the same Î-5̂-4̂ melodic gesture that characterizes the epic Judaica themes that I discussed in chapter 5. With the addition of a few ornamental arabesques, it could fit very easily into the soundscape of *The Ten Commandments* or *Ben-Hur.*

Other isolated examples such as these could undoubtedly be adduced. More important, however, are the ways in which epic films from the late 1970s up to the present day have developed certain key musical elements from the postwar bib-lical films. Although none of these elements is exclusive to the films discussed in this book, the postwar biblical epics manifested them in uniquely important ways. Four of these elements seem particularly important. Most striking, per-haps, is the way in which the motivically saturated symphonic score—whose greatest postwar exemplar, I believe, may be found in Rózsa's music for *Ben-Hur*—has endured and continued to flourish. A second point of continuity con-cerns the ways in which more contemporary film composers use ideas about mu-sical authenticity (broadly construed) in order to create a sense of place and/or historical distance. In this context, one thinks of James Horner's title theme for *Braveheart,* or the music that Hans Zimmer and Lisa Gerrard created for the North African sequences in *Gladiator.* The kind of careful attention to the inte-gration of sound effects and music that we have seen in films such as *The Robe* and *Barabbas*—needless to say—is extremely important in more contemporary epic films. Nothing in the biblical epics, of course, may compare to the elaborate soundscapes that were developed in the wake of sound designer Ben Burtt's innovative work in *Star Wars,* but the seeds of modern cinematic sound design might be found in the innovations of postwar period. The fourth point of continuity has to do with the sonic representation of the spiritual realm. Although the mainstream Judeo-Christian concept of the spirit is no longer central to the epic style, many more contemporary epics deal with spiritual and/or supernatural processes akin, at least in a general sense, to those depicted in the postwar biblical epics. The celestial choruses with which so many of the biblical epics end, for example, find later resonance in spiritualized moments from more recent films, such as the scene from *The Matrix* in which Neo awakens into the truth of his existence and sees for the first time the endless array of womb-like capsules in which most of humankind is kept. At least in terms of their music, then, we may speak of a process of partial decontextualization, whereby the various gestures in the scores of the postwar biblical epics become to a greater or lesser degree detached from their specific contexts in order to acquire new meanings as they are continually transformed and recycled.

While it is relatively easy to understand the specific ways in which certain scenes or musical gestures from the biblical epics might have influenced later films, an evaluation of the broader cultural legacy of these films is much more difficult. As spectacular embodiments of mid-century Judeo-Christian values, there is no doubt that the postwar epics shaped many Americans' ideas about biblical characters and stories, and television broadcasts of *The Ten Commandments* and *Ben-Hur* during the last decades of the twentieth century would give these films—at least for a certain segment of the American public—a special kind of enduring power. Although they have to some extent lost their iconic status, certain scenes from these films—Moses holding his staff above the raging waters of the Red Sea in *The Ten Commandments;* the crucifixion scenes in *Ben-Hur* and *The Robe*—remained central to popular American religious iconography for much of the late twentieth century. And yet even as the biblical epics were enjoying a strange afterlife in American popular culture, they were also being excised from the academic/critical account of film history. In this respect, the biblical epic stands in marked contrast to a genre such as film noir. Both film noir and the biblical epic left important legacies that influenced later movies. If we can trace the cinematic influence of *Ben-Hur* (to take one example) on subsequent blockbuster epics, so too is it easy to see how films such as *Blade Runner* and *L.A. Confidential* reference classic noir films of the forties and fifties. The legacies of these genres, of course, took different cinematic forms. But the most striking difference in their subsequent reception histories has to do with what we might call their contrasting historiographies. Unlike the biblical epics, film noir was the focus of a great deal of scholarly and critical attention during the 1970s and 1980s. At the same time that Michael Wood was dismissing the biblical epics, film noir was becoming the subject of books and articles that subsequently became foundational in the emerging discipline of cinema studies.[3] The difference between the respective reception histories of film noir and the biblical epic, I would maintain, has little to do with the intrinsic complexity of the works themselves. As I hope to have shown in this book, the scores of these epic films were often of great artistry; and several of them (Newman's music for *The Robe* and Rózsa's score for *Ben-Hur,* in my opinion) must be regarded as monuments in the history of film music. Similar claims might be made for other aspects of these films, such as cinematography and set design. The biblical epics were enormously expensive undertakings, in which many of Hollywood's most prestigious talents worked. And yet—as I noted in the introduction—the biblical epics were largely ignored by critics in the 1970s and 1980s. For all of their spectacle and grandeur, then, they seemed to pass into historical oblivion—or at least into a different cultural sphere—with extraordinary speed. Even if we replace the idea of collapse with a narrative of transformation, therefore, we are still confronted by the sense that the early 1960s witnessed a kind of sea change, after which it became nearly impossible to imagine biblical epics playing a central role in the Hollywood dream factory.

Disavowal

To hazard grand theories about the ways in which cinematic genres—or other cultural products—interact with broader social movements is far beyond the scope of this book or the competence of its author. As Leonard Quart and Albert Auster point out in the introduction to their book *American Film and Society Since 1945,* "There are no straight, clear lines to be drawn between the film industry and the popular mind—neither is it a mirror of public feelings and habits, nor can one make the vulgar, mechanistic connection that implies that the industry is some evil empire conspiratorially shaping the social values and political opinions of a supine public."[4] But even if we cannot draw a straight line between the decline of the biblical epics and the popular mind or the "political opinions of a supine public," the sea change in the cultural position of the biblical epic calls out for some kind of explanation. In these final pages, therefore, I would like to offer some thoughts about the cultural significance of the postwar biblical epic, and specifically of the music which is such an integral part of the genre.

As I have argued throughout this book, the music of the postwar biblical epics reflected and articulated a particular constellation of social forces, economic developments, and religious and aesthetic ideas. This constellation was in a state of continual flux, as Hollywood adapted to the changing landscape of the entertainment industry and ideas about America's Christian identity and its role in the world began to shift. But like other cinematic genres, the epics did not merely absorb the cultural energies of the moment. They also helped to shape and articulate these energies in particular sorts of ways. Instead of seeing the products of Hollywood as mirrors of the public mind, then, it is perhaps better to employ an acoustic metaphor. In this sense, we may imagine cinematic genres as particular kinds of resonating chambers: amplifying certain forces, attenuating others, causing others to vibrate with one another in order to create unexpected harmonies and dissonances.

In this respect, it is perhaps most appropriate to understand the history of the postwar epic as a process of cathexis, whereby certain cultural energies were amplified and channeled so that they produced an exaggerated or distorted iteration of postwar hegemonic values. It was precisely these hegemonic values that so many of the emerging cultural formations of the later 1960s and the 1970s constructed themselves. From the standpoint of the next generation, the biblical epics were the embodiment not only (as for Michael Wood) of the "myth of excess," but also of a conservative amalgam of religious and political values: of a naive and outmoded religious sensibility and of discredited and distasteful American triumphalism. In this sense, we might characterize the critical response to the epics during the 1970s and 1980s not so much as embarrassment or neglect, but rather as disavowal.

This sense of disavowal forms a strange counterpoint with the enduring legacy of these films, a counterpoint that emerges most clearly, perhaps, through a consideration of their music. As I hope to have shown in this book, this music is quite diverse: attempts to define a general biblical epic style are bound to run aground. One constant in these films, however, is simply the sheer amount of music that they contain. In the biblical epics—as in epic or fantasy films more generally—music is a vital means of suspending audience disbelief, or (to recycle Kassabian's terminology) of "assimilating" audiences into the alternative reality of distant times and places. In this respect, music was therefore central to the process of cathexis whereby the biblical epics articulated and amplified a particularly American mythos. Despite—or perhaps because of—the popular success and critical acclaim that many of the biblical epic scores enjoyed during the 1950s and early 1960s, the music did not fit comfortably into the new cultural configurations that would define themselves in opposition to this mythos. If Rózsa's comments with regard to the dodecaphonic theme that he used for the Devil in *King of Kings* are symptomatic of the ways in which he felt marginalized from the compositional avant-garde, so too, to a large degree, were the various styles employed in the biblical epics equally distant from the music of the emerging youth culture. And yet the scoring strategies articulated by composers such as Rózsa and Newman were by no means abandoned. They continued to sow new seeds in the fertile ground upon which music meets the cinematic imagination. Like other aspects of these films, then, the music of the biblical epics needed to be disavowed not because it did not succeed, but rather because it succeeded too well.

More than a half-century has passed since the biblical epics lost their preeminent position among Hollywood genres, time enough, surely, for the shadow of critical disavowal to recede. The epic sounds of postwar Hollywood biblical films are worthy of reevaluation, not simply because their intrinsic beauty and complexity makes them monuments of the art of film scoring, but also because of the ways in which they amplified and resonated with the cultural energies of a pivotal period in American history.

Notes

Introduction

1. Bosley Crowther, "The Screen: Two New Movies Shown Here; 'Darling, How Could You!' From Play by James M. Barrie, Stars Fontaine and Lund 'Quo Vadis,' Based on Sienkiewicz Novel and Made in Rome, Opens at Two Theatres," *New York Times,* November 9, 1951.

2. Bruce Babington and Peter Evans, *Biblical Epics: Sacred Narrative in the Hollywood Cinema* (New York: St. Martin's Press, 1993).

3. Martin Halliwell, *American Culture in the 1950s* (Edinburgh: Edinburgh University Press, 2007); Leonard Quart and Albert Auster, *American Film and Society since 1945,* 4th ed. (Oxford: Praeger, 2011).

4. In addition to Babington and Evans, a classic account is Gerald E. Forshey, *American Religious and Biblical Spectaculars* (Westport, Conn.: Praeger, 1992).

5. In his book *America in the Movies; or "Santa Maria, It Had Slipped My Mind"* (New York: Basic Books, 1975), Michael Wood writes about this particular quality of the epic: "Every gesture, every set piece bespeaks fantastic excess" (169).

6. Steve Neale, *Genre and Hollywood* (New York: Routledge, 2000), 85.

7. The discursive framework that distinguishes between "semantic" and "syntactic" generic markers can be traced back through the work of Rick Altman to that of Todorov and Frederic Jameson (and beyond). In his article "A Semantic/Syntactic Approach to Film Genre," *Cinema Journal* 23/3 (Spring 1984), 6–18, Altman describes how these terms might be applied to a discussion of cinema. "While there is anything but general agreement on the exact frontier separating semantic from syntactic views," he writes, "we can as a whole distinguish between generic definitions which depend on a list of common traits, attitudes, characters, shots, locations, sets, and the like—thus stressing the semantic elements which make up the genre—and definitions which play up instead certain constitutive relations between undesignated and variable placeholders—relationships which might be called the genre's fundamental syntax. The semantic approach thus stresses the genre's building blocks, while the syntactic view privileges the structures into which they are arranged" (10).

8. In his article "Bathsheba Goes Bathing in Hollywood: Words, Images, and Social Locations," *Semeia* 74 (1996), 75–101, David Gunn writes about ways in which *David and Bathsheba* may be understood as part of the genre of "women's film." Babington and Evans make a similar argument in their chapter on the film in *Biblical Epics* (70–90). I take up these specific arguments in more detail in chapter 2.

9. Wood, *America in the Movies,* 169.

10. Vivian Sobchack, "'Surge and Splendor': A Phenomenology of the Hollywood Historical Epic," in *Film Genre Reader II,* ed. Barry Keith Grant (Austin: University of Texas

Press, 1995), 280–307, originally printed in slightly different form in *Representations* 29 (Winter 1990), 24–49. A similar argument is made by Michael Wood in his *America in the Movies* (quoted by Babington and Evans, *Biblical Epics,* 9–10).

11. Sobchack, "'Surge and Splendor,'" 287. Emphasis in original.

12. The term "aspect ratio" refers to the proportional relationship between the width and the height of the projected image. The height of the image is typically expressed as "1." A common aspect ratio for "classic" Hollywood films was 1.37:1. Widescreen formats used aspect ratios such as 2.2:1 (Todd-AO system) or even 2.66:1 (some CinemaScope films)

13. The term "underscoring" is sometimes used specifically to describe music that accompanies dialogue. In this book, however, I use the term in a general sense to refer to composed music that does not have a clearly identifiable source in the narrative of the film. In this sense, "underscoring" is opposed to "source music." I treat "underscoring" as more or less synonymous with what Claudia Gorbman (and those scholars who follow her usage) calls "nondiegetic" music. I likewise regard Gorbman's term "diegetic music" as more or less equivalent to "source music."

14. Sobchack, "'Surge and Splendor,'" 281.

15. The term "suture" entered film studies through Lacanian psychology and semiotics. It has been applied to film in various ways. Here I am using it to refer to the process whereby a spectator is inserted into the discourse of the film, or—to be more true to the origins of the term—the process through which the gap between the spectator's subjectivity and the filmic narrative is "stitched closed."

16. Paul N. Reinsch, "At Least Half the Picture: Sound and Narration in the Postwar/Pre-Dolby American Film" (Ph.D. diss., University of Southern California, 2008).

17. Babington and Evans, *Biblical Epics,* 61.

18. This characterization comes from John Belton, "1950s Magnetic Sound: The Frozen Revolution," in *Sound Theory / Sound Practice,* ed. Rick Altman (New York: Routledge, 1992), 154–67. See also Belton's book *Widescreen Cinema* (Cambridge, Mass.: Harvard University Press, 1992).

19. Figures cited by Robert Ellwood in *The Fifties Spiritual Marketplace: American Religion in a Decade of Conflict* (New Brunswick, N.J.: Rutgers University Press, 1997), 1, 5.

20. William G. McLoughlin, *Modern Revivalism: Charles Grandison Finney to Billy Graham* (New York: Ronald Press Company, 1959), 8. In this book, McLaughlin looks into the future and defines the "fourth great awakening" as the period "from 1945 to perhaps 1970." In his subsequent book *Revivals, Awakening, and Reform: An Essay on Religion and Social Change in America, 1607–1977* (Chicago: University of Chicago Press, 1978), it is important to note, McLoughlin changes his chronology. In this later book, he associates the "fourth great awakening" with the new spiritualities of the 1960s and defines it as stretching from 1960 to perhaps 1990.

21. Henry S. Noerdlinger, *Moses and Egypt: The Documentation to the Motion Picture "The Ten Commandments"* (Los Angeles: University of Southern California Press, 1956), iii. The practice of buttressing a film's authority by referencing scholarly authority goes back at least to Griffith's *The Birth of a Nation* (1915). See Melvyn Stokes, *D. W. Griffith's The Birth of a Nation: A History of "The Most Controversial Motion Picture of All Time"* (Oxford: Oxford University Press, 2007), 175.

22. With regard to music, the topic of historical authenticity within the biblical epic had still another point of intersection with broader cultural trends. Rózsa's musico-

logical interest in ancient music (as is manifest in his work for *Quo Vadis*) is also manifest in the various early music ensembles that were being established during the 1950s and 1960s. It was in 1952, for example, the year after *Quo Vadis* premiered, that Noah Greenberg founded New York Pro Musica.

23. Ellwood, *Fifties Spiritual Marketplace,* 14–15.

24. Babington and Evans, *Biblical Epics,* 182. These remarks are part of a broader discussion centered on the prologue to *Quo Vadis.*

25. Maria Wyke, *Projecting the Past: Ancient Rome, Cinema and History* (New York: Routledge, 1997).

26. Melani McAlister, *Epic Encounters* (Berkeley: University of California Press, 2001). McAlister makes her point about the casting of the epics on p. 65.

27. Forshey, *Biblical Spectaculars,* 49. Forshey is basing his remarks on material from Axel Madsen, *William Wyler: The Authorized Biography* (New York: Crowell, 1973), 339.

28. There is an extensive bibliography concerning these government efforts, the most spectacular of which was the trial of the so-called "Hollywood Ten" during the late 1940s. For an account of DeMille's activities in this regard, see Tony Shaw, *Hollywood's Cold War* (Amherst: University of Massachusetts Press, 2007), 114–26.

29. Babington and Evans, *Biblical Epics,* 210–13. For a fuller and more nuanced critique of this allegorical interpretation, see Jeff Smith, "Are You Now or Have You Ever Been A Christian? The Strange History of *The Robe* as Political Allegory," in *"Un-American Hollywood": Politics and Film in the Blacklist Era,* ed. Frank Krutnik, Steve Neale, Brian Neve, and Peter Stanfield (New Brunswick, N.J.: Rutgers University Press, 2007), 19–38.

30. Geraldine Murphy, "Ugly Americans in Togas: Imperial Anxiety in the Cold War Hollywood Epic." *Journal of Film and Video* 56/3 (Fall 2004), 3–19.

31. Henry MacMahon, *The Ten Commandments* (New York: Grosset and Dunlap, 1924), 100. The frontispiece describes this work as "a novel by Henry MacMahon from Jeanie Macpherson's Story, produced by Cecil B. DeMille as the celebrated Paramount picture 'The Ten Commandments.' Illustrated with scenes from the photoplay."

32. Alan Nadel, "God's Law and the Wide Screen: *The Ten Commandments* as Cold War 'Epic,'" *Proceedings of the Modern Language Association* 108/3 (May 1993), 415–30. The article is reproduced (with minor changes) as chapter 4 of Nadel's book *Containment Culture: American Narratives, Postmodernism, and the Atomic Age* (Durham, N.C.: Duke University Press, 1995), 90–116.

1. A Biblical Story for the Post–World War II Generation?

1. Cecil B. DeMille, *The Autobiography of Cecil B. DeMille,* ed. Donald Hayne (Englewood Cliffs, N.J.: Prentice Hall, 1959), 398–99. Gerald E. Forshey recounts this story in *American Religious and Biblical Spectaculars* (Westport, Conn.: Praeger, 1992), 30.

2. According to DeMille's *Autobiography, The Ten Commandments* cost a bit over $13 million to produce, and by August 1959 (less than three years after its premiere) it had grossed nearly $84 million.

3. The widescreen format was not introduced until *The Robe* in 1953.

4. In his article "An Exotic Enemy: Anti-Japanese Musical Propaganda in World War II Hollywood," *Journal of the American Musicological Society* 54/2 (Summer 2001), 303–

57, W. Anthony Sheppard mentions Young's work in films such as *Flying Tigers* (1942) and *Sands of Iwo Jima* (1950).

5. James Buhler, David Neumeyer, and Rob Deemer, *Hearing the Movies* (Oxford: Oxford University Press, 2010), 166. The authors include an entire chapter in this book entitled "Music in Main-Title and End-Credit Sequences."

6. In his book *Music and Mythmaking in Film* (Jefferson, N.C.: McFarland, 2007), 90ff., Timothy E. Scheurer discusses the musical characterization of the figure that he calls the *femme noire*.

7. The literature on Bizet's opera is vast. A particularly influential interpretation of Bizet's music, and its implications for the characterization of Carmen, may be found in Susan McClary, *Georges Bizet, Carmen,* Cambridge Opera Handbooks (Cambridge: Cambridge University Press, 1992).

8. Janey Place, "Women in Film Noir," in *Women in Film Noir,* rev. and expanded ed., ed. E. Ann Kaplan (London: British Film Institute, 1998), 47–68. Place discusses the "two poles of female archetypes" on p. 47 of her article. Her analysis of *Out of the Past* is on pp. 60–61. For an extended discussion of the femme fatale, see Mary Ann Doane, *Femmes Fatales: Feminism, Film Theory, Psychoanalysis* (London: Routledge, 1991).

9. Vladimir Jabotinsky, *Judge and Fool* (New York: H. Liveright, 1930). The novel was also known as *Samson the Nazirite.*

10. In *Judge and Fool* this character is known as Karni. Like Miriam, she is a woman of the tribe who is in love with Samson. In the novel, however, Samson makes a proposal of marriage to her—a proposal that she rejects.

11. Jesse. L. Lasky Jr., *Whatever Happened to Hollywood?* (New York: Funk and Wagnalls, 1973), 260.

12. Ibid., 261. This account is also referenced in Anton Karl Kozlovic, "The Construction of Samson's Three Lovers in Cecil B. DeMille's Technicolor Testament, *Samson and Delilah* (1949)," *Women in Judaism* 7/1 (Spring 2010), 2–31.

13. For a provocative discussion of musical markers for Jewish identity in film, see Andrew P. Killick, "Music as Ethnic Marker in Film: The 'Jewish' Case," in *Soundtrack Available: Essays on Film and Popular Music,* ed. Pamela Robertson Wojcik and Arthur Knight (Durham, N.C.: Duke University Press, 2001), 185–206.

14. In Saint-Saëns's opera, Dalila's motivations are, of course, open to many different interpretations. For a thoughtful discussion of the character, see Ralph P. Locke, "Constructing the Oriental 'Other': Saint-Saëns's *Samson et Dalila,*" *Cambridge Opera Journal* 3/3 (November 1991): 261–302.

15. Ferdinand Lundberg and Marynia F. Farnham, *Modern Woman: The Lost Sex* (New York: Harper and Brothers, 1947), 236. The first part of this quotation is also excerpted in Harriet Sigerman, ed., *The Columbia Documentary History of American Women since 1941* (New York: Columbia University Press, 2003), 108.

16. Lundberg and Farnham, *Modern Woman,* 23.

17. Michael Stanislawski, *Zionism and the Fin-de-siecle: Cosmopolitanism and Nationalism from Nordau to Jabotinsky* (Berkeley: University of California Press, 2001), 222.

18. There is an extensive literature on the voiceover in cinema, which includes book-length explorations of the topic such as Marcel Chion's *The Voice in Cinema,* ed. and trans. Claudia Gorbman (New York: Columbia University Press, 1999), and Sarah Kozloff's *Invisible Storytellers: Voice-Over Narration in American Fiction Film* (Berkeley:

University of California Press, 1989). See also Pascal Bonitzer, "Les silences de la voix," *Cahiers du Cinéma* 256 (February/March 1975), 22–33.

19. Sometimes—as in *The Adventures of Robin Hood, David and Bathsheba,* or, for that matter, the *Star Wars* films—the position of the narrative voiceover is occupied by a script; in this case, the audience reads rather than hears the introduction.

20. Kaja Silverman, *The Acoustic Mirror: The Female Voice in Psychoanalysis and Cinema* (Bloomington: Indiana University Press, 1988), 49.

21. The *locus classicus* of this topoi is surely Wagner's score for *Lohengrin,* in which the high strings are routinely associated with the transcendent world of the Holy Grail.

22. The parallel narrative structure of DeMille's 1923 version of *The Ten Commandments* and also of Griffith's *Intolerance* (1916) is clearly related to this idea.

23. Breil's score for *The Birth of a Nation* (1915) has been the subject of extensive analysis. In his book *Music and the Silent Film: Contexts and Case Studies 1895–1924* (New York: Oxford University Press, 1997), for example, Martin Miller Marks devotes an entire chapter (pp. 109–66) to Breil's score for *The Birth of a Nation.* For a detailed exploration of the "Motif of Barbarism," see Jane Gaines and Neil Lerner, "The Orchestration of Affect: The Motif of Barbarism in Breil's *The Birth of a Nation* Score," in *The Sounds of Early Cinema,* ed. Richard Abel and Rick Altman (Bloomington: Indiana University Press, 2001), 252–68.

24. Steven P. Miller, *Billy Graham and the Rise of the Republican South* (Philadelphia: University of Pennsylvania Press, 2009), 23.

25. James Gilbert's perceptive discussion of Graham may be found in chapter 6 of his *Men in the Middle: Searching for Masculinity in the 1950s* (Chicago: University of Chicago Press, 2005). On p. 51 of his book *The Fifties Spiritual Marketplace: American Religion in a Decade of Conflict* (New Brunswick, N.J.: Rutgers University Press, 1997), Robert S. Ellwood writes: "Personal conversion is the foundation of Christian experience for Graham, and all else must stem from it. This fitted the fifties need for ways to find ways of assimilation into a cause larger and greater than oneself."

26. Billy Graham, *Peace with God* (Garden City, N.Y.: Doubleday, 1953), 105.

27. Ibid., 106. A similar sentiment (although one couched in space-age imagery) may be found in Graham's *The World Aflame* (Kingswood, Surrey: World's Work, 1965), 151: "Repentance is the launching pad where the soul is sent on its eternal orbit with God at the center of the arc. When our hearts are bowed as low as they can get and we truly acknowledge and forsake our sins, then God takes over and like the second stage of a rocket, He lifts us toward His Kingdom. The way up is down. Man got into difficulty when he lifted his will against God's. He gets out of trouble when he bows to the divine superiority, when he repents and says humbly: 'God be merciful to be a sinner.' Man's extremity then becomes God's opportunity."

28. The opening titles in *Samson and Delilah* assign the writing credits thus: screenplay by Jesse L. Lasky Jr. and Frederic M. Frank, from original treatments by Harold Lamb and Vladimir Jabotinsky, based upon the story of Samson and Delilah in the Holy Bible, Judges, chaps. 13–16.

29. Review from *Variety,* October 26, 1949, quoted in Gene Ringgold, *The Films of Cecil B. DeMille* (New York: Cadillac, 1969), 344.

30. *New Yorker,* December 31, 1949, quoted in Ringgold, *The Films of Cecil B. DeMille,* 344–45. The Jesse Lasky with whom DeMille collaborated on *The Squaw Man* was the father of the Jesse Lasky who wrote the screenplay for *Samson and Delilah.*

2. Turning Away from "Concocted Spectacle"

1. Published by Famous Music Corporation, 1619 Broadway, 1950.

2. Credit for the words and music of "David and Bathsheba" is given to Gordon Jenkins, Robert Allen, and Allan Roberts.

3. Edward Powell is credited with the orchestration for the film.

4. In her seminal study of the woman's film, *The Desire to Desire: The Women's Film of the 1940s* (Bloomington: Indiana University Press, 1987), 3, Mary Ann Doane defines the label as "a genre of Hollywood films produced from the silent era through the 1950s and early 1960s, but most heavily concentrated and most popular in the 1930s and 1940s. The films deal with a female protagonist and often appear to allow her significant access to point of view structures and the enunciative level of the filmic discourse. They treat problems defined as 'female' (problems revolving around domestic life, the family, children, self-sacrifice, and the relationship between women and production vs. that between women and reproduction), and, most crucially, are directed toward a female audience." Doane does not mention *David and Bathsheba* in her book, but the analyses of the film by Exum and Kelso (see below) are clearly informed by her discussion.

5. Bruce Babington and Peter Evans, *Biblical Epics: Sacred Narrative in the Hollywood Cinema* (New York: St. Martin's Press, 1993), 74. The authors devote an entire chapter of their book to *David and Bathsheba* (70–90). My reading of the film's generic hybridity is somewhat different from theirs.

6. In her book *Plotted, Shot and Painted: Cultural Representations of Biblical Women* (Sheffield: Sheffield University Press, 1996), 62ff., J. Cheryl Exum points out that in *David and Bathsheba* (as opposed to the biblical account) this *confrontation* is private rather than public.

7. See the discussion of this scene, ibid., 22n.5.

8. The metaphorical mapping of the music/text dichotomy onto the dichotomies of thought vs. feeling and man vs. woman is perhaps most famously developed by Richard Wagner in *Opera and Drama* (among other texts).

9. Julie Kelso, "Gazing at Impotence in Henry King's *David and Bathsheba*," in *Screening Scripture: Intertextual Connections between Scripture and Film*, ed. George Aichelle and Richard Walsh (Harrisburg, Pa.: Trinity, 2002), 155–87, 157. The idea that a male spectatorial gaze is intrinsic to cinema itself appears most famously, perhaps, in Laura Mulvey, "Visual Pleasure and Narrative Cinema," *Screen* 16/3 (Autumn, 1975), 6–18. It is developed (among other places) in Mary Ann Doane, *Femmes Fatales: Feminism, Film Theory, Psychoanalysis* (London: Routledge, 1991), especially in chapter 4, "Remembering Women: Psychical and Historical Constructions in Film Theory" (76–95); and E. Ann Kaplan, *Women and Film: Both Sides of the Camera* (New York: Methuen, 1983).

10. Exum, *Plotted, Shot and Painted*, 29.

11. Doane, *The Desire to Desire*, 5.

12. See ibid., 98–100. For a reading of this scene that focuses more explicitly on music, see Marcia J. Citron, "'Soll ich lauschen?' Love-Death in *Humoresque*," in *Wagner and Cinema*, ed. Jeongwon Joe and Sander L. Gilman (Bloomington: Indiana University Press, 2010), 167–85.

13. For a discussion of the view, prominent since the 1970s, that films typically divide into three acts, see Kristin Thompson, *Storytelling in the New Hollywood: Understanding*

Classical Narrative Technique (Cambridge, Mass.: Harvard University Press, 1999), 22–36. Thompson herself puts forward a "four-act" model, which she applies to films from the 1970s through the 1990s.

14. Indeed, Babington and Evans (*Biblical Epics,* 76) understand the pastoral setting of this scene as an allusion to the western.

15. The Genesis story (or stories), of course, can be linked to even older narratives.

16. Babington and Evans (*Biblical Epics,* 87) understand this request in Freudian terms. "As the solicited memories transport him back into childhood," they write, "making the man become the child again, she herself, not paralleling his inner journey by regression to her own childhood, becomes a mother surrogate."

17. Doane regards the 1940s as "the decade of the most intense incorporation of psychoanalysis within the Hollywood system" (*The Desire to Desire,* 45). It is certainly possible to understand David's dilemma in terms of the popular understanding of Freudian psychiatry that was so prominent in Hollywood films of this period. It is interesting to note in this regard that David was Gregory Peck's only role in the biblical epic genre.

18. 2 Samuel 1:25–27. The script quotes the King James Version.

19. See David Kopp, *Chromatic Transformations in Nineteenth-Century Music,* Cambridge Studies in Music Theory and Analysis (Cambridge: Cambridge University Press,2002). Kopp cites several seminal articles by David Lewin, including "A Formal Theory of Generalized Tonal Functions," *Journal of Music Theory* 26/1 (Spring 1982), 23–60; "Amfortas' Prayer to Titurel and the Role of D in *Parsifal:* The Tonal Spaces and the Drama of the Enharmonic C♭/B," *19th-Century Music* 7/3 (Essays in Honor of Joseph Kerman, April 3, 1984), 336–49; and "Some Notes on Analyzing Wagner: *The Ring* and *Parsifal,*" *19th-Century Music* 16/1 (Summer 1992), 49–58. My understanding of the function of these kinds of harmonic relationship owes much to the work of Frank Lehman. For a recent example of Lehman's work, see his article "Transformational Analysis and the Representation of Genius in Film Music," *Music Theory Spectrum* 35/1 (Spring 2013), 1–22.

20. In order to save space and (I hope) to increase readability, I have not included the full text of the psalm in my transcription. In the film, however, David recites the text in its entirety.

21. One of the most popular and influential of these melodramas was *Ben-Hur: A Tale of the Christ,* first produced in 1899. Based on Lew Wallace's famous novel, with a script by William Young, the drama included extensive incidental music by Edgar Stillman Kelley. One of the highlights of Kelley's score was the choral music for the final scene of the play. For a discussion of this work, see Roger Hickman, *Miklós Rózsa's Ben-Hur: A Film Score Guide* (Lanham, Md.: Scarecrow Press, 2011), 61–63.

22. Steven Cohan, *Masked Men: Masculinity and the Movies in the Fifties* (Bloomington: Indiana University Press, 1997), 125–30.

3. Spectacle and Authenticity in Miklós Rózsa's *Quo Vadis* Score

1. Roland Barthes, "The Romans in Films," in *Mythologies,* selected and trans. Annette Lavers (New York: Hill and Wang, 1972), 26–28, 26.

2. Ibid., 28.

3. Miklós Rózsa, *Double Life: The Autobiography of Miklós Rózsa,* foreword by Antal Doráti (New York: Hippocrene Books, 1982), 159.

4. See Ruth Scodel and Anja Bettenworth, *Whither Quo Vadis?: Sienkiewicz's Novel in Film and Television* (Hoboken, N.J.: Wiley, 2009).

5. Frank K. DeWald, online liner notes to *Quo Vadis, Film Score Monthly,* http://www.filmscoremonthly.com/notes/quo_vadis.html (accessed August 7, 2011).

6. Miklós Rózsa, "The Music in *Quo Vadis,*" *Film Music Notes* 11/2 (November–December 1951), 4–10. Rózsa's article has been reprinted (together with an introduction that gives useful background to the composer's life and work) in Mervyn Cooke, ed., *The Hollywood Film Music Reader* (Oxford: Oxford University Press, 2010), 165–71; all citations below are from this reprint. For the sake of consistency and legibility, I have used italics whenever Rózsa refers to the title of the film.

7. Rózsa, "The Music of *Quo Vadis,*" 167. The practice—to which Rózsa refers—of engaging academic experts to advise on matters of authenticity for big-budget epics was fairly widespread. The principal historical advisor for *Quo Vadis* (as well as for other MGM historical films) was Hugh Gray. Gray also wrote the lyrics for all the diegetic music in the *Quo Vadis* score. As I mentioned in the introduction, the most famous of these (admittedly obscure) experts is probably Henry S. Noerdlinger, who advised Cecil B. DeMille. Noerdlinger's work for *The Ten Commandments* was published as a separate volume. In subsequent years, Rózsa would continue to work closely with these advisers. For the music of *El Cid* (1961), for example, Rózsa consulted with the Spanish scholar Menendez Pidal. Pidal apparently introduced Rózsa to the twelfth-century *Cantigas of Santa Maria,* some of which appear in the film—in a manner similar to the Epitaph of Seikolos in *Quo Vadis*—as markers of historical authenticity.

8. Rózsa, "The Music of *Quo Vadis,*" 167.

9. Rózsa, *Double Life,* 23.

10. In "The Music of *Quo Vadis*" Rózsa speaks of the curved brass instrument featured prominently in the Roman processions as a "buccina," although it is actually a cornu.

11. Rózsa discusses the problem of instrumentation in "The Music of *Quo Vadis,*" 170.

12. Maria Wyke, *Projecting the Past: Ancient Rome, Cinema and History* (New York: Routledge, 1997), 120–22. Wyke reproduces *Pollice Verso* directly above a still from the 1913 film, making the connection between painting and mise-en-scène extraordinarily obvious.

13. Sol P. Levy, comp., *Motion Picture Collection, Part 1* (New York: H. S. Gordon, 1914), 18–19. I am indebted to Rebecca Eaton for pointing this source out to me.

14. Rózsa, "The Music of *Quo Vadis,*" 169.

15. Ibid., 171.

16. Christopher Palmer, *The Composer in Hollywood* (New York: Rizzoli, 1990), 213–14.

17. Martin M. Winkler, "The Roman Empire in American Cinema after 1945," *Classical Journal* 93/2 (December 1997–January 1998), 167–96, 167.

18. The literature on musical orientalism is vast. For a particularly thoughtful investigation, the fruit of more than twenty years of scholarly engagement with this topic, see Ralph P. Locke, *Musical Exoticism: Images and Reflections* (Cambridge: Cambridge University Press, 2009).

19. The only character with an explicit claim to Jewish identity in Mervyn LeRoy's film is St. Paul.

20. In Sienkiewicz's novel, Lygia is a princess from beyond the Danube, and her name is taken as a reference to her (proto-Polish) homeland. In a similar manner, "Mercia" may be taken as an (albeit somewhat anachronistic) reference to the Anglo-Saxon kingdom of the same name that flourished in the seventh and eighth centuries.

21. Henryk Sienkiewicz, *Quo Vadis? A Narrative of the Time of Nero,* trans. Jeremiah Curtin (Boston: Little, Brown, 1896, 1897, 1923), 123.

22. Sienkiewicz's description of the singing in the arena can be found in *Quo Vadis,* 430.

23. After the Production Code came into force, many of the more lurid scenes of *The Sign of the Cross* (including Ancaria's performance of "The Naked Moon") were edited out.

24. As he notes in his article, Rózsa based this musical cue on the spurious seventeenth-century "Ode of Pindar." We might then call it an "imitation of an imitation."

4. Novel and Film, Music and Miracle

1. Fulton Oursler's *The Greatest Story Ever Told* (Garden City, N.Y.: Doubleday, 1949), based on a series of radio broadcasts, was atop the nonfiction list from May to September 1949. Catherine Marshall's *A Man Called Peter: The Story of Peter Marshall* (New York: McGraw-Hill, 1950) was atop the list in September and October 1952.

2. Norman Vincent Peale, *The Power of Positive Thinking* (New York: Prentice Hall, 1952). Statistics from Ron Alexander, "Chronicle," *New York Times,* May 31, 1994.

3. Billy Graham, *Peace with God* (Garden City, N.Y.: Doubleday, 1953).

4. Lloyd Douglas's *The Robe* (New York: Houghton Mifflin, 1942) was number one on the *New York Times* best-seller list on November 22, 1942, and held that position until March 14, 1943. His next novel, *The Big Fisherman* (New York: Houghton Mifflin, 1948), was atop the list from December 1948 until April 1949.

5. Thomas B. Costain's *The Silver Chalice* (Garden City, N.Y.: Doubleday, 1952) was number one on the *New York Times* best-seller list from September 7, 1952, to March 8, 1953, remaining on the list until October 25, 1953. Costain had already had published a number-one book with *The Black Rose* in 1945 and 1946 and *The Moneyman* in 1947.

6. Rudolf Bultmann, *New Testament and Mythology and Other Basic Writings,* selected, ed., and trans. Schubert M. Ogden (Philadelphia: Fortress Press, 1984), 1–43. The original German may be found in H. W. Bartsch, ed., *Kerygma und Mythos,* vol. 1, 2nd ed. (Hamburg: Reich-Evangelischer Verlag, 1951), 15–48. See also Bultmann's "On the Problem of Demythologizing" (1952) on pp. 95–130 of Ogden's collection.

7. Bultmann was the subject of a *Time* magazine article (September 24, 1956), as well as numerous books during this period. In his 1960 book *The Scope of Demythologizing: Bultmann and His Critics* (New York: Harper and Brothers, 1960), for example, John Macquarie writes that "Bultmann's demythologizing has made a most remarkable impact upon the theological world—an impact comparable in its magnitude to that made by Barth's theology of crisis after the First World War. Since the appearance of Bultmann's essay . . . there has been a steady and voluminous stream of books and articles in which the merits and demerits of demythologizing have been debated with varying degrees of penetration. This stream has poured forth not only in Germany but in France, Britain and America; not only among Lutherans but among Presbyterians, Anglicans

and Roman Catholics; indeed, not only among theologians but in some philosophical circles as well."

8. Philip Dunne, *Take Two: A Life in Movies and Politics* (New York: McGraw-Hill, 1980), 252. Quoted in Scott Morschauser, "Watching Ancient Egyptian Poetry—Among Other Histrionics," *Journal of Religion and Film* 15/2 (October 2011).

9. Gerald E. Forshey, *American Religious and Biblical Spectaculars* (Westport, Conn.: Praeger, 1992), 85.

10. Publicity posters for *The Robe* may be viewed on "The Widescreen Museum" website: http://www.widescreenmuseum.com (accessed June 1, 2012). The website also includes detailed descriptions of the various anamorphic lens technologies that were used during this period.

11. Propp's *Morphology of the Folktale* was published in Russian in 1928 and translated into English in 1958.

12. For a fascinating description of the uses to which Newman's music was put in the context of CinemaScope, see Matthew Malsky, "Sounds of the City: Alfred Newman's 'Street Scene' and Urban Modernity," in *Lowering the Boom: Critical Studies in Film Sound,* ed. Jay Beck and Tony Grajeda (Urbana: University of Illinois Press), 105–22.

13. Harold Brown, "*The Robe,*" *Film Music* 13/2 (November/December 1953), 3–17.

14. The story of the Romans playing dice for a seamless robe can be found in John 19:23–25 and (in abbreviated form) in Luke 23:34. Douglas always capitalizes "robe" when he refers to the specific garment that Jesus wore at his crucifixion—I follow that practice here.

15. See Gordon Gow, *Hollywood in the Fifties* (New York: A. S. Barnes, 1971), 17.

16. In his analysis of Miriam's song, Harold Brown also points out the various melodic-harmonic implications of Newman's music. Brown regards Miriam's song as the highlight of the score.

17. Douglas, *The Robe,* 151.

18. Frederick Steiner, "The Making of an American Film Composer: A Study of Alfred Newman's Music in the First Decade of the Sound Era" (Ph.D. diss., University of Southern California, 1981), 322, 350–51. Steiner also points out another moment in *The Robe* (when Demetrius is freed from captivity by Marcellus) in which Newman recycled some of his score to *The Hunchback of Notre Dame.*

5. Spirit and Empire

1. Michael Wood, *America in the Movies; or "Santa Maria, It Had Slipped My Mind"* (New York: Basic Books, 1975), 174.

2. Ibid., 175.

3. With his reference to Handel, Wood might also be thinking about the (in)famous insertion of the "Hallelujah" chorus from *Messiah* into *The Greatest Story Ever Told.* I return to this insertion in chapter 9.

4. Yearly Easter telecasts of *The Ten Commandments* began during the 1970s.

5. Wood, *America in the Movies,* 169.

6. Ibid., 180–81. Wood's remarks about "cars that give you seven miles to the gallon" remind us that he was writing only a few years after the Arab oil embargo and in the same year as the fall of Saigon: harsh reminders that American appetites (to use Wood's term) for more wealth, more power, and more energy might need to be curtailed.

7. Exodus 6:4 (King James Version).

8. Exodus 19:5 (King James Version).

9. For a recent account of this relationship, see Andrew Preston, *Sword of the Spirit, Shield of Faith: Religion in American War and Diplomacy* (New York: Alfred A. Knopf, 2012).

10. We are reminded here of DeMille's staunch anti-communism, and his support for the House Un-American Activities Committee (and other groups) to root out "subversives" in Hollywood during this period. While clearly present, the allegory (that Egypt is to the ancient Hebrews as the Soviet Union is to America) breaks down when too much pressure is applied to it.

11. Alan Nadel, *Containment Culture: American Narratives, Postmodernism, and the Atomic Age* (Durham, N.C.: Duke University Press, 1995). Chapter 4 of Nadel's book (90–115) is titled "God's Law and the Wide Screen: *The Ten Commandments* as Cold War Epic," and in slightly different form was published in the *Proceedings of the Modern Language Association* 108/3 (May 1993), 415–30.

12. Melani McAlister, *Epic Encounters* (Berkeley: University of California Press, 2001).

13. Bruce Babington and Peter Evans, *Biblical Epics: Sacred Narrative in the Hollywood Cinema* (New York: St. Martin's Press, 1993), 54.

14. McAlister, *Epic Encounters*, 45.

15. Interoffice communication, now housed in the Special Collections department of the University of Southern California library. I am indebted to my brother Donald Meyer for bringing this memo to my attention.

16. Katherine Orrison, *Written in Stone: Making Cecil B. DeMille's Epic "The Ten Commandments"* (Lanham, Md.: Vestal Press. 1999), 161.

17. Ibid., 162–63.

18. Henry Noerdlinger, *Moses in Egypt: The Documentation to the Motion Picture The Ten Commandments,* introduction by Cecil B. DeMille (Los Angeles: University of Southern California Press, 1956), 71. Noerdlinger references volume 4 of Flavius Josephus's *Jewish Antiquities,* trans. Henry St. John Thackeray (Cambridge, Mass.: Harvard University Press, 1930), 275. In an interview with Katherine Orrison, Woody Strode (the actor who portrays the Ethiopian king) also references this connection, speaking of Moses as the "brother-in-law" of his character. See Orrison, *Written in Stone,* 134–35. As mentioned above, the publication of this book was essentially part of the promotional materials for the film.

19. Indeed, despite important differences in visual composition, these images from the 1956 version of *The Ten Commandments* can in many ways be regarded as an updated version of the opening sequence from the 1923 version of the story, which also shows columns of slaves laboring on heavy ropes. As Katherine Orrison points out, DeMille duplicated many of his sets from the 1923 film for his 1956 remake, and the slavery images from the 1956 prologue are only a small number of the numerous shots that can be traced back to specific precursors in the silent version. The recycling of visual and textual elements thus articulates and exemplifies what we might call the ideological continuity between the two versions of *The Ten Commandments*.

20. In his analysis of this particular scene (98–100), Nadel draws the connection between Moses and DeMille himself. In his autobiography, as Nadel points out (100), DeMille "in fact, compares his directing of over eight thousand extras to Moses' organi-

zation of subordinates" (428). Michael Wood makes a similar point in his book *America in the Movies,* where he writes that the "hero of *The Ten Commandments* is not Moses, but DeMille himself, who set up the whole show, the voice of God and the burning bush and the miracles in Egypt included" (173).

21. It is interesting to note that Olive Deering—the actress who portrayed Miriam in *Samson and Delilah*—also appears in *The Ten Commandments* as the *sister* of Moses, who coincidentally is also named Miriam.

22. Karen Brodkin, *How Jews Became White Folks, and What That Says about Race in America* (New Brunswick, N.J.: Rutgers University Press, 1998), 141.

23. Babington and Evans, *Biblical Epics,* 54.

24. Another example of the "epic Judaica topos" can be found in the theme that Rózsa wrote for the character of Rebecca in his score for *Ivanhoe* (1952).

25. James Deaville, "The *Topos* of 'Evil Medieval' in American Horror Film Music," in *Music, Meaning, and Media,* ed. Erkki Pekkilä, David Neumeyer, and Richard Littlefield (Imatra: International Semiotics Institute; Helsinki: Semiotic Society of Finland, 2006), 26–44. Philip Tagg references the association between Mixolydian mode and "wide open spaces" in his book *Everyday Tonality: Towards a Tonal Theory of What Most People Hear* (New York: Mass Media Scholars Press, 2009), 55.

26. Nadel, *Containment Culture,* 109–10.

27. The fact that Elmer Bernstein was one of the most famous and influential composers for western films lends special importance to the topic of generic hybridity between this cinematic genre and *The Ten Commandments.* Bernstein's career trajectory with regard to the epic was somewhat unusual. While some of his later films—such as *The Miracle* (1959) and *Kings of the Sun* (1963)—are generally classified as historical epics, the genre played a much less important part in his career than it did in Rózsa's or Newman's.

28. My transcription preserves the somewhat unusual metric notation of the conductor's score. It should be noted that the dotted quarter notes of the $\frac{12}{8}$ measures equal quarter notes in the $\frac{4}{4}$ measures; in other words, the basic rhythmic pulse remains constant throughout the cue.

29. The textural relationship here is in some ways similar to the interaction between a solo and a rhythm guitar in the basic four-instrument arrangement of bands like the Beatles.

30. The fact that Yul Brynner portrays both Rameses and Chris (the leader of the band of seven in *The Magnificent Seven*) makes this particular comparison even more interesting.

6. The Law of Genre and the Music for *Ben-Hur*

1. Jacques Derrida and Avital Ronell, "The Law of Genre," *Critical Inquiry: On Narrative* 7/1 (Autumn 1980), 55–81.

2. Ibid., 59.

3. In her recent book *Film and the Classical Epic Tradition* (Oxford: Oxford University Press, 2013), Joanna Paul refers to *Ben-Hur* simply as the "archetypal epic" (213).

4. Script dated February 18, 1955, currently housed as part of the Turner/MGM scripts collection at the Margaret Herrick Library, Academy of Motion Picture Arts and Sciences, Beverly Hills.

5. In the 1959 film, "Flavia"—the foreign woman of the *Ben-Hur* plot—appears only in the Roman banquet scene.

6. Marina Berti (Eunice in *Quo Vadis*) makes a brief appearance in *Ben-Hur* as Flavia.

7. Thomas Schatz, *Hollywood Genres: Formulas, Filmmaking, and the Studio System* (Philadelphia: Temple University Press, 1981), 37–38. Like many other critics and scholars from the 1970s and 1980s, Schatz passes over the postwar biblical epic virtually in silence. In the second—and by far the largest—section he explores what he calls "six dominant Hollywood genres." These include the western, the gangster film, and the musical, but not the biblical epic or even a more broadly construed category such as the epic or historical film.

8. See especially the chapter on genre theory in Steve Neale's *Genre and Hollywood* (New York: Routledge, 2007).

9. Robert Stam, *Film Theory: An Introduction* (Malden, Mass.: Blackwell, 2000), 128–29.

10. Bruce Babington and Peter Evans, *Biblical Epics: Sacred Narrative in the Hollywood Cinema* (New York: St. Martin's Press, 1993), 5–6.

11. http://www.moviegoods.com/movie_product_static.asp?master_movie_id =144&sku=271747. Accessed August 23, 2012.

12. http://sharetv.org/movies/quo_vadis_1951. Accessed August 23, 2012.

13. http://www.impawards.com/1956/ten_commandments.html. Accessed August 23, 2012.

14. http://www.yeeeeee.com/2008/09/13/112-historic-movie-posters-between-1925 -1985. Accessed August 23, 2012.

15. The challenges to the American cinema industry during this period have been widely discussed. For a succinct and useful account of these challenges, see Peter Lev, *Transforming the Screen: 1950–59* (New York: Charles Scribner's Sons, 2003), especially chap. 1, "The American Film Industry in the Early 1950s."

16. Jon Solomon, *The Ancient World in the Cinema*, rev. and expanded ed. (New Haven, Conn.: Yale University Press, 2001), 207.

17. James Buhler, Rob Deemer, and David Neumeyer, *Hearing the Movies: Music and Sound in Film History* (New York and Oxford: Oxford University Press, 2010), 165. The authors describe the conventional pattern of this introductory material (in slightly different terms from those that I use here) on 166 in the context of an analysis of *Meet Me in St. Louis*.

18. Ibid., 168.

19. The opening sequence for *The Sound of Music*—described by Buhler, Deemer, and Neumeyer on 168–70 of *Hearing the Movies*—provides yet another example of this kind of expansion.

20. Elmer Bernstein Collection, University of Southern California. These quotations are taken from the minutes to a meeting that DeMille held with Bernstein and some of his other assistants (one of many such meetings) on November 3, 1955.

21. The most obvious Wagnerian reference in *The Ten Commandments* score comes in the sequence near the very beginning of the film in which we see the infant Moses being set adrift in a wicker basket and subsequently discovered by the daughter of Pharaoh. For the underscoring to this scene, Bernstein cleverly combines an "infantilized" $\frac{6}{8}$ si-

ciliano version of his Moses theme with a reference to the opening scene of *Das Rhein-gold.*

22. William Darby and Jack Du Bois, *American Film Music: Major Composers, Tech-niques, Trends, 1915–1990* (Jefferson, N.C.: McFarland, 1990), 15. Darby and Du Bois make their comment in connection to a discussion of Max Steiner and his approach to film scoring. The supposed link between Wagner and film music is also used to cut in the opposite direction, most famously in Hanns Eisler's *Composing for the Films* (New York: Oxford University Press, 1947). Although Eisler credits Adorno in the preface to the 1947 edition of this book, in later editions (see note 29, below) Adorno is presented as a co-author. I return below to Adorno's argument about the relationship between film music and Wagner's "phantasmagoric" technique.

23. Roger Hickman, *Reel Music: Exploring 100 Years of Film Music* (New York: Norton, 2005).

24. Jeongwon Joe, "Introduction: Why Wagner and Cinema? Tolkien Was Wrong," in *Wagner and Cinema,* ed. Jeongwon Joe and Sander L. Gilman (Bloomington: Indiana University Press, 2010), 1–24; see especially 2–4.

25. See, for example, Scott D. Paulin, "Richard Wagner and the Fantasy of Cinematic Unity: The Idea of the *Gesamtkunstwerk* in the History and Theory of Film Music," in *Music and Cinema,* ed. James Buhler, Caryl Flinn, and David Neumeyer (Hanover, N.H.: University Press of New England, 2000), 58–84.

26. Hans Erdmann and Giuseppe Becce, *Allgemeines Handbuch der Film-Musik,* 2 vols. (Berlin-Lichterfelde and Leipzig: Schlesinger, 1927), 51, 52. The translation is my own.

27. Brown's keynote address was published (with modifications) as "How Not to Think Film Music," *Music and the Moving Image* 1/1 (Spring 2008), 1–18. "Music and/as Cine-Narrative; or *Ceci n'est pas un leitmotif*" appears in *A Companion to Narrative Theory,* ed. James Phelan and Peter J. Rabinowitz (Oxford: Blackwell, 2005), 456–57.

28. Eisler, *Composing for the Films,* 5.

29. Graham McCann, introduction to Eisler and Adorno, *Composing for the Films* (New York: Continuum, 2005), 26. McCann originally prepared this introduction for the 1994 Athlone Press edition of *Composing for the Films.*

30. Eisler, *Composing for the Films* (1947), 4.

31. David Neumeyer, "The Resonances of Wagnerian Opera and Nineteenth-Century Melodrama in the Film Scores of Max Steiner," in Joe and Gilman, *Wagner and Cinema,* 111–30. See especially 116–17.

32. Miklós Rózsa, *Double Life: The Autobiography of Miklós Rózsa,* foreword by Antal Doráti (New York: Hippocrene Books, 1982), 33.

33. Rózsa acknowledges this connection in his autobiography. "I had no difficulty conceiving the music [for *Ben-Hur*] stylistically," he writes. "This time I didn't go to first-century sources, but simply developed the 'Roman' style I had already established in *Quo Vadis* to create an archaic feeling" (*Double Life,* 177).

34. Roger Hickman, *Miklós Rózsa's Ben-Hur: A Film Score Guide* (Lanham, Md.: Scarecrow Press, 2011), 130. The tempo of the Panem et Circenses cue is somewhat faster than Hail Galba from *Quo Vadis.* Rózsa also transposes the march upward from F to A.

35. Although the cue is sometimes known as Circus Parade, it was excerpted under Parade of the Charioteers. I retain that usage here.

36. The cinematography for the triumphal marches in both films is also quite similar. In each, block-like cohorts of soldiers and also instrumentalists march along a wide avenue that is flanked by spectators. The brass instruments featured in *Ben-Hur* do indeed seem to be the same as those used in *Quo-Vadis*.

37. See Steven Dwight Wescott, "Miklós Rózsa's *Ben Hur*: The Musical-Dramatic Function of the Hollywood Leitmotiv," *Film Music I*, ed. Clifford McCarty (New York: Garland, 1989), 183–207. Wescott discusses the Parade of the Charioteers cue on p. 193. Hickman discusses the relationship between the Hatred theme and the main theme of the Parade of the Charioteers cue on p. 100 of his *Film Score Guide*. In this discussion, Hickman also presents the idea that Rózsa inserts elements of the Hatred theme into two other *Ben-Hur* marches as well. I find this connection to be less strong.

38. Wescott, "Miklós Rózsa's *Ben Hur*," 183–207.

39. Eisler, *Composing for the Films* (1947), 5–6. This passage appears more complex when we consider it in light of Adorno's well-known remarks about Wagner and film music in the "Phantasmagoria" chapter of his monograph *In Search of Wagner*. See Theodor Adorno, *In Search of Wagner,* trans. Rodney Livingstone (New York: Verso, 2005), 74–85.

40. Ralph Erkelenz, "*Ben-Hur*: A Tale of the Score," *Pro Musica Sana* 5/1, no. 61 (Spring 2005), 1–29; "Part Two," 5/2, no. 62 (Spring 2006), 3–36; "Part Three," 6/1, no. 63 (Spring 2007), 4–39; "Part Four," 7/1, no. 65 (Spring 2009), 3–32; and "Part Five," 7/2, no. 66 (Fall 2009), 3–49.

41. Robert Donington, *Wagner's Ring and Its Symbols,* 3rd ed. (London: Faber and Faber, 1974).

42. Erkelenz's discussion of this cue may be found in part five of his article, *Pro Musica sana* 7/2, no. 66 (Fall 2009), 5–7. Erkelenz discusses the Golgotha sequence on p. 33 of this same issue. It should be noted that in this latter sequence, the cue ends *before* the trumpet fanfares that are so prominent at the end of the Death of Messala scene.

43. Both Erkelenz and Hickman assert that Rózsa had nothing to do with the decision to use this cue for the Golgotha sequence.

44. Rózsa, *Double Life,* 153–54.

45. This complex relationship will figure even more prominently in the score to *King of Kings* that I examine in chapter 7.

46. Hickman, *Film Score Guide to Ben-Hur,* 139.

7. *King of Kings* and the Problem of Repetition

1. Miklós Rózsa, *Double Life: The Autobiography of Miklós Rózsa,* foreword by Antal Doráti (New York: Hippocrene Books, 1982), 180.

2. Quoted in Mel Martin, *The Magnificent Showman: The Epic Films of Samuel Bronston* (Albany, Ga.: BearManor Media, 2007), 58.

3. Rózsa, *Double Life,* 177.

4. For more comprehensive accounts of "Jesus movies," see Adele Reinhartz, *Jesus of Hollywood* (Oxford: Oxford University Press, 2007), and Peter Malone, *Screen Jesus: Portrayals of Christ in Television and Film* (London: Scarecrow Press, 2012).

5. Malone, *Screen Jesus,* 55. As Robert Pope points out in his book *Salvation in Celluloid* (London: T & T Clark, 2007), 67: "Jesus' presence was banned from the screen by

early censorship bodies (including the British Board of Film Censors which was established in 1912)."

6. Script dated June 8, 1960, revised June 30, 1960. Turner/MGM scripts f.K 325, Margaret Herrick Library, Academy of Motion Picture Arts and Sciences, Beverly Hills.

7. Bosley Crowther, "'King of Kings' Has Its Premiere at State," *New York Times,* October 12, 1961.

8. "Mickey-Mousing" refers to instances in which film music mimics onscreen action (much in the manner of some music for cartoons).

9. The temptation story is not present in the Gospel of John. Mark (1:13) briefly describes Jesus' forty days in the wilderness but does not mention the Devil. The temptation stories in Matthew (4:1–11) and in Luke (4:1–13) are quite similar. The specific language of the film script seems to be most closely based on Luke.

10. Rózsa, *Double Life,* 180.

11. For a discussion of Schoenberg's long and complex relationship to film, see Sabine M. Feisst, "Arnold Schoenberg and the Cinematic Art," *Musical Quarterly* 83/1 (Spring 1999), 93–113. Feisst discusses Schoenberg's op. 34 on 97–98. Schoenberg, it should be pointed out, did not write the *Begleitungsmusik* to accompany a specific film. In his article "Schoenberg at the Movies: Dodecaphony and Film," *Music Theory Online* 0/1 (February 1993), David Neumeyer subjects Schoenberg's *Begleitungsmusik* to commutation tests in order to assess its viability as cinematic music.

12. Directed by John Huston, this film is also known as *Freud: The Secret Passion.* Neumeyer discusses it as well as other examples in the introduction to "Schoenberg at the Movies."

13. Rózsa, *Double Life,* 180.

14. In this context, one might also reference the second movement of Mahler's Fourth Symphony.

15. Rózsa, *Double Life,* 180.

16. The text and music of "Victimae paschali laudes" is attributed to Wipo of Burgundy, who flourished in the early to mid-eleventh century.

17. Abraham Zebi Idelsohn, *Hebräisch-orientalischer Melodienschatz,* 8 vols. (Leipzig: Breitkopf und Härtel, c. 1914–1929), republished with translations of the prefatory material as *Thesaurus of Oriental Hebrew Melodies* (Jersey City, N.J.: KTAV Publishing House, 1973).

18. Idelsohn, *Thesaurus of Oriental Hebrew Melodies,* p. 24, no. 38. Between June 1949 and September 1950, British and American transport planes airlifted Yemenite Jews to the new State of Israel as part of what became known as "Operation Magic Carpet." The Yemenite refugees were sometimes thought to represent a more primitive or authentic stratum of Jewish culture. I touch upon this image of Yemenite Jews again in chapter 9, in connection with the Inbal dance troupe.

19. Ibid., 1:2.

8. *Suoni Nuovi, Suoni Antichi*

1. Robert S. Ellwood, *The Sixties Spiritual Awakening: American Religion Moving from Modern to Postmodern* (New Brunswick, N.J.: Rutgers University Press, 1994), 51. The famous "Is God Dead?" cover appeared on the April 8, 1966, issue of *Time* (the same

date as Good Friday). Ellwood frames his discussion of American religious life during this period in terms of a transition from "modernist" (meaning, among other things, self-confident, future-oriented, and rational) to "postmodernist."

2. Lon Jones, ed., *Barabbas: The Story of a Motion Picture* (Bologna: Capelli, 1962), 20. Capelli also published an Italian version of this work: *Barabba* (Bologna: Capelli, 1962). For this version of the book, Richard Hawkins is credited as the editor. Unlike the English version, the Italian version is lavishly illustrated with stills from the film.

3. Pär Lagerqvist, *Barabbas,* trans. Alan Blair, with preface by Lucien Maury and a letter by André Gide (New York: Random House, 1951). Lagerqvist's novel had already been adapted for the screen in the 1953 film of the same name, directed by Alf Sjöberg.

4. Lew Wallace, *Ben-Hur: A Tale of the Christ* (1880; reprint, New York: Harper and Brothers, 1959), 98–99.

5. Lagerqvist, *Barabbas,* 3.

6. The so-called "*peplum*" or "sword and sandal" films produced in Italy during this period were in many ways analogous to the spaghetti western.

7. I am indebted to Hanita Blair for her help in identifying the source for this music.

8. Jones, *Barabbas,* 167.

9. Luca Bandirali, *Mario Nascimbene: Compositore per il Cinema* (Lecce: Argo: 2004), 139.

10. My discussion here is informed by Bandirali, *Mario Nascimbene,* 139–42.

11. Quoted in ibid., 145. The translation is my own.

12. Maurizio Corbella, "Musica elettroacustica e cinema in Italia negli anni Sessanta" (Ph.D. diss., University of Milan, 2010). The translation is my own. See also Corbella's article "Paolo Ketoff e le radici cinematografiche della musica elettronica Romana" *Acoustical Arts and Artifacts; Technology, Aesthetics, Communication* 6 (2009), 65–75.

13. Claudio Fuiano, "Mario Nascimbene: The Innovative Use of Sounds. A Conversation with Mario Nascimbene," *Soundtrack Magazine* 5/20 (1986).

14. Mario Nascimbene, *Malgrè moi, musicista* (Venice: Leone, 1992), 226.

15. Jones, *Barabbas,* 168.

9. Universality, Transcendence, and Collapse

1. Ray Freiman, *From Metro-Goldwyn-Mayer: Ben-Hur: A Tale of the Christ* (New York: Random House, 1959).

2. *The Greatest Story Ever Told, a film by George Stevens* (New York: George Stevens Productions, 1965).

3. Ken Darby, *Hollywood Holyland: The Filming and Scoring of "The Greatest Story Ever Told"* (Metuchen, N.J.: Scarecrow, 1992).

4. Anahid Kassabian, *Hearing Film: Tracking Identifications in Contemporary Hollywood Film Music* (New York: Routledge, 2001), 2.

5. Ibid., 2–3.

6. Ibid., 51.

7. Included in Erno Rapée, *Motion Picture Moods* (New York: Schirmer, 1916), 10–11.

8. As I have mentioned in earlier chapters, Newman's technique for these kinds of scenes may be contrasted with the procedure that Rózsa uses.

9. Thomas Larson, *The Saddest Music Ever Written: The Story of Samuel Barber's Adagio for Strings* (New York: Pegasus, 2010), vii.

10. The "anointing of Jesus" may also be found in Matthew 6:6–13; Mark 14:3–9; and Luke 7:36–50.

11. John 12:3 (Revised Standard Version).

12. John 12:8 (Revised Standard Version).

13. The collection is housed at the Academy's Margaret Herrick Library in Beverly Hills. I am indebted to Warren Sherk for bringing these tapes to my attention, and for making it possible for me to listen to them.

14. The memos are preserved as part of the George Stevens Papers (call number 100.f-1144) in the Margaret Herrick Library. This specific reference is in a note on p. 6 of these papers.

15. Darby, *Hollywood Holyland,* 16.

16. Ibid., 205.

17. Ibid., 206.

18. Ibid., 206

19. In "The Making of an American Film Composer: A Study of Alfred Newman's Music in the First Decade of the Sound Era" (Ph.D. diss., University of Southern California, 1981), Frederick Steiner describes the music from *The Hunchback of Notre Dame* (1939) as "pseudo-Handelian" (324).

20. Although this music is not so frequently used in the cinematic context as Barber's *Adagio for Strings,* it has been employed for cinematic underscoring. It appears, for instance, as a kind of dirge to accompany the suicide/drowning of Midshipman Hollom in the 2003 film *Master and Commander: The Far Side of the World.*

Epilogue

1. Harry Medved and Michael Medved, *The Hollywood Hall of Shame: The Most Expensive Flops in Movie History* (Los Angeles: Perigree Books, 1984).

2. For an exploration of Gabriel's achievement, see Eftychia Papanikolaou, "Identity and Ethnicity in Peter Gabriel's Sound Track for *The Last Temptation of Christ,*" in *Scandalizing Jesus: Kazantzakis's "The Last Temptation of Christ" Fifty Years On,* ed. Darren J.N. Middleton (New York: Continuum, 2005), 217–27.

3. Influential scholarly works on film noir from this period include Paul Schrader, "Notes on Film Noir," *Film Comment* 8/1 (Spring 1972), 8–13; E. Ann Kaplan's edited collection *Women in Film Noir* (London: British Film Institute, 1978); and Foster Hirsch's book *The Dark Side of the Screen* (San Diego: A. S. Barnes; London: Tantivy Press, c1981).

4. Leonard Quart and Albert Auster, *American Film and Society since 1945,* 4th ed. (Oxford: Praeger, 2011), 2.

Bibliography

Adorno, Theodor. *In Search of Wagner.* Trans. Rodney Livingstone. New ed., with fore-word by Slavoj Žižek. New York: Verso, 2005.

Ahlstrom, Sydney E. *A Religious History of the American People.* 2nd ed., with foreword and concluding chapter by David D. Hall. New Haven, Conn.: Yale University Press, 2004.

Allen, Gregory Kahill Kareem. "The Word Made Cinematic: The Representation of Jesus in Cinema." Ph.D. diss., University of Pittsburgh, 2008.

Altman, Rick. "The Evolution of Sound Technology." In *Film Sound: Theory and Practice,* ed. Elisabeth Weis and John Belton, 44–53. New York: Columbia University Press, 1985.

———. *Film/Genre.* London: British Film Institute, 1999.

———. "A Semantic/Syntactic Approach to Film Genre." *Cinema Journal* 23/3 (Spring 1984), 6–18.

Anderson, Gillian B. *Music for Silent Films, 1894–1929: A Guide.* Washington, D.C.: Library of Congress, 1988.

Archibald, John B. "Reunions with Old Friends" (Recurring Thematic Materials in Herrmann, Rozsa and Newman)." *Pro Musica Sana* 39–40 (Fall 1983), 3–9.

Babington, Bruce, and Peter Evans. *Biblical Epics: Sacred Narrative in the Hollywood Cinema.* New York: St. Martin's Press, 1993.

Bandirali, Luca. *Mario Nascimbene: Compositore per il Cinema.* Lecce: Argo, 2004.

Barthes, Roland. "The Romans in Films." In *Mythologies,* selected and trans. Annette Lavers, 26–28. New York: Hill and Wang, 1972.

Baugh, Lloyd. *Imagining the Divine: Jesus and Christ-Figures in Film.* Kansas City: Sheed and Ward, 1997.

Beckermann, Michael. "Dvořák's 'New World' Largo and 'The Song of Hiawatha.'" *19th-Century Music* 16/1 (Summer 1992), 35–48.

Belton, John. *American Cinema/American Culture.* New York: McGraw-Hill, 1994.

———. "1950s Magnetic Sound: The Frozen Revolution." In *Sound Theory / Sound Practice,* ed. Rick Altman, 154–67. New York: Routledge, 1992.

———. *Widescreen Cinema.* Cambridge, Mass.: Harvard University Press, 1992.

Birchard, Robert S. *Cecil B. DeMille's Hollywood.* Foreword by Kevin Thomas. Lexington: University Press of Kentucky, 2004.

Bonitzer, Pascal. "Les Silences de la voix." *Cahiers du Cinéma* 256 (February/March 1975), 22–33.

Brodkin, Karen. *How Jews Became White Folks, and What That Says about Race in America.* New Brunswick, N.J.: Rutgers University Press, 1998.

Brown, Harold. "The Robe." *Film Music* 13/2 (November/December 1953), 3–17.

Brown, Royal S. "How Not to Think Film Music." *Music and the Moving Image* 1/1 (Spring 2008), 1–18. Reprinted as "Music and/as Cine-Narrative; or *Ceci n'est pas un leit-motif.*" In *A Companion to Narrative Theory*, ed. James Phelan and Peter J. Rabinowitz, 456–57. Oxford: Blackwell, 2005.

———. *Overtones and Undertones: Reading Film Music.* Berkeley: University of California Press, 1994.

Buhler, James, Rob Deemer, and David Neumeyer. *Hearing the Movies: Music and Sound in Film History.* New York: Oxford University Press, 2010.

Bultmann, Rudolf. *New Testament and Mythology and Other Basic Writings.* Selected, ed., and trans. Schubert M. Ogden. Philadelphia: Fortress Press, 1984.

Buscombe, Edward. "The Idea of Genre in the American Cinema." *Screen* 11/2 (March 1970), 33–45.

Chion, Michel. *Film, a Sound Art.* Trans. Claudia Gorbman. New York: Columbia University Press, 2009.

———. *The Voice in Cinema.* Ed. and trans. Claudia Gorbman. New York: Columbia University Press, 1999.

Citron, Marcia J. "'Soll ich lauschen?' Love-Death in *Humoresque.*" In *Wagner and Cinema*, ed. Jeongwon Joe and Sander L. Gilman, 167–85. Bloomington: Indiana University Press, 2010.

Clanton, Dan W. *Daring, Disreputable and Devout: Interpreting the Bible's Women in the Arts and Music.* New York: T & T Clark, 2009.

Cohan, Steven. *Masked Men: Masculinity and the Movies in the Fifties.* Bloomington: Indiana University Press, 1997.

Cohen, Ralph. "History and Genre." *New Literary History* 17/2: Interpretation and Culture (Winter 1986), 203–18.

Corbella, Maurizio. "Musica elettroacustica e cinema in Italia negli anni Sessanta." Ph.D. diss., University of Milan, 2010.

———. "Paolo Ketoff e le radici cinematografiche della musica elettronica Romana." *Acoustical Arts and Artifacts; Technology, Aesthetics, Communication* 6 (2009), 65–75.

Costain, Thomas B. *The Silver Chalice.* Garden City, N.Y.: Doubleday, 1952.

Cronin, Paul. *George Stevens: Interviews.* Jackson: University of Mississippi Press, 2004.

Crowther, Bosley. "'King of Kings' Has Its Premiere at State." *New York Times,* October 12, 1961.

———. "The Screen: 'Ben-Hur,' a Blockbuster; M-G-M Spectacle Opens at the Loew's State. Film Is Called Most Stirring of Its Type." *New York Times,* November 19, 1959.

———. "The Screen: Two New Movies Shown Here; 'Darling, How Could You!' From Play by James M. Barrie, Stars Fontaine and Lund 'Quo Vadis,' Based on Sienkiewicz Novel and Made in Rome, Opens at Two Theatres." *New York Times,* November 9, 1951.

Darby, Ken. *Hollywood Holyland: The Filming and Scoring of "The Greatest Story Ever Told."* Metuchen, N.J.: Scarecrow, 1992.

Darby, William, and Jack Du Bois. *American Film Music: Major Composers, Techniques, Trends, 1915–1990.* Jefferson, N.C.: McFarland, 1990.

Deaville, James. "The *Topos* of 'Evil Medieval' in American Horror Film Music." In *Music, Meaning, and Media,* ed. Erkki Pekkilä, David Neumeyer, and Richard Littlefield, 26–44. Imatra: International Semiotics Institute; Helsinki: Semiotic Society of Finland, University of Helsinki, 2006.

DeMille, Cecil B. *The Autobiography of Cecil B. DeMille.* Ed. Donald Hayne. Englewood Cliffs, N.J.: Prentice Hall, 1959.

Derrida, Jacques, and Avital Ronell. "The Law of Genre." *Critical Inquiry* 7/1: On Narrative (Autumn 1980), 55–81.

DeWald, Frank K. Online liner notes to *Quo Vadis. Film Score Monthly* (2009). http://www.filmscoremonthly.com/notes/quo_vadis.html. Accessed August 7, 2011.

Doane, Mary Ann. *The Desire to Desire: The Women's Film of the 1940s.* Bloomington: Indiana University Press, 1987.

———. *Femmes Fatales: Feminism, Film Theory, Psychoanalysis.* London: Routledge, 1991.

Donington, Robert. *Wagner's Ring and Its Symbols.* 3rd ed. London: Faber and Faber, 1974.

Douglas, Lloyd. *The Big Fisherman.* New York: Houghton Mifflin, 1948.

———. *The Robe.* New York: Houghton Mifflin, 1942.

Dunar, Andrew J. *America in the Fifties.* Foreword by John Robert Greene. Syracuse: Syracuse University Press, 2006.

Dunne, Philip. *Take Two: A Life in Movies and Politics.* New York: McGraw-Hill, 1980.

Eisler, Hanns. *Composing for the Films.* New York: Oxford University Press, 1947.

Eisler, Hanns, and Theodor Adorno. *Composing for the Films.* Introduction by Graham McCann. New York: Continuum, 2005.

Elley, Derek. *The Epic Film: Myth and History.* London: Routledge and Kegan Paul, 1984.

Ellwood, Robert S. *The Fifties Spiritual Marketplace: American Religion in a Decade of Conflict.* New Brunswick, N.J.: Rutgers University Press, 1997.

———. *The Sixties Spiritual Awakening: American Religion Moving from Modern to Postmodern.* New Brunswick, N.J.: Rutgers University Press, 1994.

Erdmann, Hans, and Giuseppe Becce. *Allgemeines Handbuch der Film-Musik.* 2 vols. Berlin-Lichterfelde and Leipzig: Schlesinger, 1927.

Erkelenz, Ralph. "*Ben-Hur:* A Tale of the Score." *Pro Musica Sana* 5/1, no. 61 (Spring 2005), 1–29.

———. "*Ben-Hur:* A Tale of the Score, Part Two." *Pro Musica Sana* 5/2, no. 62 (Spring 2006), 3–36.

———. "*Ben-Hur:* A Tale of the Score, Part Three." *Pro Musica Sana* 6/1, no. 63 (Spring 2007), 4–39.

———. "*Ben-Hur:* A Tale of the Score, Part Four." *Pro Musica Sana* 7/1, no. 65 (Spring 2009), 3–32.

———. "*Ben-Hur:* A Tale of the Score, Part Five." *Pro Musica Sana* 7/2, no. 66 (Fall 2009), 3–49.

Exum, J. Cheryl. *Plotted, Shot and Painted: Cultural Representations of Biblical Women.* Sheffield: Sheffield University Press, 1996.

Farnham, Marynia F., and Ferdinand Lundberg. *Modern Woman: The Lost Sex.* New York: Harper and Brothers, 1947.

Feisst, Sabine M. "Arnold Schoenberg and the Cinematic Art." *Musical Quarterly* 83/1 (Spring 1999), 93–113.

Flaxman, George A. "A Brief History of CinemaScope." Available at http://instereouk.com/Cinemascope_at_40.html. Accessed May 25, 2012. Originally published in *Movie Collector*, 1993.

Flinn, Carol. *Strains of Utopia: Gender, Nostalgia, and Hollywood Film Music.* Princeton, N.J.: Princeton University Press, 1992.

Forshey, Gerald E. *American Religious and Biblical Spectaculars.* Westport, Conn.: Praeger, 1992.

Freiman, Ray. *From Metro-Goldwyn-Mayer: Ben-Hur: A Tale of the Christ.* New York: Random House, 1959.

Fuiano, Claudio. "Mario Nascimbene: The Innovative Use of Sounds. A Conversation with Mario Nascimbene." *Soundtrack Magazine* 5/20 (1986).

Gabler, Neal. *An Empire of Their Own.* New York: Crown, 1988.

Gaines, Jane, and Neil Lerner. "The Orchestration of Affect: The Motif of Barbarism in Breil's *The Birth of a Nation* Score." In *The Sounds of Early Cinema,* ed. Richard Abel and Rick Altman, 252–68. Bloomington: Indiana University Press, 2001.

Gilbert, James. *Men in the Middle: Searching for Masculinity in the 1950s.* Chicago: University of Chicago Press, 2005.

Glancy, Jennifer. "The Mistress of the Gaze: Masculinity, Slavery, and Representation." *Semeia* 74 (1996), 127–45.

Gorbman, Claudia. *Unheard Melodies: Narrative Film Music.* Bloomington: Indiana University Press, 1987.

Gow, Gordon. *Hollywood in the Fifties.* New York: A. S. Barnes, 1971.

Graham, Billy. *Peace with God.* Garden City, N.Y.: Doubleday, 1953.

———. *The World Aflame.* Kingswood, Surrey: World's Work, 1965.

The Greatest Story Ever Told, a film by George Stevens. New York: George Stevens Productions, 1965.

Gunn, David M. "Bathsheba Goes Bathing in Hollywood: Words, Images, and Social Locations." *Semeia* 74 (1996), 75–101.

Halliwell, Martin. *American Culture in the 1950s.* Edinburgh: Edinburgh University Press, 2007.

Hickman, Roger. *Miklós Rózsa's Ben-Hur: A Film Score Guide.* Lanham, Md.: Scarecrow Press, 2011.

———. *Reel Music: Exploring 100 Years of Film Music.* New York: Norton, 2005.

Higashi, Sumiko. *Cecil B. DeMille: A Guide to References and Resources.* New York: Macmillan, 1985.

———. *Cecil B. DeMille and American Culture: The Silent Era.* Berkeley: University of California Press, 1994.

Hirsch, Foster. *The Dark Side of the Screen.* San Diego: A. S. Barnes; London: Tantivy Press, c1981.

Idelsohn, Abraham Zebi. *Hebräisch-orientalischer Melodienschatz.* 8 vols. Leipzig: Breitkopf und Härtel, c. 1914–1929. Published in English as *Thesaurus of Oriental Hebrew Melodies.* Jersey City, N.J.: KTAV Publishing House, 1973.

Jabotinsky, Vladimir, and C. Harry Brooks. *Judge and Fool.* New York: H. Liveright, 1930.

Joe, Jeongwon. "Introduction: Why Wagner and Cinema? Tolkien Was Wrong." In *Wagner and Cinema,* ed. Jeongwon Joe and Sander L. Gilman, 1–24. Bloomington: Indiana University Press, 2010.

Jones, Lon, ed. *Barabbas: The Story of a Motion Picture.* Bologna: Capelli, 1962.

Kalinak, Kathryn. *Settling the Score: Music and the Classical Hollywood Film.* Madison: University of Wisconsin Press, 1992.

Kaplan, E. Ann. *Women and Film: Both Sides of the Camera.* New York: Methuen, 1983.

Kaplan, E. Ann, ed. *Women in Film Noir.* London: British Film Institute, 1978.

Kassabian, Anahid. *Hearing Film: Tracking Identifications in Contemporary Hollywood Film Music.* New York: Routledge, 2001.

Keats, John C. *The New Romans: An American Experience.* London: J. M. Dent and Sons, 1965.

Kelso, Julie. "Gazing at Impotence in Henry King's *David and Bathsheba.*" In *Screening Scripture: Intertextual Connections between Scripture and Film,* ed. George Aichelle and Richard Walsh, 155–87. Harrisburg, Pa.: Trinity, 2002.

Killick, Andrew P. "Music as Ethnic Marker in Film: The 'Jewish' Case." In *Soundtrack Available: Essays on Film and Popular Music,* ed. Pamela Robertson Wojcik and Arthur Knight. Durham, N.C.: Duke University Press, 2001.

Kopp, David. *Chromatic Transformations in Nineteenth-Century Music.* Cambridge Studies in Music Theory and Analysis. Cambridge: Cambridge University Press, 2002.

Kozloff, Sarah. *Invisible Storytellers: Voice-Over Narration in American Fiction Film.* Berkeley: University of California Press, 1989.

Kozlovic, Anton Karl. "The Construction of Samson's Three Lovers in Cecil B. DeMille's Technicolor Testament, *Samson and Delilah* (1949)." *Women in Judaism* 7/1 (Spring 2010), 2–31.

Lagerqvist, Pär. *Barabbas.* Trans. Alan Blair, with preface by Lucien Maury and a letter by André Gide. New York: Random House, 1951.

Larson, Thomas, *The Saddest Music Ever Written: The Story of Samuel Barber's Adagio for Strings.* New York: Pegasus, 2010.

Lasky, Jesse L. Jr. *Whatever Happened to Hollywood?* New York: Funk and Wagnalls, 1973.

Lehman, Frank. "Transformational Analysis and the Representation of Genius in Film Music." *Music Theory Spectrum* 35/1 (Spring 2013), 1–22.

Lev, Peter. *Transforming the Screen: 1950–59,* History of the American Cinema, vol. 7. New York: Charles Scribner's Sons, 2003.

Levy, Sol P., comp. *Motion Picture Collection, Part 1.* New York: H. S. Gordon, 1914.

Locke, Ralph P. "Constructing the Oriental 'Other': Saint-Saëns's *Samson et Dalila.*" *Cambridge Opera Journal* 3/3 (November 1991): 261–302.

———. *Musical Exoticism: Images and Reflections.* Cambridge: Cambridge University Press, 2009.

MacMahon, Henry. *The Ten Commandments.* New York: Grosset and Dunlap, 1924.

Macquarie, John. *The Scope of Demythologizing: Bultmann and His Critics.* New York: Harper and Brothers, 1960.

Madsen, Axel. *William Wyler: The Authorized Biography.* New York: Crowell, 1973.

Malone, Peter. *Screen Jesus: Portrayals of Christ in Television and Film.* London: Scarecrow Press, 2012.

Malsky, Matthew. "Sounds of the City: Alfred Newman's 'Street Scene' and Urban Modernity." In *Lowering the Boom: Critical Studies in Film Sound,* ed. Jay Beck and Tony Grajeda, 105–22. Urbana: University of Illinois Press.

Marks, Martin Miller. *Music and the Silent Film: Contexts and Case Studies 1895–1924.* New York: Oxford University Press, 1997.

Marshall, Catherine. *A Man Called Peter: The Story of Peter Marshall.* New York: McGraw-Hill, 1950.

Martin, Mel. *The Magnificent Showman: The Epic Films of Samuel Bronston.* Albany, Ga.: BearManor Media, 2007.

Matthiesen, Thomas. *Apollo's Lyre: Greek Music and Music Theory in Antiquity and the Middle Ages.* Lincoln: University of Nebraska Press, 1999.

McAlister, Melani. *Epic Encounters.* Berkeley: University of California Press, 2001.

McClary, Susan. *Georges Bizet, Carmen.* Cambridge Opera Handbooks. Cambridge: Cambridge University Press, 1992.

McLoughlin, William G. *Modern Revivalism: Charles Grandison Finney to Billy Graham.* New York: Ronald Press, 1959.

———. *Revivals, Awakening, and Reform: An Essay on Religion and Social Change in America, 1607–1977.* Chicago: University of Chicago Press, 1978.

Medved, Harry, and Michael Medved. *The Hollywood Hall of Shame: The Most Expensive Flops in Movie History.* Los Angeles: Perigree Books, 1984.

Mikkelson, Douglas K., and Amy C. Gregg. *"King of Kings": A Silver Screen Gospel.* Lanham, Md.: University Press of America, 2001.

Miller, Steven P. *Billy Graham and the Rise of the Republican South.* Philadelphia: University of Pennsylvania Press, 2009.

Morschauser, Scott. "Watching Ancient Egyptian Poetry—Among Other Histrionics." *Journal of Religion and Film* 15/2 (October 2011).

Mulvey, Laura. *Visual and Other Pleasures.* Bloomington: Indiana University Press, 1989.

———. "Visual Pleasure and Narrative Cinema." *Screen* 16/3 (Autumn 1975), 6–18.

Murphy, Geraldine. "Ugly Americans in Togas: Imperial Anxiety in the Cold War Hollywood Epic." *Journal of Film and Video* 56/3 (Fall 2004), 3–19.

Nadel, Alan. *Containment Culture: American Narratives, Postmodernism, and the Atomic Age.* Durham, N.C.: Duke University Press, 1995.

———. "God's Law and the Wide Screen: *The Ten Commandments* as Cold War 'Epic.'" *Proceedings of the Modern Language Association* 108/3 (May 1993), 415–30.

Nascimbene, Mario. *L'impronta del suono: La mia musica per il cinema.* Ravenna: Longo, 2002.

———. *Malgrè moi, musicista.* Pref. Gian Luigi Rondi. Venice: Leone, 1992.

Neale, Steve. *Genre and Hollywood.* New York: Routledge, 2000.

———. "Questions of Genre." In *Film Genre Reader II,* ed. Barry Keith Grant, 159–83. Austin: University of Texas Press, 1995.

Neumeyer, David. "The Resonances of Wagnerian Opera and Nineteenth-Century Melodrama in the Film Scores of Max Steiner." In *Wagner and Cinema,* ed. Jeongwon Joe and Sander L. Gilman, 111–30. Bloomington: Indiana University Press, 2010.

———. "Schoenberg at the Movies: Dodecaphony and Film." *Music Theory Online* 0/1 (February 1993).

Noerdlinger, Henry S. *Moses and Egypt: The Documentation to the Motion Picture "The Ten Commandments."* Los Angeles: University of Southern California Press, 1956.

Oren, Michael B. *Power, Faith, and Fantasy: America in the Middle East, 1776 to the Present.* New York: Norton, 2007.

Orrison, Katherine. *Written in Stone: Making Cecil B. DeMille's Epic "The Ten Commandments."* Lanham, Md.: Vestal Press, 1999.

Oursler, Fulton. *The Greatest Story Ever Told.* Garden City, N.Y.: Doubleday, 1949.

Palmer, Christopher, *The Composer in Hollywood.* New York: Rizzoli, 1990.

Papanikolaou, Eftychia. "Identity and Ethnicity in Peter Gabriel's Sound Track for *The Last Temptation of Christ*." In *Scandalizing Jesus: Kazantzakis's "The Last Temptation of Christ" Fifty Years On,* ed. Darren J.N. Middleton, 217–27. New York: Continuum, 2005.

Paul, Joanna. *Film and the Classical Epic Tradition*. Oxford: Oxford University Press, 2013.

Paulin, Scott D. "Richard Wagner and the Fantasy of Cinematic Unity: The Idea of the *Gesamtkunstwerk* in the History and Theory of Film Music." In *Music and Cinema,* ed. James Buhler, Caryl Flinn, and David Neumeyer, 58–84. Hanover, N.H.: University Press of New England, 2000.

Peale, Norman Vincent. *The Power of Positive Thinking*. New York: Prentice Hall, 1952.

Place, Janey. "Women in Film Noir." In *Women in Film Noir,* ed. E. Ann Kaplan, 47–68. Rev. and expanded ed. London: British Film Institute, 1998.

Pope, Robert. *Salvation in Celluloid*. London: T & T Clark, 2007.

Prendergast, Roy M. *Film Music. A Neglected Art: A Critical Study of Music in Films*. 2nd ed. New York: Norton, 1992.

Preston, Andrew. *Sword of the Spirit, Shield of Faith: Religion in American War and Diplomacy*. New York: Alfred A. Knopf, 2012.

Quart, Leonard, and Albert Auster. *American Film and Society since 1945*. 4th ed. Oxford: Praeger, 2011.

Rapée, Erno. *Motion Picture Moods*. New York: Schirmer, 1916.

Reinhartz, Adele. *Jesus of Hollywood*. Oxford: Oxford University Press, 2007.

Reinsch, Paul N. "At Least Half the Picture: Sound and Narration in the Postwar/Pre-Dolby American Film." Ph.D. diss., University of Southern California, 2008.

Richards, Jeffrey. *Hollywood's Ancient Worlds*. New York: Continuum, 2008.

Richie, Donald. *George Stevens: An American Romantic*. New York: Museum of Modern Art, 1970.

Ringgold, Gene. *The Films of Cecil B. DeMille*. New York: Cadillac, 1969.

Rózsa, Miklós. *Double Life: The Autobiography of Miklós Rózsa*. Foreword by Antal Doráti. New York: Hippocrene Books, 1982.

———. "The Music in *Quo Vadis*." *Film Music Notes* 11/2 (November–December 1951), 4–10. Reprinted in *The Hollywood Film Music Reader,* ed. Mervyn Cooke, 165–71. Oxford: Oxford University Press, 2010.

Schatz, Thomas. *The Genius of the System: Hollywood Filmmaking in the Studio Era*. 2nd ed. New York: Pantheon, 1998.

———. *Hollywood Genres: Formulas, Filmmaking, and the Studio System*. Philadelphia: Temple University Press, 1981.

Scheurer, Timothy E. *Music and Mythmaking in Film*. Jefferson, N.C.: McFarland, 2007.

Schrader, Paul. "Notes on Film Noir." *Film Comment* 8/1 (Spring 1972), 8–13.

Scodel, Ruth, and Anja Bettenworth. *Whither Quo Vadis?: Sienkiewicz's Novel in Film and Television*. Hoboken, N.J.: Wiley, 2009.

Shaw, Tony. *Hollywood's Cold War*. Amherst: University of Massachusetts Press, 2007.

———. "Martyrs, Miracles, and Martians: Religion and Cold War Cinematic Propaganda in the 1950s." *Journal of Cold War Studies* 4/2 (2002), 3–22.

Sheppard, W. Anthony. "An Exotic Enemy: Anti-Japanese Musical Propaganda in World War II Hollywood." *Journal of the American Musicological Society* 54/2 (Summer 2001), 303–57.

Sienkiewicz, Henryk. *Quo Vadis? A Narrative of the Time of Nero*. Trans. Jeremiah Curtin. Boston: Little, Brown, 1896, 1897, 1923.

Silverman, Kaja. *The Acoustic Mirror: The Female Voice in Psychoanalysis and Cinema*. Bloomington: Indiana University Press, 1988.

Smith, Jeff. "Are You Now or Have You Ever Been A Christian? The Strange History of *The Robe* as Political Allegory." In *"Un-American Hollywood": Politics and Film in the Blacklist Era*, ed. Frank Krutnik, Steve Neale, Brian Neve, and Peter Stanfield, 19–38. New Brunswick, N.J.: Rutgers University Press, 2007.

———. "Hollywood Theology: The Commodification of Religion in Twentieth-Century Films." *Religion and American Culture: A Journal of Interpretation* 11/2 (Summer 2001), 191–231.

Sobchack, Vivian. "'Surge and Splendor': A Phenomenology of the Hollywood Historical Epic." *Representations* 29 (Winter 1990), 24–49. Reprinted in *Film Genre Reader II*, ed. Barry Keith Grant, 280–307. Austin: University of Texas Press, 1995.

Solomon, Jon. *The Ancient World in the Cinema*. Rev. and expanded ed. New Haven, Conn.: Yale University Press, 2001.

Stam, Robert. *Film Theory: An Introduction*. Malden, Mass.: Blackwell, 2000.

Stanislawski, Michael. *Zionism and the Fin-de-siecle: Cosmopolitanism and Nationalism from Nordau to Jabotinsky*. Berkeley: University of California Press, 2001.

Steiner, Frederick. "The Making of an American Film Composer: A Study of Alfred Newman's Music in the First Decade of the Sound Era." Ph.D. diss., University of Southern California, 1981.

Stokes, Melvyn. *D. W. Griffith's The Birth of a Nation: A History of "The Most Controversial Motion Picture of All Time."* Oxford: Oxford University Press, 2007.

Tagg, Philip. *Everyday Tonality: Towards a Tonal Theory of What Most People Hear*. New York: Mass Media Scholars Press, 2009.

Thompson, Kristin. *Storytelling in the New Hollywood: Understanding Classical Narrative Technique*. Cambridge, Mass.: Harvard University Press, 1999.

Wallace, Lew. *Ben-Hur: A Tale of the Christ*. 1880. Reprint, New York: Harper and Brothers, 1959.

Wescott, Steven Dwight. "Miklós Rózsa's *Ben Hur:* The Musical-Dramatic Function of the Hollywood Leitmotiv." *Film Music I*, ed. Clifford McCarty, 183–207. New York: Garland, 1989.

Winkler, Martin M. "The Roman Empire in American Cinema after 1945." *Classical Journal* 93/2 (December 1997–January 1998), 167–96.

Wood, Michael. *America in the Movies; or "Santa Maria, It Had Slipped My Mind."* New York: Basic Books, 1975.

Wyke, Maria. *Projecting the Past: Ancient Rome, Cinema and History*. New York: Routledge, 1997.

Index

MacMahon, Henry, *The Ten Commandments* (novelization of 1923 film), 15
Maderna, Bruno, 199
magnetic tape technology, 7–8, 17
Magnificent Seven, The (1960 film), 138–40
Man Called Peter, A. See Marshall, Catherine, *A Man Called Peter*
Mankiewicz, Joseph, 74, 195
Mann, Thomas, *Doktor Faustus,* 178
Marinuzzi, Jr., Gino, 200
Marshall, Catherine, *A Man Called Peter,* 96
Masetti, Enzo, 198
Matrix, The (1999 film), 118, 234
Mature, Victor, 21, 47
Mayer, Louis B., 75
McAlister, Melani, 12, 117, 118, 122, 127
McCarthyism, 13
Medved, Harry and Michael, *The Hollywood Hall of Shame,* 231
Mellotron, 200
Messiah, See under Handel, G. F.
Meyer, Donald, 138
Meyerbeer, Giacomo, *Les Huguenots,* 100–102, 186, 217
Mixerama (tape mixing machine), 200
Modern Woman: The Lost Sex. See under Farnham, Marynia, and Ferdinand Lundberg, *Modern Woman: The Lost Sex*
Montesquieu, *Considerations of the Causes of the Greatness of the Romans and Their Decline,* 84
Morricone, Ennio, 199
Moses (1951 book). *See* Asch, Sholem, *Moses*
Moses the Lawgiver (1974 television miniseries), 232
My Spiritual Diary. See Rogers, Dale Evans, *My Spiritual Diary*

Nadel, Alan, 5, 15–16, 117, 136, 139, 140
Nascimbene, Mario, 14, 17. See also *Barabbas* (1961 film); *Solomon and Sheba* (1959 film)
Neumeyer, David, 23, 147–48, 152, 254n11, 254n12
New World Symphony. *See* Dvořák, Antonin, *New World* Symphony
Newman, Alfred, 7, 9, 11, 14, 53, 119, 236; music for *Street Scene* by, 103, 186, 222, 228; transformational chromatic harmony in the scores of, 88, 100–103, 107–108, 218. See also *David and Bathsheba* (1951 film); leitmotif, in Newman's score for *David and Bathsheba;* leit-

motif, in Newman's score for *The Robe; The Robe; The Greatest Story Ever Told* (1965 film)
Noah (2014 film), 232
Noerdlinger, Henry, *Moses and Egypt,* 10–11, 124, 210, 222
North, Alex, 163
North West Mounted Police (1940 film)

Omen, The (1976–81 film series)
opening credits, 22–25, 49–50, 147–49. *See also under individual films*
Orff, Carl, *Carmina Burana,* 82–83
orientalism, 16, 22, 29, 47, 86, 93–94
Oursler, Fulton, *The Greatest Story Ever Told,* 76
Out of the Past (1947 film), 25

Paganini, Niccolò, 177
Palance, Jack, 207
Parsifal. See under Wagner, Richard
Passion of the Christ, The (2004 film), 17, 232–33
Peace with God. See under Graham, Billy
Peale, Norman Vincent, 98; *The Power of Positive Thinking,* 96
Peck, Gregory, 49, 60, 75
Phantom Menace, The (1999 film), 233
photoplay music, 79, 217
Planet of the Apes (1968 film), 176
Powell, Edward B., 105
Power of Positive Thinking, The. See under Peale, Norman Vincent
Prisoner's Dream, The. See Schwind, Moritz von, *The Prisoner's Dream*
Propp, Vladimir, 103
Psalm 23. See under *David and Bathsheba* (1951 film)

Quinn, Anthony, 191
Quo Vadis? (1895 book). *See* Sienkiewicz, Henryk, *Quo Vadis?*
Quo Vadis (1913 film), 75, 78, 144
Quo Vadis (1925 film), 75
Quo Vadis (1951 film), 1, 13, 14, 46, 181–84, 191, 196; arena sequence in, 89–91; banquet scene in, 84–87, 89–90, 93–94, 196; character of Lygia in, 26, 81, 84–86, 87, 90, 143, 173; character of Marcus Vinicius in, 9, 72, 79–80, 83, 87, 90, 143, 172–73, 194; character of Nero in, 12, 80, 83–84, 90–93; character of Poppaea in, 26, 86, 89–90; cinematography of, 12; conversion in, 72, 90; depiction of ancient Christianity in, 87, 91–93, 197–98; depiction of ancient Rome in, 79–84, 95, 153–55, 170, 197,

STEPHEN C. MEYER is Associate Professor in the Department of Art and Music Histories at Syracuse University. He is author of *Carl Maria von Weber and the Search for a German Opera* (Indiana University Press, 2003) and has published articles in numerous scholarly journals, including the *Journal of the American Musicological Society, 19th-Century Music,* the *Musical Quarterly,* and the *Cambridge Opera Journal.* His most recent articles concern the history of the sound recording of Wagner's Grail operas, the role of technology in the early music movement, and the question of medievalism in film music. In 2015 he assumes the position of editor-in-chief for the *Journal of Music History Pedagogy.*